Theories of Play
and Postmodern Fiction

COMPARATIVE LITERATURE AND CULTURAL STUDIES
VOLUME 3
GARLAND REFERENCE LIBRARY OF THE HUMANITIES
VOLUME 2068

COMPARATIVE LITERATURE AND CULTURAL STUDIES
JONATHAN HART, *Series Editor*

IMAGINING CULTURE
*Essays in Early Modern
History and Literature*
edited by Jonathan Hart

THE EDITORIAL GAZE
*Mediating Texts in
Literature and the Arts*
edited by Paul Eggert
and Margaret Sankey

THEORIES OF PLAY
AND POSTMODERN FICTION
by Brian Edwards

THEORIES OF PLAY
AND POSTMODERN FICTION

BRIAN EDWARDS

Taylor & Francis Group
New York   London

First published 1998 by Garland Publishing Inc.

Published 2015 by Routledge
711 Third Avenue, New York, NY 10017
2 Park Square, Milton Park, Abingdon, Oxfordshire OX14 4RN

First issued in paperback 2015

Routledge is an imprint of the Taylor and Francis Group, an informa business

Copyright © 1998 by Brian Edwards
All rights reserved

Library of Congress Cataloging-in-Publication Data

Edwards, Brian.
    Theories of play and postmodern fiction / by Brian Edwards.
       p.   cm. — (Garland reference library of the humanities ; v. 2068.
  Comparative literature and cultural studies ; v. 3)
    Includes bibliographical references and index.
    ISBN 0-8153-2847-8 (alk. paper)
    1. Play in literature. 2. Postmodernism (Literature). 3. Fiction—
  20th century—History and criticism.   I. Title. II. Series: Garland reference
  library of the humanities ; vol. 2068. III. Series: Garland reference library
  of the humanities. Comparative literature and cultural studies ; v. 3.
  PN56.P53E38 1998
  809.3'91—dc21   97-40346
                                            CIP

ISBN 13: 978-1-138-86437-5 (pbk)
ISBN 13: 978-0-8153-2847-6 (hbk)

For Robyn Gardner

Contents

Acknowledgments		ix
Introduction: Embracing Play		xi

Part I: **Grasshopper Antics: The Playhouse of Language**

Chapter 1:	Foreplay	3
Chapter 2:	Play: The Reader as Trickster	11
Chapter 3:	Reader Response: The Reader as Chameleon	39
Chapter 4:	Deconstruction: The Reader as Scheherazade	55

Part II: **Duplicity as Virtue: Playful Texts and Textualised Players**

Chapter 1:	The Play in Postmodernism	79
Chapter 2:	Narcissus at the Edge: The Endlessly Diddling Play of Thomas Pynchon's *Gravity's Rainbow*	91
Chapter 3:	Letters to Literature: The Epistolary Artfulness of John Barth's *LETTERS*	141
Chapter 4:	Strategies of Influence: Intertextual Infiltration in Robert Kroetsch's *What the Crow Said*	187
Chapter 5:	Revisioning the Carnivalesque: The Cultural Combinations of Angela Carter's *Nights at the Circus*	217
Chapter 6:	Deceptive Constructions: The Art of Building in Peter Carey's *Illywhacker*	247

Interlude	273
Bibliography	277
Index	301

Acknowledgments

In many ways, this study is a cooperative effort. I acknowledge the contributions in discussion of my Literary Studies colleagues at Deakin University, my students, and audiences at many conferences in Australia, New Zealand and Canada who have participated variously in the trial and development of some of these ideas. I am grateful to the English Department of the University of Melbourne for many years of courteous and friendly association, to Peter Steele and the late Vincent Buckley for their perspectives on literature and their incidental encouragement, to Chris Wallace-Crabbe and David Bennett for valuable comments on draft material for the first part of the study, and to Ken Ruthven for his most encouraging responses to the work. Earlier versions of particular chapters have appeared in *Essays on Canadian Writing*, *Australian and New Zealand Studies in Canada* and the *Canadian Review of Comparative Literature,* and I express my gratitude to the editors of those journals. I thank the English Department of the University of Alberta, especially Robert Wilson, Jonathan Hart and Doug Barbour, for providing the facilities and friendship in the summer of 1996 that enabled me to complete the project. Many friends have provided audience, advice and encouragement. In addition to those mentioned already, and in particular, I thank Robyn Gardner for her exceptionally astute readings in literature and theory and for her incisive suggestions with respect to my work. Finally, I owe a very considerable debt to Robert Wilson for first setting me out in pursuit of "play," for providing the fine example of his own scholarly research, and for maintaining a vigilant, if distant, watch over my wanderings in the field. For this variety of support I express my gratitude and, in keeping with the argument and the spirit of the project, I hope that this book will provide shifty "grounds" for continuing exchanges in the serious business of play in language, literature and culture.

INTRODUCTION

Embracing Play

Despite the impetus for innovation in recent critical theory and the rush to prefixes as competing ideas jostle for positions, *old* issues remain important. Providing connections within the discourse, they help to shape a field of activity characterised not so much by radical discontinuities as by shifts in emphasis, rhetoric and procedure so that, together with their focus on "past" definitions and practices, **de**construction, **post**modernism, **neo**-Marxism, **post**structuralism and **post**colonialism are concerned with familiar problems—with the *interplay* between traditions and change, history and aesthetics, particular instances or artefacts and the divided cultural contexts of their production and reception. Discovering particularity and difference, affording the specific its due and innovation its interest, while yet acknowledging similarity, connection and exchange is one of the major challenges facing contemporary critical theory and practice, and this challenge is complicated by tensions between models of tradition and modish attractions of the apparently new.

This study arises from a double interest in critical theory and postmodernist fiction. If postmodernist fiction is notable for its self-consciousness about language and processes of narration, questions of (re)presentation and the text's relationships with literary traditions and practices, each of which may become matters of address within the text, how may one theorise its resistances (particularly with respect to language and meaning) while acknowledging the influence of contexts? What articulations are possible between apparently opposed constructions of linguistic playfulness and cultural significance? It is my contention that the concept of play provides perspectives on language and communication processes useful not only for analysis of literary texts as cultural products but, in addition, for understanding the interactive nature of constructions of knowledge generally. Play is always already interplay, and against ideas of solitariness and singularity, fixed positions, simple binarism, privilege and truth, I present an argument for specificity, difference, pluralism and process. There is a double bind that I acknowledge, the problem of preserving the openness of play, its resistance to closure, while exploring and defining its contributions to forms, procedures, critical vocabularies and cultural interpretation. If there is no unassailable position beyond the activity, escaping play, from which authoritative pronouncements may be made, what is the status of the findings? Is it the lot of players, of contributors, to be so caught up as to be simultaneously both precipitous and belated? But, since they are antithetical to play as procedure and as value, withdrawal and silence provide no solution. An answer lies, rather, in self-consciousness and provisionality—in recognition of the interventionist and theoretically endless nature of the discourse, the place of contexts and the provisional aspect of all findings. As recent productivity demonstrates, these recognitions do not evacuate the discourse. To the contrary, and increasingly, strategies and interests in interpretation attentive to changing perceptions of aesthetics, cultural politics, identity and knowledge will continue to challenge the restrictive practices of authority systems based upon privilege and hierarchy. Just as cultural production, in its diversity, should provide amazement and opportunity, innovative theorising and interpretation are the best defence against hardening of the critical arteries.

This study is presented in two parts, the first of which argues that play is not only endemic to culture but that it helps to explain the divided operations of literary texts as cultural productions, and the second provides an analysis of the forms and styles of play in various examples of postmodernist fiction considered as interactive cultural constructions that are variously allusive, invitational and playful.

In Part I, I consider theories of game and play to argue that, as the more expansive term, "play" is more productive for appreciation of the nature of cultural engagements, including the operations of language and texts. As this work acknowledges, concepts of play and playforms are present throughout the history of Western culture. Addressed, practised, extolled or criticized, they are integral to matters of choice, debate, discourse, the operations of language and the processes of social action. It only seems that early play theorists sold play out for, as

Introduction

Mihai Spariosu demonstrates, if Plato proposed that poets be excluded from the Republic because of their *playfulness,* he also reinstates *play* at the basis of his own thought and writing. Developments in twentieth-century cultural and literary theory of ideas about play may be traced in the writings of Johan Huizinga, Roger Caillois, Jacques Ehrmann and, more recently, Bernard Suits, James Hans, Mihai Spariosu and Robert Rawdon Wilson. In consideration of their pronouncements, and against binary oppositions that devalue play by comparison with work, seriousness, utility and reality, I argue that play invades these "others," challenges the oppositional logic, and provides value in spirited activity against forms of essentialism, privilege and ending. Turning more particularly to analyses of play in language, and to the writings of Nietzsche, Wittgenstein and Derrida, I offer a perspective on language that emphasizes instability against the restrictions of simple matchings (in processes of signification) and fixed meaning. Chapters three and four extend the discussion to poststructuralist developments, with attention to reception theory and to deconstruction. The shift in attention to reception not only refigures readers as active shapers of meanings in texts; in addition, it displaces emphasis on contexts of origin to acknowledge possibilities for continuing influence and negotiation, thereby complicating appreciation of texts as divided cultural productions. While acknowledging the importance of the "original" context of production, it is necessary not only to consider its dividedness, but also to take note of the changing history of reception and, therefore, of a text's capacity for change, invitation, and reinterpretation. If there is no end to the story-telling, it is deconstruction that makes the most significant recent contribution to play theory in its application to language and to literature. Derrida's analyses of the play of signification, operations of the supplement, and the processes of decentering and *différance,* extend considerably our appreciation of the play in language and, therefore, the play in culture. In consideration of Derrida's work, and with reference to Foucault and to Barthes, I offer a definition of play as the principle of energy and difference which unsettles arrangements, promotes change and resists closure. The challenge remains to demonstrate the seriousness of play against attempts to divert it the way of easy frivolity and simple self-delight, to demonstrate its value in language, aesthetics and cultural productions as that which supports variety, enquiry and change against closed systems and hierarchical power.

xiv   *Introduction*

Amongst the different constructions of "postmodernism," this study takes those which emphasize self-consciousness, pastiche, experimentation, openness and play, or the effervescence of positive and agile responses to cultural complexity and its challenges. Thus, in their emphasis upon heterogeneity as a value, Lyotard's general attention to paralogy, dissension and difference, and Hassan's early model of "indetermanence," provide generative ideas for consideration of the range and cultural importance of forms of play in postmodernist fiction. The readings in Part II explore forms of play to consider their effects upon perceptions of literature, reading practices and the construction and evaluation of meanings. Although the main focus in each instance is a single text, the readings are comparative in the double sense that others of the writer's works as well as critical theory contribute to this reading practice. Affirming the necessity and the value of particularity, variety and difference, while acknowledging historical-cultural connections, the readings explore the ways in which these postmodernist texts are not only caught up in the complex slippages and duplicity of exercises in language, since this applies to all texts, but how they address deliberately and self-consciously the opportunities for play in language as literature. There need be no impassable chasm between notions of indeterminacy or (ultimate) "meaninglessness" and construction of meanings that are culturally and contextually significant. To the contrary, and the readings seek to demonstrate the possibilities available to writers, as well as to readers, once the barriers of determinism and simplistic notions of history, origin, context and self are down. Removing notions of *the* definitive utterance, or reading, licenses readings; and judgements about their partiality, interest and usefulness must necessarily take account of questions of ideology and context. To jettison ideas of aesthetic purity, political innocence and truth, is to open the avenues for exchange in their complexity, in their inherent and serious playfulness.

Thomas Pynchon's *Gravity's Rainbow* is a definitive example of the decentered text, a work that acknowledges and subverts the rush to closure by putting into question, through accumulation, juxtaposition and parody, such a bewildering array of systems, structures and controls. In this chapter, I suggest that playful diversity is presented as a serious tactic, that oppositional strategies offer increasing possibilities for cultural action or preterite defence against THEM, the big 'guys' of Puritan Elect, rocketmasters, cartels, the firm, the system. The forms

Introduction xv

and styles of play in *Gravity's Rainbow* are manifold—evident in the text's play with history and cultural reference, with language, and with readers and readings. Their analysis permits not fixed regulations but a provisional taxonomy since, as I argue throughout this study, the intricacies of play exceed the categories, such as those offered by Roger Caillois, by which we attempt to define it.

Offering *Gravity's Rainbow* as such a wide-ranging example of play forms, it is possible to locate other readings with reference to it. John Barth's *LETTERS,* with its formal presentation of texts within texts and its attention to literary traditions and reading strategies, may be read as another "funhouse" of language, a site of extraordinary recyclings of the prior Barth opus, together with its vast frames of reference. The play-element is foregrounded in the intricate processes of communication by which epistoleans are also readers, and language and contexts are presented as items for dissembling. Even so, I take seriously the text's repetitions on the vexed relationships between artifice and "reality," art and life, and read *LETTERS* as both entertainment and social criticism. Treating United States history, literary traditions, aesthetics and representation seriously as items for playful consideration, this text is engaged in a regenerative enterprise that is both self-delighting and invitational. Its elaborate play with cultural reference allows the complexity of that reference while demon-strating its constructed-ness and the possibilities for refigurations.

It is a commonplace in contemporary critical practice to assert the intertextuality of all texts by pointing to the divided operations of reference in post-Saussurean linguistics, fragmentation of the unitary self as any originary principle and the cultural baggage that readers of texts bring to the process of meaning construction. These factors apply to my constructions of *Gravity's Rainbow* and *LETTERS.* But Robert Kroetsch's *What the Crow Said* provides a very particular example of intertextual relationship and, for the purposes of the argument, I confine my analysis to the influence upon this text of García Márquez's *One Hundred Years of Solitude.* In contrast with the vast range of texts (including *Gravity's Rainbow* and *LETTERS)* that include allusions to other literature, and with the model of Joyce's revision in *Ulysses* of structural patterns in *The Odyssey, What the Crow Said* presents the Márquezian strategies at "play," macaws at the snowline, in a "Canadian" compliment to the definitive example of Latin American magical realism. Kroetsch emphasizes the positive possibilities of *xvi*   *Introduction*

interplay, for writers as for readers, against strict limitations of tradition, context and reference. I take *What the Crow Said* as a text that enlivens constructions of "the real" by insertions of "the fabulous," thereby complicating the genealogical issue; moreover, this two-way exchange, extended with the participation of readers, demonstrates not just the mobility of meanings but also possibilities in playing "Coyote."

Nights at the Circus varies the study by introducing a traditional figure of play, the circus, but also by offering a feminist revision of contemporary carnivalesque. In this reading, I suggest that elements of fantasy are used in Angela Carter's postmodern gothic for both entertainment and cultural criticism, that her reworkings allow the play of significant difference, and the place of distraction becomes also the place for renovation. *Nights at the Circus* is a hybrid text in which the main mode of play is combination, woman is presented as instigator rather than object, and laughter is shown to serve serious purposes. The display is complicated with the inclusion of Walser as male commentator-participant, one ideologically circumscribed register to acts of cultural revision, though not in any sense their controller.

Whereas *Nights at the Circus* offers a feminist revision of play practices and particular cultural semiotics, Peter Carey's hybrid text redresses history by introducing the lever of difference into constructions of national characteristics. Rereading the inheritance through the narrator as self-conscious liar, *Illywhacker* emphasizes the author as bricoleur and the text and its referents as bricolage. Approaching *Illywhacker* through Derrida and Barthes on the instabilities of language as signifier and through Murray Bail's deconstructions of Australian identity, I suggest that it demonstrates the artfulness in art and in cultural history. Self-reflexive in its attention to building, dealing in trickery, and exuberant in detail, it offers a postmodernist critique of naive constructions of truth-telling and authority. Again, the play is in the interaction of language and referent, and in the text's elaborate gaming with its readers.

Formal contemplation of "play" has a very long history. But whereas Plato and Aristotle regarded it primarily as a type of activity that was set apart and distinguishable from seriousness, it has been affirmed increasingly a more pervasive place in culture. These changes in perception take account of activity and attitude; but when play is located as an unavoidable characteristic of language and, therefore, of our primary systems of communication and constructions of

Introduction xvii

knowledge, the question becomes one of style, degree and effect rather than presence or absence. Associating play with movement, process and the operations of difference invites participation and exchange. And while the activities (including the texts) may be overtly exuberant, the playfulness in culture, and in literature, takes many forms and involves styles of communication over a vast range of possibilities. Displacing the ideas of absolute truth and fixed authorities emphasizes the opportunities for exchange and for change that are innate to language.

PART I

Grasshopper Antics:
The Playhouse of Language

CHAPTER 1

Foreplay

This (therefore) will not have been a book. [1]

Thomas Pynchon's story, "Entropy," includes an exchange that introduces recurrent elements in debates about the nature of textuality, reception and meaning. In response to Mulligan's suggestion that communication breakdowns are the result of a language barrier, Saul's reply offers one version of fissures in language and the problematics of meaning construction:

> "No, ace, it is not a barrier. If it is anything it's a kind of leakage. Tell a girl: 'I love you.' No trouble with two-thirds of that, it's a closed circuit. Just you and she. But that nasty four-letter word in the middle, that's the one you have to look out for. Ambiguity. Redundance. Irrelevance, even. Leakage. All this is noise. Noise screws up your signal, makes for disorganization in the circuit." [2]

But, although important, doubts about the four-letter word in the middle only begin to touch the problem, for it must also include equivocation about "I" and "you," sender and receiver, or the language users, in this simple, yet inescapably complex, communication model, as well as consideration of conventions applicable to the exchange. What does a sender intend? What will receivers understand? In what ways are meanings of an utterance shaped not only by the linguistic system but also by cultural context? Allowing Derrida's view that speech is always already writing, [3] his challenge to the prioritising which links speech with presence as a claim upon truth, the model becomes practically if not philosophically more complex as a written performance. An

4 *Theories of Play and Postmodern Fiction*

author's "absence," in addition to the instability of identity, further complicates any claim (s)he has to authority over meaning; context is destabilised and attention is drawn to the reader's task of producing meaning from the text. As Barthes' figure of the divided reader suggests, "This I which approaches the text is already a plurality of other texts, of codes which are infinite."[4] Similarly, the absent "I" who produced the text is also a plurality of codes and, most fundamentally, the medium of the message, the language text itself, is loud with "noise." This multiple disorganization in the circuit constitutes the play of signification, and the opportunities for changing engagements that deconstructionists affirm in literary discourse.[5] Meanings are plural. They oppose attempts that seek definitive meaning by second-guessing authorial intention or by discovering the timeless answer either in textual detail or in one or another context as limit. To consider reader participation in producing this pluralism is to enter the *jeu* by acknowledging the instabilities not only of texts and contexts but also of language itself. By a quirky spiral both would surely appreciate, Pynchon in 1960 anticipates Baudrillard in 1987: "If you say, I love you, then you have already fallen in love with language, which is already a form of breakup and infidelity."[6]

Because of the metaphoric flexibility of language and the variable possibilities for meanings in language acts, "partial knowledge" is, as Geoffrey Hartman has suggested, "the normal condition, then, of living in the context of words."[7] Presented within his analysis of Derrida's *Glas,* where Derrida's process of insistent interrogation and cross-referencing demonstrates the intertextuality of texts and the uncertainty of meanings, Hartman's judgement may spell despair or delight, according to one's preferences. But the mortality of determinate codes and meanings represents not the chaotic end of communication[8] (or of knowledge claims); on the contrary, because deprivileging the arbiters of authority upon the grounds for their claims encourages discourse. Ontological and epistemological uncertainties promote communication by recognising that words are allusive, gamesome and pluralistic, simultaneously both host and parasite[9] in the creation of texts by writers and by readers. But although the "deconstructive" perception complicates definitions, it cannot dispense with the question of context, with the cultural formation and political nature of meanings, with relationships between text and world. Showing the influence of intersecting contexts, the meanings that we discover in texts are

Foreplay 5

provisional and, however fiercely they may be asserted or acted upon, they have no final truth claim because the processes of communication that are their enabling condition are also the processes by which their instability can be demonstrated.

When T.S. Eliot wrote in 1921 that henceforth literature would have to be *difficult*,[10] he was responding to a perception of the variety and complexity of civilization, including its literature, and the effects of that complexity upon the writer's sensibility. Northrop Frye's 1957 proposal that literature is made from other literature, with each new work simultaneously shaped by and shaping its predecessors in the company of which it takes its place and finds its meanings, prescribes a vast grid of literary connection and explanation.[11] When, in 1967, John Barth described the "exhaustion" of literature, he defined the used-upness of certain forms and possibilities to insist on new attitudes towards returning to old things.[12] For all of their differences in these instances as cultural analyst, Jungian formalist and novelist/essayist, Eliot, Frye and Barth emphasise the intertextuality of literature and the interplay of language. They point to allusions, echoes and borrowings, to the ways in which texts depend upon one another and upon changing contexts, which are so prominent an aspect of postmodernist literature and its reception. As authors explore self-consciously the possibilities of language, the texts in turn challenge readers to enter the linguistic/cultural fields from which meanings are constructed. This formal self-consciousness is a matter of shifting emphases or fashions, as eighteenth-century fiction and the mock lament of Cervantes' Prologue to *Don Quixote* indicate:

> I have no citations for the margins, no notes for the end. To tell the truth, I do not even know who the authors are to whom I am indebted, and so am unable to follow the example of all the others by listing them alphabetically at the beginning, starting with Aristotle and closing with Xenophon, or, perhaps, with Zoilus or Zeuxis, notwithstanding the fact that the former was a snarling critic, the latter a painter.[13]

Not exclusive to postmodernist fiction but informing its wily manoeuvres, such play with the forms of fiction, and therefore with the construction of meanings, compliments readers by challenging them to

6   *Theories of Play and Postmodern Fiction*

participate in that interassociation of texts and contexts which is the play of language.

In Part I, I consider *play* as a perspective and a practice that offers valuable ideas about cultural formations generally and about literature and its reception in particular. Chapter Two presents a critical analysis of theories of play and game to argue that play is not only endemic to culture, providing impetus for change and defences against repression, but that it is, in its various manifestations, a concept which helps to explain the nature of literary texts as constructs in terms of their divided operations in cultural contexts. Consideration of these manifestations is the major task of this study.

Chapters Three and Four focus on post-structuralist developments of play theory with attention to particular examples of reader-response theory and to deconstruction. In what ways are play, reader-response and deconstruction related? What does this interrelatedness offer to theories of textuality and to critical practice? Since I am interested in play not simply as a formal component of works of literature but as an interactive process, as it is manifest in communication between texts and readers in the act of reading, reader-response studies have specific relevance in this project. Inevitably, since they are affected by matters of preference and style, institutional constraints and attitudes towards literature and culture, reader-response theories vary considerably in the extent to which they acknowledge aspects of play. But, despite their very significant differences, it is by acknowledging the reader as figure and readings as the locus of meanings that the focus on reading processes introduces the question of how play resists finality whether finality is held to be located in the text, the reading, or an academy's institutionalisation of critical practice. Deconstruction is the critical theory and practice that makes the most significant recent contribution to our understanding of play in texts, reading and writing. At risk, always, of reducing Derrida's contributions to linguistic theory and eliding the philosophical traditions within which his writings are situated, literary theory and criticism inevitably borrow with losses. Even so, the measure is not so much a question of fidelity to "origins" as evaluation of the interest and contribution of the new work to its field of study. Influenced by borrowings, it necessarily involves displacement and change and play. Interdisciplinary activity is not only a characteristic but a value in contemporary culture in its promotion of connections, changing perspectives and new opportunities for

Foreplay 7

engagement, and the impact of deconstruction upon literary studies recharges the hermeneutical enterprise.

With this focus upon play forms and practice, and with particular attention to post-structuralist developments, this study is eclectic, exploratory and incomplete. It would be a contradiction in terms to prescribe the limits; play exceeds the game. Nevertheless, definitions are possible and they help to explain the processes by which texts are constructed and acquire meanings as cultural artefacts. My procedure throughout is selective and comparative, so that practice and theory are held to be interrelated and particular examples are considered with respect to textual communication more generally.

"'How can you learn lessons in here?'" asks Alice. "And so she went on, taking first one side and then the other and making quite a conversation of it altogether. . . .'" The conversation of Part I, "Grasshopper Antics: The Playhouse of Language" is extended, first one side and then the other, suspending resolution, in the text studies of Part II, "Duplicity as Virtue: Playful Texts and Textualised Players." Itself a definitional morass, which I consider briefly as an introduction to the Part II studies, postmodernism presents so many instances of play at work against the hegemonic settlings of habit and privilege. Its self-conscious engagement with traditional forms of public discourse and its challenge to conservative ideas about disciplines, procedures, and the nature of knowledge, create a cultural arena for playful rebellion and innovation. Postmodernist fiction is our most recent and most complex literary example of play as procedure and value, and, as I attempt to demonstrate in the analyses in Part II of this study, its range addresses the broad sphere of contemporary culture.

NOTES

1. Jacques Derrida, *Dissemination,* 3.

2. Thomas Pynchon, "Entropy," *The Kenyon Review,* No. 22, 1960, 285. The story is reprinted in the collection of Pynchon's early stories, *Slow Learner.*

3. Derrida's assertion of the priority of writing over speech may be seen overtly in his analysis of Rousseau's work. See *Of Grammatology,* Part II. I discuss this matter in some detail in Chapter 3.

4. Roland Barthes, *S/Z,* 10.

8   *Theories of Play and Postmodern Fiction*

5. Discussed in Chapter 3, particularly with respect to the work of Derrida and Barthes. Although they appear to express contrasting attitudes to the situation, there are similarities between Derrida's joy, Bloom's "anxiety" (*The Anxiety of Influence: A Theory of Poetry*) and de Man's "blindness" (*Blindness and Insight: Essays in the Rhetoric of Contemporary Criticism*) as each emphasizes the disparity between sign and meaning, that condition of uncertainty which removes the epistemological supports of knowing and, against fixed knowledge, emphasizes undecidability.

6. Jean Baudrillard, *Cool Memories,* 153.

7. Geoffrey Hartman, *Saving the Text: Literature, Derrida, Philosophy,* 137. This is, of course, a central consequence for poststructuralist criticism, a position (or lack of a position) repeated in the theory and one that emphasizes play in language.

8. A view expressed by M.H Abrams, for example, when he accuses Derrida of reducing meaning to "a ceaseless echolalia, a vertical and lateral reverberation from sign to sign of ghostly non-presences emanating from no voice, intended by no one, referring to nothing, bombinating in a void" ("The Deconstructive Angel," 431). It is a view largely shared by Wayne Booth in his contribution to this discussion, 'The Limits of Pluralism', published in *Critical Inquiry.*

9. See J. Hillis Miller, "The Critic as Host."

10. T.S. Eliot, "The Metaphysical Poets." See Frank Kermode ed., *Selected Prose of T.S. Eliot,* 65.

11. Most fully expressed in his *Anatomy of Criticism,* Frye's thesis of influence and interpenetration echoes this aspect of Eliot's "Tradition and the Individual Talent." Acknowledging influence, Bloom discusses it more as a source of pressure than pleasure for poets (see *The Anxiety of Influence*).

12. John Barth, "The Literature of Exhaustion." The position Barth describes is similar to that presented by Bloom in *The Anxiety of Influence.* According to Bloom, "strong poets" feel their late arrival, their appearance at a time when earlier poets have exhausted the possibilities for writing. Bloom's view that writers must, therefore, misread their predecessors is similar to Barth's practice of re-telling those predecessors in new ways. With a change of metaphor in his later essay, "The Literature of Replenishment," Barth reaffirms within the context of postmodernist fiction the productive possibilities of the writer's communication with the past: "My ideal postmodernist author neither merely repudiates nor merely imitates either his twentieth-century modernist parents or his nineteenth-century premodernist grandparents. He has the first

Foreplay 9

half of our century under his belt but not on his back" (70).

    13. Miguel de Cervantes Saavedra, *Don Quixote,* 12.

CHAPTER 2

Play: The Reader as Trickster

The time has come to treat play seriously.

—Jacques Ehrmann[1]

It is hardly surprising that "play" and "game" recur frequently, as metaphors and as concepts, in critical theory and practice. Signalling activity, including possibilities for competition and conflict as well as cooperative exchange, favouring process against ends, they begin to suggest not only the variability (and instability) of texts and contexts but the inviting challenges that their interpretation involves. Pan-disciplinary,[2] they have a special place in aesthetics and in the study of literature. Schiller's tribute to play, to the *Spieltrieb,* sets an influential mark: "man only plays when he is in the fullest sense of the word a human being, and he is only fully a human being when he plays."[3] And as Mihai Spariosu's studies indicate, for example, ideas and uses of play and game may be seen in Western culture from the time of Hesiod and Homer to their latest incarnations in contemporary aesthetics and cultural practice, from the *agōn* in *The Iliad* to Baudrillardian precessions of simulacra and the seductions of hyperreality. But what value do the terms have for literary theory and criticism? Do they describe familiar characteristics simply by providing another set of metaphors, or do they introduce fresh perceptions in this destabilised triad of writer-text-reader? Can they serve as analytic and revelatory terms in discussion of literature, helping to locate it within an interdisciplinary focus at the centre of cultural practice? As Bernard Suits's protagonist in *The Grasshopper: Games, Life and Utopia* warns, there is "a good deal of loose talk about games these days,"[4] and, one may add, about play; but working as asshoppers and grants, with a

12   *Theories of Play and Postmodern Fiction*

combination of grasshopper verve and ant industry, we may yet provide precision while retaining variability.

At this broad level of enquiry, two general problems complicate the subject:

1. the breadth and variety of attention to game and play
    Contributing to the looseness that Suits mentions, this variability presents problems for definition and for comparative analysis. "Play" as it is used in ethnography, or by Schiller, for example, is very different from the play of Derrida's *jeu libre.*

2. the need to distinguish between game and play
    Although they are often related, game and play are not synonymous. As activities that are finite and rule-governed, games involve play but play is not bound to games.

In the following discussion, I consider game and play separately while affirming connections between them. Although texts may be about or involve games, and although "game" offers models for their study, "play" is more fundamental, wide-reaching and subversive, particularly in the cultural contexts of postmodernism where, with all barriers under pressure, the totalising parameters of game give way to the multiplicities and open-endedness of play. Although applications of game and play to literature evolve from activity in a number of disciplines, this discussion refers only selectively to those other contexts. Some reference to background and to parallels is necessary, partly to define the concepts but also because the interdisciplinary plotting is itself both recent and incomplete.

GAME

Although they vary in number, complexity and function from one culture to another, and in definition according to who produces the taxonomy and for what purpose, games are generally held to be universal cultural practices. Their study by anthropologists, psychologists, educationists, and social scientists indicates the value they are believed to have as cultural indices, as models for social practices and even as evidence for the levels of complexity in a social organization.[5] Definitions commonly include reference to organization, competition, sides, results and, therefore, rules[6] as the basic

Play
13

characteristics of games which may then be further classified according to skill levels, strategies or chance elements, for example, or according to their structure or apparent purpose. Eric Berne's *Games People Play*[7] focuses attention upon game structures and game spirit of a less formally organized type than anthropological classifications; the difference is mainly in magnitude between his attention to games in social behaviour and Kostas Axelos's omnivorous "game of the world"[8] as a figure for all human activity, a grand sweep that champions game as Schiller champions play. But it is probably because it is adaptable as well as accessible that Roger Caillois's four-part classification of games after their dominant characteristic, *agōn* (competition), *alea* (chance) *mimicry* (simulation), or *ilinx* (vertigo),[9] is the one most frequently taken up by literary critics who turn, however, fleetingly, to game theory for reference.[10] It is a simple exercise to categorize a literary text according to one or more of these figures, exploring its particularisation in terms of plot or theme or reading position. Beyond offering that signal figure, or intersection of figures, however, what does the game metaphor provide? If games are indeed rule-governed, how do rules operate in literary games? Further, to what extent may specific game references within a text (say the funeral games in *The Iliad* that reaffirm agonistic cultural practices, the Phaeacian games in *The Odyssey* that are contestatory as well as celebratory, or the chess references in Nabokov's *The Defense)* indicate either its interests or modes or parameters for its reading?

In a discussion of three studies that use game terminology, Robert Wilson observes correctly, "the current state of play in literary theory, with respect to game concepts, is characterized by considerable uncertainty over the meaning of 'game' and its related terms."[11] He attributes the interest in game concepts to four preoccupations: study of play in relation to culture, the emphasis upon rules in language and in everyday activities, the literature which stresses fantasy over realism, and the invention of mathematical Game Theory.[12] While pointing out the loose analogies drawn between games and other cultural practices, and the difficulties encountered in adaptations of Game Theory to literary theory, he is optimistic about the value of a game model. To his list of influences, I would add that scepticism within the natural and human sciences that has encouraged the questioning of values and knowledge,[13] developments in linguistics and communication theory which emphasize uncertainty, and increasing attention in reading theory

14   *Theories of Play and Postmodern Fiction*

to the reader's creative role. Contributing to the atmosphere of doubt about truth, and promoting difference, they too encourage gamesome activity with an interest in enquiry, processes and strategies.

As the following description indicates, formal Game Theory, a theoretical model derived from hypothetical two-person conflicts, has limited application to literary criticism:

> In short, what distinguishes games from non-games from the point of view of game theory is not the seriousness or lack of seriousness of a situation, nor the attitudes of the participants, nor the nature of the acts and of the outcomes, but whether certain choices of actions and certain outcomes can be unambiguously defined, whether the consequences of joint choices can be precisely specified, and whether the choosers have distinct preferences among the outcomes.[14]

Those characteristics which have made "game" fruitful in economics, political science, and resource and military planning—its precise attention to rules of procedure, clear choices and unambiguous consequences—are those which make it inappropriate in literary theory. As Wilson indicates, although the two-person model provides a suggestive metaphor for author and reader with the text as board, or playfield, its limitations are apparent: whereas game theory emphasizes rules which determine the manner of play and game, literature is more playful in its ability to transcend, by mockery, parody, or experiment, its own "rules" or conventions; whereas game theory specifies clear choice and unambiguous consequences, literature is unavoidably ambiguous by virtue of its allusiveness and its limited control over reader activity. An author may, like a gamesmaster, establish the initial field of play, the text, and guide some of the game; nevertheless, recognizing that as texts manipulate readers so readers "create" texts, readers can impose various grids (historical, philosophical, linguistic, political, feminist) in their attention to a text.

Even so, despite the limitations of criteria such as "rule-governed," "self-contained," and "definable outcomes," "game" is an attractive metaphor to apply to literature. In a less rigorous sense than strict Game Theory demands, game suggests an author's construction of a text (the author as initiator or games-controller[15]) and the view that each text challenges its readers to a contest (reading as game). It emphasizes the situation of exchange which all literature involves. Difficulties

Play   15

concerning the adaptation of game to literature may be seen in Elizabeth Bruss's "The Game of Literature and Some Literary Games."[16] Noting that there are certain works in which the reader becomes acutely aware of the reading activity, works that present influences, choices, self-conscious reflection and so on, that appear more readily game-like than some others, Bruss suggests: "A give and take, a 'game' of literature is bared in such works because in them pragmatic values outweigh the semantic and the morphological. Imaginary worlds and significant form are subordinated to the conflict or cooperation of the participants in the communicative exchange" (153). But, with the possible exception of the detective story with its standard play upon clues and choices, there is no escaping the semantic and those works that self-consciously affirm their ludic nature, from *Don Quixote, Tom Jones* and *Tristram Shandy* to the writings of Borges and Nabokov, Calvino, Barth, Pynchon and Coover, and the experimental work of Oulipo (*Ouvroir de Littérature Potentielle*) depend upon the reader's participation in the play of language. Further, as I indicate in the studies presented in Part II, this participation will be contextual—although its appropriations of other literature and cultural formations will necessarily vary from reader to reader, the matter of whether they will occur or not is not an issue. As Bruss's discussion moves between considerations of Game Theory as it might be applied to literature and more flexible descriptions of game terminology, unresolved difficulties arise from her attempt to adopt Game Theory. Her metaphor of "counters to be shifted on the board," the view that games require parity between participants, and the idea that adherence to rules constitutes the game, all severely limit the notion of literature as game. Aware of this restrictiveness, Bruss distinguishes between works that formally resemble a particular game[17] and works whose playfulness is game-like. She indicates different perspectives that arise from approaching texts as games and comments on the relationship between text and reading strategies. Her conclusion presents a summary of possibilities and limitations:

> To see the game in certain literary works is to appreciate new aesthetic dimensions, particularly the "beauty" of strategy. Game theory provides a provisional set of terms for capturing this dimension, but it remains to be seen whether it will finally prove inadequate to the full subtlety of inferred intentions and complex

16   *Theories of Play and Postmodern Fiction*

> indirect engagements that are characteristic of literary encounters.
> Many of the qualities of mind, motivation and individual behaviour
> upon which formal game theory is predicated seem primitive in
> comparison to literary treatments of these same phenomena. Even the
> notion of "game" itself may eventually prove too narrow, suggesting
> as it does a finite set of rules, a well-defined playing space, clearly
> ranked preferences, and conscious calculations. (163)

Despite the limitations, adaptations will be effective or not according to
their use in the practice of criticism. Theoretical perspectives cannot
stand as solutions to the complexities of literary texts and reading
practices. Indeed, to expect them to do so, as a justification for theory,
would be to impose conditions that literature must escape. So, for
example, although Peter Hutchinson acknowledges literature as a game
that transcends rules, his *Games Authors Play*[18] also reveals problems
in the application of game analogies. His focus on the author, and his
definition of strategies authors use to draw readers into their texts,
present examples for consideration but place too much emphasis upon
the writer as controller and too little upon the play of signification in
the text itself and in the processes of its reception. Preferring game to
play, because game "suggests more of a developed structure" (14) and a
greater challenge to readers, he offers a reductive view of texts as goal-
centred, controlled and fixed, a view that values discoverable truths and
completion above the uncertainties of play as subversive process.
Although his study defines various game-strategies used by writers, its
adherence to game and its relegation of play reduces the vitality of play
in words. It presents a limited view of the dynamics of signification.

Following citations from Wittgenstein, Suits, Sontag, Josipovici
and Steiner, Rawdon Wilson concludes that the applications assume
arbitrariness, complexity of structure and rules as the main properties of
games. But pointing out that complexity of structure is not mandatory
for games, he pursues the game/text analogy and, for literature,
distinguishes between rules and conventions, the latter offering more
flexibility and being the more accurate term for literary practice: "the
argument here will be that conventions are looser, less abstract, more
resistant to formulation, and altogether more flexible than rules" (85).
Rules may govern the construction of a sonnet but there is none that
determines the length, mode, subject matter or language of a novel, for
instance, or, as Wilson suggests in his discussion of pastoral literature,

Play 17

"Take away the flutes, the idealized setting, even the sheep, and there may still be a pastoral effect" (45). Notwithstanding the fact that many works of literature are based variously upon games (Nabokov's *The Defense,* Cortázar's *Hopscotch,* Coover's *The Universal Baseball Association,* Carroll's *Through the Looking Glass,* Calvino's *The Castle of Crossed Destinies)* and that moves, plays, challenges and ludic engagement provide attractive analogies for the processes of reading and interpretation, the wordplay exceeds the gamerules.

The time has come, as Jacques Ehrmann suggests, to treat play seriously.

PLAY

As the more expansive term, one that subsumes and transcends game, play provides insights to the operations of all literature. When Suits's grasshopper dreams that everyone alive is engaged in playing elaborate games, this dream vision underscores the ludic perspective an omniscient observer might have of the endless variability of human activity. In its most general sense, play is an attitude of mind, a perspective on life or on being in the world, together with actions manifesting this attitude. It affirms freedom and possibility against restriction, resignation and closure, thus blurring distinctions between observation and participation, and between spectators and collaborators, distinctions which are far from clear. To observe is to be involved, in activity, discourse and change, in the play of the world. It is to participate in what Derrida describes as the Nietzschean affirmation: "the joyous affirmation of the play of the world and of the innocence of becoming, the affirmation of a world of signs without fault, without truth, and without origin which is offered to an active interpretation."[19] It offers activity against the forms of essentialism, authoritarianism and ending; it offers a model for reading practice itself as for the processes of thought in culture generally. It is endemic in the operations of language.

What has been said of this "play of the world"? Although its configurations change, it is coterminous with human culture. Examining texts and cultural arrangements from Homer and Hesiod to Plato and Aristotle, Spariosu traces the predominance of specific forms of play in classical texts, using the ambiguous figure of Dionysus, the shape-shifter, half-divine and half-human, born of Zeus's lightning

18   *Theories of Play and Postmodern Fiction*

bolt, God of theatre and of wine, associated with creativity and with intoxication, this "god of many names," to stand for "the conflictive, double nature of Western humans and their play: gentle, reasonable, and peace-loving on the one hand, and competitive, intractable, and warmongering on the other" (1991, xiv). Tracing a genealogy, Spariosu emphasizes the divided concepts of play and their centrality in Hellenic thought and culture. As *paidia* (children's play) and as *agōn* (conflict), play was associated alternatively with the freedom and exuberance of innocent exploration and with serious competition and the exercise of power. In Homer's epics and in classical drama, ideas of play as exuberant movement and competition contend variously with the shifting relationship between chance and necessity. Just as *The Iliad* may be seen as a game of war between Olympian gods and their human agents, with chance circumscribed by fate (*moira*), *The Odyssey* presents Odysseus as part plaything and part free agent, a figure both moved and moving on the long journey between war's end and homeplace, between the agonistic play of battlefields and the quieter cultural interactions of work and days, between archaic and median systems of value. As Spariosu suggests, nevertheless, this is no simple evolutionary movement from primitive violence to ordered civilization (a movement that some commentators wish also to read in *The Oresteia*) but, rather, an interplay of different modes of behaviour, values and conceptions of *play*. Further, and while the exchange continues between *archaic* and *median* values, Euripides', Sophocles' and Aristophanes' attention to the battle of words foregrounds a mode of play that is endemic both in classical cultural practice, in terms of the representational and relational capacities of language and performance, and in language, in aesthetics and creativity as exploration, expression and play. Cast in *The Bacchae* as the revengeful god of ecstatic release, Dionysus plays an archaic game of power but also with dissimulation, trickery and simulacra, capacities evident again in *The Frogs* where the God of Drama who presides over the weighing of the poets' works is also the comically craven role-player whose journey to Hades is the ludic pantomime of a serious idea. But if play seemed to get off to a bad start in Western culture, the charge rests with Plato, the one who labelled poets liars, banished them from the Republic and vested control in the philosopher-kings with their authority based upon reason, truth and knowledge. Nevertheless, while regarding the play of poets with suspicion, Plato exhibits in *The Republic* and in *The Laws* his

Play 19

pleasure in verbal contest, dialectic and controlled forms of play. As Nietzsche, Gadamer, Derrida and Spariosu have noted,[20] his seriousness is inseparable from his playfulness; play as freedom, game, verbal battle, role-playing, competition, levity and ludism is a basic component of language, art, philosophy and political practice. What was repressed as mere play or as idle entertainment, as distraction and as other to work, seriousness, reason, authority and knowledge slips the noose to reassert, from the start and from the centers of human activity, its claims not just to creative attraction but also to the definition of knowledge and power. Always already, the Dionysiac rewrites the Apollonian, the two caught in a dialectic at the heartland of culture. In consideration of recent formulations, I shall begin with a critique of the Huizinga-Caillois-Ehrmann line of cultural analysis.

When Huizinga argues in *Homo Ludens* that play is meaningful, central and older than culture, with play-forms producing culture, "by allowing the innate human need of rhythm, harmony, change, alternation, contrast and climax, etc., to unfold in full richness,"[21] he accords play high value while emphasizing the fun-element as its essence. His study of expressions for play in different languages shows, in its etymological complexity, the considerable variety in conceptions of the nature of play. However, as he points out, "It is ancient wisdom, but it is also a little cheap, to call all human activity 'play'." His consequent attempt to define play by locating its main characteristics indicates, again, the difficulty of the task. What are these signal features? Huizinga suggests play's freedom, its difference from "ordinary" or "real" life, its secluded or limited nature (it is "'played out' within certain limits of time and place") and its power to create order.[22] Acknowledging the importance of this ground-breaking study, later theorists question Huizinga's definition of play, particularly his tendency to define it in opposition to both seriousness and reality, an objection made, for example, by Jacques Ehrmann,[23] George Steiner,[24] James Hans[25] and Warren Motte.[26] The definition presupposes that reality is determinate and serious so that play, despite its equivocal relationship with seriousness ("seriousness seeks to exclude play, whereas play can very well include seriousness"[27]), exists in a border zone that influences but is also apart from reality. There is a paradox in Huizinga's thesis about the relationship between play and culture: wanting to distinguish play from reality, he also argues that it is the very foundation of culture, definable not only in games, poetry, music,

20 Theories of Play and Postmodern Fiction

dance and the visual arts, but in religious ritual, war, philosophy, law and work as well. Furthermore, despite its fascination and breadth, his hymn to play depends upon an elitist view of culture, a view that champions the culture of small groups in the eighteenth century as the "full flower" of the play element in civilization and regards the democratization of life in the nineteenth and twentieth centuries as the lamentable wilting of that flower. It is because he values play so highly and wishes to savour its most effervescent moments, according to very limiting perceptions of value, that Huizinga's study presents such a nostalgic view of the past and fails to do justice to popular culture and to play in contemporary civilization.

Although Roger Caillois finds Huizinga's definition at once too broad and too narrow,[28] his own definition of play as "essentially a separate occupation, carefully isolated from the rest of life, and generally engaged in with precise limits of time and place" (6) is very restrictive as well. Like Huizinga, therefore, Caillois opposes play to "real life": "play and ordinary life are constantly and universally antagonistic to each other," (63) a position which has somehow to lift activities out of real life (for example, gambling, to which Caillois devotes considerable attention), and regard them as apart from reality, as activities in which normality is suspended. The attempt is curious and precarious. Seeing play essentially in terms of activity as free, separate, uncertain, unproductive, rule-governed and make-believe, his definition is developed within the four-part taxonomy of games that I have already considered. Even though this categorization of games provides a typology that can be used for analysis, it is because Caillois's study concentrates on games and considers play in terms of them that it is, finally, so restrictive of the possibilities of play. As Jacques Ehrmann has pointed out, both Huizinga and Caillois fail play by attempting to define it in relation to very questionable givens. He reproaches them for evaluating play in relation to reality and culture, each of which is a problematic concept, relative and changing, a construct: "the distinguishing characteristic of reality is that it is played. Play, reality and culture are synonymous and interchangeable" (55-6). The marginal usurps the center. Against the oppositional thinking that gives primacy to reality, Ehrmann's deconstructive move subverts the relationship by holding play, the secondary term and other, as one that is indissociable from "reality." It involves articulation, communication and economy in which the simple oppositions of subjectivity/ob-

Play   *21*

jectivity and play/reality are undone because they are interrelated and played through together.

For Ehrmann, then, play is the inescapable condition of life: "To define play is at the same time and in the same movement to define reality and to define culture" (55). Bernard Suits's grasshopper is Everyman/woman. Ehrmann's view celebrates flux and diversity; it is echoed by Kostas Axelos: "The whole man is both player and toy no matter what he does," (7) a perspective that places people as simultaneously manipulators and subjects of cultural systems. It is shared by James Hans: "we still play all the time, even if we are told otherwise," (154)[29] despite the way he qualifies this gesture by holding to limiting notions of value. Hans's thesis in *The Play of the World* is that play is the most meaningful of activities because it produces the world and generates values. Although he does not define play directly, his study offers such criteria as self-forgetfulness, openness, freedom, novelty, risk and change as characteristics of play. But there is a revealing disjunction between his Derridean perception of the elaborate networks and grafts of language and the modifications to freeplay represented in his attention to structures, fixing meaning and value. Although it is a matter of choice where one places the emphasis (and how one regards that emphasis) in an interminable dialectic between continuities and discontinuities, temporary stasis and inevitable change, Hans's phenomenological restrictions reduce "play" by limiting the play of language.

These attempts to define play concentrate on content, on types of activity within social contexts, attempting to say what play is and to locate it within human action in general. It is possible to look more directly at motivation as M.J. Ellis does in his psychological study, *Why People Play*. [30] Ellis locates five "classical" theories of play: play as release of surplus energy, as relaxation after stress, as instinctive response in preparation for adulthood, as instinctive recapitulation of critical responses, as an undirected instinctive behaviour. Similarly, his chapters on "recent" and on "modern" theories of play are psychological in orientation,[31] theories that sift the "classical" formulations by introducing perspectives from psychoanalysis, learning theory and recent cognitive studies. But as Ellis points out, behaviour can have many motives and the attempt to disentangle these as a means of defining play is fraught with problems: "Pure play is probably only theoretically possible and striving for a pure definition only makes

22   *Theories of Play and Postmodern Fiction*

sense in that context" (110). There remains the view that play is undefinable, a view that emphasizes heterogeneity (as both a situation and a value): "The gallant attempts to provide direct, comprehensive theories of play are inadequate partly because they attempt to define and treat play as an activity with a common core and with characteristics that distinguish it from all others."[32] Play will, by definition, elude definition. To regard play as essentially undefinable is to return to *homo ludens* and to Ehrmann's assertion that "Play, reality and culture are synonymous and interchangeable" (56).

"Play," then, is one of those alluring words, like "myth" and "art" which enjoy popular currency but which are subject to such speculation that definitions are necessarily elusive and reductive. Its range is vast, as Rawdon Wilson indicates in *In Palamedes' Shadow:*

> Drawing with it a number of subordinate concepts such as self-representation, make-believe, role, rule, move, strategy, tactics, aleatory combinations, and so forth, play has shifted from a descriptive vocabulary appropriate to the activities of children and the leisure of adults. It may be used as a model to describe and explain all kinds of human activity: learning procedures, social interaction, personal expressivity, cultural formation and transformation, as well as a wide range of activities that involve the creation and reception of works of art, simulation, dissimulation, risk-taking, strategic thinking, tactical decision making, structural experimentation, the testing or trying out of ideas. (28)

Insofar as art is often regarded as humanity's highest achievement and the quintessential expression of play in material form, what may be said about play in relationship with art? In Edmond Radar's words, "It [art] is an activity all the more infinite as it is not fixed on an object nor even on an imaginary program but on the experience of the interpretation of signs, with its unlimited potential, discoveries, unsuspected connections and continued invention" (93). For Radar, play within art is governed by the pleasure principle; it possesses a "hedonistic ascendancy" that compels both expression and response in oscillations between the pleasure principle and the reality principle. Retaining the virtues of spontaneity, exuberance and self-awareness, it tests the reality principle itself. As another perspective that points to the interconnectedness of reality and play, so that the oppositions are dismantled, it is a reminder

Play

23

of the mobility of signs, and of the play of differences within the sign, these common features of post-Saussurean linguistics. Saussure's view of language as a differential sign system[33] emphasizes not only the primacy of the word and the autonomy of language, but also the capacity for play that is indissociable from the notion of difference, a capacity that he illustrates frequently by recourse to chess metaphors. It is in Derrida's deconstruction, however, that difference is more radically transformed into an infinite play of differences for which there is no center. This mobility is innate to the discourse, existing within the signifiers and their correspondences, and it must be discovered, interpreted and remade by the spectator/participant as semiologist, as the worker of a linguistic system that offers such possibilities for meanings because there are no final grounds of arbitration. As Barthes demonstrates humorously, we are active semiologists, always creating meanings in our varied discourse with the world:

> Accidentally, Werther's finger touches Charlotte's, their feet, under the table, happen to brush against each other. Werther might be engrossed by the meaning of these accidents; he might concentrate physically on these slight zones of contact and delight in this fragment of inert finger or foot, fetishistically, without concern for the response (like God—as the etymology of the word tells us—the Fetish does not reply). But in fact Werther is not perverse, he is in love: he creates meaning, always and everywhere, out of nothing, and it is meaning which thrills him: he is in the crucible of meaning. Every contact, for the lover, raises the question of an answer: the skin is asked to reply.
> (a squeeze of the hand-enormous documentation—a tiny gesture within the palm, a knee which doesn't move away, an arm extended, as if quite naturally, along the back of a sofa and against which the other's head gradually comes to rest—this is the paradisiac realm of subtle and clandestine signs: a kind of festival not of the senses but of meaning)[34]

Werther the Lover as Bricoleur! Werther, the lover conceived by Barthes as bricoleur. Werther textual signifier, imagined by the reader as bricoleur. The discourse of lovers (and readers), as Barthes reminds us, is packed with bricolage or "the canny embezzlement of previous art."[35] Werther, endowed with our reading, is created by Fielding and

24   *Theories of Play and Postmodern Fiction*

Austen, Stendhal and Flaubert, "Don Juan" and *A la Recherche du temps perdu*!

Reading is an exemplary play situation, where the possibilities for play in pursuit of meaning are inevitably present in the text itself (through the metaphoric nature of language and the play of signification) *and* in the processes of reception. This view may be traced to Nietzsche's reflections on language in its duplicity, with its consequent destabilisation of truth claims: "What, then, is truth? A mobile army of metaphors, metonyms, and anthropomorphisms—in short, a sum of human relations which have been enhanced, transposed, and embellished poetically and rhetorically. . . ."[36] Concentrating on the centrality of language in culture, revealing the arbitrariness of words and, therefore, the relativity of meanings, his attack on fixed notions of authority (self, reason, truth, God) not only champions scepticism and uncertainty, but emphasizes as well the fragmentariness of both self and world. Most importantly, he locates this fragmentation and the provisionality of concepts in language. Emphasizing metaphor, and hence, no facts—"only interpretations"—and denying all forms of closure, Nietzsche affirms the play of texts and meanings: "Convictions are prisons. Such men do not look far enough, they do not look *beneath* themselves: but to be permitted to join in the discussion of value and disvalue, one must see five hundred convictions *beneath* oneself— behind oneself."[37] It is this activity that Derrida describes as the "Nietzschean affirmation," acknowledging its importance to his deconstructive interventions.

There is relentless probing of a different kind in Wittgenstein's *Philosophical Investigations*. Whereas the *Tractatus* offers a representational or picture-theory view of language, it is the later work's systematic critique of this view, and its denial of essence, that leads Wittgenstein to emphasize change and multiplicity against his earlier attempts to prescribe boundaries of language use. Although he criticizes Nietzsche's scepticism as the product of a deluded, and failed quest for certainty, his philosophy of language, like Nietzsche's, promotes incessant activity of interpretation against limitations. He comes to the central metaphors by reflecting upon a variety of games and the modes of play they involve, an examination in which "we see a complicated network of similarities overlapping and criss-crossing" (32) and for which he uses the expression "family resemblances" to allow for similarity with difference. Describing language itself as

Play 25

always incomplete, an ancient and labyrinthine city crossed and recrossed by the accretions of later periods of street construction and building design, his analysis demonstrates the excitement facing city visitors.[38] It is the multiplicity of styles, grammars and meanings that complicate the metaphor, destabilize texts and contexts, and subvert determinate standards of knowledge:

> There are countless kinds [of sentence]; countless different kinds of use of what we call "symbols," "words," "sentences." And this multiplicity is not something fixed, given once for all; but new types of languages, new language-games, as we may say, come into existence, and others become obsolete and get forgotten. (Item 23)

Extending the game metaphor, Wittgenstein demonstrates that no definition can account for all of the particular usages of a certain word. Usages and rules are tied to custom but if this mutability demonstrates agreements within conventions determined by time and place, it demonstrates as well the instability of concepts such as truth, knowledge, understanding and meaning. It encourages specific activity in its dividedness, particularities and fallibility against the hegemonic claims of tradition, canonicity and institutional authority.

Although the game metaphor implies rules of procedure and underscores the public nature of language, it stresses, as well, the indefinite number of possible language games. In this way, Wittgenstein explores the expansive play of meaning in language while demonstrating the arbitrary, and verifiable, framing of particular definitions. If it changes as rapidly and complexly as the world that exists by virtue of it, as Wittgenstein contends, then language is neither practically finite nor to be understood outside language itself. In this view, "reality" is not a set of knowable structures, however numerous and complex these may be, but a continuing process of articulation. Outrunning fixed structures and systems, this process simultaneously makes and questions what can be known. Wittgenstein's view holds that language is an adequate means of communication while demonstrating its dividedness and the folly of essentialist reductions. As Allen Thiher suggests, "the play metaphor functions as another heuristic axiom"[39] in Wittgenstein's work. His emphasis upon increasing multiplicity in meanings differs from the Nietzschean-

26   *Theories of Play and Postmodern Fiction*

Derridean emphasis upon indeterminacy, but these different perceptions each favour an active and open-ended linguistics.

I do not wish to include here a detailed discussion of psychoanalysis and linguistics, but Freud's theories support another and different version of the inevitability of play in language. Whether this is presented in terms of operations of the unconscious and consciousness as an explanation of ambiguities, the dreamwork model of condensation and displacement, or Lacan's linguistic revision of this model in terms of metaphor and metonymy, psychoanalytic theory emphasizes linguistic play in the production of meanings. Although it works from a ground that Derridean deconstruction questions, offering the divided self as explanatory source, it nevertheless proposes a split model of words at work. Derrida's own frequent attention to Freud's work, and particularly in "My Chances/*Mes Chances:* A Rendezvous with Some Epicurean Stereophonies,"[40] emphasizes chance, risk and contingency in psychoanalysis. Freud questions logocentric procedures while using them; while manipulating contexts, he affirms possibility in ways that also acknowledge indeterminacy. It is in their recognition of supplementarity that Freud and Derrida come together. In the interplay of language, desire, will and repression, the last word can never be the last word.

How do such views of linguistic play affect our appreciation of texts? What critical practices result? Deconstruction which I discuss in Chapter Four, is a philosophical perspective and reading practice that takes up the Nietzschean challenge in its interrogation of texts against the knowledge claims of origin, certainty and truth. According to this perspective, words and texts represent not some preordained form of presence but traces of other words, other texts. Since ultimacy is always deferred, readers will acknowledge the play of meanings in texts and the reading process, and readings will offer meanings that reflect the divided contexts of their formation while resisting closure. At this point, I would like to include a brief consideration of Mikhail Bakhtin's work because, although there are significant differences in Bakhtin's and Derrida's attention to play, particularly with respect to the relationship between cultural constraints and textual indeterminacy, Bakhtin's writing, like Derrida's, offers important perspectives upon the play of language. Whereas Derrida offers rigorous readings that demonstrate the play of meanings in language according to a perspective of indeterminacy, Bakhtin's dialogical model emphasizes

Play

multiple meanings while looking to cultural constraints upon their efficacy. When Bakhtin defines language as inherently dialogic, he suggests that words simultaneously acknowledge and transgress specific cultural constraints. Emphasizing both the historical condition of the sign and its location in a changing linguistic system, he posits it as the site of an intersection of meanings, wherein its context is intertextual, and its ambivalence is rebellious. Favouring heterogeneity and the carnivalesque, the sign subverts authority much as the institution of carnival itself transgresses normal cultural structures in its suspension of hierarchies, its mixing of all elements of life (high and low, sophisticated and billingsgate) and its consequent emphasis on variety, freedom and regeneration. When Bakhtin defines carnival as "life itself but shaped according to a certain pattern of play,"[41] and insists upon the subversive and regenerative power of laughter, he accords play a more generous cultural centrality than Huizinga and Caillois allow in their distinctions between play and seriousness. Most importantly, he locates play in language, as exemplified in his interpretation of billingsgate, the language of the market-place in Rabelais' texts. Thus Rabelais, singer of fleshly excesses, is also a celebrant of change and renewal. Light-hearted and serious at once, the carnivalesque is dialogical. There is an important distinction to be made between carnival and carnivalesque. Locating Bakhtin's work within a notion of "carnivalesque cosmogony," Julia Kristeva's description points towards this distinction:

> It [the carnivalesque] is a spectacle but without a stage; a game but also a daily undertaking; a signifier but also a signified. That is, two texts meet, contradict and revolutionize each other. A carnival participant is both actor and spectator; he loses his sense of individuality, passes through a zero point of carnivalesque activity and splits into a subject of the spectacle and an object of the game.[42]

"Game" is the appropriate metaphor for carnival in its medieval cultural context because, like a game, it was confined by rules, by a social organization that manipulated and contained its rites of reversal. Institutionalised, a fixture in the medieval calendar, carnival gave expression to political resentment but in the therapeutic forms of parody and laughter. Revolutionary in its zest, it could also function as a conservative cultural practice by permitting controlled subversions

28   *Theories of Play and Postmodern Fiction*

and thereby supporting the status quo. Robert Lavenda's case study of the relationship between carnival and social realities[43] is focussed on changes in the Caracas Carnival in the late nineteenth century, and he emphasizes not the limitations of Bakhtin's term "carnivalesque" but its appropriateness as metaphor. Carnivals as social events may indeed oscillate between spirited excess and polite decorum, between expressing a people's repressed energy and their civic achievements; the wider term "carnivalesque," on the other hand, and particularly as it is applied to the literary text, is an expression of rhetorical exuberance, of a text's spirited capacity for play that is necessarily stimulated by but not bound to "the text" as a unified concept because it concentrates upon energy and difference rather than constraint and unity.

As Robert Wilson points out,[44] Bakhtin's "carnival" undergoes changes when it is abstracted and transformed as a concept for use in textual analysis; but "carnival" is already transformed within the Bakhtinian context itself as it gives way to "carnivalesque" and to Bakhtin's definition of transgressive energy and celebration in Rabelais' work. Serving textual analysis, carnival(esque) becomes not so much a "lesser" as a "wider" concept[45] than it is in Bakhtin's discourse, a metaphor abstracted from cultural practices to function as an indicator of certain aspects of those practices, including particular modes of discourse. The extent to which analyses of carnivalesque texts will attend to social context and the extent to which these texts will be either innovative or transgressive remains more a matter of critical choice than definitional obligation. This is indicated in Bakhtin's own reading, in its movement between formalist considerations and reference to carnival traditions in specific social contexts. Although Bakhtin's attention to cultural practices recognizes a firmer contextual basis than does deconstruction for the creation of meaning, his emphasis upon the play of language, upon "polyphony" and "heteroglossia," defines interplay, exuberance and riddling as endemic to utterance. Whilst there is considerable difference between his attention to cultural constraints and Derrida's freeplay,[46] there is nonetheless a transgressive element in the carnivalesque celebration of play that simultaneously recognizes and subverts particular social determinants of meaning. Bakhtin's definition emphasizes, above all, the dialogic doublings, exchanges and reach of carnival laughter:

Play 29

> It is, first of all, a festive laughter. Therefore it is not an individual reaction to some isolated "comic" event. Carnival laughter is the laughter of the people. Second, it is universal in scope; it is directed at all and everyone, including the carnival's participants. The entire world is seen in its droll aspect, in its gay relativity. Third, this laughter is ambivalent: it is gay, triumphant, and at the same time mocking, deriding. It asserts and denies, it buries and revives. (11-12)

The at least double-plays of this definition explode simple oppositions in the attempt to include exuberant heterogeneity and transgression together with inevitable concessions to the enabling social conditions and symbolic potentialities of actual carnival celebrations.

There is much play, then, about the nature of play; it eludes nailing down. To return to my earlier overview, I am arguing that play denotes a perspective in language, together with activity manifesting this perspective, which affirms freedom and possibility against restriction, resignation and closure. Supporting open-endedness, it denies ontological anchors. Given the primacy of language and the unavoidable ambiguities in language acts, play is endemic in culture. Alternatively, culture itself forms the province for intertextual appreciation of language and literature. But it is possible to distinguish between levels of play as between different styles of language use; there are fewer possibilities for play in the language that defines our road laws than there are in literature. Nevertheless, if we concede that language and meaning are variously shaped by contexts, there remains in literary studies the problem of deciding context. Is it the frame of the book, the particular culture from which the book is written or world literature?[47] Is it none of these specifically but, rather, an intersection of them provided by generations of readers who will come to a text "already a plurality of other texts"?[48] Are these contexts mutually exclusive or do they come together as play? There is no proper context for the study of literature, not in any narrow sense. Rather, there are perspectives and modes of interpretation, and to privilege any single perspective as the definitive one for texts and criticism is not only to restrict possibilities for discourse, and for understanding, but also to confine the operations of play as discovery. In analysis of contexts and reading processes in this study, I will refer to intertextuality as it is supported by Derrida's notions of trace and supplementarity.

30   *Theories of Play and Postmodern Fiction*

It is my contention that *play*, in its inclusiveness and openness, and in its disestablishment of restrictive hierarchies, emphasizes activity that becomes, in its turn, part of a potentially infinite discourse. This is not to deny cultural context; meanings are necessarily produced within social contexts but no context can exhaust all possibilities for meaning. Conceived in terms of difference rather than identity, language is destabilised as well by operations of supplementarity; texts and meanings are caught up in the play of intertextuality. The readings in Part II concentrate on the intersection of text and reader in an attempt to bring together insights from reader-response, deconstruction and play as a focus. The play is in the text, the reader and their interaction in the processes of criticism. But what forms does this play take? What contexts do particular texts invoke, and evoke, and how do they prescribe a lexical playing field? Literature plays its characters; in what ways does it also play its reader? How useful for criticism is Ehrmann's statement that "players may be played; that as an object in the game, the player can be its stakes (*enjeu*) and its toy (*jouet*)"?[49]

The issues are best explored in each critical context and it is the activity itself, the discourse, the dialogue, the play, that constitutes the life of literature as the combined product of writers and readings. Postmodernist fiction invites analysis in terms of the impossibility of ending; but, discovering provisionality, we can yet pause, from time to time, to articulate the state of play while mindful that the articulations will be both belated and precipitous.[50] Chapters Three and Four address poststructuralist developments in play theory with respect to reader-response and deconstruction.

NOTES

1. Jacques Ehrmann ed., *Game, Play, Literature,* from Ehrmann's Introduction. This special issue of *Yale French Studies* (41, 1968) includes contributions from Kostas Axelos, Jacques Ehrmann, Eugen Fink, Michel Beaujour and Bruce Morisette. Like the special issue of the *Canadian Review of Comparative Literature* (XII.2, 1985) devoted to concepts of game and play and edited by Robert Wilson, it is an important marker in this field of study.

2. See Robert Rawdon Wilson, "In Palamedes' Shadow: Game and Play Concepts Today." This short survey provides a thorough overview with many suggestions for further reading in the fields of philosophy, anthropology, psychology, linguistics and general cultural studies. It is expanded in his book,

Play

31

In Palamedes' Shadow: Explorations in Play, Game, & Narrative Theory (1990), the most wide-ranging and exacting of recent studies in this cross-disciplinary field, in this instance with particular emphasis upon literature and language. Innovative in its attention to ideas of game and play, carnival and the carnivalesque, labyrinths, rules and conventions, magical realism, textual worlds and strategies of reading and interpretation, the study is notable for its range of literary reference and its rigorous playfulness. In addition, I recommend Mihai Spariosu's studies of the play concept in Western philosophy and culture: *Dionysus Reborn: Play and the Aesthetic Dimension in Modern Philosophical and Scientific Discourse* (1989) and *God of Many Names: Play, Poetry and Power in Hellenic Thought from Homer to Aristotle* (1991). From his analyses of play and the works of Kant, Schiller, Nietzsche, Heidegger, Fink, Gadamer, Deleuze and Derrida in *Dionysus Reborn,* Spariosu continues the investigation in *God of Many Names* to Homer, Hesiod, the Presocratics, Euripides, Aristophanes, Plato and Aristotle. Charting contributions according to "prerational" and "rational" values, he emphasizes the return in Western philosophy to prerational values and forms of play since the Age of Reason. Recent works that present more limited surveys and less emphasis upon theory, together with critical readings of a range of literary texts, are Ruth Burke's *The Game of Poetics: Ludic Criticism and Postmodern Fiction* (1994) and Warren Motte's *Playtexts: Ludics in Contemporary Literature* (1995).

3. Friedrich Schiller, *On the Aesthetic Education of Man,* 107. Published in 1795, following Kant and the French Revolution, Schiller's work asserts the importance of aesthetics and the imagination, establishing priority for play in its old oppositional relationship with work and seriousness: "how can we speak of *mere play* [*blosses Spiel*] when we know it is precisely play and play *alone* which of all man's states and conditions is the one which makes him whole and unfolds both sides of his nature at once?" (XV, 7). While setting a mark for subsequent play theorists, Schiller nevertheless keeps a rein on the play he so elevates. In contrast with Nietzsche, his idea of play involves, along with its creative energy, the cautionary presence of reason.

4. Bernard Suits, *The Grasshopper: Games, Life and Utopia,* 152. The problem of "loose talk" is complicated by the problem of interminable talk. As Robert Wilson points out, "The unwritten history of play and game concepts would probably reveal that, since Kant, nearly every thinker who has thought seriously about human life and its institutions has made some contribution to the current complexity of the subject." ("In Palamedes' Shadow," 182.)

5. For consideration of taxonomies, see Elliott M. Avedon and Brian Sutton- Smith, *The Study of Games,* 4-5.

32   *Theories of Play and Postmodern Fiction*

6. This list of factors comes from an anthropological context, in John M. Roberts, Malcolm J. Arth and Robert R. Bush, "Games in Culture," 597. Similar definitions can be seen in E.M. Avedon's 'The Structural Element of Games', in *The Study of Games*, 420-421 and Bernard Suits, *The Grasshopper: Games, Life and Utopia*, 36. Suits adds the lusory attitude.

7. Eric Berne, *Games People Play.*

8. Kostas Axelos, "Planetary Interlude," 7. Without defining it with any precision, Axelos asserts that everything is play and that, always in the process of becoming, humanity is "caught up in the game of the world" (11). He does not distinguish between game and play and, in this broad assertiveness, his work is similar in approach to Schiller's in *The Aesthetic Education of Man.* In a later article, Axelos emphasizes contradictory processes towards homogeneity and heterogeneity in the structures of play. Plurality is important in his concept. See "The Set's Game—Play of Sets."

9. Roger Caillois, *Man, Play and Games.* Within these, Caillois suggests there is a continuum from "paidia" (frolicsome exuberance) to "ludus" (determined by rules and conventions), Chapter 2: The Classification of Games.

10. Consider, for example *Auctor Ludens: Essays on Play in Literature,* edited by G. Guinness and A. Hurley. Many of the contributors to this volume refer to Callois, and to Huizinga's *Homo Ludens;* the surprising absences are Nietzsche, Wittgenstein and Derrida.

11. Robert Rawdon Wilson, "Three Prolusions: Towards a Game Model in Literary Theory," 81. The three studies that Wilson discusses are Suits, *The Grasshopper:Games, Life and Utopia,* George de Forest Lord, *Heroic Mockery: Variations on Epic Themes from Homer to Joyce,* and Robert F. Storey, *Pierrot: A Critical History of the Mask.*

12. Ibid. See his extensive footnote 11, 82-3.

13. Key works are Karl Popper's *The Logic of Scientific Discovery* and *Objective Knowledge,* Thomas Kuhn's *The Structure of Scientific Revolutions,* and Paul Feyerabend's *Against Method.* David Stove's discussion of the "irrationalists" traces the development of this movement in philosophy of science and provides a useful bibliography (*Popper and After: Four Modern Irrationalists*).

14. Anatol Rapoport, *Two-Person Game Theory.* Game theory was devised by John von Neumann and Oskar Morgenstern (see their *Theory of Games and Economic Behaviour*). For further consideration: Anatol Rapoport, *Fights, Games and Debates* and Anatol Rapoport ed., *Game Theory as a Theory of Conflict Resolution.*

Play   33

15. Consider John Fowles's term "godgame," with its emphasis on a cerebral contest in the protagonists' (and readers') search for meanings variously aware (or suspecting) their manipulation by a skilled games-controller. The bafflement in *The Magus* may also be seen in Pynchon's novels. For a discussion of this concept see Robert Rawdon Wilson, "Spooking Oedipa: On Godgames." In his later study, *In Palamedes' Shadow*, this material is expanded in Chapter 4 "The Archetype of Bamboozlement: Godgames and Labyrinths."

16. Elizabeth Bruss, "The Game of Literature and Some Literary Games."

17. Bruss points to W.K. Wimsatt's consideration of ombre in "The Rape of the Lock" ("Belinda Ludens: Strife and Play in 'The Rape of the Lock'"), Janet K. Gezari's discussion of chess problems in Nabokov's fiction ("Roman et problème chez Nabokov"), Bakhtin on games in Rabelais ("The Role of Games in Rabelais") and Bruce Morrisette's analysis of game-structures in Robbe-Grillet's work (*The Novels of Robbe-Grillet*). There is a growing body of such criticism, and works that are relevant include Kathleen Blake, *Play, Games and Sport: The Literary Works of Lewis Carroll,* Neil David Berman, *Playful Fictions and Fictional Players: Games, Sport and Survival in Contemporary American Fiction,* G. Guinness & A. Hurley ed., *Auctor Ludens,* Warren Motte, *Oulipo: A Primer of Potential Literature* and numerous articles. For an extensive bibliography to 1985, see James A.G. Marino, "An Annotated Bibliography of Play and Literature."

18. Peter Hutchinson, *Games Authors Play.* Having discussed Caillois's definition of play, he notes that literary games play loose with rules: "Of all games known to man, those in literature would seem to rely on rules the least" (5).

19. Derrida, *Writing and Difference,* 292. Nietzsche's vigorous enthusiasm for play as restless activity is apparent throughout his writings. Amongst so many articulations of its centrality and importance is the following description of play as continuing activity: "In the world only play, play as artists and children engage in it, exhibits coming-to-be and passing away, structuring and destroying, without any moral additive, in forever equal innocence. And as children and artists play, so plays the ever-living fire. It constructs and destroys, all in innocence. Such is the game that the aeon plays with itself" (*Philosophy in the Tragic Age of the Greeks,* 62). Discussing the concept of play, Gadamer also emphasizes movement, "to-and-fro" movement of play which he relates to *spiel* as dance and, in considering play in relation to art, he sees its place as inherent to "the being of the work of art itself" rather than confined to the attitude or state of mind of the creator or spectator/reader. See *Truth and*

34   *Theories of Play and Postmodern Fiction*

Method, 91. It is appropriate to include Deleuze in this trajectory with his emphasis upon the play of becoming (rather than being) and upon multiplicity, difference, heterogeneity and simulacra. See *Nietzsche and Philosophy.*

20. See Nietzsche, "Homer's Contest"; Gadamer, "Plato and the Poets" in *Dialogue and Dialectic;* Derrida, "Plato's Pharmacy" in *Dissemination;* Spariosu, Chapter 4, *God of Many Names.*

21. Johan Huizinga, *Homo Ludens. A Study of the Play Element in Culture,* 96. First published in German in 1944.

22. *Homo Ludens.* See chapter 1, "Nature and Significance of Play as a Cultural Phenomenon," particularly 26-29.

23. Jacques Ehrmann, *"Homo Ludens* Revisited." Similar objections are implicit in the work of Kostas Axelos, op. cit. and Eugene Fink, "The Oasis of Happiness: Toward an Ontology of Play." For Fink, play is fundamental: "Play is an essential element of man's ontological makeup, a basic existential phenomenon—not the only such phenomenon, to be sure, but still a clearly identifiable and autonomous one that cannot be explained as deriving from other existential phenomena" (19). In *Das Spiel als Weltsymbol* (1960), drawing upon Nietzsche and Heidegger, Fink asserts a notion of *Weltspiel* giving play priority amongst primary human phenomena. In this conceptualisation, play is, like Nietzsche's, beyond good and evil, associated with Being and with power.

24. In Steiner's introduction to *Homo Ludens.*

25. James S. Hans, *The Play of the World.* Hans suggests that "we still play all the time, even if we are told otherwise" (154), a position similar to that of Suits's grasshopper. But despite his declared wish to restore play to the centre of human activity and to assert its openness, Hans qualifies this intention by insisting on values (the point at which he contrasts his position with Derridean freeplay). I comment on this problem in a review of the text: Brian Edwards, review of *The Play of the World.*

26. Warren Motte, *Playtexts: Ludics in Contemporary Literature,* 4-5 and 17-18. Noting this common objection to Huizinga's definition, Motte nevertheless finds the study centrally important, particularly Huizinga's attention to poetry as the embodiment of ludic spirit.

27. Huizinga discusses this relationship, 24. That it bothers him is evident in the variety of statements on the relationship: "To our way of thinking, play is the direct opposite of seriousness" (5), "The contrast between play and seriousness is always fluid" (8) and so on. Of course the opposition breaks down, even as Huizinga presents a view of play that is exuberant in its breadth and yet restrictive in terms of class and period. In his attention to this issue,

Play   *35*

Gadamer both reinscribes and deconstructs the opposition: "It is more important that play contains its own, even sacred, seriousness" (91).

28. *Man, Play and Games,* 3-5. Although Caillois says that secrecy may be transformed into play, he holds that this cannot be a defining characteristic because it involves exposure. As Motte suggests, Caillois's theory of play is paternalistic and reductive.

29. Adopting Heidegger's description of the hermeneutic circle as his model to focus on the activity of play, Hans argues that production and desire are key elements. But, as I have suggested, his attempt to affirm the centrality of play is circumscribed by unspecified value judgements about what is useful.

30. M.J. Ellis, *Why People Play.* Ellis identifies three different views about how to define play: by motivation, by content or the view that it is undefinable. See Chapter 2, "Definition of Play."

31. See Chapter 4, "Recent Theories," where Ellis distinguishes Task Generalization and Compensation, Cathartic Theories, Psychoanalytic, Play Therapy, Cognitive Dynamics, Play as Learned Behaviour. In Chapter 5, "Modern Theories," he discusses "Play as Arousal-Seeking and the Competence/Effectancy Motive."

32. S. Millar, *The Psychology of Play,* 21. As a solution, Millar proposes that "play" might best be used as an adjective, not a noun, so that behaviours are defined not as play but as playful.

33. See Ferdinand de Saussure, *Course in General Linguistics.* The game metaphor is useful to explain relationships within the language system; but, as Allen Thiher points out, it does not account for changing values that occur, through time, in language systems (See Allen Thiher, *Words in Reflection. Modern Language Theory and Postmodern Fiction,* 77-79).

34. Roland Barthes, *A Lover's Discourse,* 67.

35. Geoffrey Hartman's definition, in *Criticism in the Wilderness,* 231. There are parallels between this sense of bricolage as embezzlement (intertextuality) and Eliot's thesis in "Tradition and the Individual Talent," and Northrop Frye's in *Anatomy of Criticism* about the dependence of texts upon their predecessors. The significant difference is that Barthes (and Derrida) emphasize the *reader's* creation of connections.

36. From "Truth and Lie," 46.

37. From "The Antichrist," 638.

38. Ludwig Wittgenstein, *Philosophical Investigations,* Item 18 and Item 203: "Language is a labyrinth of paths. You approach from *one* side and know your way about; you approach the same place from another side and no longer know your way about. . . ."

36 *Theories of Play and Postmodern Fiction*

39. *Words in Reflection,* 21. Thiher's discussions of Wittgenstein, Heidegger, Saussure and Derrida provide accounts of their work that retain complexity with lucidity. His is an important study.

40. Derrida's essay is published in *Taking Chances: Derrida, Psychoanalysis and Literature,* edited by Joseph H. Smith and William Kerrigan. See also, his earlier essay "Freud and the Scene of Writing" in *Writing and Difference,* 196-231.

41. Mikhail Bakhtin, *Rabelais and His World,* 7. Although Bakhtin differentiates official and religious celebrations from the carnivalesque, it is important to notice his emphasis upon their integration, as of interwoven aspects of consciousness: "The men of Middle Ages participated in two lives, the official and the carnival life. Two aspects of the world, the serious and the laughing aspect, coexisting in their consciousness" (96). This dialectical relationship is central to his concept of play as activity, the unending dialogue of possibilities which subverts stasis.

42. Julia Kristeva, "Word, Dialogue and Novel," in *Desire in Language: A Semiotic Approach to Literature and Art,* 78.

43. Robert H. Lavenda, "From Festival of Progress to Masque of Degradation: Carnival in Caracas as a Changing Metaphor for Social Reality," in Helen B. Schwartzman ed., *Play and Culture,* 19-28. Lavenda's comparison of the 1873 and 1897 carnivals concludes that the changed nature of the carnival may be explained in terms of social realities. The "real" situation in Venezuela is reflected in the carnival.

44. "Play, Transgression and Carnival: Bakhtin and Derrida on 'Scriptor Ludens'." This commentary is expanded in Chapter 2 "The Play of Carnival and the Carnival of Play" in Wilson's *In Palamedes' Shadow.*

45. Wilson emphasizes this extension and, mindful of the temptations as well as the dangers of extrapolating from particularities to general definitions and models, he presents this warning that is indeed a mark of his own careful reading practice: "There are interesting implications to removing Bakhtin's concept of carnivalization from its place in his discourse and transforming it into the hircine embodiment of linguistic playfulness and ludism. The problem that this conceptual transformation raises is brittle: *scriptor ludens,* as Rabelais, Cervantes and Shakespeare make plain, can be genuinely carnivalesque in his play, but if all linguistic play, all ludism in writing, is carnivalesque, then Bakhtin's categories will be swallowed, their force absorbed and diffused. As seems often to have been the case in discussions of play/game theory, a precise concept will have been swallowed by a larger, less precise one" (38-9).

Play 37

46. See Robert Wilson's "Play, Transgression and Carnival," and Michael Holquist's "The Carnival of Discourse: Baxtin and Simultaneity." Although Holquist allows a closer relationship between Bakhtin's dialogism and Derrida's formulations of decentering and *différance,* both he and Wilson note Bakhtin's attention to social context as a fundamental difference between his attention to linguistic play and meaning formations and Derrida's emphasis upon indeterminacy. For example: "As a term already appropriated by a textualist system, carnival might well describe Derrida's own wordplay (and has, no doubt, been used in this way), but as a dialogic term, indicating how meaning can be created out of the agon between separate monologic and incomplete utterances, carnival opposes freeplay. It does this in an essential, deeply contrastive, way" (Wilson, 83).

47. The definitions are very reductive but, as examples, I have in mind New Criticism, Marxist Criticism and Frye's schema respectively. That reductiveness is part of the activity is easily seen in the debates about critical positions themselves, in one side's rejection of positions attributed to them by the other side. Debates about the text-bound nature of New Criticism and about the nihilism of deconstruction are obvious examples. See, for example, Gerald Graff's "Fear and Trembling at Yale."

48. Barthes, *S/Z,* 10.

49. *"Homo Ludens* revisited," 55.

50. Barbara Johnson makes this point about temporal play, a comment on the nature of the work, in her "Translator's Introduction" to Derrida's *Dissemination,* xxxiii.

CHAPTER 3

Reader Response:
The Reader as Chameleon

> As no one, who knows what he is about in good company, would
> venture to talk all; so no author, who understands the just boundaries
> of decorum and good-breeding, would presume to think all: The
> truest respect which you can pay to the reader's understanding, is to
> halve this matter amicably, and leave him something to imagine, in
> his turn, as well as yourself.[1]

> You are about to begin reading Italo Calvino's new novel, *If on
> a winter's night a traveler.* Relax. Concentrate. Dispel every other
> thought. Let the world around you fade. Best to close the door; the
> TV is always on in the next room.[2]

Presenting the Reader as protagonist and the text as a collection of
discontinuous fragments, Calvino's *If on a winter's night a traveler*
dramatises the focus upon reading strategies that is so pronounced in
contemporary literary theory. Its emphasis on the act of reception not
only explores problems of meaning construction but situates the reader
as postmodernist hero. Tracking a narrative through defective editions,
translations, photocopies, fragments, academic disagreement and
divergent interpretations, the reader/narrator is a metatextual figure for
the activity of every reader of *If on a winter's night a traveler* itself.
Providing not just one but two readers, male and female, and the
reading adventure as a romance, the text raises epistemological
questions about the nature in general of textuality, context, and
meaning, and author and reader roles in the construction of possibilities
for communication. Are meanings inevitably incomplete, relative,

40 *Theories of Play and Postmodern Fiction*

subjective and multiple: "how much the word contains and conceals"(38)? Do they yield only partial mastery because, as the figure of the defective text with its blank pages suggests: "And so you see this novel so tightly interwoven with sensations suddenly riven by bottomless chasms, as if the claim to portray vital fullness revealed the void beneath"(39)? Should authorial intention be displaced as the main authority over meaning, as Calvino's *regressus in infinitum* of the vanishing text implies? By what processes do readers actually engage texts and what relationships exist between texts and readings? Does meaning exist only as it is realized, or "concretized,"[3] by a reader? What is the status of the meanings thus determined? Above all, Calvino's literary game demonstrates the opportunities for play in the activities of writing and reading. Presenting the readers' progress as an elaborate and interrupted quest, his emphasis upon acts of deception, intrigue and surprise dramatises in this text, in exaggerated forms, the cajoling, frustrations, imaginative effort and delight that characerise the act of reading.

The reader's promotion from wings to centre stage shifts the focus in literary studies from the text in its first creation to the processes of its reception or recreation. Part of that radical questioning in both the natural and human sciences which favours probability and uncertainty above deterministic explanation, truth as discoverable and language as mimetic, this shift in critical attention promotes continuing discourse against closure of meaning. It supports play. But as Susan Suleiman suggests in her introduction to *The Reader in the Text,* "Audience-oriented criticism is not one field but many, not a single widely trodden path but a multiplicity of crisscrossing, often divergent tracks that cover a vast area of the critical landscape."[4] This variety is evident in two extensive anthologies of reader-response criticism, Suleiman and Crosman's *The Reader in the Text* and Tompkins' *Reader-Response Criticism: From Formalism to Post-Structuralism,*[5] and in the readiness with which those critics represented in the anthologies attack one another's positions. For example, highly critical of Norman Holland's assumptions about the unity of the self, Jonathan Culler asserts that "the individuality of the individual cannot function as a principle of explanation, for it is itself a highly complex cultural construct—a result rather than a cause";[6] Robert Crosman attacks the positions of E.D. Hirsch and Wayne Booth for their opposition to Derrida's view that "the reader writes the text," and for their holding to a hierarchy that

Reader Response

41

gives authority to the author and to the qualified reader, indicating thereby, assumptions of determinate meaning in the literary text;[7] Stanley Fish criticises Wolfgang Iser's theory in *The Act of Reading: A Theory of Aesthetic Response* as being too generously accommodating: "The theory is finally nothing more than a loosely constructed network of pasted-together contradictions; push it hard at any point and it immediately falls apart";[8] Frank Lentricchia condemns the reductive elitism in Fish's notion of the "informed reader" within an "interpretive community," suggesting: "At the very least Fish might have pointed out that the consolidated interpretive community he is talking about is situated on the northeastern seaboard of the United States, and that most of its members are 'at home' in the English departments of Yale and Johns Hopkins."[9] And so on. Indicating the operations of ideological difference, institutional influence and individual preference, the crossfire may demonstrate a gamesome capacity in its contributors; if the divergence of opinion indicates the seriousness of the issue (the hermeneutic enterprise), it also indicates difference as a product and site of play.

Fish's reference to Iser as a phenomenon because he is influential without being controversial, one who does not appear on anyone's "list" in the ferment, neither amongst those said to be subverting standards, value and common sense, nor with those fighting the good fight against deconstructive nihilism, suggests that Iser's reputedly centrist work is a suitable focus for consideration of reader-response theories. Does Iser offer something for everyone, thereby seeming to be on no side at all, or every side at once? What is the function of play in his response theory?

When Iser differentiates the author's text, the "artistic" pole, from the reader's realisation, the "aesthetic" pole,[10] he claims that "the meaning of a literary text is not a definable entity but, if anything, a dynamic happening" (22). So his strategy is to concentrate on this happening or process, which he names "the potential of the text" (18). In common with other reader-response critics, his opposition to New Criticism's notion of the objective, self-contained text emphasises the reader's role in bringing a text "to life" (19).[11] The source of authority is both the text and the reader, and "the reader's communication with the text is a dynamic process of self-correction [. . . .] smaller units progressively merge into bigger ones, so that meaning gathers meaning in a kind of snowballing process" (67). But in this interplay between

42   *Theories of Play and Postmodern Fiction*

the text's "repertoire" (its particular strategies of representation) and the reader's expectations, there occurs, according to Iser, a process of gradual assimilation and alienation that will alter reader-consciousness. Although he concedes the reader's prior experience, he also bases his reception theory, curiously, upon an idealist concept of ideologically innocent activity: "The more committed the reader is to an ideological position, the less inclined he will be to accept the basic theme-and-horizon structure of comprehension that regulates the text-reader interaction" (202). His position may seem to be a compromise between subjective, idiosyncratic reader activity on the one hand and textual rigidity on the other: "while the meaning of the literary work remains related to what the printed text says [. . .] it requires the creative imagination of the reader to put it all together" (142). But this emphasis on the text as fixed limit differentiates his position from those of Derrida, Barthes and Fish. Granting the reader more freedom to create meanings, they not only posit the text itself as more radically indeterminate but also allow more opportunities for play throughout the processes of communication. Iser's emphasis is closer to the limited pluralism of Booth and Abrams who suggest that, while a text is open to a number of readings, there are proper textual and institutional constraints upon arbitrary readings.[12] This restriction is evident, for example, in Iser's discussion of the blank which, he says, "arises out of the indeterminacy of the text" (182) as a vacancy to be filled. Whereas Derrida and Barthes emphasise the undecidability of meaning in the freeplay of signifiers, such that responses are caught up in the play of the text, Iser conceives blanks as discontinuities between the parts of a text that the reader will link together within such systems as the text itself fixes as guidelines. While rejecting the idea of a single meaning— "the text can never be grasped as a whole—only as a series of changing viewpoints" (68)—he suggests that readings will normalise a text's indeterminacies. So Calvino's readers would eventually triumph: "Now you are man and wife, Reader and Reader. A great double bed receives your parallel readings" (205). Such modifications of reader freedom (Iser's attempt to combine flexibility with stability, to have it both ways), reveal his wavering between views of texts as determinate and indeterminate. This indecision provides the basis for Fish's strong criticism.[13] Disallowing determinate meaning and arguing that "the text is always a function of interpretation,"[14] Fish is critical of Iser's irresolution. But as his own emphasis upon degrees of consensus defers

Reader Response

to the "interpretive community" as licensing agency for readings, allowing for the social construction of acts of interpretation, he replaces one form of authorisation by another. If "interpretation is the only game in town," Fish's use of the game model illustrates the restrictiveness of allowing the game to win over the play:

> It is, in short, no easier to disrupt the game (by throwing a monkey wrench into it) than it is to get away from it (by performing independently of it), and for the same reasons. One cannot disrupt the game because any interpretation one puts forward, no matter how "absurd," will already be *in* the game (otherwise one could not even conceive of it as an interpretation); and one cannot get away from the game because anything one does (any account of a text one offers) will be possible and recognisable only within the conditions the game has established (357-8).

As Mary Louise Pratt has suggested, Fish may offer a sense of spirited reader activity but his theory ends up deferring to institutional power and privilege. [15]

There are similar problems about limitation in Iser's earlier study, *The Implied Reader.* Describing the reader's activity as an interweaving of anticipation and retrospection, and the text as a mixture of flow and gaps (or discontinuities), he concludes, "For this reason, one text is potentially capable of several different realisations, and no reading can ever exhaust the full potential, for each individual reader will fill in the gaps in his own way, thereby excluding the various other possibilities" (279). Here, too, the notion of gaps is limited (*Ulysses* would have more than *Middlemarch*) and potential readings are similarly circumscribed. But, as Pynchon's Oedipa Maas discovers, excluded middles are "bad shit,"[16] and when a reader fills gaps "in his own way" that activity need not exclude other possibilities. Barthes's reading of Balzac's "Sarrasine" serves as a model for variable possibilities;[17] it does this not so much in terms of the codes according to which Barthes discusses the text's ambiguities but through the self-awareness of this reading as a playful process and its interpretations as provisional. Readings do appropriate the text and, though not all readers concede the point, they are unavoidably ideological, each one offering a perspective amongst the many made possible in the plays between text and contexts. Since a text also survives any reading of it, thereby

44   *Theories of Play and Postmodern Fiction*

inviting any number of further engagements, it simultaneously requires and resists each reader's take-over bid. The process continues; readings accumulate.

When Fish also criticises Iser's avoidance of the choice between historical and ahistorical interpretation, he raises that perennial issue for literary theory and criticism. What "history" is and how formulations of the past influence present practice, including different conceptions of literature, are matters for continuing interdisciplinary investigation, as the work of Michel Foucault[18] and Hayden White[19] demonstrates. Necessarily central to marxist and to most feminist criticism, they should not be excluded from even the most formalist of studies. In the processes of its construction and reception, every text (and every act of interpretation) is inescapably located in a multiplicity of contexts none of which permits exhaustion of meaning. Implicit in the communication figure from Pynchon's "Entropy" with which I begin the study, this perspective underlies Derrida's deconstruction, the main subject of Chapter Four, and the general concept of play. Complicating choice, the question of context demonstrates the instability of language. Even if the rush to authorial intention is avoided, are readers contemporaneous with a work's origins especially privileged? Alternatively, is *Don Quixote* immeasurably richer when it is written in the twentieth century by Pierre Menard? In what ways does cultural context influence reader performance? How should readings take account of contexts? Although there are no definitive answers to these questions, reading is a comparative activity and constructions of meaning are indeed shaped not only by conscious ideological constraints (reading as a feminist, marxist, postcolonialist, otherwise undifferentiated WASP, and so on) but also by a reader's experiences, including experience of other literature. In this respect, as Borges implies, *Don Quixote is* a different and a richer text three hundred years after its appearance because of the intervening centuries of activity that influence its reception and change, therefore, appreciation of what the text *is*. But the ways in which readings take account of context (the writer's, the text's or the reader's) must depend upon not only definition of those variables, but reader interests and the function of the reading activity. Fish's emphasis upon interpretive communities as the context for reading leads him to oppose "subjectivist" readings because he sees the reader not as unique but as "always the product of categories of understanding that are his by virtue of his membership of a community of interpretation."[20] His

Reader Response

homogenisation of the reader contrasts with Barthes's definition of individual difference, a definition that acknowledges influence but denies the temporal and institutional constraints of Fish's idea of community: "This 'I' which approaches the text is already a plurality of other texts, of codes which are infinite."[21] On the other hand, Iser's "implied reader" locates authority in the text's frames, codes and predispositions which establish its reading guidelines, imply its reader and disestablish the influences of history or the context of reception. It is in the work of Jauss,[22] rather than Iser, that German reception theory addresses the place of history as a factor in literary studies. Proposing in his *Rezeptionsasthetik* that texts cannot be separated from the history of their reception, Jauss emphasises the flux of past and present and the importance of history in determining a "horizon of expectations." Seeking a compromise between marxist dialectics and formalist aesthetics, his theory encounters the problem of defining the influence of history while avoiding too positivistic a reading of either history or influence. I return to this issue with reference to the work of Derrida, Foucault and White, but it can be noted that Jauss's emphasis upon textual instability attends to the issue of the book's place *in* the world whereas older constructs of the text see it as a source of discoverable truth *about* the world.

What further may be said about the "reader"? In *Structuralist Poetics,* Jonathan Culler refers to literary competence as a set of conventions for reading literary texts, elaborating structuralism's concern with processes for the creation of meaning or the possibilities of interpretation. Theorising an "ideal reader," he suggests: "The question is not what actual readers happen to do but what an ideal reader must know implicitly in order to read and interpret works in ways which we consider acceptable, in accordance with the institution of literature" (123-4) and "The ideal reader is of course a theoretical construct, perhaps best thought of as a representaiton of the central notion of acceptability" (124). "We," "the institution of literature," "acceptability"? When Culler enlists Empson and his version of how "a properly-qualified mind works when it reads,"[23] the restrictive nature of this poetics is further revealed. It is an idealist model that implies a strict hierarchy of reading practice; its "reader" is an embryo scholar at least, a product of the institution of literature studies who is fitted by training for the high office of receiver/interpreter of complex cultural artefacts. Even so, and making the case against "premature

46 *Theories of Play and Postmodern Fiction*

foreclosure—the unseemly rush from word to world" (130), Culler emphasises the possibilities in interpretation for playful process and for different understandings as reasons for attention to reading procedures. When he later rejects the notion of "ideal reader," because it implies there is an ideal reading, he expands those possibilities. Proposing in this later paper that, "if we should decide that every reading of a text is markedly and unpredictably idiosyncratic, that would be the fact requiring explanation," [24] his analysis of sample readings of Blake's "London" can only partly explain the basis of their differences. This is because interpretive strategies are only one factor, though important, in the production of readings. When poststructuralist Culler clarifies in *On Deconstruction* the ambivalence expressed earlier in *Structuralist Poetics,* the later study is further acknowledgement that the final story must elude telling: "To read is to operate with the hypothesis of a reader, and there is always a gap or division within reading" (67). Similar strategies do produce different readings, in any case, because the play of difference is not only within the text but within and between readers, whatever figure is used to describe the reader or the reading process.

Although there are important differences between Iser's "implied reader," Culler's "ideal reader" and Fish's "interpretive community," [25] and in the emphases different theorists place upon the text's authority, reader-response criticism does open up the text and the reading process. Shifting the focus from text, society, self and language as determinate entities to their interaction, it reacknowledges what criticism has always known but sometimes put aside, namely that literature is not only about speaking and writing (encoding, or the sending of messages) but about hearing and reading (decoding or receiving communications). The result is an interdisciplinary bricolage, a field composed of playful connections.

Writers of fiction, themselves, have long acknowledged the instability of language and the possibilities for play in literary texts, together with their dependence on readers with whom they can initiate games of guidance or deception:

> Reader, it is impossible we should know what sort of person thou wilt be; for perhaps, thou may'st be as learned in human nature as Shakespeare himself was, and, perhaps, thou may'st be no wiser than some of his editors. Now, lest this latter be the case, we think proper,

Reader Response 47

> before we go any further together, to give thee a few wholesome admonitions. . . . [26]

> I know there are readers in the world, as well as many other good people in it, who are no readers at all, who find themselves ill at ease, unless they are let into the whole secret from first to last, of everything which concerns you. It is in pure compliance with this humour of theirs, and from a backwardness in my nature to disappoint any one soul living, that I have been so particular already. [27]

and

> Never mind what your predecessors have come up with and never mind that in a sense this "dialogue" is a monologue, that we capital-A Authors are ultimately, ineluctably and forever talking to ourselves. If our correspondence is after all a fiction, we like, we *need* that fiction: it makes our job less lonely. [28]

As Geoffrey Hartman suggests: "through the work of reading the work of art never comes to a rest."[29] Although readers play the text, so too the text manipulates the reader who "for his part, must lose himself for a while in a hermeneutic infinitizing that makes all rules of closure appear arbitrary" (244). Best exemplified in Derrida's work, this perspective is the subject of the following chapter. Whatever refinements, confusions and disagreements are noted within reader-response and reception theory, it moves readers, and the act of reading, from the margins to the centre of literary studies as items for analysis. No longer regarded as passive recipients of a text's message but as active shapers of its meanings, readers participate in an activity characterised not by finalities but by process. Although it is possible to hypothesise multiple readings from a model that posits the text as determinate and readers as variable (a New Critical paradigm), thereby attributing variation to reader difference, the game is complicated (and it becomes a more accurate representation of the exchange) when variability is located within the text itself as well. While many reader-response theorists emphasise gaps and indeterminacies in language and in texts, this perception especially characterises deconstruction. In its concentration on the "freeplay" of signifiers, deconstruction's

48   *Theories of Play and Postmodern Fiction*

affirmation of play locates readers as self-interpreting co-creators of texts, each of which is necessarily a construct that invites its own, further, continuing disassembly. Iconoclastic *and* rigorous, deconstruction promotes enquiry by concentrating on the dynamics of language.

This chapter begins with reference to Calvino's playful opening to *If on a winter's night a traveler*. Although the novel must come to an end as a material production, its exploration of reading positions does not. And the inconclusive dialogue between readers is situated appropriately, as the penultimate rather than last chapter and within a library, the house of books and readings. Assembling this range of critical positions in amicable exchange, it licenses them in an egalitarian representation that favours continuing discourse above power:

Reader 1   "If a book truly interests me, I cannot follow more than a few lines before my mind, having seized on a thought that the text suggests to it, or a feeling, or a question, or an image, goes off on a tangent and springs from thought to thought, from image to image, in an itinerary of reasonings and fantasies. . . ."

Reader 2   "Reading is a discontinuous and fragmentary operation [. . . .] my reading has no end: I read and reread, each time seeking the confirmation of a new discovery among the folds of the sentences."

Reader 3   "At every rereading I seem to be reading a new book, for the first time. Is it I who keep changing and seeing new things of which I was not previously aware?"

Reader 4   "Every new book I read comes to be a part of that overall and unitary book that is the sum of my readings."

Reader 5   "There is a story that for me comes before all other stories and of which all the stories I read seem to carry an echo. . . ."

Reader Response 49

Reader 6   "The moment that counts most for me is the one that precedes reading. At times a title is enough to kindle in me the desire for a book that perhaps does not exist."

Reader 7   "For me, on the other hand, it is the end that counts [. . .] but the true end, final, concealed in darkness, the goal to which the book wants to carry you."[30]

And not even the Reader hero who comes upon this group has any particular privilege. His statement is stodgy, and the text runs on: "I like to read what is written, and to connect the details with the whole, and to consider certain readings as definitive; and I like to keep one book distinct from the other, each for what it has that is different and new; and I especially like books to be read from the beginning to end." The text itself frustrates each of the Reader hero's preferences in turn. Parodying the desire for neat narrative order and a clear ending, it regenerates the figure of the divided text, the reader as both player and played, and the "communication" as a gamesome exchange.

NOTES

1. Laurence Sterne, *The Life and Opinions of Tristram Shandy, Gentleman,* 134.

2. Italo Calvino, *If on a winter's night a traveler,* 3.

3. Ingarden's use of this figure presupposes the text as a potential or skeletal structure whose gaps and indeterminacies shall be filled out, or concretized, by the reader in exploration of its capacity for meanings. Concretizations of the text involve experience, creativity and effort and, as Ingarden allows, they will necessarily reflect the individual variations of readers. It is curious, however, that while emphasizing indeterminacies in the text, he postulates the determination of boundaries for acceptable acts of concretization, revealing an idealist aesthetics which his emphasis upon variabilities otherwise questions. See Roman Ingarden, *The Cognition of the Literary Work of Art.*

4. Susan R. Suleiman and Inge Crosman, ed., *The Reader in the Text: Essays on Audience and Interpretation.* For the purposes of her introductory exposition, for example, Suleiman distinguishes six varieties of audience-oriented criticism: rhetorical, semiotic and structuralist, phenomenological, subjective and psychoanalytic, sociological and historical, and hermeneutic. As

50   *Theories of Play and Postmodern Fiction*

she points out, however, and as the readings indicate, the approaches are not mutually exclusive. For example, the rhetorical and structuralist/semiotic approaches share a model of the literary text as a form of communication, but whereas the former concentrates on meanings the latter analyses the codes and conventions which determine readability; Stanley Fish, whose emphasis is structuralist/semiotic, emphasizes the individual reader's place within an "interpretive community," a temporal concern which overlaps the sociological/historical concentration on specific cultural context. Further, at the more general level of descriptive categorization, a distinction may be drawn between "reader-response criticism" and "reception theory," the term commonly applied to German studies of reader-oriented perspectives. For an overview, see Robert Holub, *Reception Theory: A Critical Introduction.* Although there is a clearer sense of tradition and contact covering German reception theory than applies to reader-response criticism, there is a shared focus on reading and an overlap of influence. Iser's work, for example, though situated in the German context, has been prominently considered within Anglo-American reader-response criticism. In *The Return of the Reader,* Elizabeth Freund provides a general overview and useful introduction. Like others, she emphasizes the "disorderly scene crowded with explorers whose discrepant maps rechart the topography"(6-7). To explain such attention to readers and to acts of reading, she notes a "self-conscious moment" that has produced reassessments of primary concepts, the return to studies of textuality, reading and meaning construction prompted by various dissatisfactions with formalism and ideas of truth and objectivity.

Many studies of readers and reading use the rhetoric of play. Gadamer suggests that the "true being of the work of art is the play of interpretation"; Barthes writes in *S/Z* that "rereading is no longer consumption but play" (16) and later, in *The Rustle of Language:* "To open the text, to posit the system of its reading [. . .] is [. . .] to gain acknowledgement that there is no objective or subjective truth of reading, but only a ludic truth; again 'game' must not be understood here as a distraction but as a piece of work—from which, however, all labor has evaporated" (31). In his book *Rereading,* Matei Calinescu devotes a section to play, exploring with reference to play theory, psychological studies and framing processes (after Goffman's *Frame Analysis*), specific ways in which reading may be conceived as play. In this context, he notes studies by analytic philosophers and literary theorists on fictionality, make-believe and possible worlds, referring specifically to Kendall Walton's work on make-believe that focuses on games, fictional worlds and reading as variable processes of individual make-believe. In such 'as if' thinking, it is necessary to

Reader Response 51

question relationships between reality and fantasy, seriousness and play, replacing simple oppositionality with open-ended interaction.

5. Jane P. Tompkins ed., *Reader-Response Criticism. From Formalism to Post-Structuralism.*

6. Jonathan Culler, "Prolegomena to a Theory of Reading," 56. The paper supports Culler's structuralist emphasis on systems and codes that readers use—see his *Structuralist Poetics.* Favouring a poetics concentrating on structures or systems or conditions of meaning, his perspective contrasts pointedly with the psychoanalytic models, for example, of David Bleich, *Subjective Criticism* and Norman Holland, *5 Readers Reading.* There are obvious problems in Holland's shifting unity to the reader's "self," attributing to the reader a solidity so variously challenged by attention to linguistic practices and contextual change. In *The Pursuit of Signs,* Culler is critical of Holland's homogenising practices, suggesting that the "free" (individual) associations of his readers in *5 Readers Reading* are "the clichés of the various subcultures and cultural discourses that work to constitute the consciousness of American college students" (53). William Ray is also critical of Holland's brand of psychoanalytic criticism.

7. See Crosman's "Do Readers Make Meaning?" His objection supports critics who favour a more openly dialetical model, for example Derrida, and the Yale deconstructionists. In a move that further complicates the interweavings, Hartman includes Riddel, Said, Fish, Holland, Jauss and Jameson (a varied collection) as fellow sympathizers for "a more 'dialogic,' 'dialectic' or transactive model for the interpretive activity" (Geoffrey Hartman, "Literary Criticism and Its Discontents," 207).

8. Stanley Fish, "Why No One's Afraid of Wolfgang Iser," 12.

9. Frank Lentricchia, *After the New Criticism,* 147. His Marxist perspective notwithstanding, Lentricchia's reminder about institutional and intellectual politics points to the changing ideological climates within which all such judgements operate.

10. Terms introduced in Iser's earlier book, *The Implied Reader: Patterns in Prose Fiction, Bunyan to Beckett,* 274. They are developed in *The Act of Reading: A Theory of Aesthetic Response.*

11. Iser's emphasis differs from Ingarden's, the precursor whose text-reader concentrations are otherwise similar. Although he attends to reader work in its variable creativity, Ingarden's deterministic focus on the text connects his work rather more with Anglo-American New Criticism.

12. Expressed in Booth's and Abrams' contributions to "The Limits of Pluralism," *Critical Inquiry,* 3.3 Spring 1977.

52   *Theories of Play and Postmodern Fiction*

13. Consider Fish's paper, "Literature in the Reader: Affective Stylistics," *New Literary History*, 2.1 Autumn 1970, 123-62 (and reprinted in Tompkins, *Reader-Response Criticism*). Susan Suleiman discusses ambiguities in Iser's theory (see *The Reader in the Text*, 23-4). Similar criticisms are offered by Terry Eagleton, *Literary Theory: An Introduction*, 81-2, and by Robert Holub, *Reception Theory*, 84-5.

14. Stanley Fish, *Is There a Text in This Class?*, 342. Debate will inevitably continue about the shifting *grounds* of interpretation, particularly in an intellectual climate which has questioned so radically ideas of authority while (and by) emphasizing meanings as provisional constructions resulting from the dialectical interplay of authors, texts and readers, each notable more for its heterogeneous possibilities than its unequivocal consistency.

15. Mary Louise Pratt, "Interpretive Strategies/Strategic Interpretations: On Anglo-American Reader-Response Criticism," in Jonathan Arac ed., *Postmodernism and Politics*. In this paper on interpretative strategies, Pratt focuses on the writings of Prince, Culler and Fish. See also Elizabeth Freund's *The Return of the Reader*, chapter 4. Fish's earlier distinction between "rhetorical" and "dialectical" texts is very similar in meaning to Barthes's "readerly"/"writerly" and claims differences between modes of textuality while holding a focus on the act of reading. Inevitably, attempts to define the structure of the reader's experience remain linked to specificities of the text. Between 1970 and 1980, Fish's emphasis upon interpretive communities returned priority to intellectual/institutional influence in the continuing interplay between systems of analysis and individual reading experience: "meanings are the property neither of fixed and stable texts nor of free and independent readers but of interpretive communities that are responsible both for the shape of the reader's activities and for the texts those activities produce" (1980, 322).

16. Thomas Pynchon, *The Crying of Lot 49*, 138. I consider Pynchon's deconstructive manoeuvres in Part II, with particular attention to *Gravity's Rainbow* as decentered text.

17. Roland Barthes, *S/Z*. Barthes's 'erotics of reading', as presented in *S/Z* and *The Pleasure of Text* contrasts pointedly with Iser's response theory.

18. See *The Archaeology of Knowledge* or Foucault's "archaeological" studies of health, prisons, madness and sexuality in texts that uncover both the workings of ideology in language and the artifice of history.

19. See his *Metahistory: The Historical Imagination in Nineteenth-Century Europe* and *Tropics of Discourse: Essays in Cultural Criticism*.

Reader Response 53

20. "Interpreting the Variorum," *Critical Inquiry,* 2 (Spring 1976), 465-485 and reprinted in Tompkins, *Reader-Response Criticism.* Fish collapses the form of the reader's experience, formal units in the text and structures of intention into one, suggesting that questions of priority and independence do not arise because these factors operate simultaneously. It is a strange homogenisation.

21. *S/Z,* 10. With its emphasis upon heterogeneity, multiplicity and difference as cause for excitement in conception of the reader, and of readings, Barthes's attention to intertextual influence has been important in poststructural aesthetics. It is a more radical restatement of the theses about influence presented by Eliot in "Tradition and the Individual Talent" and Bloom in *The Anxiety of Influence.*

22. Hans Robert Jauss, *Toward an Aesthetic of Reception.*

23. William Empson, *Seven Types of Ambiguity,* 248. Quoted by Culler, 125. Despite misgivings about the idea of determinate text, one should concede, nevertheless, the subtlety and importance of Empson's work in this study.

24. "Prolegomena to a Theory of Reading," in Suleiman and Crosman, *The Reader in the Text,* 51. I agree with Culler's criticisms of Holland's free association technique and transference of unity from text to person. See Norman Holland, *5 Readers Reading.* Similar objections can be made to Holland's psychoanalytic model in "Unity Identity Text Self." Describing interpretation as a function of identity, he presents a model that depends precariously upon a notion of individual unity and text as mirror.

25. Figures for the reader multiply. A larger survey would take account of Michael Riffaterre's "superreader," Gerald Prince's "narratee," Erwin Wolff's "intended reader," each fiddling the boundaries of definition.

26. Henry Fielding, *Tom Jones,* 446.

27. Laurence Sterne, *Tristram Shandy,* 6.

28. John Barth, *LETTERS,* 655. Barth's most overt self-conscious attention, in his fiction, to textual artifice and to the processes of writing and reading make him an obvious candidate for attention in this study. *LETTERS* is my main focus in Part II, Chapter Three.

29. *Criticism in the Wilderness,* 180.

30. Calvino, *If on a winter's night a traveler,* 200-03.

CHAPTER 4

Deconstruction:
The Reader as Scheherazade

> O my sister, relate to us a story to beguile the waking hour of our night. Most willingly, answered Scheherazade, if this virtuous king permit me. And the king, hearing these words and being restless, was pleased with the idea of listening to the story; and thus, on the first night of the thousand and one, Scheherazade commenced her recitations.[1]

Depriviledging Daedalus the builder and affirming Ariadne's thread as not one but infinitely multiple, deconstruction appropriates the labyrinth, that already popular figure for the mesh of language and the ways of postmodernist fiction, and locates Theseus in an unending maze of forking pathways. In the freeplay of signifiers, the questing reader participates in a game removed from ontological authorities, one in which the magical threads, far from pointing to the exit, become the complex tracery of the labyrinth itself. For the deconstructionist, as for Scheherazade, there can be no end to the story-telling.

Of all developments in critical theory and practice over the last two decades, deconstruction makes the most significant contribution to play theory in its application to literature. Its attention to language and textuality, to reading strategies, subjectivity, and the constitution of knowledge, demonstrates the pervasiveness of play in discourse. The post-structuralist contributions of Derrida and Barthes have promoted a large critical industry of use and abuse, citation, excitation and occasional premature vilification. The following discussion seeks neither to redisplay the range of their work, for that is offered in so many studies, nor to engage the varieties of debate about it. Rather, I

56 *Theories of Play and Postmodern Fiction*

wish to concentrate selectively on their contribution to play theory and practice. Against criticisms that their work is formalist and apolitical, and altogether too little concerned with cultural issues, I will argue its specific cultural relevance via attention to play.

Although deconstruction may be regarded as a philosophical position, a political or intellectual strategy or a mode of reading, each of these can be only a starting point because of their interrelationship in practice. As Vincent Leitch suggests, Derrida is the one who stole the referent.[2] His work as arch-villain is philosophy *and* cultural strategy *and* reading instruction. Following Kierkegaard's concentration on uncertainty and incompletion,[3] Nietzsche's attention to the play of differences in language,[4] and Wittgenstein's emphasis upon the open-endedness of language games,[5] Derrida's dismantling of ideas of truth and identity is not so much a singular wild card in philosophy's pack as part of that larger movement of "deconstruction" against the totalising pressures of certainty as a principle of operation. Unsettling the Kantian emphasis upon reason and unity, Hegel's dialectic is itself reinterpreted and displaced, in its movement to synthesis and resolution, by this tradition that rethinks difference and includes, in addition to Kierkegaard, Nietzsche and Wittgenstein, contributions from Husserl, Saussure, Sartre, Merleau-Ponty, Bataille and Blanchot. At risk, as he acknowledges, of erring towards continuity and coherence by compiling an anthology devoted to difference, Mark Taylor's *Deconstruction in Context: Literature and Philosophy* presents a valuable reading of the philosophical context of Derridean deconstruction. Similarly motivated, aiming to retrieve Derrida's writings against their alleged misappropriation for deconstructionist criticism, Rodolphe Gasché's *The Tain of the Mirror,* by reading Derrida "philosophically," also demonstrates the attractions in Derrida's work for literary theory and criticism. Interpreting Derrida as putting 'literature' in parenthesis, as requiring "a connection of deconstruction and scholarship, of deconstruction and tradition" (268) in which specificity of the object of attention in its undecidability is paramount, Gasché presents a case not for separation of Derrida's philosophy from literary criticism but, rather, for rigor in the processes of extrapolation: "the very future of the institution of literary criticism hinges on its deconstruction" (266). What does Derridean deconstruction offer to play theory and to appreciation of literature?

Deconstruction 57

In his insistent attention to writing and the *play*[6] of signification, Derrida's deconstruction of the metaphysics of presence refocuses critical attention upon reading practice and knowledge claims by analysing textuality. When appeals to history, reality, author, speech, being and God are denied authority as sources for definitive meaning, by being textualised, by being revealed as constructs and not givens, the renewed emphasis upon writing, the text and the play of its signifiers, promotes interpretation and re-interpretation as a continuing activity. In the emphasis on supplementarity and operations of the trace ("there have never been anything but supplements, substitutive significations which could only come forth as a train of differential references"),[7] and substitution of fragmentariness for unity, and process for ends, deconstruction supports a view of the text as writing without ontological status and of reading as a process of shifting negotiation and re-adjustment. Derrida describes this movement in *Of Grammatology:* "One could call *play* the absence of the transcendental signified as the limitlessness of play, that is to say as the destruction of ontotheology and the metaphysics of presence" (50); this "play" is exemplified in his deconstructive analyses of the writing of Saussure, Lévi-Strauss and Rousseau in *Of Grammatology,* as in his readings of Freud,[8] Hegel,[9] Plato,[10] Husserl[11] and Heidegger.[12] Taking up the implications of Nietzsche's perception of the "death of God" and his concentration upon language as metaphor (and truth as illusion[13]), Derrida's critique of logocentrism emphasizes not only the play of signifiers against determinate meaning but the possibilities for rigorous idiosyncratic reading. Offering the play of *différance* with its notions of infinite substitutions and endless deferral, he asserts that it "must be conceived without nostalgia; that is, it must be conceived outside the myth of purely maternal or paternal language belonging to the lost fatherland of thought. On the contrary, we must affirm it—in the sense that Nietzsche brings affirmation into play—with a certain laughter and a certain dance."[14] His challenge to traditional authorities deprivileges (or alternatively "privileges") all in its refusal of a hierarchy of appeal so that readings thereby constitute another chain of signifiers in a theoretically endless play of substitutions. They will no longer be considered right or wrong but, rather, interesting or not interesting, useful or not useful, as part of a cumulative discourse.

It is by attending so closely to the operations of language in a text itself besieged by proliferating contexts, and via a perspective attuned

58   *Theories of Play and Postmodern Fiction*

to the duplicities of the medium, that Derridean deconstruction displaces the concept of ending. Destabilising the sign, by noting the removal (and textualisation) of the signified ('*Il n'y a pas de hors-texte*' 1976, 158) as that which would offer closure, and emphasizing the incessant interaction of subjectivities and contexts, or intertextuality, Derrida's denial of origins, of originary fullness and presence as explanation, supports the indeterminate text: "This interweaving, this textile, is the *text* produced only in the transformation of another text. Nothing, neither among the elements nor within the system, is anywhere ever simply present or absent. There are only, everywhere, differences and traces of traces" (1981, 26). In the double sense of *différance*, with its spatial and temporal connotations of simultaneously differing and deferring, Derrida resituates within operations of the sign itself the element of difference that Saussure locates between signs. Thus, whether it is in search of ideological inscriptions, authority or meaning claims, the act of reading produces its *textual* transformation; and this, in turn, invites further deconstruction in the spiral of discourse whereby texts are made and re-shaped, constructed and disseminated. Meanings exist *sous rature;* but, it must be emphasized, they are not less tenacious for that.

In his enthusiastic analysis of *Glas,* Geoffrey Hartman finds the spirit of game and play in the agility of Derrida's intertextual interrogation of Hegel, the arch-Christian, and Genet, the antichrist: "the mobility itself is what is remarkable in Derrida, and the sense of a serious unending game, both in the writer who plays language against itself and in the reader who must uncover, without losing track, the gamut of language: rules, conventions, sedimentations, intersecting themes, crossing texts. . . ." (1981, 5). Not only in *Glas,* but in all of Derrida's readings this double sense of seriousness and game that marks the process of interrogation serves, inevitably, to complicate the text. It is evident throughout *The Post Card: From Socrates to Freud and Beyond,* this radically divided book with its consideration of questions of order and priority, sequencing, chronologies, exchange, influence, communication and meaning. So "Envois" with its plays upon the names and significance of Plato and Socrates, post cards and the sending of messages with the emblematic image of "*Plato,* teacher, in erection behind *Socrates,* student" (22) providing the inspiration for reflections upon relationships, language and communication: "As soon as, in a second, the first stroke of a letter divides itself, and must indeed

Deconstruction 59

support partition in order to identify itself, there are nothing but post cards, anonymous morsels without fixed domicile, without legitimate addressee, letters open, but like crypts. Our entire library, our entire encyclopedia, our words, our pictures, our figures, our secrets, all an immense house of post cards. A game of post cards. . . ." (53). Suggesting that the reader consider "Envois" as "the remainders of a recently destroyed correspondence" (3), Derrida presents a remarkable interplay of levity and seriousness operating upon the *as if* of an exchange that uses *Plato* and *Socrates* to re-explore issues to do with language and meaning that have remained central to his work from the beginning:

They are dead and they travel through us in order to step up to the cashier, not them, their name, at every instant. At this very moment. How they resemble each other. Never forget that they have existed outside their names, truly.—How is that, you say.—Well, like you and me.—Not possible?—*Mais si, mais si.* And then every word must be franked in order to be addressed to whomever. Au-to-ma-tic-al-ly.Whatever I say, whatever I do, I must paste on myself a stamp with the effigy of this diabolical couple, these unforgettable comperes, these two patient impostors. A little engraving with this royal, basilical couple, sterile but infinite in its ideal progeniture. Cynically, without a cent, they have issued a universal stamp. A postal and fiscal stamp, by making themselves appear to advance funds. And on the stamp both are to be seen in the course, the one in front of the other, in the course, *en train,* of drawing a stamp and of signing the original. And they plaster themselves on the walls. An immense poster. This is a stamp. They have signed our I.O.U. and we can no longer not acknowledge it. Any more than our own children. This is what tradition is, the heritage that drives you crazy. People have not the slightest idea of this, and they have no need to know that they are paying (automatic withdrawal) nor whom they are paying (the name or the thing: name is the thing) when they do anything whatsoever, make war or love, speculate on the energy crisis, construct socialism, write novels, open concentration camps for poets or homosexuals, buy bread or hijack a plane, have themselves elected by secret ballot, bury their own, criticize the media without rhyme or reason, say absolutely anything about chador or the ayatollah, dream of a great safari, found reviews, teach, or piss against a tree. They can even

60   *Theories of Play and Postmodern Fiction*

never have heard the name of p. and of S. (hey, I see them as very chirpy, suddenly). Via all kinds of cultural, that is, postal, relays they pay their tax, and no need for that to be taxed with "platonism," and even if you have overturned platonism (look at them, turn the card, when they write upside down in the plane). Of course the tax goes only to the names, that is to no one (for the "living," notice, this is not absolutely, rigorously different), since the two pilots are no longer there, only subject, submitted, underlying their names, in effigy, their heads topped by their names. No more than Hegel, Freud or Heidegger, who themselves had to put themselves into the position of legatees, from the front or the back. Standing or lying, not a movement, not a step without them. I even would like to believe that those who liberate themselves better and more quickly, those at least who desire to pay the least and to "acquit" themselves most properly, are those who attempt to deal directly with them, as if this were possible, the patient philosophers, historians, archivists who are relentless over the issuing of the stamp, who always want to know more on this subject, dream of the original imprint. Me, for example. But naturally, the busier one gets liberating oneself, the more one pays. And the less one pays, the more one pays, such is the trap of this speculation. You will not be able to account for this currency. Impossible to return it, you pay everything and you pay nothing with this Visa or Mastercharge card. It is neither true nor false. The issuing of the stamp is simultaneously immense, it imposes and is imposed everywhere, conditions every other type, *timbre,* or tympan in general; and yet, you can barely see it, it is miniscule, infinitely divisible, composes itself with billions of other obliterating positions, impositions, or superimpositions. (99-101)

This is the divisible and intricate relationship conceived between signifiers, between past and present, tradition and change, parent and child, teacher and student, *fort* and *da* centered (which is also to say *decentered)* upon language and upon messages as influence. As Derrida insists, whether the ways are held to be fascinating or trivial, they *exist.*

Whereas Hartman values the mobility, praises its refusal of authorities beyond the text and welcomes the wit in Derrida's work, M.H. Abrams attacks these characteristics in accusing Derrida of reducing meanings "to a ceaseless echolalia, a vertical and lateral reverberation from sign to sign of ghostly non-presences emanating

Deconstruction

61

from no voice, intended by no one, referring to nothing, bombinating in a void."[15] From within the same platform as Abrams, "The Limits of Pluralism," Wayne Booth's warning demonstrates a similar view of meaning: "A critic who denies authority either of author or text is trying to fly without a supporting medium. He thus subjects himself to a peculiarly dangerous test: he must prove his own equality or superiority" (1977, 422). Despite their claims for pluralism, Abrams' and Booth's statements reveal anxieties about authority and meaning, and a desire for hard limits to discourse. Although interpretation is always "misreading," Booth's misreading of Derrida reveals not only a conservative attitude to authority and to play but an inadequate interpretation of decentering. Derrida's work does not deny "authorities" and "centres"; rather it refuses their power to specify limits to meaning.[16] Of course they remain operative in cultural situations but, the Derridean view insists, they must be subjected to rigorous interrogation in order to reveal the operations of power in discourse. As Lentricchia suggests, it is at this point that "our historical labors have just begun."[17] Their relative status and their intertextuality affirmed, those decentered authorities shall be interrogated within the deconstructive work. It follows, of course, that all statements of interpretation can be provisional only, responses which are themselves relative to a range of socio-cultural, political and psychological criteria and another set of signifiers in the discourse. Against finality, play continues; latent in texts it is activated in reading. That the misreadings of Derrida's texts also continue is evident in his "Afterword: Toward an Ethic of Discussion" within the context of the exchange with John Searle republished as *Limited Inc:*

> A few moments ago, I insisted on writing, at least in quotation marks, the strange and trivial formula, "real-history-of-the-world," in order to mark clearly that the concept of text or of context which guides me embraces and does not exclude the world, reality, history. Once again (and this probably makes a thousand times I have had to repeat this, but when will it finally be heard, and why this resistance?): as I understand it (and I have explained why), the text is not the book, it is not confined in a volume itself confined to the library. It does not suspend reference—to history, to the world, to reality, to being, and especially not to the other, since to say of history, of the world, of reality, that they always appear in an experience, hence in a

62   Theories of Play and Postmodern Fiction

> movement of interpretation which contextualizes them according to a
> network of differences and hence of referral to the other, is surely to
> recall that alterity (difference) is irreducible. *Différance* is a reference
> and vice versa. (137)

To claim that "the finiteness of a context is never secured or simple"
(137) denies neither the existence nor the importance of contexts as
shaping forces upon texts and meanings. Deconstruction can not exist
outside of its work, in play, in contexts.

That deconstruction is not mere formalist play, a postmodernist
New Criticism for those with time for games of elaboration, may be
seen by considering its articulations with marxism, feminism and the
cultural archaeology of Michel Foucault. Links between deconstruction
and marxism allow a number of positions, and this is because of the
varieties within each,[18] together with the range of practices that their
association produces. Although with his concern for material culture,
ideology and political change, Eagleton evaluates literary theory and
criticism with specific attention to rhetoric as social action, he approves
of Derrida's deconstruction of the metaphysics of truth and criticizes,
for its carelessness, the view that deconstruction denies the existence of
anything but discourse.[19] There is no necessary antithesis between
deconstruction's attention to the unending play of signification and a
marxist program for economic and political change. That marxist
analysis which unpicks the workings of ideology in historical
constructions necessarily, itself, dismantles ideas of the "natural" or
"transcendental" by its concentrations on power and position. It uses
strategies of "deconstruction" just as, alternatively, Derrida's critique of
sovereign meaning invites a participatory mode of social analysis and
action. Whether in a text or in a social structure, to dismantle
logocentrism, in its concentration on binary oppositions is to displace
authority by revealing it as a process or function rather than an
unassailable given. That which has been regarded as external and
secondary, a poor relation to the principal term whether this term is
male or upper class, presence or universality, can be shown to be
internal, repressed and the means by which the relationship can be
challenged. Not simply reversing but displacing the hierarchy by
emphasizing difference, the critiques offer decentered pluralism as a
strategy for political action as well as for reading practice. Never
completed, the work proceeds against concepts of textual rigidity, on

Deconstruction 63

the one hand, and fixed power relations in society on the other. Favouring heterogeneity and difference over resolution and its institutionalisation, it keeps texts and social arrangements open to participation and exchange. Progress does not depend upon affirmations of absolute knowledge, either in reading practice or in political action. Diversity does not mean anarchy. This point of view is summarised by Michael Ryan in his analysis of possible articulations between marxism and deconstruction:

> Deconstruction criticizes the attempt to establish the truth of reality as positive, factual, ideal, or objectively natural identity by revealing scission and difference to be the constituents of identity. Marxism characterizes this scission as a class antagonism and this difference as a difference of social forces and conflicting political—economic interests. Marxism thus adds a missing dimension to deconstruction by extending it into social and political-economic theory. But deconstruction also is crucial for the marxist critique because bourgeois ideology, in social science and social policy, has been able to write off the marxist contention that the social world is politically conflictual through and through as a merely external, sociological point unrelated to the internal, essential, purely philosophical or scientific, technical pursuit of true knowledge detached from politically interested, sociologically motivated concerns. Deconstruction, operating from within the outlines of bourgeois philosophy, shows how what that philosophy excludes is in fact internal to its makeup.[20]

Such summaries inevitably cut the corners of important differences, as Ryan's study acknowledges in his discussion of the range of marxist and deconstructive definitions. Nevertheless, in broad terms, intersection of the "philosophical" with the "political" indicates that deconstruction is not an apolitical parallel to marxist criticism but a mode of reading practice that is, itself, immediately cultural and political. There are close similarities, in findings as well as procedure, between Derrida's readings of philosophy and Marx's deconstruction, in the *Grundrisse,* of objectivist ideas of political economy. Each attacks ideologies that claim objective or natural laws as the ground and justification for systems. Their critiques invite vigilant, and continuing, differential analysis. The point is that whether deconstruction becomes

64   *Theories of Play and Postmodern Fiction*

a political weapon, following Derrida, or a conservative aesthetic, as in most of the Yale critics' work, will depend on its use.

Although "feminism" too includes so many practices that to speak generally is to speak fallaciously, feminist criticism involves frequently a "deconstructionist" form of decentering. Its subversion of the idea of neutral criticism (the male neuter) involves, against phallogocentrism, investigation of gender constructions and their political inscription in texts and discourse. While it may concentrate on the recovery of women's writing and women's experience previously neglected by a male-authorised discourse, it also serves other expressly political purposes. In Judith Fetterly's description, feminist criticism "is a political act whose aim is not simply to interpret the world but to change it by changing the consciousness of those who read and their relation to what they read" (viii). So, for example, Gayatri Spivak's combination of feminism, marxism and deconstruction offers "a reading method that is sensitive to gender, race and class" (81), a method that uses deconstructive strategies to read against the grain. Opposing all forms of essentialism, including "female," she proposes, as methodology, that unsettling and incessant interrogation characteristic of deconstruction, along with precise attention to the particularities of difference in line with feminist and marxist readings. Spivak's politicisation of texts and reading practice acknowledges subject positions while resisting reduction to any one of them. In her work, the tactics of deconstruction present subversive reading as process against the discovery of conclusions. As she suggests in the essay "Feminism and Critical Theory": "Feminism lives in the master-text as well as in the pores. It is not the determinant of the last instance. I think less easily of 'changing the world' than in the past. I teach a small number of the holders of the can(n)on, male or female, feminist or masculist, how to read their own texts, as best I can" (92). While there is no unified feminist theoretical system, just as there can be no single female position, feminist criticism has made gender an important consideration for literary and cultural analysis; and deconstruction, along with marxism, psychoanalysis and linguistics, provides feminist practice with important strategies as well as perspectives on language, texts, and ideology.

In this intersection, and to serve its political interests, feminist criticism follows the deconstructive practice of putting into question all grounds of authority against the reductive and debilitating effects, not

Deconstruction 65

only of simple hierarchical oppositions, but also of homogenisation. Challenging the system that supports male-female oppositions, deconstructive feminist criticism, by definition, favours the pluralism that Annette Kolodny advocates against monolithic feminism: "a playful pluralism, responsive to the possibilities of multiple critical schools and methods, but captive of none."[21] As Kolodny observes, to favour pluralism is not to surrender the search for patterns and connections but, rather, to give up "the arrogance of claiming that our work is either exhaustive or definitive." Against unity, this pluralism acknowledges not only the complexities of language and texts but also the necessary variety of positions within feminist ideology. Licensing eclecticism in the general cause of feminist critical practice, favours French theories of the feminine, as developed by Julia Kristeva, Hélène Cixous, Luce Irigaray and Monique Wittig, alongside Anglo-American reconsiderations of women's writing and the places of women in literature and culture.[22] Although the French feminists take different positions in their concentrations on language, it is notable that where language is seen as an instrument of the oppression of women it is also the principal means of countering that oppression. In Irigaray's *Speculum de l'autre femme,* the *différence* of subjugation gives way to celebration of the specific *jouissance* of female experience; Cixous's *écriture feminine* emphasizes female difference as a mode of deconstructive writing against closure. Across disciplines, creativity and liberation are expressed in play with, and against, concepts, writings and practices.

On the subject of provisional meaning, Michel Foucault's archaeology of the text points up the particularity of Derrida's deconstruction. Like Derrida, Foucault follows Nietzsche in questioning systems that would disguise their will to power as claims of objective truth. Each emphasizes difference and discontinuities within the fields of discourse and Foucault's transgressive history, like Hayden White's "metahistory" and Edward Said's analyses of cultural formations,[23] treats "history" as linguistic construct rather than seamless record. Although Foucault's emphasis upon textuality and his reading strategies are similar to Derrida's, his view of the text as an archaeological site includes the possibility of locating the historical condition of signifiers by painstakingly interpreting context. Concerned about the processes of opposition, exclusion, incorporation and control in cultures, Foucault holds that rigorous analysis of the "discursive

66   *Theories of Play and Postmodern Fiction*

formation" can reveal the particularities of power operating in text and context and provide, thereby, the means for a deconstructive politics of subversion and transgression. Theorised in *The Archaeology of Knowledge* and in such essays as "What Is an Author?" and "Nietzsche, Genealogy, History," this linguistic archaeology (and genealogy) is the method used in his studies of madness, medicine, prisons and sexuality.[24] Studies of cultural practices, they are studies of the operations of power in discourse which reveal not essences or truths or unalterable laws but the processes of selection, discontinuities and influence by which inequalities become institutionalised. Although Derrida emphasizes the instability of meaning in its slippage in proliferating spirals of discourse—whereas Foucault turns to the "gray, meticulous and patiently documentary"[25] work of genealogy in pursuit of meaning within a social context—they nevertheless produce complementary deconstructive readings against the totalising operations of logocentrism. Together, they demonstrate different purposes for deconstruction and, because their work is armed with scepticism and rigor, a critical appreciation of textuality and of cultural practice. Foucault's description of genealogy shows the connections between his perspective on language and culture and the perspectives of Nietzsche and Derrida; it refutes allegations of formalist play to the neglect of cultural pressures: genealogy "disturbs what was previously considered immobile; it fragments what was thought unified; it shows the heterogeneity of what was imagined consistent with itself" (147). Whether the focus is on prisons or philosophy, the material object or the discourse, Foucault's emphasis upon the ways in which these are particular cultural constructions indicates, thereby, avenues too for deconstructive analysis and, in all seriousness, the dissimulations of play in culture.

Roland Barthes's post-structuralist work, particularly *S/Z* and *The Pleasure of the Text,* complements Derridean deconstruction. As one whose interests in the play of language are so evident, Barthes commands a place in this attempt to focus reader activity and deconstruction in "play":

> To read is to find meanings, and to find meanings is to name them;
> but these named meanings are swept towards other names; names call
> to each other, reassemble, and their grouping calls for other naming: I

Deconstruction 67

> name, I unname, I rename: so the text passes: it is a nomination in the
> course of becoming, a tireless approximation, a metonymic labour.
> (1975a, 11)

This definition of reading as process, like Derrida's, emphasizes not only instability as the condition of language and texts but also the activity of reading as a challenge to readers. Barthes's declaration of "the death of the author" deprivileges authorial intention as the guide to meaning in order to elevate the reader: "the birth of the reader must be at the cost of the death of the Author" (1977,148); but it also includes a particular focus on intertextuality:

> We know now that a text is not a line of words releasing a single
> "theological" meaning (the "message" of the Author-God) but a
> multidimensional space in which a variety of writings, none of them
> original, blend and clash. The text is a tissue of quotations drawn
> from the innumerable centres of culture.[26]

This definition of intertextuality goes beyond Frye's attention to archetypes, and to texts as variations on pre-existent forms. Whereas Frye's aesthetic posits basic structural paradigms underlying individual works, Barthes and Derrida concentrate on the minutiae as always intertextually riven. Barthes's theory of intertextuality points up the influence of cultural signs and codes as historical determinants of meanings yet also the deconstructive means that subvert closure. Through the operations of "quotations," the text is always destabilised, its meanings caught in the play of difference that Derrida defines via the figures of supplement, trace and graft.[27] Hillis Miller's figure of the critic as host provides a descriptive model of this intricate interplay of language in texts and readings. Referring to the inevitable presence of old texts in new, Miller points out that "the parasite is always already present within the host"[28]; the new text is both host and parasite because it gives place to, while drawing sustenance from, its predecessors. Accordingly, readings host one another in a flexible interplay mediated by the activities of readers as co-creators and co-writers. A radical reformulation of Eliot's observations about influence in "Tradition and the Individual Talent," it takes account of the instability of the sign itself as well as lines of allusion and repetition. However one reads the Yale School's adaptations of Derridean

68   *Theories of Play and Postmodern Fiction*

practice, or Miller's ambiguous place between phenomenology and deconstruction, the intertextual figure can be put to a variety of tactical uses that acknowledge play as opportunity in the practice of reading.

In what has become a demonstration piece, Barthes's *S/Z* provides a deconstructive model which suggests that we read "invariably for a ludic advantage: to multiply the signifiers, not to reach some ultimate signified" (165). His description of the writerly text as a "galaxy of signifiers" (5) emphasizes indeterminacy; compelling reader participation and absorbing interpretations it resists closure by affirming the duplicity of language. The reader becomes a "producer" rather than a "consumer" of the text because of this poststructuralist perception of difference within the text itself. When, in *The Pleasure of the Text,* Barthes defines "pleasure" as "value shifted to the sumptuous rank of the signifier" (65), he, like Derrida, emphasizes reader activity as a playful pursuit that offers the possibility of *jouissance:* "the subject gains access to bliss by the cohabitation of languages working side by side" (3), and "it is not the reader's 'person' that is necessary to me, it is this site: the possibility of a dialectics of desire, of an 'unpredictability' of bliss: the bets are not placed, there can still be a game" (4). Even as Barthes moves to an erotics of textuality and reading,[29] his opposition to mimesis and to authorial control over meaning affirms plurality against closure. Far from constituting any reinscription of identity, and therefore essentialism, this invocation of the "reader" as site of a "dialectics of desire," emphasizes ludic activity in erotic dress. Barthes's "erotic" variety of deconstruction varies the Derridean mainsong but in support and not subversion of it.

What, then, is the relevance of deconstruction for literary theory and criticism? What can it offer to an appreciation of the literary text generally and to the reading of postmodernist fiction in particular? Jonathan Culler's four-point definition of "critical consequences"[30] includes some overlapping:

1. deconstruction's impact upon critical concepts
2. identification of important topics for criticism
3. provision of reading strategies
4. influence upon the goals of critical enquiry

Deconstruction 69

Derrida's concentration upon writing (over speech) and upon the subversion of other hierarchies (particularly the opposition of centre/margin, truth/fiction and serious/playful) not only extends the boundaries of 'literature' by including historical and philosophical writings; it re-emphasizes, as well, the play of rhetoric in discourse and the power of discourse in culture. While it might be argued that this changes not so much literature (since it is always read as figurative language) but perceptions of history and philosophy, it does bring different discourses into communication with one another. One result is to refocus attention on the problematics of truth and knowledge, context and language, or the complex processes of representation themselves and the relationships between text and world. It should be noted that Derrida's work does not deny the existence of signifieds but removes their authority as agents of closure. Although, as Culler reminds us, deconstruction emphasizes writing (and speech), presence (and absence), origin, marginality, representation and indeterminacy as matters for concentration, it is not the case that only particular types of texts lend themselves to consideration in such terms nor, of course, that these are matters of concern exclusive to deconstruction. Marginality and centrism, for example, are as much of interest to marxism and feminism, in their attention to the operations of ideology, as to deconstruction. Although the conclusions drawn and the purposes to which they are put are different, the matter for concentration is common and strategies for its analysis are shared. If deconstruction is "the careful teasing out of warring forces of signification in the text,"[31] as Barbara Johnson's formulation suggests in a view that applies to her readings of literary texts in *The Critical Difference,* to Barthes's *S/Z* and to Derrida's textual analyses, what strategies are involved? Culler's six can be restated as four: deconstruction of oppositions via their inversion and interrogation, persistent analysis of figures that combine different arguments or values, attention to the marginal and secondary with particular emphasis upon the play of supplementarity, and consideration of exclusions that may be reinscribed to elucidate not only the operations of power and meaning but also the ways in which a text differs from itself. These tactics for close reading combine deconstruction's aversion to truth claims, unity and closure with its interest in the play of language. It is because they are situated within markedly different views of textuality that deconstruction's concentration on gaps and undecidability may be differentiated from

70 *Theories of Play and Postmodern Fiction*

New Criticism's concentration on irony and ambiguity as double-voicedness in texts.[32] Whereas New Critical practice proceeds from perceptions of unity and identity, and discoverable meanings, deconstruction recognizes only provisional starting points and theoretically incessant activity. Following the practice that Culler describes as a "systematic and comprehensive putting in question" (1982, 223), its strategy of always complicating the text not only refuses the comfort of closure but offers the attractions, and the challenges, of subversive reading as a tactic and as reward.

In terms of both its philosophy of meaning and its strategies for reading, deconstruction has much to offer to consideration of works of postmodernist fiction, the focus of Part II of this study, which themselves confront epistemological issues often through decidedly ludic processes of representation. There are connections between reader-response theories and deconstruction in their focus on the text, the reader and processes of their intersection. As Derrida observes, scepticism invites play: "Play is always play of absence and presence, but if it is to be thought radically, play must be conceived of before the alternative of presence and absence. Being must be conceived as presence or absence on the basis of the possibility of play and not the other way around" (1978, 292). What are the possibilities of this "play"? Under what terms, and with what authority, does play co-exist with work and seriousness, not as some repressed other, a displaced joker in the pack, but as the enabling factor itself, the principle of energy and difference? These questions are addressed in the studies of Part II, "Duplicity as Virtue: Playful Texts and Textualised Players."

NOTES

1. *The Thousand and One Nights.* Emphasizing story-telling against ending, the frame situation is not only one of the most famous in world literature but also a persuasive emblem of linguistic riches. John Barth's favourite story-teller, coming to her task so steeped in lore and narrative invention, keeps the language in play.

2. From Vincent Leitch, *Deconstructive Criticism,* 116. It is by focussing upon the play of signification, by complicating the relationships between language and referents, that Derrida disturbs easy identification.

3. Kierkegaard's emphasis upon existence in time and identity as becoming sits against the hypothesised permanence of abstract thought.

Deconstruction 71

Correlating reality with subjectivity and temporality, and holding the pursuit of objectivity as to be in error, he anticipates Nietzsche's view of 'truth' as a fiction. See Soren Kierkegaard, *Concluding Unscientific Postscript.*

4. When Nietzsche asserts the impossibility of certainty, he emphasizes duplicity as a play of differences that can never be resolved. Interpreting the search for truth as "the will to power" working against fragmentation and incompleteness, he presents not only a rebuke to "Nay-sayers" (whose quest for transcendent values is held to be a negation of life) but also a perception of language that is later taken up by Wittgenstein and Derrida: "What, then, is truth? A mobile army of metaphors, metonyms and anthropomorphisms. . . ." (*The Portable Nietzsche,* 47). See also *The Will to Power.*

5. As in Wittgenstein's *Philosophical Investigations.* I refer to Wittgenstein's view of language in chapter two.

6. Consider Derrida's, "There is not a single signified that escapes, even if recaptured, the play of signifying references that constitute language. The advent of writing is the advent of this play. . . ." (*Of Grammatology,* 7).

7. *Of Grammatology,* 159. Derrida's emphasis on the irreducibility of *différance* in the operations of language and meaning is evident throughout his writings, though see particularly "The White Mythology: Metaphor in the Text of Philosophy." From this perception comes his opposition to the idea of a system that can be closed or complete.

8. See "Freud and the Scene of Writing" in *Writing and Difference,* 196-231, a reading that elicits the play of metaphors and tropes in Freudian texts and, in addition, *The Post Card: From Socrates to Freud and Beyond* with Derrida's intertextual and allusive reading of *Beyond the Pleasure Principle.*

9. "From Restricted to General Economy: A Hegelianism without Reserve," *Writing and Difference,* 251-277. Derrida, reading Hegel via Bataille, emphasizes Hegel's association with various forms of continuity and totality.

10. "Plato's Pharmacy," *Dissemination,* 61-171. Derrida's subversive reading of Plato's logocentrism offers not only particular detail of his definition of the play of the supplement but also a range of strategies for deconstructive analysis.

11. *Speech and Phenomena: And Other Essays on Husserl's Theory of Signs.* Including close attention to Derrida's concept of *différance.*

12. See "Différance" in *Speech and Phenomena.*

13. Nietzsche's statement is widely quoted; its relevance to Derrida's thought is obvious:

72 *Theories of Play and Postmodern Fiction*

> What, then, is truth? A mobile army of metaphors, metonyms, and anthropomorphisms—in short, a sum of human relations, which have been enhanced, transposed, and embellished poetically and rhetorically, and which after long use seem firm, canonical, and obligatory to a people: truths are illusions about which one has forgotten that this is what they are; metaphors which are worn out and without sensous power; coins which have lost their pictures and now matter only as metal, no longer as coins.

From "On Truth and Lie," *The Portable Nietzsche,* 47. In his *Deconstruction: Theory and Practice,* Christopher Norris provides a useful discussion of Nietzsche's influence in Derrida's work. Contrasting the Nietzschean emphasis upon undecidability in the play of signification with Marxist historical materialism, he introduces the common debate over deconstruction's value as a mode of historical-cultural criticism. It is, of course, a consideration guiding Eagleton's critique of deconstruction (see his *Literary Theory,* Chapter 4) and is addressed at length in Michael Ryan's very useful comparative study, *Marxism and Deconstruction.* Ryan argues convincingly that various aspects of Derrida's work can be used in critical Marxism. I take this up, briefly, later in the chapter.

14. "Différance," *Speech and Phenomena,* 159. See also Derrida's accounts of *différance* in the 1967 and 1968 interviews in *Positions.*

15. M.H. Abrams, "The Deconstructive Angel," 431. As Walter Benn Michaels notes, in his comments on this debate, Abrams insists on the primacy of determinate meaning, suggesting at least three strategies for its location: authorial intention, the linguistic reality of the text itself, the professional competence of trained readers. Homogenising approaches usually seen as competitors, Abrams presumably sees such divisions as trivial. See Walter Benn Michaels, "The Interpreter's Self: Pierce on the Cartesian Subject."

16. Answering a response similar to Booth's, Derrida said "I didn't say there was no center, that we could get along without the center. I believe that the center is a function, not a being—reality but a function. And this function is absolutely indispensable. The subject is absolutely indispensable. I don't destroy the subject; I situate it." ("Structure, Sign and Play," 267). Similarly, in "The Double Session" he remarks "reference remains" (*Dissemination,* 211), but how it operates in any example is an issue for analysis. This debate about authority will certainly continue, with debaters variously supporting authors, texts, contexts or one or another formulation of reader. For a traditionalist case in support of authorial intention, see E.D. Hirsch, *Validity in Interpretation.*

Deconstruction

17. *After the New Criticism,* 175. In this valuable discussion of American poststructuralist criticism and its sources Lentricchia prefers what he sees as an engaged and worldly rhetoric (in the work of Foucault particularly) to the textcentric work of Derrida and, moreso, his American followers.

18. The most discussed differences within deconstruction are those between Derrida's work and its transformations in the writings of the Yale school. Major studies of deconstruction by Culler, Norris and Leitch discuss these variations, but see particularly *The Yale Critics: Deconstruction in America* edited by Jonathan Arac, Wlad Godzich and Wallace Martin for analyses of the American work. In his important study, *Marxism and Deconstruction: A Critical Articulation,* Michael Ryan begins with Gouldner's identification of two major schools of Marxism, "scientific," grounded in the USSR's dialectical materialism, and "critical" as the provisional label for a variety of movements which, in their anti-authoritarianism, can be more readily associated with deconstruction (Alvin Gouldner, *The Two Marxisms*). Ryan emphasizes the range of different "Marxisms" included within critical Marxism. It is notable that Althusserian Marxism (see, particularly, the writings of Pierre Macherey and Terry Eagleton) shares many reading strategies with deconstruction.

19. Terry Eagleton, *Literary Theory. An Introduction.* See chapter 4, 144-150. Contrasting the work of American deconstructionists with Derrida's lead, Eagleton writes of Derrida, "deconstruction is for him an ultimately *political* practice, an attempt to dismantle the logic by which a particular system of thought, and behind that a whole system of political structures and social institutions, maintains its force" (148). As my emphases indicate, I read Derrida's deconstruction in terms of political engagement not withdrawal, a reading that applies not only to such later texts as *The Ear of the Other* but to the early texts as well. See *The Ear of the Other: Texts, and Discussions* and Christopher Norris's review article, "Deconstruction Against Itself: Derrida and Nietzsche."

20. *Marxism and Deconstruction,* 63. See also Chapter 2, "Marxism *Redivivus"* in Howard Felperin's *Beyond Deconstruction. The Uses and Abuses of Literary Theory.*

21. Annette Kolodny, "Dancing through the Minefield: Some Observations on the Theory, Practice and Politics of a Feminist Literary Criticism,"17. The essay is reprinted in *The New Feminist Criticism,* edited by Elaine Showalter.

22. For useful discussions of the increasing range of feminist critical practice, see Toril Moi, *Sexual/Textual Politics: Feminist Literary Theory,*

74 *Theories of Play and Postmodern Fiction*

Gayle Greene and Copelia Kahn ed., *Making A Difference: Feminist Literary Criticism* and Showalter's *The New Feminist Criticism.*

23. See Edward Said's *Orientalism, The World, the Text and the Critic* and *Culture and Imperialism.*

24. See *Madness and Civilization: A History of Insanity in the Age of Reason, The Birth of the Clinic: An Archaeology of Medical Perception, Discipline and Punish: The Birth of the Prison,* and *The History of Sexuality.*

25. "Nietzsche, Genealogy, History," in *Language, Counter-Memory, Practice,* 139.

26. Ibid, 146. There are many formulations of this view, for example: "A literary text is not a thing in itself, 'organically unified,' but a relation to other texts which are relations in their turn. The study of literature is therefore a study of intertextuality" (J. Hillis Miller, "Stevens' Rock and Criticism as Cure, II," 334).

27. For consideration of the "graft," see Derrida's "The Double Session," in *Dissemination,* 173-285. He uses graft to describe the operations of combinations, insertions and conjunctions in discourse. *Glas,* with its Hegel-Genet combination, provides a large-scale example of the grafting that, like the processes of supplement and trace, operates in the minutiae of texts.

28. J. Hillis Miller, "The Critic as Host," 446. For a short analysis of Miller's *Critical Inquiry* "debate" with M.H. Abrams, the debate that occasioned this "deconstructive" defence, see Donald Pease, "J. Hillis Miller: The Other Victorian at Yale" in *The Yale Critics,* 69-74.

29. This movement in Barthes's work includes, as well, *Roland Barthes by Roland Barthes* and *A Lover's Discourse: Fragments.* Vincent Leitch's "From a Poetics to an Erotics of the Text" offers an analysis of this range of work (See his *Deconstructive Criticism: An Advanced Introduction,* 102-115). As Leitch notes, psychoanalytic discourse is an important component of these later texts, but this is not at the expense of radical intertextuality. Richard Howard's "A Note on *S/Z,*" is interesting in this context for its attribution of "erotic" to Barthes's meditation: "Essentially an erotic meditation, then, because it concerns what is inexpressible (which is the essence of eros), Barthes's essay is the most useful, the most intimate, and the most suggestive book I have ever read about why I have ever read a book" (*S/Z,* xi–xii).

30. Jonathan Culler, *On Deconstruction: Theory and Criticism After Structuralism,* 180-225.

31. In her introduction to *Dissemination,* xiv. I assume that Derrida would approve of the statement with its emphasis on process. Amongst his responses to questions about what deconstruction *is,* he has suggested:

Deconstruction 75

There is no one, single deconstruction. Were there only one, were it homogeneous, it would not be inherently either conservative or revolutionary, or determinable within a code of such oppositions. That is precisely what gets on everyone's nerves. I see very well in what respects certain of my writings, or certain of my practices (for example), have something conservative to them and I assume it as such. I am for safeguards, for memory—the jealous conservation—of numerous traditions, for example, but not only in the university and in scientific, philosophical, literary theory. I am actively committed to such safeguards. But at the same time, I could also show how certain of my writings (sometimes the same ones) or certain of my practices (sometimes the same) seem to call into question the foundations of this tradition, and I assume that as well. . . . As deconstruction is inherently neither "conservative nor the contrary, the political evaluation of each of the gestures called deconstructive will have to depend, if it is to be rigorous and in proportion to what it is addressing, upon analyses that are very difficult, very minute, very flexible with regard to the stereotype of political-institutional discourse. Deconstruction does not exist somewhere, pure, proper, self-identical, outside of its inscriptions in conflictual and differentiated contexts; it "is" only what it does and what is done with it, there where it takes place." (*Limited Inc,* 141)

See also his contribution to "The States of 'Theory'," edited by David Carroll: "Some Statements and Truisms about Neologisms, Newisms, Postisms, Parasitisms and Other Small Seismisms."

32. See Christopher Norris's brief discussion of structuralism and New Criticism in the opening chapter of *Deconstruction: Theory and Practice.*

PART II

Duplicity as Virtue: Playful Texts and Textualised Players

CHAPTER 1

The Play in Postmodernism

> Postmodern knowledge is not simply a tool of the authorities; it refines our sensitivity to differences and reinforces our ability to tolerate the incommensurable. Its principle is not the expert's homology, but the inventor's paralogy.[1]

According to Lyotard's construction, postmodernism affirms difference, resists appropriation and manifests itself in playful invention. As the denial of metanarrative, or transcendence, it is the expressive principle of heterogeneity realized in language games of the *petit récits* which are held to deny legitimation by recourse to the grand narratives of totalising rhetoric or to consensus as authority. Thus constructed, postmodernism acknowledges the mazes of contemporary communication, dismantles tradition and the truth claims of reason and the scientific method, and asserts, against teleological perspectives, avant-garde expression, radical democratization and eclectic cross-disciplinarity or the moment and the event as experimental opportunity. Open in principle, in its resistance to hierarchies, it deconstructs the idea of an autonomous subject by emphasizing the interplay of networks, grafts, configurations and instances. Similarly, the sayings of postmodernist expression, will, in their critical difference, challenge taxonomic imperatives. Resisting incorporation into totalizing systems, narratives or histories, they emphasize particularities as playful opportunity and potential transgression.

In the unlimited ink business of the debate about postmodernism, Lyotard's heuristic formulation is one offering, though an important one, in the multidisciplinary accumulation of participants and instances. Whether the examples are taken from architecture, painting, music, film, literature, TV, philosophy, aesthetics or psychoanalysis, whether

80   *Theories of Play and Postmodern Fiction*

the markers are held to be temporal or economic, national or global, and whether the instances are seen to acknowledge or to resist the past, through nostalgia, irony, pastiche or parody, the definitional confusions of "postmodernism" are ancient history, matters of bemusement and entertainment and intellectual exchange however serious the stakes. In this expansive context of interplay, avoidance and contradiction, Lyotard's continuing dispute with Habermas presents one indication of the difficulty of deciding "grounds" of exchange, with the contrast between Habermas's allegiance to an ideal of knowledge legitimated by consensus and Lyotard's emphasis upon paralogy and dissension demonstrating rival conceptions of knowledge and radically different measures of value in cultural action. It is because he sees true "modernity" as the realization of Enlightenment ideals of Reason and Progress that Habermas describes the avant-gardes of Modernism as "empty reactions" and postmodernism as neo-conservative:

> When the containers of an autonomously developed cultural space are shattered, the contents get dispersed. Nothing remains from a desublimated meaning or a destructured form. [2]

But this is not a nothing from which nothing will come. As Robyn Gardner suggests, in a paper whose influence I acknowledge in my focus on this exchange, "from a Lyotardian perspective, Habermas was not paying attention when Philosophy announced 'the Death of the Subject'"[3] as the way to a proliferation of meanings against the institutionalisation of Knowledge. His arguments for an autonomy based upon an ideal of self-conscious subjectivity and agreed pragmatics are held, therefore, to smack of idealist aesthetics and hierarchical legitimation. To the extent that the Lyotard-Habermas exchange provides "sides" in the battle about postmodernism, this study endorses various points in Lyotard's argument. His emphasis upon difference and abundance accentuates the deconstructive *jouissance* in postmodernism, a restlessness and energy that are manifest, for instance, in language games conceived as part of a "general agonistics" in culture:

> to speak is to fight, in the sense of playing, and speech acts fall within the domain of a general agonistics. This does not necessarily mean that one plays in order to win. A move can be made for the sheer

The Play in Postmodernism

81

> pleasure of invention . . . Great joy is had in the endless invention of turns of phrases, of words and meanings, the process behind the evolution of language on the level of *parole*. But undoubtedly even this pleasure depends on a feeling of success won at the expense of an adversary—at least one adversary, and a formidable one: the accepted language or connotation. (10)

Dismissing Habermas's consensus politics as inherently conservative, as an outmoded perception of cultural action and knowledge formation, Lyotard supports the revolutionary potential of avant-garde expression and abundant heterogeneity. An accommodation with multinational consumerism, this eclecticism links with Baudrillard's "precession of simulacra" and with what Jameson refers to as "the new depthlessness" in contemporary culture. But whereas they find cause for alarm in the loss of "the real" (or in the simulacra become the real), Lyotard responds more positively. In his description in "Answering the question: what is postmodernism?" it is:

> the degree zero of contemporary general culture: one listens to reggae, watches a western, eats McDonald's food for lunch and local cuisine for dinner, wears Paris perfume in Tokyo and "retro" clothes in Hong Kong; knowledge is a matter for TV games. It is easy to find a public for eclectic works. By becoming kitsch, art panders to the confusion which reigns in the "taste" of the patrons. Artists, gallery owners, critics, and public wallow together in the "anything goes," and the epoch is one of slackening. (334-5)

In this formulation, the postmodern is that turn or moment in which the creative inspiration, the play, exceeds the constraints of tradition, consensus, or institutional approval, the rules of the game. Collapsing traditional boundaries between elite and popular, conservative and idiosyncratic, and exceeding geographical and national restrictions, it is inevitable that cultural production so often reflects the mass consumerism provided by revolutions in technology and communications. It is a leading irony of postmodernism, in its emphases upon change, reproduction and availability, that successful local innovation is so likely to be transformed into mass-marketed global production. That figures of difference will be collared in their turn, and canonised or rejected, is an inevitable consequence not only of

82   Theories of Play and Postmodern Fiction

the normalising processes of cultural politics but also of the market forces of multinational consumerism. As Pynchon observes in *Gravity's Rainbow,* after Weber, routinisation is that against which charisma, in the instances of its difference, must struggle. But, paradoxically, those normalising processes in economics and cultural exchange, those processes that transform the one into the many, simultaneously promote creative innovation and playful transgression.

It is not my intention here to survey either the history of "postmodernism" or interventions of the last two decades in their extension across the range of contemporary cultural production. Rather, since this study focuses on concepts of play and their manifestation in postmodernist fiction, I consider the place of play in postmodernism. To emphasize play, in constructions held to be postmodernist and in constructions of postmodernism itself, is not to deny questions of period, politics, economics, gender, nation and globalism their relevance in the debate. If it is broadly perceived as the multidisciplinary struggle against received forms, in which modernist ideas of design, unity and autonomy are displaced for uncertainty, heterogeneity and difference, postmodernism can be seen to support the poststructuralist dismantling of binary operations. In this construction, there is an emphasis upon irresolution which is itself, as Jameson observes, always liable, in turn, to commodification and incorporation.[4] Whether the instances are taken from film, music, theatre, architecture, advertising or literature, these are material cultural artefacts analysable in terms of production and exchange whereby the analyst may choose to emphasize class, gender, economics, technology or national politics as the point of particular interest, of entry. When Jameson links postmodernism with late capitalism, and insists that "it is not just another word for the description of a particular style"[5] but a periodizing concept, his reading of multinational capitalism as a state of social and economic malaise, antipathetic to regenerative aesthetic production, is the basis for declaring an anti-aesthetic, an end to meaningful stylistic innovation. The characteristics by which he defines postmodernism—reaction, dissolution of the boundaries between high and popular culture, interdisciplinary "theoretical discourse," pastiche and inward turning aesthetics—are held to indicate, therefore, not critical interrogation and progress but the depthless simulacra of a dispirited culture with a weak sense of history. Asserting that "aesthetic production today has become integrated into commodity production

The Play in Postmodernism

generally,"[6] Jameson holds that art is controlled by the same consumer logic as fashion with the result that it is vacuous. But this totalising rhetoric takes little account of difference as a regenerative cultural value and, as the alternative to his conception of postmodern culture, he offers a negative formulation of potted deconstruction: "a view of history as sheer heterogeneity, random difference, a coexistence of a host of distinct forces whose effectivity is undecidable" (72). It is not simply the high seriousness of Jameson's emphasis upon consumerism and cultural politics but the totalities in which he deals that devalue the exuberance and invention in postmodernist production. His is a gloomy postmodernism, a view that not only interprets the postmodern hyperspace of the Bonaventure Hotel in terms of alarming disorientation rather than pleasurable pastiche or invitational mazes but which holds that this cultural dominant is depthless, schizoid and bereft of critical distance.

Articulating the play in postmodernism involves, at the level of theory, acknowledgement of the poststructuralist writings of Derrida, Barthes, and Foucault, discussed in Part 1, and attention to the functions of such ideas as *différance,* "displacement," "bricolage" and the archaeology of texts. Delegitimating limiting notions of unity, origin, and hierarchy, and the operations of binary logic, their emphasis upon interplay and irresolution underscores the playful turn in postmodernist practice. From this perspective, the practices of pastiche, reaction and self-consciousness, which constitute for Jameson a negative mode of production, offer opportunities not only for variety and exuberance but also for cultural critique and regeneration, for what Barthes calls *jouissance,* Derrida "the Nietzschean affirmation" and John Barth "replenishment." The concentrations on language and on complexities in exchange emphasize possibilities in communication for variable discourse and, against prior determinations of form, identity, value and meaning which they must acknowledge, texts and readings produce their subversions. The work of postmodernist art that Jameson is in danger of reducing to empty pastiche and puns is not only available for interpretation but also for readings of history, politics and culture.

The range and meanings of postmodernism have shifted considerably from its 1950s origins in the vocabularies of architecture and literary criticism to the global conceptual levels of the 1980s. Both Charles Jencks and Lyotard acknowledge Ihab Hassan's contributions

84   *Theories of Play and Postmodern Fiction*

to early discussion of postmodernism, contributions that move towards a poststructuralist position in the late 1970s. Hassan situates postmodernist fiction within a concept of postmodernism that allows for heterogeneity while affirming "a number of related cultural tendencies, a constellation of values, a repertoire of procedures and attitudes."[7] Noting such agreed conceptual problems as the relationship between postmodernism and modernism, semantic slippage, multidisciplinarity, general cultural definitions and whether postmodernism is a term of commendation or denunciation, he avoids sharp totalities and their rhetoric of inclusions and exclusions by employing a model of "indetermanence." Allowing an open-ended interplay in postmodernism of the "constitutive tendencies" of indeterminacy and immanence, the neologism advances the cause of significance without finality:

> —as an artistic, philosophical, and social phenomenon, postmodernism veers toward open, playful, optative, provisional (open in time as well as in structure or space), disjunctive, or indeterminate forms, a discourse of ironies and fragments, a "white ideology" of absences and fractures, a desire of diffractions, an invocation of complex, articulate silences. Postmodernism veers towards all these yet implies a different, if not antithetical, movement toward pervasive procedures, ubiquitous interactions, immanent codes, media, languages. (1982, 271)

Incorporating deconstruction's emphasis upon indeterminacy together with recognition of cultural structures, needs and immanences (which deconstruction interrogates but does not deny), Hassan proposes a meaningful liaison, one that notes connections while acknowledging the instabilities that *should* prevent their becoming unassailable imperatives of tradition, the academy, consumerism or the technologies of multinational capitalism.

This double perspective continues to mark Hassan's later observations, defining the combination of "excitement" and "unease" he expresses towards the disestablished imagination of postmodernism. Excited by the zest it promises, he does not declare simple nostalgia for lost authorities (God, King, Father, Reason, History, Humanism) but concern for the ways of constructive and rigorous action in a revolutionary practice: "At worst, postmodernism appears to be a

The Play in Postmodernism

mysterious, if ubiquitous ingredient—like raspberry vinegar, which instantly turns any recipe into *nouvelle cuisine.*"[8] Readdressing from this 1986 perspective the question "what is postmodernism?" his eleven-point "catena" is designed to present "a region of postmodern 'indetermanences' (indeterminacy lodged in immanence) in which critical pluralism takes shape" (1987, 168). So far as such a thing is possible in a "field" where one primary characteristic is its resistance to the boundaries that definitions involve, it is a useful summation:

1. Indeterminacy
2. Fragmentation
3. Decanonization
4. Self-less-ness, Depth-less-ness
5. The Unpresentable, Unrepresentable
6. Irony
7. Hybridization
8. Carnivalization
9. Performance, Participation
10. Constructionism
11. Immanence

Thus Hassan enfolds nine elaborations within the Indeterminacy and Immanence of his 1982 neologism. There is irony in his "schematic" articulation of postmodernism's non-schematic practice; but, even so, in this anatomy the overlapping parts support critical difference and the possibilities of play. In their explosion of absolutes, and in the positive rhetoric of possibility that follows as correlative, one may detect that which Derrida described so long before as: "the Nietzschean *affirmation,* that is the joyous affirmation of the play of the world and the innocence of becoming, the affirmation of a world of signs without fault, without truth, and without origin which is offered to an active interpretation" (1978, 292). But this exuberance must somehow contend too with ideas of decadence, scepticism, weariness and wariness, not as hypothetical others in a simple binary construction, the darker sides of becoming, but as explicit cultural considerations. Hassan's narrative of the postmodernist turn includes a "postlude," and "immanence" wins a round over "indeterminacy" as he turns *back* to the pragmatism of Rorty and William James in the name of moral and social concern. This concern is implicit in postmodernism's critical

86   *Theories of Play and Postmodern Fiction*

pluralism, despite Hassan's re-turn and despite Jameson's view of postmodernism as "an alarming and pathological symptom of a society that has become incapable of dealing with time and history."[9]

The play in postmodernism, then, may be read as simultaneously destructive, in its subversion of totalities (including "postmodernism" itself as an entity), and constructive, in its affirmation by theory and demonstration of the positive cultural effects of difference. Working against unity, it opens history, artefacts and authority to continuing interpretation; and whether or not this activity is held to be progressive or reactionary will depend not upon its "postmodernism" but upon analysis of the performance detail in its reception by the heterogeneous audience. Where some see *jouissance,* others see bourgeois decadence. One person's progressive instance is another's empty gesture. As David Bennett asks, for example, what happens to the "postmodernist" point of Christo Javacheff's huge exercises in wrapping, to their critique of commodification, when one considers the consumerism (mass-produced postcards, photographs, and drawings) that furnishes their budget?[10] Does that irony alter the message? Jameson selects the Bonaventure Hotel as an emblem of "postmodern hyperspace" which can symbolize "the incapacity of our minds, at least at present, to map the great global multinational and decentered communicational network in which we find ourselves caught as individual subjects."[11] But, alternatively, such architectural transmutations may signify, in their (con)fusions, a hybridisation that is as much entertaining as alienating, as much an indication of playful pastiche in building construction as a reminder of our subject-ness in the face of bewildering cybernetic systems.

Although it is hardly the dominant cultural expression of postmodernism, the postmodernist novel partakes of features associated with postmodernism as period and as style—its fusion of styles, interrogation of totalities, concern with ontological questions, displacement of fixed referents, emphasis upon innovation, and self-conscious attention to the artifice of presentation and of representation. Treating reality, history, identity, culture and reference not as unified discourses but as fields of discursive practices, postmodernist fiction emphasizes particularly the operations of play in language, aesthetics and cultural constructions. The following readings explore instances of play in texts and reading with the intention of analysing their effects

The Play in Postmodernism

upon perceptions of literature, reading practices and construction of meanings. Although the readings are offered as evidence of the immanence, importance and particularities of play, they may contribute to critical theory by providing support for a provisional taxonomy. The most rewarding play, for players, is in the practice, but it may serve, as well, as cultural example. In particular, and by emphasizing slippage, difference and duplicity, the readings seek to affirm variety against reduction as not only "true" to texts in their complexities but also important for cultural practice and development.

NOTES

1. Jean-François Lyotard, *The Postmodern Condition: A Report on Knowledge,* xxv. Lyotard's study remains influential. When he defines the postmodern as "incredulity towards metanarratives" (xxiv), denying those supposedly transcendent truths that underpin western culture, his work coincides with French poststructuralism of the 1970s in the emphasis upon writing, textuality and local processes against centers of authority. Turning also to Wittgenstein, for the notion of proliferating "language games," he attacks the principle of transcendent legitimation to argue for diversity, uncertainty and multiplicity—this attention to process that puts his work in opposition to the Habermasian emphasis upon consensus. It is against such consensus that he holds modern and postmodern aesthetics to be an aesthetics of the sublime as the unrepresentable. Although in *Le Différend,* Lyotard drops "game" and "player" because they may imply liberal humanist definitions of subjectivity and intentionality, his perceptions of the postmodern continue to favour radical openness and experimentation.

2. Jurgen Habermas, "Modernity—An Incomplete Project" (1980) in *The Anti-Aesthetic: Essays on Postmodern Culture,* edited by Hal Foster, 11. Developed in *The Theory of Communicative Action,* his theory of "communicative reason" or "communicative rationality" is based in ideas of intersubjectivity and consensus. While acknowledging that modernity had faltered, Habermas nevertheless argues a continuation and working out of the Enlightenment faith in reason as the proper guide to progress. See Richard Rorty's "Habermas and Lyotard on Postmodernity" for an analysis of the Lyotard-Habermas debate. Based upon a pragmatic view of representation and social action, and optimistic faith in consensus, Rorty's sympathies are with Habermas.

88   *Theories of Play and Postmodern Fiction*

3. Robyn Gardner, "Saying the Subject (or Slaying the Subject) of Postmodernism," 11. Unpublished paper presented to Honours Seminar, "Cultural Theory/Cultural Practice," Deakin University, 1988. This paper provides a fine, and detailed, analysis of the exchange, situating it within philosophic traditions and with specific reference to Kant, Hegel, and Feyerabend.

4. Fredric Jameson, "Postmodernism and Consumer Society," in *Postmodernism and Its Discontents* edited by E. Ann Kaplan. Jameson points out how artefacts of high modernism, once held to be revolutionary in their strategies and effects, have become canonical and part of that against which newness must define itself. First printed in Foster's *The Anti-Aesthetic,* the essay marks Jameson's entry to theorizing the postmodern and work that is extended in the essay held by Douglas Kellner to be the most quoted and debated article of the 1980s, "Postmodernism, or, the Cultural Logic of Late Capitalism." Kellner's *Postmodernism/Jameson/Critique* presents a fine collection of analyses of Jameson's attempts to find an articulation between marxism and postmodernism. It is in the 1980s that postmodernism attracts the attention of an impressive range of philosophers and leftist critics, including Habermas, Lyotard, Jameson and Baudrillard, extending the mode and range of earlier commentary.

5. "Postmodernism and Consumer Society," 15. Jameson's attempt to create an articulation between marxist theory and postmodernism shares with Baudrillard his emphasis upon a causal relation. Such characteristics of multinational consumer capitalism as the ephemera of styles and fashion, planned obsolescence, advances in electronic technology, mass media communication and globalization are related to pastiche, depthlessness, simulacra and schizoid discontinuities in art, notions popularized by Baudrillard.

6. Jameson, "Postmodernism, or the Cultural Logic of Late Capitalism," 56. Kellner's anthology provides a useful context of responses to Jameson's work, including Jameson's "Afterword—Marxism and Postmodernism" in which he describes his totalizing approach to the postmodern.

7. Ihab Hassan "Postface 1982: Toward a Concept of Postmodernism" in the second edition of *The Dismemberment of Orpheus,* 260.

8. Hassan, "Pluralism in Postmodern Perspective" (1986) in *The Postmodern Turn: Essays in Postmodern Theory and Culture,* 173.

9. Fredric Jameson, "Postmodernism and Consumer Society," in *The Anti-Aesthetic: Essays on Postmodern Culture,* edited by Hal Foster, 117.

The Play in Postmodernism   *89*

10. David Bennett, "Wrapping Up Postmodernism: The Subject of Consumption Versus the Subject of Cognition," in *Postmodern Conditions* edited by Andrew Milner et al., 15-36.

11. Jameson, "Postmodernism and Consumer Society," in *Postmodernism And Its Discontents,* 25.

CHAPTER 2

Narcissus at the Edge:
The Endlessly Diddling Play of
Thomas Pynchon's
Gravity's Rainbow

THE SUNSHINE OF UNCERTAINTY

> Is there a single root, deeper than anyone has probed, from which
> Slothrop's Blackwords only appear to flower separately? Or has he
> by way of the language caught the German mania for name-giving,
> dividing the Creation finer and finer, analysing, setting namer more
> hopelessly apart from named, even to bringing in the mathematics of
> combination, tacking together established nouns to get new ones, the
> insanely, endlessly diddling play of a chemist whose molecules are
> words. . . . [1]

It is commonplace in Pynchon criticism to emphasize the metatextual
link between his protagonists' roles as displaced questers and our
assigned task as readers.[2] When ONE/THE WORD/THE CREATION are
dismantled, divided "finer and finer," deconstructed, there is indeed a
match between the work of those eccentrics who try to put it all
together against the maddening, alluring forces of fragmentation and
the activity from readers that the beguiling detail demands, applauds
and mocks. But attempting to string together V-connections, excited
and afraid that V might tie in with "The Big One, the century's master
cabal" (V 226),[3] Stencil is, of course, seduced by his own detective
work; chasing signs of Tristero and finding such bizarre links, there is
always the possibility that sorting demon Oedipa is sorting the divided
spirals of her own demon; and although Slothrop's rocket search is

92   *Theories of Play and Postmodern Fiction*

legitimised by centuries of patriarchal tradition and political organisation, his is another "Holy-Center-Approaching" (GR 508), a genealogical exercise, that fixes on the abused and abusing interpretative self as divided center and reading kit. Pynchon's texts light up crazily, splendidly, like Alfonso Tracy's pinball machines, and of course the play is rigged. It always is. In each, the dialectics of desire is energised by disorder, and characters, and readers, become frequent callers at the Lost and Found counter of the Department for Connections. Freed from the prisonhouse of totalising explanation, from God's rule and simple mimesis, we are liberated from cause-and-effect mechanics and the beginning-middle-end tyranny of reductive narrative instruction into the narcissistic temptations of our own systems of partial explanation. Commonplace in postmodernist fiction, these perceptions of radical division, change, uncertainty and exchange have a long history as Barth's Henry Burlingame suggests to Eben Cooke, worldliness to innocence, in instructing him that the single and unified self "lives only in your fancy, as doth the pointed order of the world. In fact you see a Heraclitean flux: whether 'tis we who shift and alter and dissolve; or you whose lens changes color, field and focus; or both together. The result is the same, and you may take it or reject it" (SWF 349). Multidisciplinary complications of the world, and of our processes of understanding, recommend we "take it." When *Gravity's Rainbow* offers "the insanely, endlessly diddling play of a chemist whose molecules are words" (GR 391), it offers not only amazing diversion between beginning and ending, between the rocket birth scream of the opening line and its imminent and deferred fall at novel's end, but a model of deconstructive defence against authoritarian practice. As legions of contributors to the Pynchon Critical Industry show, its "mindless pleasures" (GR 270) are packed with mindfulness,[4] the "whole" serious playful play existing always *sous rature.* In the busy text and in the Heraclitean flux, or in the wake of Heisenberg's Uncertainty Principle, that is its/our condition. It is not that "There is time" (GR 760) simply cancels "It is too late" (GR 3); but if we are always both belated and precipitous, caught up in processes that are death-serving and life-supporting, we can yet direct desire to life, to the mazy middle ground, unpacking the binaries, knowing that "excluded middles are bad shit" (L49 138),[5] making hay in the sunshine of uncertainty. The text acknowledges while it subverts the rush to closure. This is, I believe, the overriding message and strategy of

Narcissus at the Edge 93

Gravity's Rainbow, if one may be permitted such impudent language in the face of such complexity: "There is time, if you need the comfort, to touch the person next to you, or to reach between your own cold legs. . . ." (GR 760, Pynchon's ellipsis). "Now everybody—" (GR 760), the bouncing ball is in our court.

How is it that *Gravity's Rainbow* with its concentration upon control, manipulation, alienation, fear, resignation and death-structures as leading aspects of contemporary Western civilisation is not a bleak and nihilistic work?[6] This is primarily because of the zest with which it deals with such weighty matters; one of postmodernism's most politically searching texts, it is also one of its most exuberant and agile, a text that reminds us throughout not only of language's capacity as play-medium, but that ideas, as well as characters and readers, can be played. Entering its world is to enter an elaborate cerebral game but one in which laughter is so fused with seriousness, and textual moves with such a range of contexts, that reader disorientation signals not the play of a smart-arsed author at dumb reader's expense but the first part of a collaborative enterprise, a WELCOME sign to transgression as positive activity and with the temptation of pleasure along the way. Reading the text for its playful diversity, I wish to argue that its playfulness is inseparable from its seriousness and that this interdependence is a function of Pynchon's decentering. Displacing the centre need not loose mere anarchy upon the world; when the holding (binary) logic of centrism is displaced and the barriers are down (between literature and philosophy, reality principle and pleasure principle, sober reconstruction and gleeful deconstruction), the labyrinth of subjection becomes the labyrinth of possibility, with bamboozlement both a condition and a tactic, both wonder at the text's and the world's variety and a strategy for their preservation. If *Gravity's Rainbow* is to be perceived as a conceptual and linguistic god-game, its moves set in play by a magus figure with superior intelligence and a mean streak, it is one in which the author-god's authority is decapitalised, not only by the text's dismantling of authority-systems and its sudden changes in manner, but by its embrace of "this dancing Preterition" (GR 548). With old primal innocence and the Real Text gone (it never was a generous concept), and warned that "jokers around the table be sneaking Whoopee Cushions into the Siege Perilous, under the very descending arse of the grailseekers" (GR 321), our readings will proceed against the unbearable condition of anti-paranoia in search of

94   *Theories of Play and Postmodern Fiction*

not the word that dispels all doubt[7] but connections that offer the comfort of contact and provisional understanding. Against closure, we are offered possibilities; against the story, we are offered stories. The critique of mimesis does not dispense with the world for the sake of the text; rather, it is by offering such historical/cultural weight in displaced forms that it questions the real and mimesis, inviting us to reconsider (as *the* unending task) the ways of not only a text's but culture's "critical difference from itself."[8] This is the business of scepticism and play.

Against its sorrowful, and angry, reading of history, and in the face of the anticipated but deferrable end-game of Apocalypse, *Gravity's Rainbow* offers not simply HERE and NOW but a deconstructive reading program that provides strategies to counter those grim traditions. Despite the death-serving obsessions, and such instances of imperialistic darkness as Puritan colonisation of America, German genocide of Hereros in southwest Africa and destruction of the Kirghiz culture in Central Asia, together with the toll of WWII, there are acts of compassion, acts of resistance, surprises, accidents, opportunities. . . . Tchitcherine takes not Enzian's life but "half a packet of American cigarettes and three raw potatoes" (GR 735), Ludwig finds Ursula and Pynchon narrators have always cared for the preterite.

Above all, there is the restless play of the decentered text and in this discussion of strategies in *Gravity's Rainbow,* I will concentrate on decentering and inclusiveness, specific references to games and to modes of play, and language as a medium of play that can as well provide exaltation as imprisonment. Against those readings that emphasize gloom, there is a case to be made for the text's extraordinary exuberance (*jouissance*), an exuberance that is realized in formalist terms but which is indissociable, I believe, from perceptions of social context. In its interests and procedures, *Gravity's Rainbow* catches the excitement of deconstructive interrogation and play, epitomising the spirit that Derrida describes in "Structure, Sign and Play"as "the Nietzschean *affirmation,* that is the joyous affirmation of the play of the world and of the innocence of becoming, the affirmation of a world of signs without fault, without truth, and without origin which is offered to an active interpretation" (292).

Narcissus at the Edge 95

THE DECENTERED TEXT, OR "THE DOMAIN BETWEEN ZERO AND ONE" [9]

"The absence of the transcendental signified extends the domain and the play of signification ad infinitum": [10] for Derrida, as we have seen, decentering and play are fellow travellers. Associating centre with the idea of fundamental ground, origin and permanence, or that which would be beyond the play of *différance* and be seen as the place and the guarantee of certitude, he emphasizes its restriction of the play of discourse and, conversely, its displacement as the way to deconstructive freeplay: "the moment when language invaded the universal problematic, the moment when, in the absence of a center or origin, everything became discourse." [11] But when he points to Nietzsche's critique of the concepts of Being and truth, Freud's subversion of self-presence and consciousness, and Heidegger's attack upon the metaphysics of presence as examples of decentering, he points as well to the inevitability of centers as concepts of authority. These shall be centers within and not beyond the discourse, however; textualised, subjected themselves to the instabilities of discourse, their authority is provisional, not absolute. Decentering is, therefore, an always incomplete act of deliberate dislocation, of resituating by putting into question the authority of all centers to speak with the forked tongue of truth. As a form of scepticism and an important reading strategy, it re-emphasizes the many and the variable, or, in Derridean terms, the plays of *différance* and the supplement, against the one. It is, I suggest, a major strategy in *Gravity's Rainbow*. Evident in Pynchon's deconstruction of binary logic with its processes of determination, valuation and exclusion, decentering is the very condition of the text's vast inclusiveness and *Gravity's Rainbow* is contemporary Western culture's definitive example of the decentered text, a leading reminder of not only the complexity of ordering systems but also of play as a multi-faceted form of resistance to them, a tactic merry with the possibilities of evasion and of self-assertion.

In Leni Pökler's attempt to explain to Franz her sense of the existential complexity, Pynchon provides a figure for abundance which is not only self-reflexive of the text's arrangements but also a guide to the deconstructive strategies that characterise its inclusiveness: "'Not produce', she tried, 'not cause. It all goes along together. Parallel, not series. Metaphor. Signs and symptoms. Mapping on to different

96 *Theories of Play and Postmodern Fiction*

coordinate systems, I don't know. . . .' She didn't know, all she was trying to do was reach" (GR 159). Antithetical to the cause-and-effect man, its attention to uncertainty as principle, metaphor as process and searching as life condition, presents a picture of confusion that the text affirms against simple binary elegance and closed-shop determinism. Leni Pökler, street revolutionary, is a spokesperson for the decentered text. Returned, much later, as prostitute Solange, she confirms the incessant play of change and multiplicity:

> "This is some kind of plot, right?" Slothrop sucking saliva from velvet pile.
> "*Everything* is some kind of plot, man," Bodine laughing.
> "And yes but, the arrows are pointing all different ways," Solange illustrating with a dance of hands, red-pointed fingervectors (GR 603).

Re-cycled from "Low-lands"[12] and *V,* Pig Bodine is caught up in at least three "plots." How the puns proliferate. And, seeing that "the Zone can sustain many other plots besides those polarized upon himself" (GR 603), Slothrop envisages going with the flow, becoming this text's Benny Profane, to ride the els and busses of the Raketenstadt's elaborate transport system because "this network of all plots may yet carry him to freedom" (GR 603). In this "Ellipse of Uncertainty" (GR 427), rhetorical questions such as "What th' fuck's going on?" (GR 187), "What's happening?" (GR 310) and "Do you have any idea what's going on?" (GR 611) are not simply metafictional reminders of the text's gamesome intellectual challenge, of its "progressive *knotting into*" (GR 3); they also point up uncertainty as both the preterite condition *and* a defence against THEM, against Puritan Elect, Rocket masters, Cartels, the Firm, the System, the Man, Pernicious Pops and Mother Conspirators, controllers whose controls are everywhere and insidious, based upon the processes of division and exclusion that constitute THEY and WE systems, Elect and Preterite, screwers and screwees,[13] these textual recreations (and subversions) and our own contextual reading arrangements. Emphasizing plurality and openness, Leni's perception of the streets points to the text: "It all goes along together. Parallel, not series. Metaphor." But what forms does the decentering take? In what ways and with what consequences are systems deconstructed? In this discussion of the text's emphasis

Narcissus at the Edge 97

upon displacement and proliferation, I shall consider the Pointsman-Mexico opposition as an example of the deconstructed binary; Puritanism and paranoia, with reference to Slothrop, as a locus for text/context operations; and the decentering of History as part of the text's strategies of inclusion.

Franz Pökler's difference from Leni parallels the central Pointsman-Mexico conflict that puts in opposition the Pavlovian to the statistician, determinism to probability theory and the one's death-serving obsession with control to the other's life-serving preference for chance and possibility: "in the domain of zero to one, not something to something, Pointsman can only possess the zero and the one. He cannot, like Mexico, survive any place in between" (GR 55). In Mexico's ability to cope with a riotous present there are links with Meatball Mulligan and Benny Profane amongst Pynchon's earlier characters, whereas Pointsman, like Callisto[14] and Stencil, is caught in the grip of negative history and a fascination with pattern and control. While Pointsman, like Stencil, "must go about grouping the world's random caries into cabals" (V 153), and without the soft-pedalling of Stencil's "Approach and avoid" (V 55) tactic, Mexico's philosophy of indeterminacy and his attention to randomness resemble the text's strategies of displacement and proliferation. That Pointsman's position is held to be both repressive and uncreative is elaborated in metaphors of perversion and sterility; that it is also farcical is emphasized in the contrast between his plodding and the Faustian vision of Blicero as the text's other main representative of sterility. Won into Pavlovian service by "The Book" (GR 87), having abandoned Harley Street "for a journey more and more deviant, deliciously on, into a labyrinth of conditioned reflex work" (GR 88), and dreaming of the Minotaur he would find and destroy, Pointsman is no Theseus nor Maudie Chilkes an Ariadne. When Harvey Speed and Floyd Perdoo foul up surveillance of Slothrop by getting side-tracked into "mindless pleasures" (GR 270), and Spontoon and Muffage castrate Marvy not Slothrop, this Pavlovian's progress moves towards ignominy rather than glory, "left only with Cause and Effect, and the rest of his sterile armamentarium" (GR 752). In the name-plays and the parody, Pynchon not only ridicules Pointsman but also deconstructs the repressive binary logic of deterministic practice in its association with control and with "structures favouring death" (GR 167).

98   Theories of Play and Postmodern Fiction

This tactic of subversion by parody, displacement and the play of supplementation may be seen most strikingly in representations of the "Puritan reflex of seeking other orders behind the visible" (GR 188). Offering paranoia, 'the discovery that *everything is connected*' (GR 703), as a secularised form of Puritan consciousness and a variant upon the Pavlovian version of mechanistic connected-ness, the text emphasizes the ambiguities of system-making as a mode of explanation. These comic-serious subversions are exemplified in the range of references that intersect to present Slothrop as Nalline's boy and the text's play-object. Whereas for his early Puritan ancestors meaning centered on God, for Slothrop the paranoid search for explanation is centered on the Rocket, archetypal symbol and system, new threatening presence (absence)[15] in the sky, and upon Father Broderick, Laszlo Jamf, Lyle Bland and IG Farben as representatives of a secular elect whose power defines and subjects the preterite. But is Slothrop the victim of some "real" plot—a Father Conspiracy, Pavlovian experiment or industrial cartel—or of the paranoid's trained imagination? Is the Rocket merely a figure, its "presence" the sign of a vacancy, a lack that must be filled?

> Proverbs for Paranoids, 1: You may never get to touch the Master,
> but you can tickle his creatures (GR 237).

Are things strictly determined, as Pointsman hopes they are, or subject to the laws of probability and the vagaries of chance, Mexico's position? What does this curious relationship between the behaviour of Slothrop's penis and rocket strikes mean? Is there a relationship? Proverb 3: "If they can get you asking the wrong questions, they don't have to worry about the answers" (GR 251). Of course, the alternatives are not plot or meaninglessness, which is another form of the zero-one binary that the text deconstructs so busily, because in fragmentariness there are always meanings, and connections. Though who is making them, and for what purpose? Like Stencil and Oedipa Maas, Slothrop is curious for explanations: "Either they have put him here for a reason, or he's just here. He isn't sure that he wouldn't, naturally, rather have that *reason*. . . ." (GR 434). Not quite so careless of fixed forms as Mexico, nor so obsessed with them as Pointsman, Slothrop is Pynchon's leading figure of contradictions, a comic "Saint George after the fact" (GR 24) in whose wanderings the related issues of influence, allusion and

Narcissus at the Edge

meaning can be explored. To detail his cultural baggage as a loaded textual signifier is to point up the processes of his deconstruction, to perceive the figure as locus for a variety of manoeuvres that place in question, while not denying, factors that influence behaviour and meaning. Text and context necessarily displace one another in this reading process; metaphors reveal their ambiguities, providing fixes within, while contributing to, the play of differences in the text, this "tissue of quotations."[16]

These processes are evident in the manner in which the quest pattern is used and displaced. What does Pynchon's use of quest-romance motifs signify? What are the effects of their displacement by other frames of reference? Sent forth into the perilous zone, the knight's phallic lance actually becomes his penis, tracking the V2, and variously aided and distracted, Slothrop is a mock quester; but the traditional framework provides difference, in addition to structure, by including a set of figures that together contribute to the processes of putting into question. Some of the complications are signalled in the layers of rubbish on Slothrop's desk, "Elm Throat Lozenges sent by Slothrop's mother Nalline" (GR 18), as well as ukelele chords and a busted ukelele string, as first indicators of the oedipal tensions and orphic characteristics that become part of Pynchon's play with systems of analysis. Parodying Watson's Infant Albert and early behaviourist psychology, "Infant Tyrone" is heir to and victim of three centuries of Puritanism: "There is in his history and likely, God help him, in his dossier, a peculiar sensitivity to what is revealed in the sky. (But a hardon?)" (GR 26). The "great bright hand reaching out of the cloud" (GR 29) that shaped his ancestors' repressive austerity and obsession with death becomes the V2. A metamorphosis wrought by technology, it replaces one mythology, the Puritan, with another, the Rocket as symbol and system, while criticizing their negative effects. In the text's terms, these are death-serving structures because they inhibit individual freedom, inviting fear and manipulation. Real and imagined, their power is multiplied by the mysteries of presence in absence, by the palimpsestic ghostings of desire and fear, by the ways in which victims conspire in their own shackling:

> The Man has a branch office in each of our brains, his corporate emblem is a white albatross, each local rep has a cover known as the

100   *Theories of Play and Postmodern Fiction*

> Ego, and their mission in this world is Bad Shit. We do know what's
> going on, and we let it go on (GR 712-3).

Religious authority multiplying in secular structures, paranoia as
comfort and as terror, changing patterns in the dance of screwers and
screwees. . . . the play of *differánce* in language.

In this representation of a contemporary grail knight, the traditional
forms are complicated by references to Puritanism, psychoanalysis,
technological and economic determinism, and events of World War II.
As the references intersect, the systems qualify one another,
decentering representation, replacing "truth" with speculation, placing
the text and its contexts *sous rature*. In addition to filling out the 1940s
context and providing more laughter, Pynchon's attention to popular
culture further complicates the patterns. When Slothrop reads a
Plasticman comic he daydreams the role (GR 206) and his cry
"Plasticman where are you?" (GR 314) is both a pop cultural joke and a
further play upon the "plasticman" sorcerer from his own past, Laszlo
Jamf. He can be "the Cagney of the French Riviera" (GR 222), Errol
Flynn (GR 381), Siegel and Shuster's early Superman (GR 380) or a
momentary Lone Ranger (GR 435). He perceives a Sherman tank (GR
248) and the Reichstag building (GR 368) as King Kong, sees Mickey
Rooney (GR 382) and maybe hears the Andrews Sisters (GR 382)!
Inscribing context, providing playful intertextuality, such allusions also
define Slothrop's preterition, supporting his position as a Tannhaüser or
Orpheus figure rather than a St. George or Galahad, or indeed an Elect
in any system. There is no need to trace Slothrop's comic progress for
that has been done amply in Pynchon criticism, and with careful
attention to the substitutive collage. Rather I wish to emphasize the
effect of Pynchon's voluminous intertextuality as a process of radical
decentering. Deconstructing the invidious binary logic of zero and one,
preterition and election, and bringing literature, film, comic books,
science and history into the context, the proliferation of reading frames,
in their intersection, "extends the domain and the play of signification
ad infinitum."[17] As a strategy that promotes inclusiveness, it favours
"loving the people" (GR 547), even in the mildly pornographic and
necessarily incomplete (but we get the drift) picture from the horny
Anonymous, and in Katje's and Pirate's dissolve "into the race and
swarm of this dancing Preterition" (GR 548). A text down the track, it
is an answer to the narrator's lament in *The Crying of Lot 49*, "how had

Narcissus at the Edge 101

it ever happened here, with the chances once so good for diversity?" (L49 136).[18] Before leaving Slothrop, and despite labouring the connections, it is worth noting that his rediscovery of trees as the living green (GR 552-3) reverses the Puritan regard of paper as a medium for "shit, money and the Word, the three American truths" (GR 28), and that the recovery of his harmonica, and the Orpheus association, 560 pages on from its loss down a toilet at the Roseland ballroom (GR 63), suggests an alternative "grail" to the mysterious S-gerät of rocketry. It is appropriate that these images follow references to nationalities on the move in the Zone, "a great frontierless streaming" (GR 549) where the barriers are down and the signifiers come crowding in. But, lest we slip back into old habits of order and into reading narrative (and history) as linear pattern:

> He's been changing, sure, changing, plucking the albatross of self now and then, idly, half-conscious as picking his nose—but the one ghost-feather his fingers always brush by is America. Poor asshole, he can't let her go. She's whispered *love me* too often to him in his sleep, vamped insatiably his waking attention with come-hitherings, incredible promises. One day—he can see a day—he might be able finally to say *sorry,* sure and leave her . . . but not just yet. One more try, one more chance, one more deal . . . (GR 623).

It is not just that this reference evokes the seductive ambiguities, and long literary-cultural tradition, of the American dream, though it does this poignantly enough, but that its particular concentration on guilt and desire emphasizes, again, the complexities of connection that Pynchon invokes in the term "paranoia." These are psychological and linguistic, manifest in the workings of individual consciousness and in the text as construct. They ensure, always, the interplay of text and the contexts it both creates and evokes; *Gravity's Rainbow* is an elaborate play in words *and* a social-political tract.

The work's social-political "consciousness" can be seen in the manner of Pynchon's recreation of history, via a process of "quotation" and of putting into question. In this discussion, I will argue that judicious quotation and displacement produce not a denial but a reinvestigation of history and historiography. This reading supports Lyotard's view of the postmodern as the subversion of totalising structures, including traditional history, in favour of difference:

102   *Theories of Play and Postmodern Fiction*

> A postmodern artist or writer is in the position of a philosopher: the text he writes, the work he produces are not in principle governed by preestablished rules, and they cannot be judged according to a determining judgement, by applying familiar categories to the text or to the work. Those rules and categories are what the work of art itself is looking for. [19]

I have argued that inclusiveness is directly related to strategies of decentering, and this serious playfulness applies to Pynchon's use of history. It is by displacing "familiar categories" that *Gravity's Rainbow* is able to appropriate the historical, taking the past as a source for evocative borrowings which are used to question not the power of history but its ideological inscriptions and its role as the common model for linear construction and causal explanation. It is indeed the case that "History is not woven by innocent hands" (GR 277).

Most commentators on *Gravity's Rainbow* acknowledge Pynchon's meticulous historical research.[20] But of course the research is selective, for that is inevitable, and there are such varieties of invention in this text's deconstructive reconstruction of versions of past-ness. As John Krafft has noted, it is the elites who are more narrowly "historical" as the apparent shapers and exploiters of *History*.[21] Pynchon presents these as forces (Puritanism, the cartels, scientific research and technological development) while reading back against the text of capital-H History, "the humility, the multitudes who are passed over by God and History" (GR 299), including the carnivalesque variety of popular culture. In one respect, then, Pynchon provides an archaeological revision of traditional history. The appropriateness of Foucault's metaphor is evident in the repeated play in *Gravity's Rainbow* between the expansive narrative surface and ideas of layering, with search as an excavation of historical sedimentation, as applicable to the mess on Slothrop's desk as to waste, London in the blitz, the unconscious, Herero ideas of the Center beyond time, and to white corporate organisation as a surface replication of the black mineral world below.[22] But it is also appropriate in its attention to discontinuities: "The uses of concepts of discontinuity, rupture, threshold, limit, series and transformation present all historical analysis not only with questions of procedure but with theoretical problems."[23] Foucault addresses these in specific contexts in *Madness and Civilization, The Birth of the Clinic, Discipline and Punish,* and *The*

Narcissus at the Edge 103

History of Sexuality,[24] archaeological explorations of the often insidious workings of discourse that trace the ways in which "human beings are made subjects."[25] Pynchon, as I have argued, addresses them by the related processes of decentering, fragmentation and inclusiveness; and there are similarities in his and Foucault's concentrations upon language and upon power in discourse, upon the processes that create the changing daisy chain of screwers and screwees. Foucault's description of genealogical work could well be a description of Pynchon's text: "[it] disturbs what was previously considered immobile; it fragments what was thought unified; it shows the heterogeneity of what was imagined consistent with itself."[26] "Worldly" and "historical,"[27] *Gravity's Rainbow* is a postmodernist text that directs our attention to epistemological questions, inviting us not to ignore history but to analyse it as construct, force and influence. As an "historian," Pynchon is closer to Hayden White's metahistory than to logocentric renditions of neat causal connections:

> Properly understood, histories ought never to be read as unambiguous signs of the events they report, but rather as symbolic structures, extended metaphors, that 'liken' the events reported in them to some form with which we have already become familiar in our literary language.[28]

White argues that history is not only selective, signifying the choices and mode of interpretation of its makers, but that it is subject to the instabilities of language as discourse. To regard it as a narrative form, "a verbal structure in the form of a narrative prose discourse,"[29] is to emphasize the strong function of tropes in discourse, a function that he explains in terms of Freud's analysis of dreamwork. While "condensation," "displacement," "representation" and "secondary revision" allow for the relativities that destabilise simple truth-claims, they also point towards a text's imaginative appeal in its play between the historical and the mythical, or in representations of "myth" as "history."

Discussions of Pynchon's use of history in *Gravity's Rainbow* commonly point to the contrast between Enzian's search for "the Center without time" (GR 319) and "the one-way flow of European time" (GR 724), the contrast between perceptions of time as cyclical and linear, or between tribal myth and Western history.[30] And the

104   *Theories of Play and Postmodern Fiction*

textual play *is* dazzling: Rocket 00001, assembled by the Schwarzkommando, endowed with mandala symbolism, associated with regenerative impulses and carrying Enzian, black preterite and dying God, seems potentially redemptive; Rocket 00000, assembled under Blicero's direction, its symbolism accentuating death, associated with destruction and carrying Gottfried, white Nordic youth and sacrificial bride in death, threatens annihilation. They may seem to fulfil the dualistic conception of Manichaeans: "who see two Rockets, good and evil, who speak together in the sacred idiolalia of the Primal Twins (some say their names are Enzian and Blicero) of a good Rocket to take us to the stars, an evil Rocket for the World's suicide, the two perpetually in struggle" (GR 727), or to be explicable in terms of Eros and Thanatos, the Dionysiac and the Apollonian, feminine and masculine, intuition and rationality, and so on. But, again, binary alternatives are shown to be unsatisfactory; they are introduced but they are also dismantled, mainly by the myriad checks and confusions to reductive logic in the play of ideas but also in simple narrative terms: "each day the mythical return Enzian dreamed of seems less possible" (GR 519). The Schwarzkommando's mandalic projections are variants of another mandala, "The great Serpent holding its tail in its mouth, the dreaming Serpent which surrounds the world" (GR 412) of Kekulé's 1865 dream of the benzene ring which revolutionised chemistry and made IG Farben possible;[31] by further transference, the Uroboros becomes the V2, the serpent whispering ambiguous messages in a garden whose innocence is already destroyed. So the unities are undone, and scepticism replaces trust: "Before the Rocket we went on believing, because we wanted to. But the Rocket can penetrate, from the sky, at any given point. Nowhere is safe, we can't believe them any more" (GR 728). Situating this deconstructed opposition, tribal return and Western linearity, within space-time research in contemporary physics, we find with Pynchon, and as Steven Weisenburger suggests, that history "does not march inexorably forward by goose-steps, nor does it gyrate in circles."[32]

Seanced, communicating from the *other* side, Walter Rathenau announces the future:

> "All talk of cause and effect is secular history, and secular history is a diversionary tactic. Useful to you, gentlemen, but no longer so to us here. If you want the truth—I know I presume—you must look into

Narcissus at the Edge 105

> the technology of these matters. Even into the hearts of certain molecules—it is they after all which dictate temperatures, pressures, rates of flow, costs, profits, the shapes of towers. . . .
>
> You must ask two questions. First, what is the real nature of synthesis? And then: what is the real nature of control?" (GR 167).

But the dismantling of history does not mean escape from history. The preterite defence against synthesis (incorporation) and against control (subjugation) lies not only in Murphy's Law, "*When everything has been taken care of, when nothing can go wrong, or even surprise us . . . something will*" (GR 275); it lies as well in the associated processes of decentering and inclusiveness, in the possibilities between the zero of annihilation and the one of assimilation that the text's tactics of vigorous accumulation and diversion demonstrate. These deconstructive processes are political as well as linguistic; in their subversive analysis of the structures of repression, they constitute a positive critique of historical crisis, a critique that offers awareness as the way of resistance. I cannot agree with Thomas Smith's judgement that "the book's refusal to systematise any form of thought, its denigration of history as the paranoid, fear-ridden construct of an omnipresent 'them,' represents a form of quietism, an abject surrender to exactly those forms of violence and exploitation which the author has spent 700 pages denouncing."[33] If systematisation is perceived as hardening into power plays and the oppositional antics of division and subjection, as it is in *Gravity's Rainbow,* then its refusal is not surrender but part of a strategy of denunciation and recouperation. Who wants to play the power game on THEIR terms!

In this very brief consideration of Pynchon's use of history, I have not traced sources because, fascinating as the back-tracking is, my interest here is not the particular accuracy or otherwise of details, not the specific edge between verified "fact" and fictitious spinoff, but the ways in which "history" can be read back against History; the linguistic nature of the past as an influential construct; and the types of play for which Pynchon uses history, treating it not as an essence but taking advantage of its variety. Certainly, as critical studies show,[34] Pynchon's research is precise. *Gravity's Rainbow* is a history book, but one in which the brilliant local colour is used, in serious play, to displace structures, practices and ways of perceiving that it cannot help but

106   *Theories of Play and Postmodern Fiction*

acknowledge. Pynchon lifts a lot from the world, but the dialectical play between the book and the world resists synthesis.

RIGGED GAMES AND THE POINT OF PLAY

> —it's here that saturation hits him, it's all this playing games, too much of it, too many games: the nasal obsessive voice of a croupier he can't see—messieurs, mesdames, les jeux sont faits—(GR 205)

So, Slothrop set up at the Casino Hermann Goering! But while the metaphors provide inklings of Slothrop's gathering paranoia and another reference to manipulative processes, they also describe the gamesome text in which "les jeux sont faits" and the opportunities for play are so prodigious. With particular reference to Derridean deconstruction, I have argued that play is endemic in language; *Gravity's Rainbow* makes such overt reference to the rhetoric and strategies of game and play that it constitutes a source book of play as concept. Reading the narrative self-consciousness as a metafictional reminder of the text's status as artefact, we are necessarily involved, as well, in considerations of its relationship with "reality". The concentration can be both formalist and contextual, a study of textuality and of social processes. It finds shelter within Ehrmann's generous overview, "To define play is at the same time and in the same movement to define reality and to define culture,"[35] but this requires further analysis of the styles of play and the philosophy of meaning. What forms does play take in *Gravity's Rainbow?* How do these conjure realities? In this brief discussion, I wish to point to Pynchon's use of "play" as a concept to denote both text and culture. It decenters and questions restrictive systems of authority by affirming difference and heterogeneity, subversion, accumulation, parody and laughter. Although Eros may never break free from Thanatos, this acknowledgement, despite the accumulated weight of negative history and repressive structures, can be life-enhancing rather than death-serving.

In Part 1, I suggest that play denotes an attitude of mind (and subsequent activity) which affirms freedom and possibility against restriction, resignation and closure—and that while it transcends game, games necessarily involve play. In this general sense, *Gravity's Rainbow,* by virtue of its vast inclusiveness and the exuberance with

Narcissus at the Edge

which ideas are introduced and played with, is one of postmodernism's most playful texts. Raiding cultural forms, not just for reference but for metaphors that he uses figuratively, Pynchon works and compliments the reader. The inventiveness is challenging and playful, so much of it turning about the connections that we are invited to make as we "go on blundering inside our front-brain faith in Kute Korrespondences" (GR 590) sifting the layers, tracking metaphors out to other contexts, and making links across the text's changing narrative lines and modes. To read is to be a sorting demon. And to play, that is to be an activist, appears to hold out not only the best possibilities for reading satisfaction, but also the best opportunities for defence, or at least for contact and life-nourishing surprise, in the face of those repressive forces that the text identifies as the death-serving structures of Western civilisation. While not disparaging high culture, nor the value of knowledge (though suspicious of its institutionalisation), *Gravity's Rainbow* conducts its salvage operation on behalf of the preterite of humanity and of cultural forms. It is part of the play, an irony of text and history, that to have been passed over may be life-preserving: Mbakayere, "a mantra for times that threaten to be bad" (GR 362).

Pynchon's explicit references to games and play are extremely varied. Chess, pinball, roulette and cards, games in which the player's success depends upon different degrees of knowledge, skill and luck are used as metaphors for power and control, with reference to the ubiquitous They and to manipulation of preterite by elect. Or is it a dramatisation of preterite paranoia? Both. Chess is a popular source of metaphor in fiction and in language theory, not only because it provides such figures as board, players, moves and contest but because, above other two-person board games, it places such emphasis upon strategy and multiple choices. Providing, "raggedy pawns, the disgraced bish-op and cowardly knight" (GR 173) to suggest terror in the Blitz, and the figure for von Göll, der Springer, as the knight who leaps "across the chessboard of the Zone" (GR 376), it provides as well explanatory images for drug-salesman Wimpe's description of organic chemistry: "how each molecule had so many possibilities open to it, possibilites for bonding, bonds of different strengths, from carbon the most versatile, the queen, 'the Great Catherine of the periodic table', down to the little hydrogens numerous and single-moving as pawns" (GR 344). But, most extensively, the relationship between Blicero (Weissmann), visionary magus at the centre of the Rocket program, and Pökler, long-

108 *Theories of Play and Postmodern Fiction*

serving engineer on the V2 project, becomes a game of brute and unequal strategy with Blicero, the chess-master, shifting Ilse-pawns on the board of the Zone, withholding the Queen Leni, moving inexorably towards an end-game fixed on Rocket 00000:

> But that night in the cubicle, only breathing—no moon-wishes this year—from her cot, he was awake wondering, one daughter, one impostor? same daughter twice? two impostors? Beginning to work out the combinations for a third visit, a fourth . . . Weissmann, those behind him, had thousands of these children available. As the years passed, as they grew more nubile, would Pökler even come to fall in love with one—would she reach the king's row that way and become a queen-substitute for lost, for forgotten Leni? The Opponent knew that Pökler's suspicion would always be stronger than any fears about real incest. . . . They could make up new rules, to complicate the game indefinitely. How could any man as empty as Pökler felt that night ever be flexible enough for that? (GR 418)

In the intersection of two sets of metaphor, chess pawn Ilse is also, like film, a succession of stills to counterfeit movement: "The only continuity has been her name, and Zwölfkinder, and Pökler's love—love something like the persistence of vision, for They have used it to create for him the moving image of a daughter, flashing him only these summertime frames of her, leaving it to him to build the illusion of a single child" (GR 422). It is a deliberate irony on Pynchon's part, as grand master of riddling connections, that this summertime Ilse conceived in film images relates to the "real" Ilse, who is one of the generation of shadow-children "fathered" upon film-star Greta Erdmann, her conception inspired by Erdmann's role in *Alpdrücken*.[36] That this Pökler episode is one of the most moving, and most verisimilitudinous parts of the text, is attributable to the interweaving of motifs (with chemical and technological added to those I have mentioned) but also to our perception of historical context against which it is received. The chess metaphors convey very well the idea of moves in a game of power, with Pökler as the one who is used, more played than player. Though textual signifiers may all fit Ehrmann's formulation, Pökler does so doubly: "as an object in the game, the player can be its stakes ('enjeu') and its toy ('jouet')."[37]

Narcissus at the Edge

One of the most brilliantly developed game metaphors of conspiracy is the rigged pinball machine. Shipped from Chicago to Alfonso Tracy and housed secretly within a monolithic Masonic Hall in Mouthorgan, Missouri, details which announce a multi-directional play of signification, every one of the huge stack of machines "'is fucked up', sez melancholy Tracy":

> "Look at this." It's a Folies-Bergères: four-colour lovelies doing the cancan all over it, zeros happening to coincide with eyes, nipples, and cunts, one of your racy-type games here, a little hostile towards the ladies but *all in fun*! "You got a nickel?" *Chungg,* boing there goes the ball just missing a high-scoring hole, hmm looks like a permanent warp there *ahnnnggghk* knocks a flasher worth 1000 but only 50 lights up on the board—"You see?" Tracy screams as the ball heads like a rock for the bottom, outside chance get it with a flipper *zong* flipper flips the other fucking *way,* and the board lights up TILT.
> "Tilt?" Bland scratching his head. "You didn't even—"
> "They're *all* like that," Tracy watering with frustration. (GR 583)

The section is a sustained example of Pynchon's brand of exuberant fun serving a serious thematic purpose, an example of the interpenetration of playfulness and seriousness that characterizes this text. Set within the discussion of American entrepreneur Lyle Bland, who symbolises the insidious manipulators at the heart of the huge international cartel and who is connected via IG Farben, General Electric and Laszlo Jamf with Slothrop's peculiar conditioning, the faulty pinball machines provide another figure for the central determinism-freewill opposition. It is according to this opposition that characters are aligned and the force of conceptual systems (religious, scientific, economic and cultural) is represented:

> Outside the temple, the organisation reps from Chicago lurk, play morra, drink Canadian blends out of silver hip-flasks, oil and clean 38s and generally carry on in their loathsome ethnic way, Popish inscrutability in every sharp crease and shadowy jowl. No way to tell if someplace in the wood file cabinets exists a set of real blueprints telling exactly how all these pinball machines were rewired—a randomness deliberately simulated—or if it has happened at real random, preserving at least our faith that each machine, individually,

110   *Theories of Play and Postmodern Fiction*

> has simply, in innocence, gone on the blink, after the thousands of roadhouse nights, end-of-the-world Wyoming thunderstorms that come straight down on your hatless head, truckstop amphetamines, tobacco smoke clawing at insides of eyelids, homicidal grabs after some way out of the year's never-slackening shit . . . have players forever strangers brought about, separately, alone, each of these bum machines? (GR 586)

Genuine malfunction or wear, or the work of organisation reps with, beyond them, mysterious higher level reps like Bland, and beyond them . . . such a chain of command? Are thoughts of conspiracy merely delusions of preterite paranoia? The possibilities reflect upon the narrator's earlier assertion that the Blands of the world are such influential shapers of reality that, "those like Slothrop, with the greatest interest in discovering the truth, were thrown back on dreams, psychic flashes, omens, cryptographies, drug-epistemologies, all dancing on a ground of terror, contradiction, absurdity" (GR 582). Within this context, Pynchon's attention to magic and the supernatural, in scenes of communion with spirits of the dead, dreams, drug-induced visions, Tarot cards, alchemy, astrology, Freemasonry, Kabbalist interpretations and so on, constitutes a challenging observation about realities of life in the twentieth century. Following Freud and Jung particularly, with their views of the divided psyche, and of dreams and myths as symbolic products of the unconscious, his emphasis upon the interrelationships of magic, the occult, dream and myth, while a rich source of mystery, metaphor and play, explicitly deconstructs a Western orthodoxy based upon the priority of reason. If "reason" presumes to be the guiding intelligence that would hold it all together, that would be the source of social control, its "mindful" authority is challenged not only by "mindless pleasures" as alternative and subversive behaviour but also by the continuing fear that they really are the signs of energy, play and creative possibility, positive others in an ancient dialectic.

Examples are numerous of game used more loosely, as both a structural metaphor and an indicator of playful contest. They include the White Visitation's surveillance of Slothrop, Gottfried and Katje's "oven-game" with Blicero in occupied Holland, Enzian's pact with Blicero, the Schwarzkommando's search for the True Text and the Enzian-Tchitcherine opposition, in addition to more confined "games" such as Slothrop's with Greta Erdmann and Geli Tripping,[38] Greta and

Narcissus at the Edge   111

Bianca playing "stage mother and reluctant child" (GR 465), Saüre's debate with Gustav over the merits of Rossini versus Beethoven, the singing-duel and the Mother of the Year contest. Game terminology and options in the play are emphasized most clearly in Katje and Gottfried's Hansel-and-Gretel game in the forest with witch Blicero:

> though it is never discussed among them openly, it would seem Katje, Gottfried, and Captain Blicero have agreed that this Northern and ancient form, one they all know and are comfortable with—the strayed children, the wood-wife in the edible house, the captivity, the fattening, the Oven—shall be their preserving routine, their shelter, against what outside none of them can bear—the War, the absolute rule of chance, their own pitiable contingency here, in its midst . . . (GR 96).

As the fattening figure in this sado-masochistic ritual, Gottfried shall become the S-gerät, the sacrificial victim entombed ecstatically in the Rocket 00000 of Blicero's Faustian dreams of transcendence. Cast as the witch and combining both male and female, SS Captain Blicero is a negative anima figure, both Terrible Mother and sadistic warlord, the one who plays the game out, combining science and technology with numinous magic in his role as master of the phallic Rocket. But exercising a player's choice, Katje quits the game:

> Indeed, why did she leave Schuhstelle 3? We are never told why. But now and then, players in a game will, lull or crisis, be reminded how it is, after all, really play—and be unable then to continue in the same spirit. . . . Nor need it be anything sudden, spectacular—it may come in gentle—and regardless of the score, the number of watchers, their collective wish, penalties they or the Leagues may impose, the player will, waking deliberately, perhaps with Katje's own tough, young isolate's shrug and stride, say *fuck it* and quit the game, quit it cold . . . (GR 107).

Becoming planted "damsel-in-distress" in the White Visitation's observation of Slothrop on the French Riviera, Mistress of the Night in Brigadier Pudding's humiliation, the White Goddess attending the Schwarzkommando's assembly of Rocket 00001, and dissolving with Pirate Prentice into the "swarm of this dancing preterition" (GR 548),

112   *Theories of Play and Postmodern Fiction*

Katje's role changes are presented as those of a drifter within the war zone's arrangements and the text's narrative strands. Whether in representation of Katje Borgesius, Slothrop, Pökler, Blicero or Greta Erdmann, each of whom plays a number of different parts, role-play is presented as ambiguous action, as both a response to repressive structures and a tactic for survival. Operating, therefore, as a commentary on systems and the divided psyche, on perceptions of character and on social structures, it is also an important tactic in Pynchon's making and unmaking of the text. Supporting the processes of fragmentation, displacement and change by which such variety is accumulated, it is a textual play and a commentary. Thus in Katje's final meeting with Enzian, and following their reminiscences of Blicero:

> Feedback, smile-to-smile adjustments, waverings: What it damps out to is *we will never know each other.* Beaming, strangers, la-la-la, off to listen to the end of a man we both loved and we're strangers at the films, condemned to separate rows, aisles, exits, homegoings (GR 663).

But lest the play of alternatives becomes too alienating, too complex and too broken for comfort, "There are things to hold on to . . ." (GR 659).

There is also the play of laughter, specifically the comic in those scenes in *Gravity's Rainbow* that offer the exaggerations of farce, slapstick or the carnivalesque. Adding to the linguistic variety, they are also subversive. Their energy and their vulgarity constitute a challenge to notions of conventional decorum and to order as both a characteristic and an object of communication. Defining carnival laughter, Bakhtin emphasizes its dividedness; it is derisive and regenerative:

> Carnival laughter is the laughter of all the people. Second, it is universal in scope; it is directed at all and everyone, including the carnival's participants. The entire world is seen in its droll aspect, in its gay relativity. Third, this laughter is ambivalent: it is gay, triumphant, and at the same time mocking, deriding. It asserts and denies, it buries and revives. Such is the laughter of carnival.[39]

Narcissus at the Edge 113

This dividedness is central to the *Gravity's Rainbow* slapstick. It marks the excesses of Pointsman's dog-napping, Raoul's party, the Marvy-Slothrop chase scenes, Frau Gnabb as Pirate Queen of the Baltic, Marvy's castration and Mexico's revenge upon Pointsman and the other controllers in Mossmoon's office. It is a form of pointed exuberance that appears in the earlier novels, for example in Suck Hour at the Sailor's Grave (*V*) in Oedipa's wild meeting with Metzger (*The Crying of Lot 49*) and in the later mad antics of Zoyd Wheeler (*Vineland*). A Pynchon trademark, these scenes of wild narrative combine point with excess, message with vulgarity, by offering variations on a theme rather than mere diversion. So, for example, the scene in which Mexico urinates on the poker-faced assembly and makes his escape through London streets may be orchestrated as a mixture of Marx Brothers farce and a Douglas Fairbanks chase scene, a combination of old film memories and narrative excess, but *in its sheer extremity* it represents an affront to Them and to their passion for control. Such scenes offer the energy of billingsgate with a pattern to the play, a pattern that favours the folk (the preterites), and subversive action, against repressive authority-structures.

SO AT THE MERCY OF LANGUAGE . . .

> —all right, say we *are* supposed to be the Kabbalists out here, say that's our real Destiny, to be the scholar–magicians of the Zone, with somewhere in it a Text, to be picked to pieces, annotated, explicated, and masturbated till it's all squeezed limp of its last drop . . . (GR 520).

Ah, the Word, the Text, this patriarchy . . . but what if a feminine principle is insinuated, the metaphors all changed, male order junked . . . then, maybe then, the multiplicities unfold, and keep on, extending opportunities for play and for pleasure, infinitely. . . . But Nietzsche's, Derrida's and Pynchon's challenges to logocentrism question the categories themselves. The text invites the reader to mock jittery Pointsman when he is appalled at Mexico's emphasis on symbols of randomness: "What if Mexico's whole *generation* have turned out like this? Will Postwar be nothing but 'events,' newly created one moment to the next? No links? Is it the end of history?" (GR 56). And the result of the loss of ONE is not zero. In this analysis of the *play of*

114   *Theories of Play and Postmodern Fiction*

language in *Gravity's Rainbow,* I shall consider: the relationship between language and meaning; style as thematic commentary; film work as one example of serious play in words; and the narrator and the reader, a volatile relationship.

There is something to be said for a commentary with which one disagrees at almost every point: in choice and definition of key terms, in the authority accorded "authorities" cited for the analysis, in judgements about effects and, in sum, in perspectives on what may be worthwhile and why in literature. In "Linguistic Distancing in *Gravity's Rainbow,*"[40] Brooke Horvath locates *Gravity's Rainbow* "in the modernist camp" and asserts that it is uninhabitable by readers of "traditional fiction"; cites a waspish snippet from Gore Vidal and slabs of E.D. Hirsch with approval; judges that Pynchon's strategies of copious allusion, varied styles, fragmented narrative, mixed vocabulary and bad grammar keep the readers ever outside any empathy, with characters or with message; and concludes that the text "negates any 'real world' concerns on the reader's part," presumably because it is "too convoluted, too valueless, too absurd, too grim." The case is peculiarly judgemental as well as anachronistic. Where are poststructuralism and postmodernism as contexts for discussion, or some reader-response theory besides Hirsch's pedantry about short-term memory as the determinant of what can constitute "good prose"? Good heavens. But I cite the article not so much to enter into battle as to note how contrary conclusions can arrive from similar definitions of the evidence, apparently because of differences in literary preference; although we agree that the text has multiple vocabularies, syntactic complexities, interlocking frames of reference and the juxtaposition of different styles, tones and genres, Horvath and I disagree entirely, it seems, about their effects. Whereas Horvath defines these as "a wall between reader and work," I have argued that they are, on the contrary, an invitation into the work and that, furthermore, in their difficulty they compliment the reader as having intelligence as well as a sense of play. The chances of our agreeing are shaky when Horvath can quote Hirsch on style in the face of Pynchon's prose: "we should choose the most economical expression from among these different expressions which serve the same purpose"[41]—exemplary good sense if we are talking about road signs.

Narcissus at the Edge 115

What is the relationship between language and meaning in Pynchon's work? The exuberant mix of language styles in each of the novels demonstrates that, just as play is innate to language, in the forms of ambiguity and multiplicity, so too language is an object of play in the processes of shaping and communicating meanings. Pynchon's texts exemplify Nietzsche's perception that "truth" is "a mobile army of metaphors, metonyms and anthropomorphisms,"[42] or Oedipa Maas's "discovery": "The act of metaphor then was a thrust at truth and a lie, depending where you were: inside, safe, or outside, lost" (L49 97).[43] Saul's references in "Entropy" to ambiguity, redundancy, irrelevance, leakage, or noise, in language; Fausto Maijstral's in *V* to the poet's consciousness that metaphor "has no value apart from its function; that it is a device, an artifice" (V 326); Leni Pökler's sense of metaphor and difference in *Gravity's Rainbow*—these much-quoted references *are* self-reflexive of the linguistic artifice of the texts that contain them. And if language denotes an absence it also denotes an abundance: in the absence of simple identification (of the word with the object, or of the signifier with the signified, or of the "transcendental signified" as legitimating presence), an absence to which we have been alerted increasingly in post-Saussurean linguistics, there is the shifting availability of complex possibilities. For Pointsman, uncertainty promotes dread; in Pynchon's texts it promotes multiplicity, not the loss but the proliferation of meanings and, thus, the inevitable play within discourse between texts and contexts in inescapable awareness that texts are material objects with a political presence. Like Derrida and Barthes, and Foucault, Pynchon is interested in the nature and the control of meaning-formation. It is presented as his characters' leading obsession.

The inescapability of language and, with it, of systems of conditioning and power is addressed in varieties of nostalgia for "the Center without time" (GR 319). Already caught in language, Enzian and the Schwarzkommando search for the "holy Text" (GR 520), assuming it to be the Rocket, a text that might yet enable them to recover the lost Centre beyond (Western) time. In the Kerghiz Light episode, Tchitcherine's mission to bring alphabet to an illiterate culture presents both the utopian idea of originary naturalness and the impossibility of any return to it. Similarly, Slothrop's dream of a radical reversal of history, of a way back to "a single set of coordinates from which to proceed, without elect, without preterite, without even

116   *Theories of Play and Postmodern Fiction*

nationality to fuck it up" (GR 556) emphasizes not so much the dream vision as the intricate processes of history and of cultural conditioning operating through the medium of language. It is suggested that "words are only an eye-twitch away from the things they stand for" (GR 100): with the narrator's observation situated within the description of Blicero's first meeting with Enzian in the Südwest, and with Blicero feeling the potency of every word, we are reminded of both authority and difference in language. Words are potent, yet how important the "eye-twitch" is; it allows the act of linguistic and political displacement that makes Blicero "Njambi Karunga" (God) to Enzian, white overlord to Black African, and it is a figure too for the general mobility of words as they are crossed by contexts none of which, as Derrida says, permits saturation of meaning.[44] So keen has been the critical picking and annotation, that most of the words in *Gravity's Rainbow* seem squeezed almost to the "last drop"; the zealousness is a compliment to the text. Even so, I would like to take just two examples, *black* and *labyrinth*.

Colour of "the Word made printer's ink" (GR 571), black's cultural baggage is huge, and, as we would expect, Pynchon exploits it. Treacle's reaction to the Schwarzkommando uses and parodies Freudian perspectives while shifting the black focus by a double associative move:

> He had not meant to offend sensibilities, only to show the others, decent fellows all, that their feelings about blackness were tied to feelings about shit, and feelings about shit to feelings about putrefaction and death. It seemed to him so clear . . . why wouldn't they listen? Why wouldn't they admit that their repressions *had,* in a sense that Europe in the last weary stages of its perversion of magic has lost, had incarnated real and living men, likely (according to the best intelligence) in possession of real and living weapons, as the dead father who never slept with you, Penelope, returns night after night to your bed, trying to snuggle in behind you . . . or as your unborn child wakes *you,* crying in the night and you feel its ghost-lips at your breast . . . they are real, they are living, as you pretend to scream inside the Fist of the Ape . . . but looking over now at the much more likely candidate, cream-skinned Katje under the Wheel of Fortune (GR 276-7).

Narcissus at the Edge

Picking up traditional imagery linking blackness with excrement, racism and death, as presented in the drug-induced trip into the sewerage system of Slothrop's unconscious (GR 63-7) and in Pudding's masochistic humiliation at the hands of the Mistress of the Night (GR 233-6), the passage introduces King Kong as archetypal black figure of popular mythology and collective projection of phantom figures in Western humanity's nightmares. And in this play with possibilities, the cinematic figure (itself a significant "projection"!) generates offspring; art shapes reality: "And so, too, the legend of the black scapeape we cast down like Lucifer from the tallest erection in the world has come, in the fullness of time, to generate its own children, running inside Germany even now—the Schwarzkommando, whom Mitchell Prettyplace, even, could not anticipate" (GR 275). King Kong, the Schwarzkommando and racial destruction in the African Südwest are linked as products of Western culture's repressions (The White Visitation has an Operation Black Wing! (GR 74)), and Fay Wray in the Fist of the Ape becomes an archetypal image of this entrapment, the problem that Freud, in *Civilization and Its Discontents*,[45] perceived at the heart of Western civilization. The reference to Katje prefigures the role she will play as substitute Fay Wray to the Zone's black rocket troops, and both Jessica Swanlake (GR 275) and Slothrop do Fay Wray numbers (GR 688).

But "black" is radically split. In its link with individual repression and social control, it is the darkness of nightmare and of death-serving controllers: Puritanism, Pointsman, Blicero and the tyrant-figures played by Rudolf Klein-Rogge in Fritz Lang movies, the admired of Franz Pökler, Rocket-servant, and forerunners, it is implied, of Hitler:

> Klein-Rogge was carrying nubile actresses off to rooftops when King Kong was still on the tit with no motor skills to speak of. Well, one nubile actress anyway, Brigitte Helm in Metropolis. Great movie. Exactly the world Pökler and evidently quite a few others were dreaming about those days . . . (GR 578).

Black is for power-mongers. On the other hand, Pynchon plays upon both the romantic tradition of the "noble savage" and the potential fertility of waste. The Schwarzkommando's and King Kong's comparative innocence and nobility are important ("'you know, he *did* love her folks,'" GR 275); Queequeg is his text's regenerative figure—

118   *Theories of Play and Postmodern Fiction*

like Enzian here; and, furthermore, waste, as the expressed (shit *and* words), the repressed (the unconscious), the passed-over (preterites) and the victimised (tribal nations), these black figures, offers hope as, to switch texts, We Await Silent Tristero's Empire (W.A.S.T.E.). Even riddling keeps things moving. There are black contrasts to be made with white, in its association with Weissmann (white man), with Gottfried as pale sacrificial victim, with North as the land of death, with Christian Europe as the order of analysis, repression and death (GR 317), and with the destruction of Hiroshima—"a giant white cock, dangling in the sky straight downward out of a white pubic bush" (GR 693). But in this text, as in Melville's, white is the gap that must be filled, the blank upon which inscriptions gather, and "in a matter like this, subtlety appeals to subtlety, and without imagination no man can follow another into these halls."[46] Although white is the erasure towards which Gottfried is impelled in Rocket 00000, "what is this death but a whitening, a carrying of whiteness to ultrawhite, what is it but bleaches, detergents, oxidizers, abrasives" (GR 754), it signifies too the cinema screen of the text's final image: "The screen is a dim page spread before us, white and silent" (GR 760), and this white invites performance. Again the text deconstructs its own processes of signification; black and white are not so much simply opposed as separately divided. Loaded signifiers, they are playful and played.

Already a pervasive figure in postmodernist literature,[47] associated with intricate structure and the promise of uncertainty, labyrinth is an important image in *Gravity's Rainbow*. Squalidozzi's lament to Slothrop, about the Argentinian's obsession with building labyrinths, is not only a metaphor for civilisation myths, for developments from Garden innocence to City of Pain; it points as well to subject and method in the text:

> "It is our national tragedy. We are obsessed with building labyrinths, where before there was open plain and sky. To draw ever more complex patterns on the blank sheet. We cannot abide that openness: it is terror to us. Look at Borges. Look at the suburbs of Buenos Aires" (GR 18).

Look at the London underworld of Prentice's dream, the Mittelwerke tunnels where one may trace the Rocket's becoming, and the image of Hell, the World and the Book in which "its labyrinthine path turns out,

Narcissus at the Edge

like Route One where it passes through the heart of Providence, to've been set up deliberately to give the stranger a tour of the city" (GR 537). Although Slothrop's reply to Squalidozzi, "'you can't have open range forever, you can't just stand in the way of progress'" (GR 264), has the ominous sound of an old catch-cry, one that has led Western society to assume its superiority and caused the spread of its "order of Analysis and Death" (GR 722), there is no easy return to Garden innocence or the blank page. Besides, who really wants to make that trip? Who wants to reverse this long-running film, run it backwards through the projector? John Barth has pointed out that, for Borges, the labyrinth is the place in which all the possibilities of choice are embodied.[48] And this is so for *Gravity's Rainbow,* with the labyrinthine form offering images of culture, positive and negative, and symbolising the play of signification itself.

So, labyrinths are permissive and restrictive. In opposition to the penis of Rocket and cathedral, technological and religious systems, the earth-womb of the labyrinth is regenerative. Alternatively, there is the array of metaphors and sequences that present visions of life as labyrinth and humanity trapped. Characters caught in the cellulose of film, rats running mazes, dogs salivating, the ball stuck in a pinball machine, pigs led to slaughter, the annihilation of dodos, and lemmings rushing to sea provide variations on the theme. They are supporting images to the text's concern with ideas of manipulation and control exemplified in the labyrinthine networks of IG Farben and Shell. But complex structures can trap readers as well as citizens and some of us, suckers for tracery, would rather stay in than take Ariadne's thread out: "'passages out there are dangerous, chances of falling so shining and deep. . . . Gravity rules all the way out to the cold sphere, *there is always the danger of falling'*" (GR 723). No exit, really. Only interpretation.

> It was stated at the outset, that this system would not be here, and at once, perfected. You cannot but plainly see that I have kept my word. But I now leave my cetological system standing thus unfinished, even as the great Cathedral of Cologne was left, with the crane still standing upon the top of the uncompleted tower. For small erections may be finished by their first architects; grand ones, true ones, ever leave the copestone to posterity. God keep me from ever completing

120   *Theories of Play and Postmodern Fiction*

anything. This whole book is but a draught—nay, but the draught of a draught. Oh, Time, Strength, Cash and Patience![49]

The comparison between *Gravity's Rainbow* and *Moby Dick* is an obvious one.[50] Another grand erection, the Rocket system is unfinished too. Although Melville writes, partly, about whales and Pynchon, partly, about rockets, the vast allusiveness and shape-switching of their texts guarantee an "intellectual chowder."[51] Each invites the reader's writerly interventions, making a virtue of "enterprises in which a careful disorderliness is the true method."[52] Style *is* text, inseparable from plot, ideas, character, and place; in these two big books it is defined by diversity and change, formal characteristics that uphold uncertainty as the condition of meaningfulness.

I have discussed decentering, the play of supplementation and intersecting fields of reference. Pynchon's style is to play with ideas, and with language, and this activity offers the possibility of laughter while serving the serious thematic purpose of destabilising authority structures and claims. The fragmented narrative lines, odd juxtapositions, and mixture of forms, generic models and moods create a designedly schizoid text. As Thomas Schaub says:

> The experience of ambiguity in the reading of Pynchon is essential. It is a necessary result of his design to bring readers to the uncertainties of the precarious balance where possibilities abound, where the familiar is strange, where the benign is evil, and where the rage for order is persistently denied. This is the effect of reading Pynchon.[53]

It is in this sense of radical ambiguity that *Gravity's Rainbow* is a post-structuralist work, one that promises but denies balance between detail and pattern. The text withholds the possibility of resolution precisely because it is antithetical to its view of the provocative instabilities of language and the world. It is not that the conflicting sources and styles of information cancel one another out, that uncertainty theory cancels determinism, that Tchitcherine balances Enzian, that Pökler's act of kindness to the dying woman in Dora prison-camp obliterates Blicero's sadistic manoeuvering, or that Rossini replaces Beethoven, and so on, because "'It all goes along together'" (GR 159) though not all with equal approval. Physics, mathematics, cybernetics, history, philosophy, religion and the occult, psychology, music, film, literature, comic books

Narcissus at the Edge

and cartoons. . . . At this stage of Pynchon criticism, and with the "discoveries" repeated time and again, the point is not the list but the manner and effect of juxtaposition, integration, displacement, of how the philosophical treatise is cut by farce, or the jeremiad by music hall. *Gravity's Rainbow* is "a film,"[54] "a musical,"[55] a history book, an "encyclopedic narrative,"[56] or—as the text itself invites—"it's all theatre" (GR 3). But territorialising zeal is undone, of course, by the text's refusal to provide any form as *the* definitive form. As a charismatic figure, its protean nature resists routinisation.

The final section, from the last seven-squares text break to the end, indicates the ways in which style is commentary. As the narrative lines cut or interweave, and metaphors pick up earlier details of character, event and idea, sentences typically twist through half-pages of associative representation in which the riddling play of structure at large is replicated in the typography itself, with italics, capitalisation, dashes, ellipses and brackets creating their graphic impression of the exuberant text. The formal intricacies embody Pynchon's concentration on social structures, systems and the complexities of individual identity and meaning, creating the complex structure of labyrinth, cityscape and zone or of the text as archaeological site. The final fragmentations can be read as a formal parallel to Slothrop's scattering, and to its interpretation as escape from the forces of subjugation; but this is a limited perspective. Fixed more upon the firing of Rocket 00000, these pages provide impressions of a waiting world, of the kaleidoscope of what may yet be possible beneath the threatening death-arc of this gravity's rainbow, the arc of ASCENT and DESCENT that joins the forest setting of PRE-LAUNCH, COUNTDOWN AND THE CLEARING with Richard M. Zhlubb (Richard M. Nixon), Los Angeles Theatre Manager, and "this old theatre" (GR 760) where the audience (U.S.A., the world) waits in darkness. The collective image repeats, for a world target, the numinous shape in the sky that earlier links Katje in Holland and Slothrop in London, Bodenplatte and target, "a curve each of them feels unmistakably" (GR 209). But the new secular mythology is imbued with traditional religious iconography, each a manifestation of deep psychic needs, and, as their juxtaposition implies, Gottfried in Rocket 00000 "is linked with Isaac under the blade" (GR 750). Although Blicero completes the ritual sacrifice of his surrogate son, this is a variation upon the theme of parents' "betrayal" of children to mortality: "The victim, in bondage to falling, rises on a promise, a

122   *Theories of Play and Postmodern Fiction*

prophecy of Escape . . ." (GR 758). In the biblical reference, Pynchon conceptualises the two alternatives that are presented so often in the text, Abraham's position or Isaac's, holding the knife or under the knife, the one active and masculine and the other "dark and female, passive, self-abandoning" (GR 75). Another play upon the Puritan idea of Election and Preterition, it is the organising metaphor for "the Apollonian Dream" (GR 754) and the implied Dionysiac other.

CHASE MUSIC provides not only an interruption, with witticisms about pop cultural heroes, but also commentary on power and preterition. Do they really lose their charisma? Who is making the play?

> There'll be a thousand ways to forget. The heroes will go on, kicked upstairs to oversee the development of bright new middle line personnel, and they will watch their system falling apart, watch those singularities begin to come more and more often, proclaiming another dispensation out of the tissue of old-fashioned time . . . (GR 752).

But nor does ageing Pointsman succeed, "left only with Cause and Effect, and the rest of his sterile armamentarium" (GR 752); and von Göll's continuous movie under the rug is not watched by regulars but "only visitors passing through" (GR 746), a reference that mocks his megalomanic pretensions about films creating reality. Blicero's tarot, repeated references to the kazoo (Slothrop's instrument),[57] Fritz Lang's *Die Frau im Mond* as source of the countdown, Steve Edelman and Kabbalist interpretation, CATCH with its suggestion of film running through a projector, late references to Byron the Bulb and to Ludwig that recall their narratives and the notion of story-telling. . . . As the modes and sources of allusion pile up, we are reminded of the text's concentration upon the making of connections and also of variety itself as both a feature of play and a form of resistance to closure. Sharp changes in language and mood, as well as in the sources of allusion, create style and, taken together, they are gamesome, subversive of all forms of ending, and invitational. The text's style leads us towards choosing, to the final reference to Slothrop's seventeenth-century ancestor William and thus back to *On Preterition:* "Could he have been the fork in the road America never took, the singular point she jumped the wrong way from?" (GR 556). It also withhlds the answer. We are invited to search among the preterite.

Narcissus at the Edge

"Springer, this ain't the fuckin' *movies* now, come on."'"Not yet. Maybe not quite yet. You'd better enjoy it while you can. Someday, when the film is fast enough, the equipment pocket-size and burdenless and selling at people's prices, the lights and booms no longer necessary, *then* ... then ..." (GR 527).

Pynchon as cinema buff: with a text so addicted to surprises and a critical industry addicted to tracking them, it is no surprise at all that *Gravity's Rainbow* spawns so much film commentary:

> film is more to the novel than a source of culturally rich allusion: it is its ostensible medium. *Gravity's Rainbow* purports to be a movie itself (David Cowart, 1980). [58]

> the medium of the text underlines the book's opening conviction that "it's all theatre" (Thomas Schaub, 1981).[59]

> Like a rainbow, *Gravity's Rainbow* spans the entire arc of cinema: from technical processes of invention to the writer's script to motion picture-making to final appreciation by an audience (Charles Clerc, 1983).[60]

> Rather than being merely a part of the content and plot of the novel, it [film] is the underlying complex metaphorical matrix along which various rhetorical positions are developed (Hanjo Berressem, 1993).

The range of Pynchon's emphasis upon Hollywood films to the early 1940s and upon German films of the 1920s and 1930s is finely documented in criticism. It is the case that film provides metaphors, strategies, and entertainment, while serving the text's concentration upon shaping forces in culture, the nature of power and subjection, and the incessant play between reality and illusion. It is one part of his postmodernism that Pynchon's texts include such a vast range of reference to popular cultural forms, in particular to film and in deference not only to its influence but also because of its specific usefulness in drawing attention to ideas about representation, meaning, and communication. Seeming to present reality as image but in fact presenting simulations or displacements of "the real," films offer vivid examples of processes in cultural construction. "Old fans who've

124   *Theories of Play and Postmodern Fiction*

always been at the movies (haven't we?)" (GR 760)—certainly. Including film addicts, film-stars (and occasional performers), and such a range of film reference,[61] it is to be expected that the text's filmmaker is important. In this discussion, I shall concentrate on film-maker von Göll, with particular attention to the place of film as a play-concept.[62]

In film reviews of Pynchon's epic, there is no shortage of attention to film as a preterite cultural form that has a profound effect upon the images and the attitudes of generations.[63] When it is noted that the relationship between art and life is not to be defined in illusion/reality terms but in each-way displacements of them, the importance of artforms as components of the real can be considered. Von Göll's megalomania is placed by an ironic narrative framework when, learning of the Schwarzkommandos, he asserts that "My images, somehow, have been chosen for incarnation" (GR 388). This perspective should be read in conjunction with details of his role as director of Greta Erdmann. While we are invited to read sceptically his claim that he can produce an Argentinian reversal, take Pain City back to Garden State, von Göll *has* directed Erdmann "through dozens of vaguely pornographic horror movies. 'I knew he was a genius from the beginning. I was only his creature'" (GR 393). He *named* his stars, "'the Reich's Sweethearts—Greta Erdmann and Max Schlepzig, Wonderfully Together—'" (GR 395), and it is *Alpdrücken* that inspires the generation of shadow-children fathered on Erdmann's screen image. In a further displacement that also draws attention to interpenetrations of art and life, Slothrop and Greta Erdmann's "reenactment" of the sadomasochistic scene from *Alpdrücken* complicates ideas of reality through its cinematic focus on artifice:

> Slothrop puts the whip down and climbs on top, covering her with the wings of his cape, her Schlepzig-surrogate, his latest reminder of Katje . . . and they commence fucking, the old phony rack groaning beneath them, Margherita whispering *God how you hurt me* and *Ah, Max . . .* and just as Slothrop's about to come, the name of her child: strained through her perfect teeth, a clear extrusion of pain that is not in play, she cries, *Bianca . . .* (GR 397)

Cut to Pökler inspired by the film image, fucking Leni, begetting their daughter Ilse (Bianca's "twin"), his "movie-child" (GR 398), whose

Narcissus at the Edge

annual visits to Zwölfkinder he perceives in terms not only of chess moves but also of film images and technology:

> So it has gone for the six years since. A daughter a year, each one about a year older, each time taking up nearly from scratch. The only continuity has been her name, and Zwölfkinder, and Pökler's love— love something like the persistence of vision, for They have used it to create for him the moving image of a daughter, flashing him only these summertime frames of her, leaving it to him to build the illusion of a single child. . . . (GR 422)

A "succession of frames to counterfeit movement." Susceptible to the Rocket-Master's manipulative tactics and influenced by film, Pökler's sense of the real is effectively decentered. It is a confused product of deprivation, nostalgia and technology.

Presented in association with great directors of the Expressionist period in German cinema, Lang, Pabst and Lubitsch (GR 112), von Göll as image-maker is a specialist in Pynchon's list of controllers. Film director and black marketeer, he is "der Springer," "'the knight who leaps perpetually [. . .] across the chessboard of the Zone'" (GR 376) and, in his explanation to Slothrop, he is one of the elite who define the preterite:

> "mistakes are part of it too—everything fits. One sees how it fits, ja? learns patterns, adjusts to rhythms, one day you are no longer an actor, but free now, over on the other side of the camera. No dramatic call to the front office—just waking up one day, and knowing that Queen, Bishop, and King are only splendid cripples, and pawns, even those that reach the final row, are condemned to creep in two dimensions, and no Tower will ever rise or descend—no: *flight has been given only to the Springer!*" (GR 494).

The alternative positions, in front of or behind the camera, acting or directing, being controlled or controlling, pick up the oppositions (under the knife or holding the knife) that are most extensively presented as Elect and Preterite.

Pynchon's presentation of von Göll is marked by comic exaggerations, and he is ridiculed finally for his last project, "New Dope," a "really offensive and tasteless film" (GR 745) that goes on

126   *Theories of Play and Postmodern Fiction*

twenty-four hours a day, under the rug. But with his zany irresponsibility and disruption of official market arrangements, von Göll escapes condemnation and the parody does not qualify the text's general insistence on the cultural influence of film and film-makers. Represented in the amazing variety of film personnel, scenes, language and techniques that are used as points of definition by characters, this influence is vast not only in the text but also in the cultures that it quotes, creates and prefigures. And even "New Dope" picks up earlier references to the arc and filming of Rocket flight, to the waste cycle of life and death perceived as a chronological trip, and to the one-way flow of European time:

> It is the dope that finds *you* apparently. Part of a reverse world whose agents run around with guns which are like vacuum cleaners operating in the direction of life—pull the trigger and bullets are sucked back out of the recently dead into the barrel, and the Great Irreversible is actually reversed as the corpse comes to life to the accompaniment of a backwards gunshot . . . (GR 745).

The riddling continues in even the most absurd details, and it is no small part of it, of course, that the text lampoons our "academic" textual masturbation, our will to discover connections and significance everywhere.[64] But this home movie trick as a victory over time does connect with a number of obsessions, notably Pökler's dreams of rocket travel "'We'll all use *it,* someday, to leave the earth, To transcend'" (GR 400), and Blicero's Faustian vision:

> "Will our new Edge, our new Deathkingdom, be the Moon? I dream of a great glass sphere, hollow and very high and far away . . ." (GR 723).

However, gravity rules, the ascent is betrayed, the victim rises "in bondage to falling" (GR 758), and, as he is shown to understand, the myopic rocket master cannot bequeath transcendence. On the other hand, the text-master bequeaths the text with its formal play as release from the great irreversible of one-way plot arrangement and final things. It is a considerable gesture, a gift including such mindful possibilities along with its "mindless pleasures." So many of these (in both categories) turn about film in fiction.

Narcissus at the Edge

Film is a productive treasurehouse for writers of fiction, as many recent works demonstrate. In the fiction of Gilbert Sorrentino (*Mulligan Stew*), Manuel Puig (*Betrayed by Rita Hayworth, Kiss of the Spider Woman*) and David Thomson (*Suspects*), it provides a rich source of allusion and opportunities for intertextual and cross-media play in recognition of the strength of films as a cultural influence. But, as Charles Clerc suggests, although Pynchon is not the first to realise the potential of films for fiction, "he is clearly in the forefront in exploiting new blends."[65] Fiction has long provided plots for films but, as *Gravity's Rainbow* demonstrates, films and cinematic strategies can be appropriated for fiction.

> The night room heaves a sigh, yes Heaves, a Sigh—old-fashioned comical room, oh me I'm hopeless, born a joker never change, flirting away through the mirrorframe in something green-striped, pantalooned, and ruffled—meantime though, it is quaint, most rooms today hum you know . . . (GR 122).

The narrator as harlequin: although just one image, it points up role-play as well as humour, each of which is essential to any conception of narrator in *Gravity's Rainbow*. The *Gravity's Rainbow /Moby Dick* comparison involves more than a meeting of two major symbols in encyclopaedic narratives. Like Ishmael, who occasionally disappears from Melville's text and who is given to parading in such a variety of linguistic dress, Pynchon's "narrator" is also a self-regarding quick-change artist whose diversity of language styles, moods and perspectives effectively destroys narrative unity and mocks any attempt to construct an identifiable narrator-figure and a stable narrative base. A strategy of difference that creates ennabling uncertainty, it is an appropriate narrative equivalent to the disappearance of the author. Although Barthes has sounded the author's death-knell,[66] I expect that Pynchon readers, made curious by his much-publicised absence, would nevertheless like to know more about the man-as-author, to have something to add to this image of a sorting demon with serious ideas and a sense of humour. But that 'something' would not ground the texts. If "the birth of the reader must be at the cost of the death of the Author,"[67] what relationship with its narrator does the text offer readers? Or, to re-formulate the question, what guiding strategies for its reading are provided in *Gravity's Rainbow?*

128   *Theories of Play and Postmodern Fiction*

I have argued throughout this study that the proliferation of meanings in *Gravity's Rainbow* is a product of decentering and uncertainty. Appreciating that play is intrinsic to language, Pynchon's style accentuates the space between signifiers and signifieds and crowds this space with possibilities for meaning, holding the idea of complete design always in abeyance. Against the closure of design, the Word, God, the visionary moment, or singularity,[68] there is the play of signification that Thomas Schaub describes in the phrase "prose at the interface":

> Meaning in Pynchon is always a medium, not an answer; his goal is to induce that medium, verging on psychosis, whereby the sterile and false world of "official" forms is given the lie by a protective and inquisitive alertness, leaving an uncertain reality which both terrifies and releases [...] the threshold is the proper relation to meaningfulness.[69]

Language signifies; there is always the problem of its being firmed too readily into The Word of Explanation, of its serving Pointsman's "stone determinacy of everything" (GR 86). Against this threat, and in service of "inquisitive alertness," the text offers its formal discontinuities and changes in language style. Pynchon's guffawing puns, bursts of loud song and belly-laugh vulgarities cannot be explained away as mindless pleasures within a serious major novel; rather, they function as linguistic equivalents to an ambiguous wink or a nudge in the ribs and, like a Brechtian reminder, they refocus attention upon the performance *in its dividedness* while grabbing some diversion along the way. If Melville's Ahab needs an Ishmael to vary the furious reading of clues, so too do Pynchon's world-readers, and in *Gravity's Rainbow* this check is provided by the dissimulating narrative voice(s) as reader's guide.

Pynchon's particular creation of a third-person omniscient mode, broken occasionally by first-person interruptions, avoids the limitations of first-person perspective while retaining its vulnerability and intimacy in expanded forms. Adopting different language styles, and moving in and out of the points of view and speech patterns attributed to other characters in the text, the narrator position is filled by an intimate commentator not reducible to any particular identity or perspective, save a sharp satirical edge and a general sympathy for changeability

Narcissus at the Edge 129

and for the preterite. Along with the continuous present tense, this strategy creates, against endings, the text's immediacy of action as well as its uncertain possibilities.

> Holy shit it's *moving*—an octopus? Yes it is the biggest fucking octopus Slothrop has ever seen outside of the movies, Jackson, and it has just risen up out of the water and squirmed halfway onto one of the black rocks. Now, cocking a malignant eye at the girl, it reaches out . . . (GR 188).

> . . . yes, bitch—yes, little bitch—poor helpless bitch you're coming can't stop yourself now I'll whip you again whip till you *bleed* . . . . Thus Pökler's whole front surface, eyes to knees: flooded with tonight's image of the delicious victim bound on her dungeon rack, filling the movie screen—close-ups of her twisting face, nipples under the silk grown amazingly erect, making lies of her announcements of pain—*bitch!* (GR 397).

Pynchon presents not only a particular character's point of view, but adopts that character's speech within the third-person mode. In this way, the text offers its profusion, and confusion, of perspectives. Paradoxically, the process produces a strong impression of positions while disallowing their solidification into definite authority-structures. In the Octopus Grigori sequence, Slothrop's increasing paranoia is located within plots revealed only gradually to the reader, and Pökler's response to the film image prefigures the concentration on his submissiveness and dreaming. In each instance the diffusion of styles emphasizes play *in* language while demonstrating play *with* language. It helps to create indeterminacy and keeps the reader active. Rhetorical jibes and questions are similarly subversive, with some of them directed specifically at the "you" reader position, a position which seems to include the narrator's perspective as well, in a sharing of the joke, confusion or possibility—

> Is the baby smiling, or is it just gas? Which do you want it to be?(GR 131) (following the narrator's reflections upon the Christ-child's reaction to the War's likely gifts).

130   *Theories of Play and Postmodern Fiction*

> No: what the Serpent means is—how's this—that the six carbon
> atoms of benzene are in fact curled around into a closed ring, *just like
> that snake with its tail in its mouth,* GET IT? (GR 413) (lest the
> reader miss the connection between the uroboros and the aromatic
> ring).

> Who would have thought so many would be here? (GR 537)
> (prefacing the description of Pirate Prentice and the dancing
> preterition in Hell, and in the Book).

> You will want cause and effect. All right. (GR 663) (preceding the
> absurdist story of Thanatz's rescue at sea by a Polish undertaker).

Deconstructing the narrator, and the idea of reliable narration, such
fragmentations promote reader activity by avoiding the restrictions of
realist narrative convention. Whether particular metatextual messages
are read as compliment or taunt, they redirect attention to textuality and
to the *act* of attributing meaning. Changing tone, working the language,
the flexible narrative voice orchestrates its own "nonstop revue" (GR
681).

How does the text situate the reader? Those features that make
Gravity's Rainbow so challenging, its dislocation of all plot lines,
manifold allusiveness, the coming and going of so many characters, and
its unending play with concepts and with language, do not deny reader
access. On the contrary, the complexities ask for collaboration,
acknowledging a relationship that is energised by the discontinuities.
Unlike a conventionally ordered work of mimetic realism, where the
reader's position is, as it were, outside the text as spectator of the
narrative, *Gravity's Rainbow's* awareness of the reader is manifest
throughout. As the narrative voice prompts, questions, amuses,
beguiles, challenges, cajoles or entertains, the reader is situated *within*
the text's concerns, invited by the correlation of uncertainty and
incompletion, and always by the insistent address of this divided voice,
into the process of considering possibilities and exploring meanings.
Almost any page of the 760 can provide examples of this combination
of immediacy and intimacy; the following are from the opening scene:

> No, this is not a disentanglement from, but a progressive *knotting
> into*—(GR 3)—direct address, a statement.

Narcissus at the Edge

131

> There is no way out. Lie and wait, lie still and be quiet. (GR 4)—an imperative.
>
> His name is Captain Geoffrey ('Pirate') Prentice. (GR 5)—introduction.
>
> What is it? Nothing like this ever happens. (GR 6)—rhetorical question.
>
> You can't see a vapor trail 200 miles, now, can you. (GR 6)—assertion.
>
> That would be fuel cutoff, end of burning, what's their word . . . Brennschluss. We don't have one. Or else it's classified. (GR 6)—reflection.
>
> How could there be a winter—even this one—gray enough to age this iron that can sing in the wind, or cloud these windows that open into another season, however falsely preserved? (GR 7)—musing.
>
> It travels faster than the speed of sound. The first news you get of it is the blast. Then, if you're still around, you hear the sound of it coming in. (GR 7)—explanation.

"You," "we," the implied I, the changing mode of address draws the reader into the prose and the scene. It is a finely modulated voice, even in this short example, and in the range of the text as a whole the variations are extraordinary if we care to notice them. And, as Schaub points out:

> The present tense of *Gravity's Rainbow* is the essential characteristic of Pynchon's voice and the primary source of the uncertainty and transience which readers experience. It is more than the appropriate stance of an Orphic narrator, for the present tense emphasizes the tentative conditional location of the "real presence" of the reader.[70]

It acknowledges perspective and context, and also their changeability, as important influences in the creation of meanings. Readers *are* coded differently and can be expected to situate themselves differently in response to the protean narrator and to the changes in style. The decentered text creates the opportunities.[71] This game has many plays:

132 *Theories of Play and Postmodern Fiction*

[the] text is made up of multiple writings, drawn from many cultures and entering into mutual relations of dialogue, parody, contestation, but there is one place where this multiplicity is focused and that place is the reader. . . . [72]

NOTES

1. Thomas Pynchon, *Gravity's Rainbow,* 1973 (London: Picador, 1975), 391. Subsequent references are to the Picador edition.

2. Consider Thomas Schaub, *Pynchon: The Voice of Ambiguity,* 103ff. Schaub suggests that the characters are situated on the conditional ground between the facts of their situation and the meaning of those facts, and that, similarly, readers are stalled at the interface between facts—the printed words—and what they might mean. It is the conditions for meaning that are problematic and final answers are withheld. This view offers a parallel to deconstructive concentration on the operations of language in which meaning is buried in meanings. Amongst earlier analyses of the reading problem, see particularly David Leverenz "On Trying to Read *Gravity's Rainbow."* See also Peter L. Cooper, *Signs and Symptoms: Thomas Pynchon and the Contemporary World,* chapter 7.

3. Thomas Pynchon, *V,* 1963 (London: Picador, 1975). Page references are to the Picador edition.

4. A view expressed in the title of the Levine and Leverenz collection of essays. It is well known that Pynchon intended originally to name the book *Mindless Pleasures*—see Mark Siegel, *Pynchon: Creative Paranoia in Gravity's Rainbow,* note 12, 126. Repeated twice in the text, on pages 270 and 681, the phrase is both a gloss for zany possibilities and a diversionary smokescreen for the seriousness in Pynchon's project.

5. Thomas Pynchon, *The Crying of Lot 49,* 1966 (Harmondsworth: Penguin, 1974). Page references are to the Penguin edition.

6. There is a spectrum of critical response on this issue, ranging from interpretations that emphasize Pynchon's concentration on the Rocket and apocalypse as a narrowing world reality to the more positive readings that emphasize the text's multiplicity and exuberance (and "There is time") as offering hope in the face of death structures. Mark Siegel provides a general overview of this range of responses.

7. Compare Oedipa's "having lost the direct epileptic Word, the cry that might abolish the night" (L49,88).

8. The phrase is Barbara Johnson's, *The Critical Difference,* 5.

Narcissus at the Edge

9. *Gravity's Rainbow*, 55. In deconstructive fashion, Pynchon acknowledges the binary basis of language and definitions while also challenging the reductive binarisms to emphasize variety, complication and the play of possibilities in constructions of meanings.

10. Derrida, "Structure, Sign and Play," in *Writing and Difference*, 280.

11. Ibid. Amidst indulgence of Derridean *jeu libre*, that frequently misinterpreted concept, it is necessary to remember that Derrida does not deny the existence of centres of authority in discourse, in cultural arrangements, or in the operations of power in the world. Rather, and particularly in his deconstructive analyses of language and meaning, he questions their authority to claim the high ground of "truth," "origin," "finality."

12. First published in *New World Writing* 16, March 1960, and now available in Pynchon's *Slow Learner* 53-75.

13. Using this figure in *V,* Pynchon has Rachel Owlglass suspect that these relativities change, that is, that one is a "screwer" or a "screwee" depending on one's place at any point in time (and with respect to others and to the operative criteria) in "this long daisy chain of victimisers and victims, screwers and screwees" (*V* 49). Although screwers manipulate the connections, while screwees are manipulated, the connections can be both life-enhancing and enslaving. It is, therefore, distinguishable from traditional Puritan ideas of election which are held to exclude the possibilities for change.

14. See "Entropy," republished in *Slow Learner*, 77-94. The contrast between Callisto's hermetically-sealed upstairs apartment and Mulligan's open-house downstairs party prefigures sets of oppositions in the later texts that turn about control versus chaos and the search for middle alternatives. Pynchon's double use of the concept of entropy, in terms of thermodynamics and information theory, has been discussed extensively. See, for example, Schaub, Chapter 2, for a discussion of Pynchon's sources and the ambiguities of entropy as it is used in the short story and in *The Crying of Lot 49,* and Joseph Slade's "'Entropy' and Other Calamities" in Edward Mendelson, ed., *Pynchon: A Collection of Critical Essays,* 69-86, an abridgement from Slade's fine early study *Thomas Pynchon* published in 1974.

15. The text offers a number of double-plays on this theme, and they turn about the relationship between illusion and reality, or between systems of belief or hopes or fears, on the one hand, and empirical data on the other. Typically the categories are confused. How absent is the signified? Consider, for example: "But just over the embankment, down in the arena, what might that have been just now, waiting in the broken moonlight, camouflage paint from fins to point crazed into jigsaw . . . is it, then, really never to find you again?

134   *Theories of Play and Postmodern Fiction*

Not even in your worst times of night, with pencil words on your page only delta t from the things they stand for?" (GR 510)

16. Barthes' phrase, "The Death of the Author," 146. He offers similar poststructuralist formulations in *S/Z,* emphasizing, against conventional notions of originality and authorial control, the play of linguistic and textual influences and connections. As I have suggested in Part I, the shift away from ideas of originality and that form of "truth" liberate the text and readings.

17. Derrida, "Structure, Sign and Play,"*Writing and Difference,* 280.

18. See Molly Hite, *Ideas of Order in the Novels of Thomas Pynchon,* Chapter 1, "Including Middles."

19. Jean-Francois Lyotard, *The Postmodern Condition: A Report on Knowledge,* 81.

20. See Edward Mendelson's "Gravity's Encyclopedia," in *Mindful Pleasures,* 161-95 for a discussion of the range of reference. Steven Weisenburger, "The End of History? Thomas Pynchon and the Uses of the Past," provides sources for the V-2 and Herero references. Marcus Smith and Khachig Tololyan, "The New Jeremiah: *Gravity's Rainbow,*" trace the form and detail of Pynchon's Puritan borrowings to the old Puritan jeremiad. See also David Cowart's *Thomas Pynchon: The Art of Allusion* for discussion of sources in film, music and literature. The manner in which *Gravity's Rainbow* presents history is suggested in Robert Scholes's argument: "It has happened while we were unaware. The major novels of the past decade or so have tended strongly toward the apparently worn-out form of the historical novel [. . . .] But they are not novels based upon empirical concepts of history that dominated Western thought in the nineteenth century. The North American works, in particular, bristle with facts, and smell of research of the most painstaking kind. Yet they deliberately challenge the notion that history may be retrieved by objective investigations of fact" (*Fabulation and Metafiction,* 206). Scholes includes Barth's *The Sot-Weed Factor,* García Márquez's *One Hundred Years of Solitude,* Fowles's *The French Lieutenant's Woman* and Coover's *The Public Burning* in this category along with *Gravity's Rainbow.* They are, he suggests, fabulative fictions, a title that emphasizes the surreal manner of their play with versions of the past.

21. John M. Krafft, "Historical Imagination in the Novels of Thomas Pynchon," 254.

22. Geological layers are variously used as metaphors of deep structure repeated in human organisations. See, for example, the context of this description of Shell "with no real country, no side in any war, no specific face or heritage: tapping instead out of that global stratum, mostly deeply laid, from

Narcissus at the Edge

135

which all the appearances of corporate ownership really spring?" (GR 243). Shell and IG Farben recur most frequently as examples of the powerful (and faceless) cartels that exercise controls international and 'subterranean' in nature. They are faceless from a preterite point of view.

23. Michel Foucault, *The Archaeology of Knowledge*, 21. Although there are variations in their positions, Hans Georg Gadamer (*Truth and Method*), Jurgen Habermas (*Knowledge and Human Interests*) and Wilhelm Dilthey (H.P. Rickman, *W. Dilthey: Selected Writings*), by emphasizing the problematic nature of language and context against deterministic notions of meaning construction, support Foucault's meta-historical perspectives.

24. Each of the Foucault texts is referred to in Part II, Chapter 4, "Deconstruction: The Reader as Scheherazade."

25. Michel Foucault, "The Subject and Power," in *Michel Foucault: Beyond Structuralism and Hermeneutics*, 208.

26. Michel Foucault, "Nietzsche, Genealogy, History," in *Language, Counter-Memory, Practice*, 147.

27. I am using Said's terms. See Edward Said, *The World, the Text, and the Critic*, 5.

28. Hayden White, *Tropics of Discourse. Essays in Cultural Criticism*, 91. See also White's *Metahistory. The Historical Imagination in Nineteenth-Century Europe.*

29. White, *Metahistory*, ix. See his discussion of poetic elements in both historiography and the philosophy of history. Although the schema is necessarily reductive (like Northrop Frye's in the *Anatomy of Criticism* with which it has a number of resemblances), White provides reminders about the relationship between history, philosophy and linguistics. Predominantly formalist, his method in historical work may be compared with Derrida's in philosophy and Foucault's in the human sciences.

30. Weisenburger, "The End of History?," discusses Pynchon's borrowing of material for the Herero sections, in *V* and *Gravity's Rainbow*, from Rex Hardinge's *South African Cinderella: A Trek Through Ex-German Southwest Africa* (London: Herbert Jenkins, 1937). Although Pynchon may not have used Eliade, his writings are particularly relevant to appreciation of Herero mythology. See M. Eliade, *Cosmos and History. The Myth of the Eternal Return* and *Myths, Dreams and Mysteries*. Also consider Schaub, *Pynchon: The Voice of Ambiguity*, 83-8.

31. *Gravity's Rainbow*, 410. Pynchon's criticism of the multinationals, IG Farben, Shell, Standard Oil and the like is sustained. Although this criticism is often presented in zany satire, he aligns their operations with exploitation and

136 *Theories of Play and Postmodern Fiction*

repression, with power-mongering, environmental pollution and with manipulation of individuals and populations.

32. Weisenburger, "The End of History?," 154.

33. Thomas S. Smith, "Performing in the Zone: The Presentation of Historical Crisis in *Gravity's Rainbow*," 253. As Smith points out, Scott Sanders offers a similar reading in "Pynchon's Paranoid History." Smith draws attention to Slothrop's foundering as a negative image; but that fragmentation, following Slothrop's rejection of at least some Puritan repressions, can be read as a symbol of preterite resistance.

34. See note 20. In addition, see in particular Steven Weisenburger's *A "Gravity's Rainbow" Companion: Sources and Contexts for Pynchon's Novel.*

35. Jacques Ehrmann, *Game, Play and Literature,* 55.

36. Franz Pökler's susceptibility to film images is most powerfully established via his adoration of German actor Rudolph Klein-Rogge, "Whom Pökler idolized, and wanted to be like" (GR 578). He dreams about connections, power and transcendence: "Metropolitan inventor Rothwang, King Attila, Mabuse der Spieler, Prof.-Dr. Laszlo Jamf, all their yearnings aimed the same way, toward a form of death that could be demonstrated to hold joy and defiance . . ." (GR 579). Desire bespeaks lack in this Freudian portrait, and engineer Pökler is created as one especially susceptible to the controllers, as to dream images.

37. Ehrmann, *Games, Play and Literature,* 55.

38. The pointed contrast between these two female characters represents another play upon stereotypes, with complications to the traditional patterns. Whether as guilt-ridden sacrificer of boys to the black mud at Bad Karma, inspiration of male sexual fetishes, screen image, masochistic lover or sadistic mother, Greta Erdmann is associated with perversion, paranoia and death. On the other hand, Geli Tripping, aptly named young witch, is a figure of rural simplicity and regenerative possibilities.

39. Bakhtin, *Rabelais and His World,* 11-12. According particular importance to Bakhtin's carnivalesque in his analysis of models and concepts of play and game, Rawdon Wilson emphasizes the necessity to consider the contexts in which any uses or readings of the carnivalesque are made. See *In Palamedes' Shadow,* chapter 2.

40. Brooke Horvath, "Linguistic Distancing in *Gravity's Rainbow.*"

41. From E.D. Hirsch, *The Philosophy of Composition,* 144.

42. *Viking Portable Nietzsche,* edited by Walter Kaufmann, 46.

43. Although, as *The Crying of Lot 49* and *Gravity's Rainbow* demonstrate in their emphases upon uncertainty, "inside safe" provides provisional security

Narcissus at the Edge

via the *act* of language, but not full meaning. The act of metaphor is a bridging between event and meaning, between signified and signifier, and not complete identification.

44. Derrida "Living On: Border Lines," in *Deconstruction and Criticism* edited by Harold Bloom, et al., 81.

45. Sigmund Freud, *Civilisation and Its Discontents:* "It is impossible to overlook the extent to which civilization is built upon a renunciation of instinct, how much it presupposes precisely the non-satisfaction (by suppression, repression or some other means?) of powerful instincts. This 'cultural frustration' dominates the large field of social relationships between human beings. As we already know, it is the cause of the hostility against which all civilizations have to struggle" (34).

46. Herman Melville, *Moby-Dick,* 167.

47. See Robert Rawdon Wilson's discussion, "Godgames and Labyrinths: The Logic of Entrapment." In this paper, Wilson relates godgames to labyrinths "as a genus to a species" and looks at literary labyrinths in terms of game. Borges is his main source, with passing attention to Pynchon, along with Cervantes and Robbe-Grillet. He suggests: "A narrative can be a labyrinth if it seeks to capture its reader in the perplexities of interpretation," a definition that makes *Gravity's Rainbow* a definitive example. In his later study, *In Palamedes' Shadow: Explorations in Play, Game, & Narrative Theory,* the distinction between "strong" and "weak" labyrinths offers a range of useful models and suggests that the strong textual labyrinth will be experienced as a godgame, a conceptualisation that emphasizes mystery, manipulation and the sense of play and of being played. Labyrinthine structures within structures are common in the writings of Borges, Nabokov and Barth, as well as Pynchon, and the implications vary from emphases upon the complexities of knowledge (and apprehension of the processes) to technologies, corporate systems, power and paranoia.

48. John Barth, "The Literature of Exhaustion." Barth's essay and its later companion piece "The Literature of Replenishment" are discussed in the next chapter of this study.

49. Melville, *Moby-Dick,* 127-8.

50. Many Pynchon commentators refer to *Moby-Dick* as a text that, in many ways, "prefigures" *Gravity's Rainbow.* See, for example, Schaub in *Pynchon: The Voice of Ambiguity* 118ff. Richard Poirier (in *Saturday Review of the Arts,* March 1973) points to *Moby-Dick* and *Ulysses* as obvious comparisons; Tony Tanner (in *Thomas Pynchon)* refers to Melville, and then to

138 *Theories of Play and Postmodern Fiction*

a line of Sterne, Rabelais, Cervantes. Certainly, for varieties of narrative play, and for size, the comparisons hold.

51. The phrase is Evert Duyckink's from his 1851 review of *Moby-Dick:* 'Melville's *Moby-Dick;* or, *The Whale'* New York *Literary World* 9 (November 22, 1851) 403-4. Reprinted in Norton *Moby-Dick*, 613-6.

52. Melville, *Moby-Dick,* 304. From its multiple frame to the cetological "asides," the gams, shifting narrative perspectives and ludic displacements, *Moby-Dick* presents "careful disorderliness" as a measure of energetic and exuberant enquiry.

53. Schaub, *Pynchon: The Voice of Ambiguity,* ix-x.

54. "the novel is indeed a film"—Mack Smith, "The Paracinematic Reality of *Gravity's Rainbow,"* 28. It is a conception well entertained by Schaub and Cowart as well.

55. "Basically *Gravity's Rainbow* is a musical"—Scott Simmon, "Beyond the Theatre of War: *Gravity's Rainbow* as Film," 352.

56. Edward Mendelson, "Gravity's Encyclopedia."

57. The instrument that Slothrop loses down the toilet of the Roseland Ballroom and rediscovers in a mountain stream hundreds of pages later, it also provides the sound for the opening of Part 4, The Counterforce. Pynchon obviously associates it with simplicity and pleasure; it is a preterite of the music world. The instrument's special place in Pynchon's view is emphasized in his blurb for Richard Farina's *Been Down So Long It Looks Like Up To Me* (New York: Random House, 1966). He describes the book as coming on "like the Hallelujah Chorus done by 200 kazoo players with perfect pitch, I mean strong, swinging, skillful and reverent—but also with the fine brassy buzz of irreverence in there too. Farina has going for him an unerring and virtuoso instinct about exactly what, in this bewildering Republic, is serious and what cannot possibly be." *Gravity's Rainbow* is dedicated to Farina.

58. David Cowart, *Thomas Pynchon: The Art of Allusion,* 33.

59. Thomas Schaub, *Pynchon: The Voice of Ambiguity,* 45.

60. Charles Clerc, "Film in *Gravity's Rainbow,* in *Approaches to 'Gravity's Rainbow,"* 105.

61. For discussions, see Cowart Chapter 3; Clerc's "Film in *Gravity's Rainbow"*; Simmon's "Beyond the Theatre of War: *Gravity's Rainbow* as Film"; Mack Smith's "The Paracinematic Reality of *Gravity's Rainbow"*; Berressem's "*Gravity's Rainbow:* Text as Film—Film as Text" in his *Pynchon's Poetics.*

Narcissus at the Edge

62. An earlier and differently situated version of this analysis appears in my article "Mixing Media: Film as Metaphor in Pynchon's *Gravity's Rainbow.*"

63. In addition to the studies by Cowart, Clerc, Simmon and Smith mentioned in Note 61, see George Levine's "V-2" in *Pynchon: A Collection of Critical Essays,* edited by Edward Mendelson; John D. Stark, *Pynchon's Fictions: Thomas Pynchon and the Literature of Information,* Chapter 6; Bertram Lippman, "The Reader of Movies: Thomas Pynchon's *Gravity's Rainbow.*" Like others, and particularly David Cowart, I have found Siegfried Kracauer's *From Caligari to Hitler: A Psychological Study of the German Film* an invaluable source of information about German films and film-makers referred to in *Gravity's Rainbow.*

64. See Joseph A. Cosenza, "Reader-Baiting in *Gravity's Rainbow.*"

65. Clerc, "Film in *Gravity's Rainbow,*" 148.

66. Roland Barthes, "The Death of the Author," *Image Music Text.*

67. Ibid.,148.

68. It is notable that *design,* or the locus of meaning, is what Pynchon's major characters seek and miss: Stencil, Oedipa Maas and the questers of *Gravity's Rainbow.* Borrowing "singularity" from Henry Adams, Pynchon uses it often in the text and nowhere more tellingly than in Slothrop's meeting with Greta Erdmann on the *Alpdrücken* film-set. See p. 396.

69. Schaub, *Pynchon: The Voice of Ambiguity,* 104.

70. Ibid., p.132. Schaub's attention to the processes of language in *Gravity's Rainbow* is, I believe, accurate. It is a view that can acknowledge the variety of text-reader moments while holding to the overall invitation that this work extends, by virtue of its awareness of readers.

71. Tony Tanner's formulation of *Gravity's Rainbow* as "an exemplary experience in modern reading" makes this point succinctly. His view supports the argument I have presented. He suggests: "The reader does not move comfortably from some ideal 'emptiness' of meaning to a satisfying fullness, but instead becomes involved in a process in which any perception can precipitate a new confusion, and an apparent clarification turn into a prelude to further difficulties. So far from this being an obstacle to appreciating the book, it is part of its essence" (75).

72. Barthes, "The Death of the Author," 148.

CHAPTER 3

Letters to Literature: The Epistolary Artfulness of John Barth's *LETTERS*

TEARS AND CINDERS, OR THE PERSISTENCE OF INCORRIGIBLE RAILROAD BUFFS

To be a novelist in 1969 is, I agree, a bit like being in the passenger-railway business is the age of the jumbo jet: our dilapidated rolling stock creaks over the weed-grown right-of-ways, carrying four winos, six Viet Nam draftees, three black welfare families, two nuns, and one incorrigible railroad buff, ever less conveniently, between the crumbling Art Deco cathedrals where once paused the gleaming Twentieth Century Limited. Like that railroad buff, we deplore the shallow "attractions" of the media that have supplanted us, even while we endeavour, necessarily and to our cost, to accommodate to that ruinous competition by reducing even further our own amenities: fewer runs, fewer stops, fewer passengers, higher fares. Yet we grind on, tears and cinders in our eyes, hoping against hope that history will turn our way again. [1]

Presented in *LETTERS* within an Author to Todd Andrews exchange, this comment on context picks up issues that Barth addresses in the sixties, in "The Literature of Exhaustion" and *Lost in the Funhouse*. But whether the challenge is perceived to come from new media or from the "used-upness"[2] of certain forms and possibilities, his answer to the "exhaustion" rhetoric is, self-consciously, and with variations upon the Borges model in mind, again to turn those "ultimacies" back upon themselves, making new texts from old fare. Although he may

142   *Theories of Play and Postmodern Fiction*

decide in 1980 that the influential 1967 essay, "The Literature of Exhaustion," was about "the effective exhaustion not of language or of literature, but of the aesthetic of high modernism,"[3] the new metaphor, "replenishment," is implicit in the earlier rhetoric and, besides, "print-oriented bastards"[4] have a legacy of 4,500 years or so that is a defence against, rather than an instigator of, burn out. It is but one part of the play, one component of the shifty capital-A Author persona, to write in this context, within this postmodernist variation upon "the old-time epistolary form" itself, about the decline of the novel. History has never really turned away.[5] The writer may choose whether or not to aim at fewer passengers and higher fares, in practice of an aesthetic that limits access,[6] against the false "democratisation" of cultural forms and products.

If Pynchon is a contemporary Daedalus, Barth is the novelist as conservationist. Everything is recycled (and the service is to literature and society). Whereas from the earlier works, *The Sot-Weed Factor, Giles Goat-Boy, Lost in The Funhouse* and *Chimera* involve varied transformations of literary/mythical motifs, patterns and stories, *LETTERS* offers not just the audacious plays of Barth recycling Barth but a re-exploration of the genre itself which is also, necessarily, an analysis of history as process. It is easy to situate Barth as a formalist and funhouse-proprietor, as an author whose texts offer the entertainment of very clever play with the resources of language and literature. Selective reference to his commentaries on literature and reality can be adduced to support this perspective.[7] In this study, however, I wish to concentrate on "the world" as well, not in denial of the novelist's role as entertainer but in demonstration of the false antithesis in Barth's work between entertainment and history, art and life. Despite the competition, the "rolling stock" is not really so dilapidated, and there are enough buffs about to sustain the business, to prevent that spiral into obsolescence or silence.

It is curious now, more than three decades and eight Barth books later, to reread his 1964 interview, an interview conducted when he was part-way through the writing of *Giles Goat-Boy:*

> One ought to know a lot about Reality before one writes realistic novels. Since I don't know much about Reality, it will have to be abolished. What the hell, reality is a nice place to visit but you wouldn't want to live there, and literature never did, very long.[8]

Letters to Literature 143

Barth always provides good copy, partly because of his appreciation of literature but also because of the riddling that adds conscious ambiguities to exploratory pronouncements. Treating capital-R Reality as a construct is already to invite its deconstruction, and small-r reality necessarily fragments into realities. While literary history locates Realism (realism) in certain examples of the nineteenth-century European novel, it acknowledges both a disposition and a practice, a way of perceiving the world and strategies for its representation in language. With its emphasis upon "real" events and accuracy in their representation, and in its differentiation from romanticism, the imaginary and the mythical, realism retains links with the idealist aesthetics of universal forms, objectivity and truth. But as Barth's comment implies, and I read it as both playful and serious, the distinctions are not only problematic but fraudulent in their second-hand book store zeal for categorisation. It is the sort of reading practice which, having defined novelist Barth as a fabulist, places *The Floating Opera* and *The End of the Road* as early realist aberrations,[9] a stutter in the writer's refinement of his "voice." Or, defining the fabulist, it writes off history, seriousness, and society, by reading the later works as entertainments. What definition of "realism" accepts *The Floating Opera* with its achronological design, parodies of literary conventions, elaborate artifice, chats to reader from self-conscious narrator Todd Andrews as an ageing Hamlet, and such representations of the text as:

> It's a floating opera, friend, fraught with curiosities, melodrama, spectacle, instruction, and entertainment, but it floats willy-nilly on the tide of my vagrant prose: you'll catch sight of it, lose it, spy it again; and it may require the best efforts of your attention and imagination—together with some patience, if you're an average fellow—to keep track of the plot as it sails in and out of view.[10]

In terms of technique, this first novel finds congenial company in the eighteenth century, with the comic self-consciousness and digressive manner of Fielding, Sterne and Smollett. Like those riverbank watchers of "Adam's Original and Unparalleled Floating Opera," readers of *The Floating Opera* are invited to use their imaginations "to fill in the gaps" (FO 7) because, even in this early "realist" work, Barth follows his later prescription, "*affirm* the artificial element in art (you can't get rid of it anyhow), and make the artifice part of your point. . . ."[11]

144   Theories of Play and Postmodern Fiction

And part of the point, my point throughout, is that affirmations of artifice do not separate the text from the world, or play from reality. Rather, as acknowledgements of the processes of textual construction they redirect our attention not only to the nature of the text as an artefact but also to the complexities of its relationship with social contexts. Barth's fiction generally, and *LETTERS* in particular, turns about these matters. His comment upon the eighteenth-century reading preparation for the writing project illustrates both the importance and the ambiguity of artifice so manifest in the text itself:

> When I was re-reading Richardson, Fielding, Smollett and the rest, I was impressed with that spookily "modern" awareness they had that each novel was a document. They manifestly were aware that a novel wasn't life itself. It was an imitation, a convention for imitating life and, especially in their case, a convention for imitating life's documents.[12]

So, *LETTERS,* with its cryptographic title formed from the 88 letters which spell "An old time epistolary novel by seven fictitious drolls and dreamers, each of which imagines himself actual" (scheme, refrain, and ironic comment on the relationship between art and life), and its pages consisting of the 88 letters attributed to those drolls and dreamers. Each of the 88 signifiers is and stands for a "letter." Letters are, of course, one of the most significant of all forms of life's documents, and the epistolary novel is one of the most overtly artificial of literary forms. The artifice of this postmodernist version is affirmed at every point—in the seven-part structure, each part of which represents a month from March to September 1969, the year which is not only a sexual pun[13] but which also presents *LETTERS,* in one of its guises, as a farewell to the decade; in the arrangement whereby the correspondents always write in the same sequence and always on the same day of the week, an arrangement which, because of its basis in calendar patterns, disrupts simple chronological sequence and packs the text with signposts, retrospectives, frames, gaps and alternative versions of "common" events; in the artifice of the epistolary form itself, about which the capital-A Author writes in parodic apology: "(I blush to report) I am smitten with the earliest-exhausted of English novel-forms, the 'epistolary novel,' already worked to death by the end of the 18th century. Like yourself an official honorary Doctor of Letters, I take it as

Letters to Literature 145

among my functions to administer artificial resuscitation to the apparently dead" (L 654). And so this Doctor of Letters produces doctored letters, a modest 88 compared with the 537 of *Clarissa* (L 654).

LETTERS is a curious phenomenon, a postmodernist work that addresses, interrelatedly, three aspects of past-ness—American history, Barth's previous writings and the history of the novel—in one of the earliest of novel forms, the epistolary. Although it is intricately formalist, it is also open-ended and this in a number of senses. It resists closure by integrating different aspects of the past and different narrative strands thereby complicating ideas of origin, by creating variations upon received patterns of history, by offering incompletion against resolution in major plot-lines and, above all, by emphasizing the capacity of language for play. In "The Literature of Replenishment," Barth suggests, "The ideal postmodernist novel will somehow rise above the quarrel between realism and irrealism, formalism and 'contentism', pure and committed literature, coterie fiction and junk fiction."[14] The novel transcends those debates in its mockery of the category distinctions, subsuming them within its metafictional deliberations and such ontological plays as "the relation between fact and fiction, life and art, is not imitation of either by the other, but a sort of reciprocity, an ongoing collaboration or reverberation" (L 233). Attributed to Lady Amherst, the observation follows speculation about the 1812 War, Napoleon's role in European politics (and possible role in American), A.B. Cook's ideas, the author's fiction and Reg Prinz's continuous film in progress. The interplay submits History/Fiction/Film, subjects and forms, to a deconstructive unsettling, questioning not their potential for entertainment, and even instruction, but their claims upon truth. Barth's strategies of proliferation and interweaving serve Nietzsche's dictum, "No facts, only interpretations." *LETTERS* is a literary funhouse constructed from the inventive replay of literature and history. It is a "narcissistic narrative,"[15] and, if the tale is to be trusted, an example of metafiction that flaunts mimesis of its own process, demonstrating in this process that "art" is part of "life."

In this analysis, I will concentrate on the modes and style of Barth's play with resources, including the resource of language itself. As well as instructing readers in their work as co-producers of meanings, self-conscious texts can be instructive about the nature of fiction itself, in its status as text and in its relationships with other

146   *Theories of Play and Postmodern Fiction*

fiction and with social contexts. Because of its attention to literary history and to social history, to texts and to contexts, *LETTERS* offers reconsideration along with replay. In the "discovery" attributed to Ambrose Mensch, Barth underscores relationships that the text explores throughout. It is significant that the passage is included in Ambrose's final letter to Yours Truly, concluding his attempts as wordsmith to "fill in the blank":[16]

5.   If one imagines an artist less enamored of the world than of the language we signify it with, yet less enamored of the language than of the signifying narration, and yet less enamored of the narration than of its formal arrangement, one need *not* necessarily imagine the artist therefore forsaking the world for language, language for the processes of narration and those processes for the abstract possibilities of form.

6.   *Might he/she not as readily, at least as possibly, be imagined as thereby (if only thereby) enabled to love the narrative through the form, the language through the narrative, even the world through the language.* Which, like narratives and their forms, is after all among the contents of the world.

7.   And, thus imagined, might not such an artist, such an amateur of the world, aspire at least to expert amateurship? To an honorary degree of humanity? (L 650-1)

It is by careful design, of course, that Ambrose's love for Lady Amherst, and his attempts to impregnate her (the result uncertain), match not only male and female but also writer and muse, American letters and the European Great Tradition. It is notable that in his later fiction, in each of *Sabbatical, The Tidewater Tales* and *The Last Voyage of Somebody the Sailor,* the plays continue apace upon male-female cooperation in sexual/textual production, in romantic couplings whose primary offspring are indeed the texts that contain them. Though Kate Sagamore's twins end a run of outs in the parallel biological conception stakes, in each instance books are produced. Loving the world through language involves creating the world in language. Barth's "letters to literature," my title for this chapter, are letters about "the world" and in the process he not only deconstructs simple oppositions between play and seriousness, art and reality, literature and

Letters to Literature 147

the "facts" of social existence but offers a persuasive case for his postmodernist fiction as a repository of cultural analysis and commentary.

SEVEN EPISTOLEANS: THE READER'S ROLE AS VOYEUR

Reading other people's private correspondence is an activity approved for historians and biographers, and, so our culture tells us, favoured by private detectives and secret service agencies. The epistolary novel exploits our prurient interest in the confidential, even when, as in that first famous example, the form is indeed all artifice and the intention is nobly didactic: "a series of Familiar Letters from a Beautiful Young Damsel to her parents. Now first published in order to cultivate the Principles of Virtue and Religion in the Minds of the Youth of Both Sexes."[17] Offering Pamela's letters to "Dear Father and Mother," and the parents' much less frequent replies, Richardson's *Pamela* casts the reader as voyeur, for our instruction. In this first-person intimate mode of narration, we are doubly invited by being excluded from the form of address at the head of each letter.

Richardson, and his early imitators and parodists, responded to a culture that cultivated the art of letter-writing. It was more public an accomplishment for genteel people of the eighteenth century than in the late twentieth. However, since Richardson's letters are not "authentic" but fabricated documents, including texts within texts because Pamela shares with her parents a range of letters written by others, the novel is set up like a game. Despite his apparent intention to present a portrait of injured innocence, Pamela's protests run as readily to fascination as to fear and, filling in the writerly blanks in Richardson's text, we can speculate on how it slips his moralistic guard. The heroine's virtue contends with guile, the text's didacticism with titillation. The "reward" is in the play not the moral, the game not the result. In its overt self-consciousness, Barth's postmodernist revision of the eighteenth-century model extends considerably not only the range of voices and subjects, but also the complexity of reading positions. Commenting on the plan for *LETTERS,* he suggests: "I wanted to write about second cycles, about reenactments, and I hoped the novel would include texts within texts [. . .] So once I realized I needed several letter writers, I found myself with another, a ventriloquistic task: that of devising separate and believable voices."[18] One reenactment is the formal one; *LETTERS*

148   *Theories of Play and Postmodern Fiction*

reworks an early form of the English novel. Richardson's *Pamela* and *Clarissa* are ghostly presences in Barth's novel and, retrospectively, Barth's text alters our perception of Richardson's, a factor of intertextual influence that Eliot defines cogently in "Tradition and the Individual Talent." But, at this point, I wish to concentrate on the "ventriloquistic task," on reenactment with difference of the earlier fiction via the separate voices of these seven epistoleans. Although *LETTERS* does not depend upon the reader's acquaintance with the earlier works, that acquaintance nevertheless enriches the reading process by taking us out to and back from the other texts. This cumulative process offers pleasure in old acquaintances and variations upon recurrent themes; it is a mode of writerly play that turns about ontological questions to do with the nature of literary texts and their relationships while offering literature for provocation and entertainment.

SEVEN days in the week, colours of the rainbow, Snow White's dwarfs, Ages of Man, Wonders of the World, letters in LETTERS (and in NUMBERS) etc. etc.—and Barth's seventh book. Catalogue as a form of representation and the dominant structural motif, Barth's play upon sevens affirms the artifice.[19] It is appropriate to the spirit of play in this recycling that the number symbol for consummation and unity should also be quite undone, not only by the appearance of *Sabbatical: A Romance,* Barth's Number 8, *The Tidewater Tales* as Number 9, and *The Last Voyage of Somebody the Sailor* and *Once Upon a Time: A Floating Opera,* Numbers 10 and 11, but also by the refusal of *LETTERS* to grant all connections and tie up all ends, matters that I take up in discussion of metafiction and metahistory. For the moment, seven epistoleans—

Todd Andrews

Despite their differences in age, circumstances and disposition, and the 200 years of cultural change, Todd Andrews, of *The Floating Opera,* and Tristram Shandy address the reader with similar affection, and duplicity. Todd's mock humility could be pointing to the digressive tricks of Sterne's text:

> Good heavens, how does one write a novel! I mean, how can anybody
> stick to the story, if he's at all sensitive to the significance of things?

Letters to Literature

149

As for me, I see already that storytelling isn't my cup of tea: every new sentence I set down is full of figures and implications that I'd love nothing better than to chase to their dens with you, but such chasing would involve new figures and new chases, so that I'm sure we'd never get the story started, much less ended, if I let my inclinations run unleashed. (FO 2)

The text is a performance, a floating opera. Repeating this concern with technique in the flashbacks and delays, and in the narrator's discursive chats with the reader "about" the project, Barth associates theme with mode. Todd's transition from rake to saint to cynic, and to a pervasive sense of uncertainties, his movement from existential angst to postmodernist equivocation, is represented in a text in which formal variations embody the state of flux.

The self-consciousness and digressive mode apply to his letters too, to these 1969 reconsiderations of why he changed his mind in 1937 and did not commit suicide, his relationships with Harrison, Jane and Jeannine Mack, communication problems with his father who hanged himself in the basement in 1930, the Tragic View of History, and so on. Since six of Todd's eight letters are addressed to his long dead father, he conforms ironically to the perspective described in an Author to Mensch letter:

Never mind what your predecessors have come up with, and never mind that in a sense this "dialogue" is a monologue; that we capital-A Authors are ultimately, ineluctably and forever talking to ourselves. If our correspondence is after all a fiction, we like, we *need* that fiction: it makes our job less lonely. (L 655)

His opening address, "Brr! Old fellow in the cellarage, what gripes you?" (L 12), is a play on old oedipal tensions, a variation on the general theme of communication problems and indicative of the black humour recycled from the early fiction. Borrowings are emphasized also in the plays upon 1969 and Todd's being the century's child, beginning in letter one "'Soixante-neuf' once more with this kinky crone of a century, here in my old hotel room" (L 12), and concluding in his last letter soixante-neuf aboard "Osborn Jones" with Jeannine Mack, possibly his daughter, in a variation upon his old relationship with her mother Jane Mack, itself reenacted in detail in *LETTERS*.

150   *Theories of Play and Postmodern Fiction*

The text depends upon and discusses connections: Todd Andrews is an ageing Hamlet ambivalent about his absent father; his letters to dad recall Kafka's; languishing for Jane Mack he imagines himself "a superannuated Jay Gatsby awaiting his Daisy's visit" (L 400); his nihilism of the 1930s, "Nothing has intrinsic value" (FO 218), is replaced by his nostalgia and weeping for all things at 69, "they are all precious" (L 96); and this time round the symbolic "O" of nothingness becomes the musical "O" of Jane Mack's orgasm (L 276), a return that has him feeling "a grateful indulgence of that Sentimental Formalist, our Author, for so sweetly, neatly—albeit improbably—tying up the loose ends of his plot" (L 178). As he says, "Events recycle like turkey buzzards" (L 561) and "poop preserved in pickle jars" (L 15) so important in the settlement of an estate in *The Floating Opera* times becomes Harrison Mack's "freeze-dried faeces" in *LETTERS*. Sensing that the second half of his life is reenacting the first, his suggestion is self-reflexive of the text: "God the novelist was hard enough to take as an awkward Realist; how shall we swallow him as a ham-handed Formalist?" (L 256).

Like Todd Andrews, the reader is invited to see patterns everywhere, and to question their significance:[20] "If (as Marx says in his essay 'The 18th Brumaire') tragic history repeats itself as farce what does farce do for an encore?" (L 255) In *LETTERS* one thing it does is have itself filmed by Reg Prinz and his ubiquitous film crew in a continuous reenactment of the past, but in such elaborate parody that it constitutes a reminder of the arbitrariness of "history" and "reality." The recycling of Todd Andrews involves his Inquiry, Letter to Dad, the replays in his "imagination" of *Floating Opera* relationships and their reenactment with variations in *LETTERS*. It is an intersection of texts and forms. As a focus of patterns, he is also their interrogator and, however else we read the character—as melancholic, nostalgic, cynical[21]—he is also a storyteller given a sophisticated frame of literary and political reference,[22] and considerable charm. As this text's sailor, navigator of the Chesapeake, his voyages marked by sailing lore and favourite anchorages, as well as the watch upon relationships and memories, Todd Andrews spans the Marylandiad of Barth's opus, prefiguring too the Chesapeake Bay concentration of *Sabbatical, The Tidewater Tales* and *Once Upon a Time.*

It is formally and thematically appropriate, and another indicator of Barth's precise attention to detail, that Todd's last letter should end

Letters to Literature 151

with farewells and greetings "6:53: Good-bye, Polly; good-bye Jane; good-bye Drew. Hello Author; hello, Dad. Here comes the sun. Lights! Cameras! Action!" (L 738). The double play upon Author/Dad signifies not only Todd's long correspondence with his dead father, his "author"; it acknowledges, as well, the character as child to the Author, and hence the text in its representations of the forms of life. Encastled in Schott's "Tower of Truth" as the young revolutionaries prepare to blow it up, he is left facing the "suicide" and the explosion that were deferred in *The Floating Opera*. "Truth" is under siege throughout; the ending is incomplete. As Derrida reminds us, texts beget further texts and the contexts are never saturated. The play of language and meaning continues and it is in not only the Author's hands but also the Reader's. Using Todd Andrews as focus for deliberations upon the novel form, Barth incorporates reminiscences about American literary history and such stylish invitations as:

> Let's not press further the historicity of our "encounter." Given your obvious literary sophistication, you will agree with me that a Pirandelloish or Gide-like debate between Author and Characters were as regressive, at least quaint, at this hour of the world, as naive literary realism: a Middle-Modernist affectation, as dated now as Bauhaus design. (L 191)

But it is the task of *LETTERS* to recycle and invigorate the "out-of-date."

Jacob Horner

In *The End of the Road*,[23] the meaninglessness that cripples Jacob Horner makes him another character as player-victim of patterns. Confined to a Jack Horner corner, his "identity" in doubt and with reality displaced by artifice, he is a portrait of the nihilist as a succession of masks. In *LETTERS,* the ontological uncertainty is replayed in Barth's having Horner write mainly to himself. Variations upon "In a sense, I am Jacob Horner" recreate the opening line of the earlier text, and, immobilized again at the Remobilization Farm, Fort Erie, Ontario, Horner repeats his textual history.

So, the reader finds, it was as part of the Farm's "Scriptotherapy"[24] that patient Horner wrote "What I Did Till the Doctor Came," the

152   *Theories of Play and Postmodern Fiction*

manuscript of his "Hundred Days"[25] (and parody of Napoleon's), which fictitious Barth discovered while on a skiing holiday![26] The author used it to create *The End of the Road,* a fiction about an "ontological vacuum" (L 339) named Jacob Horner, that fiction in turn forming the basis for a film of the same title. According to Horner to himself, the film is "as false to the novel as was the novel to your Account and your Account to the actual Horner-Morgan-Morgan triangle as it might have been observed from either other vertex" (L,19). The formal play is a variation upon that in which the Author discusses with Todd Andrews the genesis of a novel called *The Floating Opera,* about an imaginary 54-year old Maryland lawyer named Todd Andrews. . . . But in this self-reflexive spiralling, the Author consoles him, "No matter. Life is a shameless playwright (so are some playwrights) who lays on coincidence with a trowel" (L 189). Indeed, as the text demonstrates relentlessly, for the reenactments include the replay and filming of Horner's Hundred Days as "Der Wiedertraum," with Horner (in a sense) and Joe Morgan playing themselves: "You Do Not quite understand what's going on. You suspect that in a sense you Are its Focus—read Target—yet at the same time but a Minor Figure in some larger design" (L 403). While Horner's paranoia is part of the representation of character, the statement also describes the reading role produced by the text's mode of construction. Presented with this complex cross-referencing of plot-lines that not only spiral about their first-person narrators but gather meanings from such a range of sources, the reader becomes a sorting demon. In contrast, however, with Stencil's, Oedipa Maas's, or Slothrop's roles as searchers and sifters, *LETTERS* does not hold out the teasing metaphor of a revelation to place all clues and provide the answer to the puzzle. As in Pynchon's texts, the play of reference and meanings expands against the idea of ending.

Each "bequeathed" to the Author for his consideration for the *LETTERS* project, Horner's "Anniversary View of History" and "Principle of Alphabetical Priority" emphasize reenactments while providing more catalogues that add to the "pretty interlacings" (L 101) of past and present, plot and plot. A.B. Cook VI's enquiry about this Horner practice, "A piquant coincidence of anniversaries—but so what?" (L 406), is also the reader's question; but while it allows Barth to slip in another anniversary list, it directs attention to the operation of this lexical playfield. The "so what?" is given one answer in *The End of*

Letters to Literature 153

the Road, in Horner's reading the World Almanac as part of the "Informational Therapy" designed to draw him out of his corner. But the catalogues do suggest the flux of culture as well as the possibilities and limitations of signifying systems. Placing the text "in the world," with references to Ted Kennedy and Chappaquiddick, man on the moon, US troop withdrawals from Vietnam and the latest Wall Street figures, they extend its playful range as a cultural artefact while posing an implicit "so what?," the always imminent rhetorical question, in the act of juxtaposing so varied a range of markers.[27]

Some of Barth's most inventive play with character and texts is evident in the "Hornbook." Horner's therapeutic "Catalogue of Cuckolds" provides Alphabetical Priority (in its arrangement from Agamemnon to Zeus), intertextual games (as a score chart of sexual behaviour for *LETTERS* and the preceding six works together with inclusions from myth, literature and history generally), and conceptual invention:

> You sat in your stiff Ladderback, Contemplating the empty U page in your Hornbook. The inclusion of Odysseus among the O's was questionable enough in the first instance: it is only a scurrilous early variant of the myth which holds Penelope to have cuckolded him with all 108 of her suitors, plus nine house servants, Phemius the bard, and Melanthius the goatherd. To cross enter him as Ulysses Seemed a Cheap Shot (L 195).

Its place as a structural motif is emphasized in the Horner-Joe Morgan relationship where the elaborate game leads to Morgan's retribution on the night of Horner's marriage to Pocahontas/Marsha Blank. Horner's own name goes into the "Cuckold" column, and "All scores settled" in the "Remarks" column; but Barth parodies storytelling when Joe Morgan declares his real grievance to be not that Horner had done A, B, C with Rennie Morgan causing D, but that he had *"Written It All Down"* (L 743).

The End of the Road survives the "events" it "records"; later texts do not obliterate earlier. *LETTERS* (and the telling of Joe Morgan's revenge) does not cancel *The End of the Road.* It is a literature of replenishment.

154 *Theories of Play and Postmodern Fiction*

A.B. Cook

Henry Burlingame III's assertion in *The Sot-Weed Factor,* "I am a Suitor of Totality, Embracer of Contradictories, Husband to all Creation, the Cosmic Lover,"[28] speaks as well for those descendants who are correspondents in *LETTERS,* A.B. Cook IV of the early nineteenth century and A.B. Cook VI of the twentieth century. The three sets of Cook letters[29] reenact and extend the mock picaresque form and burlesque style of *The Sot-Weed Factor.* Its attention to relationships between history and fiction, analyses of literature and story-telling, patterns of intrigue and counter-intrigue, metamorphosis and play-acting are their interests. Having A.B. Cook IV write to his unborn child in 1812, and discuss the family affliction of small peckers, uncommon sexuality and endless interests, with particular reference to Henry Burlingame III, Barth reminds readers of the range and energy of *The Sot-Weed Factor,* while commencing the play upon patterns in this presentation in *LETTERS* of succeeding generations of Cooks and Burlingames. Their gift for forgery, disguise, political intrigue, fine conversation, and love-making recycles and addresses Burlingame III's perceptions of change:

> "Your true and constant Burlingame lives only in your fancy, as doth the pointed order of the world. In fact you see a Heraclitean flux: whether 'tis we who shift and alter and dissolve; or you whose lens changes color, field, and focus; or both together." (SWF 349)

and of action:

> "One must needs make and seize his soul, and then cleave fast to 't, or go babbling in the corner; one must choose his gods and devils on the run, quill his own name upon the universe, and declare, 'Tis I, and the world stands such-a-way!' One must *assert, assert, assert,* or go screaming mad." (SWF 365)

Jacob Horner is the one who babbles in a corner; when the ABC's take up their quills, the alphabetical play that their initials introduce is large in design and gusto—a twentieth-century revisitation upon eighteenth-century forms.

Letters to Literature 155

Barth crowds the A.B. Cook IV letters with an unofficial version of the early nineteenth century. Typically, the revision mixes political and literary history in a rewrite that might be produced by Sterne upon street gossip. In this version, A.B. Cook IV loses his virginity in a carriage with Madame de Staël fleeing Paris at the height of The Terror (L 283), chats in the Hustler Tavern with Midshipman J.F. Cooper "freshly expell'd from Yale for insubordination" (L 198) who makes copious notes for a friend hoping to write novels about Indians, deplores the waste of powers in the pattern whereby Cooks and Burlingames cancel each other in successive generations (L 323), proclaims this "the tragical view" (L 315) of family history, and plays the "Game of Governments" that is the family's obsession. Defining A.B. Cook IV's world as a place of "conspiracy, counterconspiracy, double and triple agentry" (L 625), Barth creates a "political" equivalent to the literary duplicity of *LETTERS* generally. In repetition of the patterns "behind" the letters of Todd Andrews and Jacob Horner, or the process by which texts beget or frame other texts, the A.B. Cook IV letters reenact patterns from *The Sot-Weed Factor,* A.B. Cook VI reenacts both and is, in turn, replayed in the film crew's strange work. Master of disguise, Cook VI, Laureate become lecturer at Marshyhope State University, is also (it seems) André Castine once married to Lady Amherst, Baron André Castine or Lord Baltimore who woos Jane Mack, and Monsieur Casteene who manipulates Jerome Bray in the course of the "Second American Revolution." Such is the play where the patterns reflect all ways, that "he" can gloomily imagine himself, "my namesake's pallid parody, and in my own second cycle the impersonator of myself" (L 636). The interplay of fact and fiction, past and present, is compounded in these letters with their references to the late sixties, Kennedy, the moon project, Vietnam demonstrations, civil rights action, assassinations and political games.

The Cook letters deconstruct "reality." As in *The Sot-Weed Factor,* extensions and plays upon the "real" of historical events and persons displace "history" by emphasizing the processes of construction. History and identity are matters of negotiation. In the Cooks' family capacity for disguise, trickery, and byzantine adventures, and the stories-within-stories structure artifice is paramount. Fixing attention upon language as both the means of representation and a source of play, the letters recall, while qualifying, Ebenezer Cooke's discovery that "the sound of Mother English [is] more fun to game with than her sense

156   *Theories of Play and Postmodern Fiction*

to labor over" (SWF 13). But in their concentration on action in the world, they convey Henry Burlingame's assertiveness rather than Eben Cooke's abstractions. Henry's "I love the world, sir, and so make love to it! I have sown my seed in men and women, in a dozen sorts of beasts, in the barky boles of trees and the honeyed wombs of flowers" (L 348), and not Eben's idealist aesthetics as virgin and poet, defines the recycling.

In its Rabelaisian play upon the texts of history and fiction, a play that questions the truth-claims of historical documents and affirms the energy of the eighteenth-century picaresque, *The Sot-Weed Factor* offers a deconstructive return to the past. As if "begotten by Don Quixote upon Fanny Hill,"[30] which is a fair gesture towards its parody and bawdiness, it shows Barth mixing "history" with fiction, spinning new tales upon old and in ways that demonstrate the text's contemporary relevance. Although "late seventeenth-century," its replay is a re-exploration of faith, creativity, mythopoesis, protean shape-shifting, the forms of representation and the uses of language. Eben Cooke and Henry Burlingame are figures of the artist as shaper of the world. Recycling Cooks and Burlingames, Barth again creates audacious variations upon received historical narrative and, in particular, upon revolutionary history. A.B. Cook VI's proposal to the author that "The Second American Revolution" be the grand theme of his book gathers the "family tradition" and places one frame of the many that intersect in *LETTERS*. The Author's rejection of his suggestion that they collaborated on *The Sot-Weed Factor,* thanks for the family's later history, and withdrawal of his invitation that Cook be one of the seven correspondents, all at page 533, complement the structure and complicate the formal riddling as texts interweave with texts.

Jerome Bray

Barth is a close critic of Barth, and the opportunities for dissimulation are sharpened when the critiques are presented as meta-perspectives and included "in disguise" within the works. "Editor B's" comment within the introductory mirrors of *Giles Goat-Boy* is also an appropriate introduction to J.B. Bray's role in *LETTERS:*

Letters to Literature

> this author has maintained (in obscure places understandably) that language *is* the matter of his books, as much as anything else, and for that reason ought to be "splendrously musicked out"; he turns his back on what *is the case,* rejects the familiar for the amazing, embraces artifice and extravagance; washing his hands of the search for Truth, he calls himself "monger after beauty" or "doorman of the Muses' Fancy-house." [31]

Descendant of not only Harold Bray, Grand Tutor, but also of the American Bonapartes, recycled from "Bellerophoniad," cousin of the Cook/Burlingames, disciple of Harrison Mack imagining himself to be George III, ex-patient of the Remobilization Farm, dedicated to a Second Revolution to restore the dominion of fiction (scientific fiction) and bizarre extra in film scenes, Jerome Bonaparte Bray is the work's weirdo, aptly described by Lady Amherst as "the lecherous Lily Dale lunatic" (L 540). [32] Although his links are mainly with *Giles Goat-Boy,* Bray is a phantom figure of cumulative points of reference, existing in the words and symbols of "computerese."

In another variation upon Marx's observation in "The 18th Brumaire," the tragedy of the myth hero becomes farce in *Giles Goat-Boy;* in its reenactment in *LETTERS,* farce is compounded with WESCAC becoming LILYVAC, Bray's computer, housed in the barn on goat farm COMALOT (intentional sexual pun), itself, in turn, a parody of George Giles' goat-farm origins (and mysterious parentage). Barth's obfuscation over ancestry in the representation of character is repeated at large in his extravagant attention to allusion and quotation. As the theory and practice of deconstruction affirm, and strategies of metafiction support, this play of reference and meanings is endemic in language and, mocking the idea of single origin, it emphasizes the processes of accumulating reference. In Barthes' description, "the text passes: it is a nomination in the course of becoming, a tireless approximation, a metonymic labor." [33] Whereas the reference list for *Giles Goat-Boy* includes Greek tragedy, the Bible, *The Divine Comedy, Don Quixote* and *Ulysses,* and constructions of the traditional myth-hero from Raglan's *The Hero* and Campbell's *The Hero with a Thousand Faces,* LILYVAC is fed with entries from Thompson's *Motif Index of Folk Literature, Masterplots* and *Monarch Notes,* or a reference list as indicator of the *reductio ad absurdum* of Bray's farcical antics. But the verbal tricks of "computerese" show Barth's

158   *Theories of Play and Postmodern Fiction*

propensity for puns, anagrams, codes, alliteration games and cryptic word-play; and Bray's plan for NOTES (L 147), with its five letters coinciding with a 5-year plan and things in fives, provides a preamble to NUMBERS, seven letters, 7-year plan, catalogues of sevens and the war against *LETTERS*. Bray's feud with John Barth, Author, commencing in his first letter with reference to the plagiarism suit against Barth for his appropriation and perversion of Harold Bray's 'Revised New Syllabus' into *Giles Goat-Boy,* continues:

> You think to make us a character in yet another piece of *literature!* You, "sir"—now we have your number programmed into LILYVAC—will be a character in our 18 14 (a.k.a. R.N.): the world's 1st work of Numerature! (L 527)

R.N.? Not only "Revolutionary Novel" but also Bea Golden (Jeannine Mack) who will play "**R**egina de **N**ominatrix" to Bray's "**R**e**g** Numerator." In this cause, 1 2 3's are set against A B C's. His letter to the Author concludes wittily:

> P.S.:   . . . Eat your heart out *writer!*
> P.P.S.:   . . . Our last to you. An end to letters!
>   ZZZZZZZ! (L 528)

As the last letter, "Z" is an end to letters (and dismissal of the *LETTERS* project); but as the sound of a bee (or a gadfly), it is another reference to Bray's role as Gadfly and a reminder of his weird sexual antics, his manufacture and use of Honey Dust, and his plan to fertilize the Queen to usher in a New Golden Age, this time with a Bee-Girl (Bea Golden), not a Goat-Boy! (L 756-7). When his final words list the ingredients of the miraculous aphrodisiac as a Macbethian witches' brew, together with royal jelly of Queen Bea and the freeze-dried faeces of George III (Harrison Mack mad), the list not only typifies Bray's mad cunning in the role but also reminds us that Barth's allusions keep most things cycling.

Is Bray's computerese and the promise that LILYVAC can repeat any author's style, a jest at new technology and McLuhanite predictions of an end to traditional letters? A.B. Cook VI, with no more claim than Bray to authorial trust, warns his son that Bray "may have abilities, capacities, as extraordinary as yours and mine" (L 746). Bray is a figure

Letters to Literature 159

whose intertextual range and capacity for plotting match A.B. Cook's and, as Charles Harris points out, "In the Bray passages language mediates between opacity and transparency, abstract formalism and 'contentism,' self-consciously directing attention to itself while still managing to *signify.*"[34] Foregrounded so overtly in Bray's style, this linguistic self-consciousness is, nevertheless, evident throughout *LETTERS.* It is a reminder of the capacities of language as a flexible system of signification which, against simple mimesis, offers choice, invention, and not an absence but a proliferation of styles and meanings.

Ambrose Mensch

The liveliness of the Ambrose Mensch letters is fitting for Barth's portrait of the artist as correspondent, the writer whose sexual antics, like his literary, are a source of fun and frustration and are finally "handed over" incomplete. In their inventive parodies, language games and literary reference, the letters revive motifs not only from *Lost in the Funhouse,* Barth's metafictional tribute to art and the artist,[35] but also *Chimera, Giles Goat-Boy* and *The End of the Road* as the spirals take shape in *LETTERS.* There are obvious connections, furthermore, between this text's struggling writer and the story-making writers of the later works, Fenwick Scott Key Turner of *Sabbatical,* Peter Sagamore of *The Tidewater Tales* and William Behler of *The Last Voyage of Somebody the Sailor,* all of them revived as literary ghostings of the author figure in Barth's latest "water message" of life and literature, *Once upon a Time.*

Ambrose's main form of address, "To Yours Truly" is a triple reminder: first, of "Water-Message" from *Lost in the Funhouse,* partly recycled in the first letter (L 39); second, of the attempts of Ambrose Mensch, and John Barth (each symbolising the labour of every writer), to fill in the blank space between "To Whom it May Concern" and "Yours Truly"; and third, of the idea that writers talk/write eternally to themselves, the notion addressed brilliantly in "Anonymiad"[36] and directly in an Author to Mensch letter (L 655). Making the law of reenactment both a central subject of discussion and an organisational strategy, Barth again invites readers to explore the connections. Typically, some of the tracery is explicit, in the manner of self-parody, some is implicit. Ambrose discusses the principle that Ontogeny

160   Theories of Play and Postmodern Fiction

recapitulates Phylogeny, announces this as the working principle of his next fiction about Perseus (the fiction that Barth has created already as the novella "Perseid" in *Chimera)*, perceives his own second cycle as a recapitulation of his first (a play upon the "Perseid" model), tells how he threw his early work "The Amateur" into the Choptank sealed in a bottle where it stayed seven years until he fished it out (a parodic replay of both "Water-Message" and "Anonymiad") and worries about the Mensch family's recycling of stones in the building of "Mensch's Folly" and Marshyhope's Tower of Truth. His mock lament, "Nothing lost, alas. All spirals back recycled!" (L 427) is placed in the context of a reference to the swarm of bees[37] described in "Ambrose His Mark," the event that alludes to Zeus's descent upon Danaë in a shower of gold to beget Perseus and to Barth's play upon the myth in creating Ambrose Mensch; it is also a variation on the recurrent references in Todd Andrews' letters to the past fertilizing the future; further, it comments on the Prinz film crew, Ambrose's ambivalent participation in the reenactment of his past and his refusal to replay his marriage to Marsha, asserting, "closed-circuit history is for compulsives: Perseus and I are into spirals [. . . .] The question of the plot is clear: How transcend mere reenactment?" (L 429). Self-reflexive art indeed. Writing about the "problem" is the answer to the problem. While it is central to Barth's idea of "exhaustion" and the plan to recycle old stuff, the question is implicit throughout *LETTERS*, posed in the reenactments and presented explicitly by the Capital-A Author. As I have noted already, the revisitations create a literature of "replenishment," via a practice that uses other literature and invigorates it in the process. The spiral metaphor also recalls "Dunyazadiad" and strategies of literary creation that the novellas of *Chimera* discuss and enact. Setting out the official Perseus myth alongside Ambrose's projected fiction (L 648-9), and within the analysis of Raglan's and Campbell's definitions of the myth-hero's life pattern, Barth typically mixes styles, roles and perspectives on myth, history and narrative, to play with the ideas in demonstrating their arbitrariness but also their tenacity.

Like Perseus at his imagined mid-life crisis, Ambrose exterminates his taskmaster, "Yours Truly," bequeaths his Perseus/Medusa notes to Author John Barth to write the story, suggests that the Author postpone his plan for an epistolary opus and write a "quickie sixth" (because Lady Amherst has read the first five and is waiting), and contemplates his life's Second Cycle. Not only does Barth comment in this way on

Letters to Literature

161

the plan of *Chimera,* he also attributes to Ambrose the idea that the theme of *LETTERS* be not "revolution" but "reenactment" (L 652) and has "him" describe off-handedly a possibility that provides yet another way of looking at *LETTERS:*

> perhaps I'll commence *my* Second Cycle—with a novel based on the movie that was meant to be based on *your* novels but went off in directions of its own. Or perhaps with a crab-and-oyster epic: a *Marylandiad*? (L 653).

LETTERS is both of these, and more. There are revealing ironies in the Author's thanking Ambrose for these ideas, noting the closeness of their literary apprenticeships, "we served each as the other's alter ego and aesthetic conscience" (L 653), and asking permission to recycle him "out of the Funhouse and into LETTERS" (L 655), all in Part 6, having had him there from the "start." The Funhouse mirrors reflect reflections of reflections of reflections.

The major omission from this short discussion of Ambrose is Lady Amherst and his obsession with impregnating her, the obsession that produces so many variations about his low motile swimmers and her old egg as Barth extends the twin concentrations on procreation and artistic creativity of *Lost in the Funhouse.* I will consider the implications of this union under the later heading of "Metafiction/ Metahistory." But the interrelationship of Ambrose's roles as artist and lover is sustained through the letters:

> For your patience wherewith, Art and Germaine, once again my thanks.
>
> A.

and

> P.S.: Adieu Art. Now: Will you, dear Germaine, circa 5 P.M. Saturday, 13 September 1969, take me Ambrose as your lawful wedded husband, in dénouements as in climaxes, in sevens as in sixes, till death do us et cet.? (L 764)

"Adieu Art"? Does "legitimation," or the triumph of love, signify silence and the blank page? How can the reader not applaud the union

162 *Theories of Play and Postmodern Fiction*

of Ambrose Mensch and Lady Amherst, writer and muse, but not at the expense of art. And so the text taunts the reader. But Barth's plays upon the figure of the writer, and upon the closeness of Ambrose Mensch and John Barth, extend beyond this penultimate Mensch letter. Blanks are still being filled: *Sabbatical* succeeds *LETTERS* and that Chesapeake and literary voyage is succeeded by another, *The Tidewater Tales,* which incorporates anew and differently many of the main features of *Sabbatical* and in which the story-telling imperatives produce new inventions upon such old Barth familiars as the figures of Odysseus, Scheherazade, Don Quixote and Huck Finn. They are succeeded by *The Last Voyage of Somebody the Sailor,* with its extravagant literary voyaging and the central storytelling *mano a mano* between Scheherazade's Sindbad and William Behler (Somebody), and *Once upon a Time* as Barth's latest literary voyage, the hybrid text that intermingles autobiography, fiction and literary-cultural analysis and concludes, in deference to both the preciousness of "now" and its invasion by what is past and yet to come: "The time is once upon" (398).

Lady Amherst

As the one correspondent newly created for *LETTERS* and most prolific of all, since as Saturday writer she has to fill in the horizontal lines at the top of the capital letters L-E-T-T-E-R-S, Lady Amherst is garrulous, learned and elegantly vulgar. Describing her early life as a literary grand tour, and embroiled so variously with characters recycled from Barth's earlier works, she is (like the reader) the "discoverer" of their fictionalisation as systematic reader of novelist Barth's works and leading commentator on the art of fiction and relationships between aesthetics and life.

English by background, figure of the European Great Tradition, she is a stylish and gossipy treasure-house of literature, the figure for Barth's selective allusions to literary background and primary means of the links between this European tradition and American letters. Descendant of Byron and Madame de Staël, deflowered at fourteen by H.G. Wells's fountain-pen, introduced to Mr. Sinclair Lewis, admirer of Joyce, unimpressed by Hemingway, sceptical of Eliot's neo-orthodoxy, distressed by Pound's anti-semitism, befriended by Gertrude Stein and Alice Toklas, pregnant to aged Herman Hesse and packed with Elizabethan allusions, she is the representation of character

Letters to Literature 163

as a network of playful borrowings, both a reaffirmation and selective critique of the past. The literary references constitute neither a checklist of European literature and American offspring nor the focus for detailed critical analysis; rather, as Lady Amherst's familiars, they are signs of her characterisation and reading role as well as markers in the text's intertextual play with the reader. This is a play of artful correspondences in Barth's recycling of his own works: as Lady Amherst "writes" about her ancestor and namesake Madame de Staël, not only do her descriptions of parallels between their lives interweave with A.B. Cook IV's descriptions of Madame de Staël's activities, but her relationship with André Castine in the twentieth century reenacts the A.B. Cook IV and Madame de Staël liaison in the late eighteenth century; her recollection of an abortion at Fort Erie, Ontario, echoes Rennie Morgan and *The End of the Road;* created as an old friend of Harrison and Jane Mack, her role as Lady Pembroke to Harrison's George III (Harrison Mack mad believing himself George III sane) recalls *The Floating Opera;* her descriptions of the Menschhaus recycle, from another perspective, "The Amateur" by Ambrose Mensch as A.M. King; her participation in the Prinz film reintroduces her to the Remobilization Farm, to characters from various fictions, to the farcical reenactments of fiction's treatment of history and vice versa, and to the formal battle between writer and director, fiction and film. As reader of author John Barth's work, her words to the Author are principal examples of the metafictional play. She comments on *The Floating Opera,* "I felt a familiar uneasiness about the fictive life of real people and the factual life of 'fictional' characters" (L 58); during *The Sot-Weed Factor,* "what am I to do with these 'coincidences' of history and your fiction with the facts of my life [. . . .] No more games!" (L 198-9); and after *Lost in the Funhouse,* "I enjoyed the stories—in particular the 'Ambrose' ones. Your Ambrose, needless to say, is not my Ambrose—but, then, mine isn't either!" (L 438). In these ways, Barth focuses the organisational principles and aesthetic questions of *LETTERS* in the letters of the text's "qualified" literary critic. Having Lady Amherst address generic and theoretical questions, amidst her commentaries on events and relationships, Barth can play paradoxically with them, adding frames, while presenting a mixture of learning, levity and frankness as her signature as character:

164   *Theories of Play and Postmodern Fiction*

> A. assures me that you do not yourself take with much seriousness
> those Death-of-the-Novel or End-of-Letters chaps, but that you *do*
> take seriously the climate that takes such questions seriously; you
> exploit that apocalyptic climate, he maintains, to reinspect the origins
> of narrative fiction in the oral tradition. Taking that cue, Ambrose
> himself has undertaken a review of the origins of *printed* fiction,
> especially the early conventions of the novel. More anon. To us
> Britishers, this sort of programme is awfully *theoretical,* what? Too
> French by half, and at the same time veddy Amedican. (L 438)

Not only does the form thereby meet itself, but the reference picks up,
in Lady Amherst's seventeenth letter, a theoretical issue introduced in
her first (L 5). It is also the central theoretical issue of *Lost in the
Funhouse* and, as in the earlier text, the answer is presented in a
sexual/textual interrelationship. In *LETTERS,* Barth's attempts to
refertilise the present via the past, explicitly the literary tradition, focus
symbolically and playfully upon Lady Amherst's old egg; the uncertain
voyage of the sperm of "Night-Sea Journey" becomes the riotous
repetitions of Ambrose's swimmers, "High count but low motility, like
great Schools of dying fish" (L 64). Is she pregnant at text's end? If so,
to whom? Although the result of that exhaustively orchestrated attempt
remains uncertain, the larger answer, the formal answer, is the existence
of *LETTERS* itself, this not so old-time epistolary novel. While
LETTERS might induce readers to return to Richardson and Fielding,
more important is the sustenance contemporary literature may draw
from earlier literature. There is an analogy to be made between this
relationship and Prinz's filming of "The Second American War of
Independence": "it is, anyroad, not the *war* we're interested in but its
reenactment—in which 1969 and 1812 (and 1669, 1776, and 1976) are
tossed together like salad greens" (L 445).

   Barth has commented upon the special place he conceived for Lady
Amherst: "Despite the unusual nature of the fiction I was putting her
into, I wanted to make her as believable as possible. The other
characters, to me at least, are clearly ancillary, complementary,
supplementary; her voice is the sustaining one."[38] Created as
literature's intimate, and as a correspondent given to explicit detail and
energetic rhetoric, her letters "to the Author" focus the connections
between *LETTERS* and other literature, including Barth's own. She is,
after all, the character as reader, as well as lover, and writer.

Letters to Literature 165

The Author
It is appropriate that the capital-A Author be last in sequence, filling in the bottom line, Sundays, on the LETTERS grid. Authors, *in a sense,* have final say *in* texts. Barth creates a most polite author, one who writes courteous letters not only to the reader but to each of his major characters in turn, discussing their previous careers in fiction, the fine distinctions between Art and Life ("a boundary as historically notorious as Mason and Dixon's line" (L 51-2)), and inviting their participation in a new project, "a longish epistolary novel" (L 341). The trick, of course, is that the letters passing back and forth between the drolls and dreamers about a project are the project. *LETTERS* is an elaborate fiction about fictions and Fiction.

In this funhouse, the mirrors are multi-directional. What is the relationship between John Barth author of *LETTERS* and capital-A Author John Barth character in *LETTERS,* who describes himself as "a fabricator, not a drawer-from-life" (L 194) but who also holds that "Art and life are symbiotic" (L 341)? Presenting a version of the author, signified by his name, the text's attention to the concept of authorial identity, and to the question of responsibility, is extended in the deconstructive proliferation of JB's (John Barth, Jerome Bray, Joel Barlow, J.A. Beille, Jean Blanque). JB-author is another construct, a figure who is well-acquainted with Barth's writing, surprised to discover the existence in "life" of some of the characters of "fiction," and able to mix firm admonitions with polite discourse. Such foregroundings are more a process of authorial self-effacement than self-advertisement because they deconstruct the site of authority. Acknowledging the text's artifice as a construct and its dependence upon the reader for its meanings, they paradoxically subvert the author's authority by throwing it into the ring as an item of contemplation. They confirm Roland Barthes' perception of the difference at play within a text:

> We know now that a text is not a line of words releasing a single 'theological' meaning (the 'message' of the Author-God) but a multi-dimensional space in which a variety of writings, none of them original, blend and clash. The text is a tissue of quotations drawn from the innumerable centres of culture.[39]

166   *Theories of Play and Postmodern Fiction*

Extensive as the quotations are in *LETTERS,* it is also the case that readers inevitably bring others to their part in the creative exchange. In a letter to Jacob Horner about the project, the Author suggests that "it will hazard the resurrection of characters from my previous fiction, or their proxies, as well as extending the fictions themselves, but will not presume, on the reader's part, familiarity, with those fictions, which I cannot myself remember in detail."[40] Nevertheless, although specific familiarities are not an essential reading preparation, they necessarily extend the text as well as help to define the manner and effects of its replays. *LETTERS* is enriched by Barth's other work, as it is by Richardson and Fielding, Sterne and Smollett, contemporary "postmodernist" fiction, and the classical literature to which Barth returns again, and again.

In the first Author-to-the-Reader letter, the Author reminds the Reader that letters in epistolary fiction have three times—their actual date of composition, letterhead date and time of reading:

> It is *not* March 2, 1969: when I began this letter it was October 30, 1973: an inclement Tuesday morning in Baltimore, Maryland. The Viet Nam War was "over"; its peacemakers were honored with the Nobel Prize; the latest Arab-Israeli war, likewise "over," had preempted our attention, even more so the "energy crisis" it occasioned, and the Watergate scandals and presidential-impeachment moves. . . . (L 44-5)

Reminding us of what we should know, the details also prefigure the style of contemporary referencing that situates the text in a sixties American context. The lists of events create a 1969 farewell to the decade, while affirming how perspectives interweave and while emphasizing the arbitrariness of facts and values, patterns and connections. Re-enacting these reminders in the short final letter, second of two in the Author-to-the-Reader series, the Author says that he has spent time between outlines, drafts, typescripts and galleys, "rewriting, editing, dismantling the scaffolding, clearing out the rubbish, planting azaleas about the foundations, testing the wiring and plumbing, hanging doors and windows and pictures, waxing floors, polishing windows and windowpanes" (L 771). The game continues to the last letter because the scaffolding's not dismantled and the azaleas don't really hide the foundations. The waxed floors, pictures and

Letters to Literature

167

windows reflect images and all the mirrors have curved surfaces. He has built a funhouse. Describing the Bonaventure hotel in downtown Los Angeles as a definitive example of "postmodern hyperspace," a spectacle that induces bewilderment in visitors, Fredric Jameson emphasizes its reflective glass skin, labyrinthine interiors and exhibitionist escalators and elevators.[41] Barth's funhouse is a literary analog, but whether a visitor to this elaborate communicational network is frustrated or fascinated by the "postmodernist" challenge is a matter of individual disposition.

METAFICTION/METAHISTORY: THE FRAGMENTED TEXTS OF ART AND LIFE

The reader is reminded frequently in *LETTERS* that "art" is not separable from "life."[42] Variations upon the statement itself, and the work's integration of social-historical references with its attention to aesthetics, emphasize the relationship as a close interrelationship. Literary texts *are* cultural constructions, though not in any simple reflectionist sense; the "unseemly rush from word to world"[43] is as problematic as denial of the connection. With its references to an "immediate" 1960s American cultural context, and representations of late eighteenth and nineteenth-century history, *LETTERS* addresses Social, Historical and Literary issues, treating each not as a given but as an open subject for continuing speculation. In this discussion, I wish to argue that Barth's *play* with the received narratives of literature and history is a process of acknowledgement and displacement, both a tribute to the past and subversive of endings. Against Fiction and History, *LETTERS* offers meta-perspectives and the fragmented text. Its deconstructions are thematic as well as formal; while they invite the reader to cross-reference and create patterns, they emphasize process and pluralism against idealist notions of the one. As always, the potential for play exceeds any particular configuration of it.

As Edward Said suggests, "texts are worldly, to some degree they are events, and, even when they appear to deny it, they are nevertheless a part of the social world, human life, and of course the historical moments in which they are located and interpreted."[44] The statement might have been written by the Author in *LETTERS* who reminds the Reader of precisely these things.[45] But since the ways are various, the manner of this worldliness is always the point at issue. In a 1965

168   *Theories of Play and Postmodern Fiction*

article, in which he differentiates his work from the Black Humorists'
by emphasizing their responsibility as satirists, Barth concludes:

> But I say, Muse spare me (at the desk, I mean) from Social-
> Historical Responsibility, and in the last analysis from every other
> kind as well, except Artistic. Your teller of stories will likely be
> responsive to his time; he needn't be responsible to it. [46]

As *Giles Goat-Boy* was published in 1966, the statement is made within
the context of this work and the earlier three, none of which is a social
documentary novel but all of which are responsive to social-cultural,
including philosophical-aesthetic, issues. But *LETTERS,* this most
seriously playful of texts, offers a new rapprochement in the art-life
dialectic. It does so, not by conceding the novel's subservience to the
weighty business of Society and History but, rather, by incorporating
this business as itself fragmentary and *sous rature.* The effect is not to
deny but to question and to game with "the world" as it is represented
in texts.

Judgements of Barth's attention to history vary:

> One can think of no American novel seizing "'the pen of History"
> (p.750) that covers so much American territory and history as
> *LETTERS.* [47]

> For a novel with so much history in it, *LETTERS* is oddly
> unhistorical. [48]

But so much depends upon one's definition of history, since the past, in
any example of its reconstruction, is inseparable from the theory of
history and the mode of representation by which it is shaped. Hayden
White's work on metahistory offers a parallel theory of history to
contemporary theories of metafiction. Challenging history's claims to
scientificity (and truth), and defining historical work, as "a verbal
structure in the form of a narrative prose discourse," [49] he emphasizes
not only the processes of selection and speculation in historians'
reconstructions of the past but also the importance of poetic elements in
historiography and philosophy of history. In his view, the dominant
"tropological mode" and its attendant linguistic style constitute the
metahistorical basis of each historical text—or that element by which,

Letters to Literature

169

consciously or unknowingly, it reveals its processes and opens itself to deconstruction. *LETTERS* incorporates different perceptions of the past, ranging from its repudiation, a perception based upon linear arrangement and causal relationships, to its repetition with difference, either in the Eliadean[50] sense of cyclic patterns or in Marx's view that tragic history repeats itself as farce. Barth incorporates these as organizational concepts and as indicators of character, since those revolutionaries and schemers who attempt to triumph over history see it as a linear development whereas those caught in repetitions or reenactments are more inward turning.[51] Appreciation of such meta-perspectives is attributed to Todd Andrews, the "Bourgeois-Liberal-Tragic-Viewing Humanist":

> as a connoisseur of paradoxes, he understands to the bone that one of St. Augustine's concerning time: that while the Present does not exist (it being the merely conceptual razor's edge between the Past and the Future), at the same time it's all there is: the Everlasting Now between a Past existing only in memory and a Future existing only in anticipation. (L 88-9)

He locates the Drew Macks and H.C. Burlingames, the revolutionaries, with the future and situates himself, "ever for Reform," upon that conceptual razor's edge.

There is a Game of History in *LETTERS*. It is conducted in a number of different ways and its effect is to deconstruct versions of the past:

First, the text's attention to its dependence upon earlier fiction and its incorporation of its own history (it is its own history). *LETTERS* works interventions, and extensions, upon received narratives, and its duplicity about origins is represented in the whole process of reenactment. This metafictional strategy is also metahistorical. It is addressed frequently and explicitly: "The past manures the future" (L 15); A.B. Cook VI's action historiography is "the *making* of history, as if it were an avant-garde species of narrative" (L 73); stung by the mocking reception of his "Columbiad," Joel Barlow "agreed now with his former tutor that History is your grandest fiction" (L 319); Ambrose Mensch reflects "History is a code which, laboriously and at ruinous cost, deciphers into HISTORY. She is a scattered sibyl whose oak-leaf oracles we toil to recollect, only to spell out something less than

170   Theories of Play and Postmodern Fiction

nothing: e.g. WHOL TRUTH, or ULTIMATE MEANIN" (L 332); and, from Lady Amherst, "History really *is* that bird you mention somewhere, who flies in ever diminishing circles until it disappears up its own fundament!" (L 381). Typically, the characters protest about inaccuracies in representation. Their historian does not get it all right. "History" depends upon language and is subject to its capacity for dissembling.

Second, the text's references to historical "fact." Although *LETTERS* is set in the present of the American sixties, the Cook letters incorporate selective versions of the Indian Wars and westward expansion, and plotting in the courts of Europe from the late eighteenth century to this sixties detail of political protest, Vietnam withdrawals, men on the moon, and domestic America. Creating the sixties ethos, and a mythicised version of nineteenth-century history, *LETTERS* draws attention to the processes of signification, or the markers of history, by its mode of summary notation. This calendar plotting, which is like a shorthand version of leading details from the *World Almanac* and *Time* magazine, provides the US cultural framework for such narratives of historical reenactment as Drew Mack's revolutionary activities and campus politics at Marshyhope State University. In either case, Barth *plays* with history. A.B. Cook IV's ribald versions of the late eighteenth century spin out new inventions upon the events of text-book history, and the catalogues of sixties events provide bizarre juxtapositions of the clutter of a culture:

> Every fourth day of the year, on the average, an airliner had been hijacked: fifteen so far. Before the month expired, so would Mr. Eisenhower; and before the year, Senator Everett Dirksen, Levi Eshkol, Ho Chi Minh, and Mary Jo Kopechne, with difficult consequences for Senator Edward Kennedy. Tom Mboya would be assassinated in Nairobi, Sharon Tate and her friends massacred in California . . . (L 43).

In deference to the endlessness of detail and perspectives, this three-page list "ends" with, "the National Committee on violence would describe the 1960s as one of the most violent decades in United States history, but the French wine-growers association would declare '69 a vintage year" (L 44). Although one could read the lists for their concentration on acts of violence, and extract some thesis about cultural

Letters to Literature

171

apocalypse against which to set Barth's advocacy of love and creativity, the variety (and, indeed, the comic exuberance) of his cultural notation subverts such reductions. Our attention is diverted to frameworks for the organisation of culture and of texts, but not at the expense of that variety which slips the frames and beckons the players. Despite such headliners as the Vietnam War, Apollo II and Chappaquiddick, there are interest rates, postage costs and people in the streets.

The metahistorical and the metafictional meet in the figure of Lady Amherst. Her history embraces European revolutions (and their impact upon the revolutionary history of America) and she is the "Fair Embodiment of the Great Tradition" (L 39) of European letters; but, in addition, her roles as reader and self-conscious commentator focus upon connections between history and fiction. Allegorising her love affair with Ambrose Mensch as a meeting of Europe and America, the Great Tradition and contemporary fiction, muse and writer, Barth addresses not only the twinning of literary creativity and sexual activity, again, [52] but also the history of narrative fiction itself. Representing to Ambrose "Literature Incarnate, or The Story Thus Far" (L 40), she is the muse to whom his exhortation is addressed, "Speak love to me, Mother Tongue" (L 41), and upon whom words six and seven, "fornication" and "generation," are projected. His first letter is addressed to Lady Amherst, but also to literature and to language. Prefiguring the stages of this central relationship between characters in *LETTERS*, it is another example of a writer's address to his art, of his talking to himself or musing in print. Barth does it in *Lost in the Funhouse;* John Fowles does it often, but most explicitly in *Mantissa* [53] where the quirky Miles Green-Erato, writer-muse, confrontations are situated, conceptually, within the grey rooms of the writer's brain. In Fowles's comic parody, the plays go either way, against the male writer's clichéd superiority but also against the female muse's intellectual shallowness and seductive tricks. Erato protests but capitulates (she is a male writer's toy). Miles's attempts to up-date the muse both discuss metafiction and are an example of it:

> The reflective novel is sixty years dead, Erato. What do you think modernism was about? Let alone post-modernism. Even the dumbest students know it's a *reflexive* medium now, not a reflective one! (M 116).

172   *Theories of Play and Postmodern Fiction*

In *Mantissa* and in *LETTERS,* self-reflexive concentrations upon textuality provide a mimesis of process in their formalisations of writer-muse relationships. But whereas Fowles concentrates on literary reference, *LETTERS* looks to literature and history. Erato refers lightly to her past lovers (Virgil, Ovid, Horace, Shakespeare, Mallarmé, T.S. Eliot . . .) and irreverently to their art, a sample of which she wrote herself—*Men, Will They Ever Grow Up?*—publishing it under a pseudonym as *The Odyssey.* Lady Amherst, on the other hand, represents a rapprochement between literature and politics, art and social life.

Potentially promiscuous in her role as the Great Tradition, she receives invitations not only from Ambrose Mensch but also from the Author: "It is as if Reality, a mistress too long ignored must now settle scores with her errant lover" (L 52). Since Ambrose has taken letters F (fornication) and G (generation), the Author offers number nine from the *New England Primer,* an Invitation, "Will you consent to be A Character in My Novel?" (L 52). Although she protests her designations as Literature, The Great Tradition, and Muse of the Realistic Novel, "Lady Ambrose" writes, and writes, inscribing within the text the meandering story of her former literary life and lovers alongside the stages of her relationship with Ambrose. As the formalist who is obsessed with patterns in his life, and in art, Ambrose has conducted "a running warfare against the province of Literature" (L 333), a battle involving retreats and experiments:

> Tranquilly I turned my back on Realism, having perhaps long since turned it on reality. I put by not only history, philosophy, politics, psychology, self-confession, sociology, and other such traditional contaminants of fiction, but also, insofar as possible, characterization, description, dialogue, plot—even language, where I could dispense with it. (L 151)

But his relationship with Lady Amherst represents a regeneration of character and form, of letters as *LETTERS,* said to be inspired by love and respect of the "last-ditch provincial Modernist" for this "fancied embodiment (among her other, more human qualities and characteristics) of the Great Tradition" (L 767). The symbolic child of their literary union is the text itself, in its postmodernist version of epistolary narrative.

Letters to Literature 173

The metafictional play is extraordinarily various. Represented overtly in the text's elaborate formal organization, and in the numerous discussions of the project, it is also explicit in the self-consciousness with which every epistolean addresses the relationship between art and life, alternative fictions and the interweaving of characters in the notional present of 1969 within frames provided by earlier relationships, reenactments, and different forms. Jerome Bray's call for a revolution to restore fiction's supremacy is located within such speculative commentary as, "Thus Art is as natural an artifice as Nature; the truth of fiction is that Fact is fantasy; the made-up story is a model of the world" (L 33). The meta-perspective marks his computerese, the transition from NOTES to NUMBERS, and his role as purveyor of Honey Dust and possible impregnator of female characters in preparation for a "2nd American Revolution." There is a parallel observation about the low status of contemporary fiction in Todd Andrews's second letter:

> Nowadays the genre is so fallen into obscure pretension on the one hand and cynical commercialism on the other, and so undermined at its popular base by television, that to hear a young person declare his or her ambition to be a capital-W Writer strikes me as anachronistical, quixotic, as who should aspire in 1969 to be a Barnum and Bailey acrobat, a dirigible pilot, or the Rembrandt of the stereopticon. (L 84)

Literary references vie with the Chesapeake Bay and characters from *The Floating Opera* (*literary* characters) for a place in his letters. The ageing lawyer as sailor is another literateur. Jacob Horner's Scriptotherapy, Hornbook and Anniversary View of History provide intertextual repetitions on the linked explorations of fact and fiction, and the shaping of texts. This concentration is evident, as well, in the sets of Cook letters where the parody of A.B. Cook VI as "self-styled Laureate of Maryland" (L 6) signifies a family tradition and all three sets of letters gather references to literature alongside their variations upon two hundred years of political history.

Having A.B. Cook VI write to the Author about his "awakening to sex, literature and history together" (L 423), Barth underscores their interrelationship in these letters, in *The Sot-Weed Factor,* and in most of his writing. The triumvirate succeeds *LETTERS* in the allusiveness

174 *Theories of Play and Postmodern Fiction*

and formal exuberance of the story of Fenn and Susan. Transforming "The Tempest," revisiting American literature, history, mythology, and paranoia, *Sabbatical* offers *love* [54], again, and story-making itself, as the key to the treasure. The world *is* all that is the case, and in Barth's writing it is a construct motivated by love as well as curiosity—love between people and between their literary imagos, and love for the signifying systems that allow expression in life and art, in the art of life. Although, in disenchantment with her role and with the darkness of contemporary culture, Susan aborts her pregnancy, the text is a replacement offering for those twins: "The doing and the telling, our writing and our loving—they're twins. That's our story."[55] It is in *The Tidewater Tales,* despite continuing emphases upon dark political plotting, the CIA, and the dangers of toxic waste, that genesis of the text as offspring incorporates, as well, the birth of Kate's twins in a productive association between sex, literature, and history, that looks to the future of society while re-exploring its genealogy.

THE REGENERATION OF LITERATURE

Metafiction regenerates fiction. Its attention to sources, as well as to strategies, keeps material cycling and changing; and allusions to other texts not only recall them as items of attention but invite their consideration in a new dialectic. As Brecht would have it for drama and the theory of metafiction for prose narrative, acknowledgements of process also strengthen the text-reader relationship by inviting readers to participate co-creatively in the making of the text's meanings.[56] No longer treated as recipients of the completed representation, but as "confidantes" who may be entrusted with its scaffolding, readers can be involved specifically in a text's evolution and in wider generic and aesthetic reflections. It is not the case that meta-perspectives, in fiction, theatre, film or history, replace conventions that do not foreground the processes of representation. But their inclusion is provocative, a ruse by which seriousness may be interleaved with laughter and the parameters of play shifted to a new level of engagement, one that includes artifice not as a repressed other but as the very condition of the lexical playing field itself.

The Author's resuscitation of "that earliest-exhausted of English novel-forms" (L 654) tends not only to the epistolary form but to fiction and to prose narrative in general. Its "reenactments" are a process of

Letters to Literature 175

revival by allusion but also a means of extension. As Ambrose suggests: "Cycle II must not reenact its predecessor: echo, yes; repeat, no" (L 767); and spiral rather than circle is, as *LETTERS* acknowledges, the more appropriate metaphor for reference as the basis for regeneration. Barth's reappropriation is a reinterpretation of literary traditions, and it involves not only the epistolary form but the range of literary texts, conventions and historical contexts addressed in *LETTERS*. The text incorporates such early narrative forms as the picaresque, the travel book, the historical novel, the journal and autobiography, in addition to its play with manuscripts, self-conscious rhetoric, disguise, coincidence and the convoluted plot.[57] Although their inclusion is a parodic reaffirmation of literary traditions, it also signals, in this postmodernist context, a reconsideration of the processes of fictional representation. The variety refuses resolution and this refusal itself is regenerative. *LETTERS* celebrates the novel tradition by presenting together such an array of discourses and procedures. It is a roll call of old practice but also a self-conscious remaking under new conditions of productive uncertainty. The regenerative possibilities of conflation are evident in the scene that presents Ambrose Mensch and Lady Amherst fucking in the Tower of Truth. Inspired by their rehearsal of the contents table of *Clarissa,* and by Lady Amherst's remembrance of Madame de Staël's breathless doting upon Richardson's novels, the meeting of writer and muse incorporates its own literary model. But, another event in "the *mano a mano* between Author and Director, Fiction and Film" (L 453), it is filmed by Reg Prinz, film-maker and figure of film's challenge to print:

> My Zeus sprang off me as if galvanised, snatched up Vol.I and winged it staircaseward with a curse. Now I heard the whirrs and clicketies over there! By the time I got my legs together and my hem pulled down, he had armed himself with the sack of Vols II, III and IV and, bare-arsed with his spigot still adrip, was whamming in a rage at Reg Prinz, perched there with his hand-held! (L 441).

It is not just that the writer flings *Clarissa* at the film-maker in the Tower of Truth, all so obvious as to constitute its own self-parody, but that the scene picks up the formal play that is presented throughout the text: "for what Prinz truly wants to record the destruction of is not any historical city, but the venerable metropolis of letters" (L 223), and "No

176   *Theories of Play and Postmodern Fiction*

question but moviemakers have the world in their pocket in our century, as we like to imagine the 19th Century novelists did in theirs" (L 381). But, of course, they do not cancel one another and literature's accommodations with film are various. As Manuel Puig's *Kiss of the Spider Woman* and David Thomson's *Suspects* show,[58] this relationship, like those between past and present, fact and fiction, and art and life, is another "two-way street" (L 96).

LETTERS not only addresses such serious matters as United States history and the history of fiction, relationships between art and life, and the artifice of representation, it also treats them seriously as items of play. I have argued that this play is regenerative: the past may fertilize the future, but Barth demonstrates that the present can re-fertilize the past, while keeping open the opportunities for new developments upon old things. This overtly self-conscious text also *addresses* the reader.

Throughout this discussion, I have used the term "reader" in a general sense, while defining the reader's position as voyeur and referring to the two letters addressed to the Reader. It is part of the artifice that readers are invited by being "excluded," that the privacy of letters as documents of limited communication is both used and displaced in epistolary fiction. The "as if," as if real, is qualified in so many ways. Barth's introduction of the 'Dear Reader' convention substantiates the artifice by attributing a reading position as both frame and commentary. It is not simply that verisimilitude is disrupted but that it is offered, duplicitously and affectionately, in notations to the reader about the text and as a reminder of the reader's role as participant:

> Dear Reader, and Gentles all: *LETTERS* is now begun, its correspondents introduced and their stories commencing to entwine. Like those films whose credits appear after the action has started, it will now pause. (L 43)

Sop to tradition, philosophical nicety, pedantry, a game—in its attention to time, and to the acts of writing and reading, the letter is all of these. Urbane and inviting, it is another display piece and a critique, both a reinforcement of the clever play of allusions and ideas in the letters "written" by Barth's characters and their corrective. But if the Reader is cautioned about matters of perspective, readers are expected

Letters to Literature

177

to be interested in literature and writing. Despite the text's disclaimers, knowledge of Barth's other writing enriches *LETTERS,* and, in the cross-fertilization, readerly appreciation of eighteenth-century epistolary fiction, classical literature and movements in twentieth-century fiction enables readers to play more writerly[59] roles in *LETTERS.* Just as it is possible to theorise about writing as rewriting, so too reading is re-reading, the summons of accumulated experience to new and changing configurations.

Most significantly, *LETTERS* thematizes reading via its major characters, each of whom is not only a writer but also a reader involved in the creative processes of reception and response, processes that are shown to engage predispositions and to involve self-analysis. They read fiction, particularly Barth's fiction, as well as letters. Their activity parallels the reader's; as reader surrogates, they lead our responses by referring to literary underpinnings and by puzzling over connections between the work of art and the patterns and detail of public life. Whereas Pynchon's major characters read the world like a text, Barth's letter-writers read texts and trace their relationship with the worlds they evoke. Deconstructing the simple binary of real and fictitious in the elaborate artifice of its triple[60] play upon "letters," *LETTERS* implicates the reader as historian, philosopher, philologist, literary critic, and as visitor to the "funhouse." The discontinuous text is, in fact, a plethora of texts all of them fragmentary, self-conscious and allusive. Its concentration upon reading is similar to Calvino's postmodernist attention to eighteenth-century conventions. In an address that recalls Borges's "The Library of Babel," Calvino begins the penultimate chapter of *If on a winter's night a traveler:*

> Reader, it is time for your tempest-tossed vessel to come to port. What harbor can receive you more securely than a great library? Certainly there is one in the city from which you set out and to which you have returned after circling the world from book to book.[61]

His emphasis upon linguistic uncertainty, and the construction of a text from elusive literary sources that both invite and resist appropriation, parallels Barth's in *LETTERS.* Linking the search and the act of reading with the love affair between its readers, this fiction about fictions, like Barth's, associates textual construction and sexual communication. Writing and reading are acts of love, and Calvino's *If on a winter's*

178   *Theories of Play and Postmodern Fiction*

night a traveler is a covert epistolary effort, a love letter to readers
about literature.

Self-consciousness about the artifice of fiction is communicated to
readers in so many ways: formal variation (Sorrentino's *Mulligan Stew,*
Pynchon's *Gravity's Rainbow*), critical discussions (Nabokov's *Pale
Fire,* Barth's *Sabbatical,* Bowering's *Burning Water*), ostentatious
reference or parody (Coover's *The Public Burning,* Barth's *Chimera*),
explicit affirmation of readers and reading (Calvino's *If on a winter's
night a traveler,* Findley's *Famous Last Words*), and so on. Just as the
list can be extended and sub-divided, it is also clear that the ways
interrelate and that particular texts are more likely to exhibit a variety
of these characteristics together than any one as their definitive
metafictional marker. *LETTERS* exhibits each of the characteristics
included in this list. As Patricia Waugh argues, metafiction involves
play: "It aims to discover how we each 'play' our own realities."[62]
Although its self-consciousness about language and texts directs
attention to the interpenetration of "reality" and "fiction," it allows that
endings are only pauses. The plays of text construction and
interpretation, while meaningful in contexts, exceed restriction to any
specific context. Despite its inventive play with language, *LETTERS*
does not forsake the world for words. It is typical of Barth's fiction that
it offers answers to the problems it addresses, this time posed as a
rhetorical question in Ambrose's musings about the artist: *"Might
he/she not as readily, at least as possibly, be imagined as thereby (if
only thereby) enabled to love the narrative through the form, the
language through the narrative, even the world through the language?'*
(L 650).

NOTES

1. John Barth, *LETTERS* 191. Subsequent references are marked by the
abbreviation L and the page number.

2. The phrase is from Barth's essay "The Literature of Exhaustion,"
Atlantic Monthly, August 1967, 29-34. The "exhaustion" Barth defines may be
compared with Harold Bloom's descriptions of the "anxiety" of "influence"
(see *The Anxiety of Influence*) to the extent that each perceives the pressure of
past achievement as, in certain respects, stultifying of present endeavor.
Whereas Barth emphasizes the exhaustion of forms and possibilities, Bloom's
definition of the influence of strong predecessors sets up a psychoanalytic

Letters to Literature

model in which the "child" must necessarily contend with the tyrannical parent. Offering Beckett and particularly Borges as exemplary answers to the problem of exhaustion, Barth suggests that one tactic is to go back to the sources themselves, to address them in new ways. As he points out, Borges' "Pierre Menard, Author of the *Quixote*" encapsulates this perception. Menard's verbatim discovery of Cervantes' text is "almost infinitely richer" because of three hundred years of interventions that influence the "text." Borges' playful attribution of contextual influence defines the place of temporal difference in the nature of textuality:

"Menard (perhaps without wanting to) has enriched, by means of a new technique, the halting and rudimentary art of reading: this new technique is that of the deliberate anachronism and the erroneous attribution. This technique, whose applications are infinite, prompts us to go through the *Odyssey* as if it were posterior to the *Aeneid* and the book *Le jardin du Centaure* of Madame Henri Bachelier as if it were by Madame Henri Bachelier. This technique fills the most placid works with adventure." (Jorge Luis Borges, *Labyrinths* 71).

As Campbell Tatham points out, Ortega y Gasset predicted, in 1925, the coming death of the novel: "if it is not yet irretrievably exhausted, [it] has certainly entered its last phase." Ortega's essay, "The Dehumanization of Art" is published in *The Dehumanization of Art and Other Essays on Art, Culture, and Literature*. Tatham emphasizes the strength of Barth's self-conscious response to "exhaustion" (see his "John Barth and the Aesthetics of Artifice"), taking up Barth's pronouncements about affirming the unavoidable artifice in art. But, from a later perspective, Charles Harris acknowledges Ortega's exhaustion rhetoric and asserts one crucial difference: whereas Ortega says art can only survive by dehumanizing itself, Barth insists upon its moral relevance to human conditions: "Barth, then, is not—nor has he ever been—the strict formalist that both his supporters and detractors have sometimes portrayed him as being" (Charles B. Harris, *Passionate Virtuosity: The Fiction of John Barth,* 3). My reading of Barth's writings supports this view.

3. John Barth, "The Literature of Replenishment: Postmodernist Fiction," *Atlantic,* January 1980, 71.

4. An expression that Barth uses in "The Literature of Exhaustion," to represent the McLuhanite view of the writers. When the phrase is directed at the reader, we assume that there is more than a little collective affection in its use:

"The reader! You, dogged, uninsultable, print-oriented bastard, it's you I'm addressing, who else, from inside this monstrous fiction. You've read me

180   *Theories of Play and Postmodern Fiction*

this far, then? Even this far? For what discreditable motive? How is it you don't go to a movie, watch TV . . .?" ("Life-Story," *Lost in the Funhouse,* 123).

It is significant that the catalogue of alternatives thrown up to the insistent reader begins with film and television, leading "new" media competitors implicit in the extract from *LETTERS* with which I commence this chapter.

5. What counts as evidence? It seems fatuous to point to new titles, book sales, publishers' catalogues and the like. It is pertinent to point to late twentieth-century practice continuing in the "old" forms that are never really used up, as Borges and Barth, for example, demonstrate. And Ron Sukenik's response, *The Death of the Novel,* a novella, underscores the case. Barth's earlier commentary, "The Literature of Exhaustion," is not a prophecy of doom but a celebration of developments, a "reading" that his subsequent contributions as novelist support. For Barth's own, much later, analysis of his intentions and the circumstances of his writing this 1967 essay, see Charles Reilly, "An Interview with John Barth," 5-8.

6. In both "The Literature of Replenishment" and the Reilly Interview, Barth points specifically to High Modernism, to the writings of Joyce, Proust and Kafka, as a literature of difficult access. While not dismissing the demands his own works make upon readers, he nevertheless hopes that they are accessible to a wide readership and looks to a postmodernism (with *LETTERS* as his postmodernist offering) that will "embody a kind of literature which can find a way to transcend that quarrel between the cultural aristocrats and the pop novelists" (Reilly Interview, 7).

7. Consider the following interviews with Barth: John Enck, "John Barth: An Interview"; Alan Prince, "An Interview with John Barth"; "Having it Both Ways: A Conversation between John Barth and Joe David Bellamy"; James McKenzie, "Pole-Vaulting in Top Hats: A Public Conversation with John Barth, William Gass and Ishmael Reed."

8. Enck Interview, 11.

9. See, for example, John Stark, *The Literature of Exhaustion: Borges, Nabokov and Barth.* Stark refers to these two works as "quite conventional and realistic," 118. A number of earlier studies are limited by their definition of the works as nihilistic (Richard W. Noland, "John Barth and the Novel of Comic Nihilism"; Beverley Gross, "The Anti-Novels of John Barth"). On the other hand, there are readings that provide consideration of formal inventiveness and parodic self-consciousness against the limitations of conventional realism (Thomas Le Clair, "John Barth's *The Floating Opera:* Death and the Craft of Fiction"; Jac Tharpe, *John Barth: The Comic Sublimity of Paradox;* David

Letters to Literature   181

Morrell, *John Barth: An Introduction;* Stan Fogel and Gordon Slethaug, *Understanding John Barth;* Zack Bowen, *A Reader's Guide to John Barth*).

10. John Barth,*The Floating Opera.* Subsequent references are marked by the abbreviation FO and the page number.

11. Enck Interview, 6.

12. Reilly Interview, 3. The comment virtually reenacts another in *LETTERS,* 52-3.

13. Most significant of the many plays upon this meaning of 69 are the intersexual, intertextual associations of Ambrose Mensch and Lady Amherst, American postmodernist and the great Tradition, writer and muse. These associations are discussed later in the chapter.

14. Barth, "The Literature of Replenishment," 70.

15. See Linda Hutcheon, *Narcissistic Narrative: The Metafictional Paradox.* Hutcheon's distinction between "mimesis of product" (the manner of mimesis applied to traditional realism) and "mimesis of process" (metafiction) not only salvages the term mimesis from its conventional limitation to forms of realism in the arts, it directs attention to the making of texts in ways that acknowledge both their artifice and the participation of readers in creating meanings. Further, this emphasis helps to erode distinctions between text and context, art and life, opening the way not only to formalist analyses but also to considerations of the product *in* the world.

16. See "Water-Message" in Barth's *Lost in the Funhouse,* 53. The "blank" between "To Whom It May Concern" and "Yours Truly" invites both the writer and the reader (as "writer"). It functions analogously to Derrida's metaphor of gaps in language itself, and to operations of the trace, to the extent that each of the figures emphasizes incompletion against closure.

17. Samuel Richardson, *Pamela, or Virtue Rewarded.* First published in 1740. The quotation is from the title page.

18. Reilly Interview, 13.

19. And, as the Weixlmanns have pointed out, Giles performs seven trials in *Giles Goat-Boy,* Barth provides seven additional author's notes to *Lost in the Funhouse,* seven concentric stories comprise "Menelaiad" and "Dunyazadiad," there are seven sections in Chimera . . . and lots of sevens in "Perseid" and "Bellerophoniad." See Joe Weixlmann and Sher Weixlmann, "Barth and Barthelme Recycle the Perseus Myth: A Study in Literary Ecology."

20. See, for example, *LETTERS,* 255. Like *Gravity's Rainbow, LETTERS* abounds in connections. As characters in each text pursue patterns as a means of explaining phenomena, Pynchon and Barth focus the reader's attention on the act of making and unmaking explanatory links. But Barth's formal play is

182   *Theories of Play and Postmodern Fiction*

more overt, and his emphasis upon recapitulation less threatening than Pynchon's representation of paranoia.

21. Consider Harris, *Passionate Virtuosity*, 191-3. His reading acknowledges this Todd Andrews as a more humane character than his predecessor of *The Floating Opera* but emphasizes his "lack of authentic care for and involvement in a world he ultimately fears" (192). It is a tribute to the "believability" Barth sought in creating the characters (see Reilly Interview, 13), that in such a fragmented and artificial text, readers will adopt this "as if real" strategy, constructing character as unity. The point is that Todd Andrews' character, is (like people in real life) a construct containing many contradictions, manifesting uncertainties, capable of acting "out of character." In *The Floating Opera,* variability is discussed in terms of stages and masks (see 15); it is supported too by the emphasis upon change as the condition of the world.

22. His letters contain a range of literary allusions and, as lawyer to Marshyhope University, saviour of Drew Mack and observer-participant with respect to the film work, he is a reporter of the Sixties' protest politics.

23. John Barth, *The End of the Road.* Page references to the Penguin edition.

24. Barth has his Horner note a difference between therapy in *The End of the Road* times and hollow practice in *LETTERS:*

"When you Were, in a sense, Jacob Horner, you Interested yourself, at the Doctor's prescription, in such events. Now you Merely Acknowledge calendric resonances, the anniversary view of history, and Catalogue them by Alaphabetical Priority" (L 98).

Repetition of the earlier text is, explicitly and implicitly, repetition with difference.

25. Horner's 100 Days at Wicomico Teacher's College, beginning with his appointment and ending with his departure after Rennie Morgan's funeral, and Napoleon's 100 Days (Elba to St. Helena). Barth plays upon the "relationship" in terms of Marx's view that tragic history repeats itself as farce.

26. See the Author to Horner letter 338-42. Are we to believe, from the fiction, Author John Barth's claim that people wrote letters to him about therapies concocted in *The End of the Road?* "Art and life are symbiotic" (L 341).

27. I take up the implications of this strategy later in the chapter, in discussion of metafiction and metahistory.

28. John Barth, *The Sot-Weed Factor,* 1960. Subsequent page references are to the Grosset and Dunlap edition.

Letters to Literature

183

29. The "prenatal" and "posthumous" letters of A.B. Cook IV and the letters of A.B. Cook VI.

30. Denham Sutcliffe, "Worth a Guilty Conscience," reprinted from *The Kenyon Review* 1961, in Joseph J. Waldmeir, *Critical Essays on John Barth.* See 113.

31. John Barth, *Giles Goat-Boy,* 11. Subsequent page references are marked GGB and are to the Penguin edition of the text.

32. Labels for Bray mix madness and insight: "madman," "solicitous mosquito," "amateur Stanislavski-Method actor, and amateur historian" (Lady Amherst); "Sodomite" (Merry Bernstein, MBl); "Certainly mad but as certainly not simply mad" (A.B. Cook VI); "Gadfly," "Godflow," "Gadflaw" (Bray).

33. Barthes, *S/Z,* 11.

34. Charles Harris, *Passionate Virtuosity,* 178.

35. I provide a deconstructive analysis of this doubling, in comparison with Italo Calvino's *If on a winter's night a traveler,* in "Deconstructing the Artist and the Art: Barth and Calvino at Play in the Funhouse of Language."

36. Another story about a writer creating a story, "Anonymiad" provides a striking figure for the reception of stories as well as for the genesis of all story-telling. Marooned on the rocky outcrop, addressing his muse and creating his last story, the isolated narrator can only launch it upon the sea: "Will anyone have learnt its name? Will everyone? No matter. Upon this noontime of his wasting day, between the night past and the long night to come, a noon beautiful enough to break the heart, on a lorn fair shore a nameless minstrel Wrote it" (LF 194).

37. The bee-swarm is also associated with Saint Ambrose, providing the name that Barth links with the Ambrose Lightship outside New York harbour and with ambrosia, food of the Olympian gods.

38. Reilly Interview, 15. Barth has expressed his enthusiasm for the character: "Germaine Gordon Pitt is a remarkable woman, whom I'm proud to have conceived and brought to light. You'd like her." Interview with Angela Gerst, "Speaking of *LETTERS,*" *The Friday Book,* 174.

39. Barthes, "The Death of the Author," 146.

40. Reilly Interview, 9:

"I have no business assuming my readers have pored over my previous works, so the rule in my house is that it's okay to bring back or refer to past characters if you don't presume for even one sentence that even one reader has so much as heard of any of them. The corollary to the rule is that everything the reader needs to know must be right there in the text at hand. That was my intention, at any rate; I hope I was successful."

184   *Theories of Play and Postmodern Fiction*

41. Fredric Jameson, "Postmodernism and Consumer Society," in Kaplan ed., *Postmodernism and Its Discontents,* 21-5.

42. See 191, 223, 252, 341.

43. The expression is Jonathan Culler's. See his *Structuralist Poetics: Structuralism, Linguistics and the Study of Language,* 130.

44. Edward Said, *The World, the Text, and the Critic,* 5.

45. Note, particularly, the two Author to the Reader letters, 42-5, and 771-2.

46. John Barth, "Muse, Spare Me," 28.

47. Max F. Schulz, "Barth, *LETTERS,* and the Great Tradition," 107.

48. Gerald Graff, "Under our belt and off our back: Barth's *LETTERS* and postmodern fiction," 160. Graff's view that *LETTERS* contains no theory of history, and his doubt that Barth (in contrast with Borges) has anything to say about the twentieth century, sit in opposition to my view of the text and its evocation of contexts. But we start with different perceptions of "truth," "history" and the nature of texts in their relationships with the world. To suggest, as Graff does (153), that "Literary forms become obsolete when they no longer tell, or are thought to tell, the truth about the world," is to reduce to misleading simplicity the state of contemporary debate about truth, texts and language.

49. White, *Metahistory,* ix. In this study, White explores the styles of four historians, Michelet, Ranke, Tocqueville and Burckhardt, in terms of four philosophers of history, Hegel, Marx, Nietzsche and Croce respectively. See also his *Tropics of Discourse.*

50. In his studies of comparative religion and mythology, Eliade emphasizes the sense of Great Time in a number of tribal religions and repetitions that are conceived as a recreation of that time. See, particularly, Mircea Eliade, *The Myth of the Eternal Return: Or, Cosmos and History.*

51. See Harris, *Passionate Virtuosity,* 162.

52. The relationship of particular concern in *Lost in the Funhouse* and *Chimera.*

53. John Fowles, *Mantissa,* 1982. Subsequent references are to the Triad/Panther edition, signified by the letter M and the page reference. Although Erato is the most overt example, there are various muse-figures in Fowles's writings: Miranda in *The Collector,* Sarah Woodruff in *The French Lieutenant's Woman,* Mouse in *The Ebony Tower* and Jane in *Daniel Martin.* While he riddles self-consciously about the artifice of fiction, choice and authorial control, his metafictional works are not so much self-effacing as

Letters to Literature

invitations to a number of plays in which the author-magus enjoys his authority. Writing about his lack of control over filming of *The Magus,* Fowles adds:

"I come back with a sort of relief, a re-affirmation in my faith in the novel. For all its faults, it is a statement by one person. In my novels I am the producer, director, and all the actors; I photograph it. This may seem a megalomania beside which the more celebrated cases from Hollywood pale to nothingness. There *is* a vanity about it, a wish to play the godgame, which all the random and author-removing devices of avant-garde technique cannot hide."

(John Fowles, "Notes on an Unfinished Novel," in Malcolm Bradbury ed., *The Novel Today,* 144).

54. Problematic four-letter word it may be, but Barth returns to it persistently, and even as Helen's answer to Menelaus's persistent "Why?" at the extravagant formal centre of "Menelaiad." See *Lost in the Funhouse,* 150.

55. Barth, *Sabbatical: A Romance,* 365.

56. This emphasis upon the invitational aspect of meta-perspectives is not new, of course. As one would expect, studies of metafiction characteristically analyse the text's "placing" of the reader. See, for example, Hutcheon's discussion in *Narcissistic Narrative,* 138-142. Metafiction makes the act of reading self-conscious, and it may do this in a number of different ways. The ways range from overt "Dear Reader" messages to more covert strategies of narrative discontinuity which induce reflection about the process.

57. I do not wish to discuss each of these via examples in the text. The point is well made by Charles Harris, in *Passionate Virtuosity,* 168-9.

58. Fiction has so often provided fare for films, so that the "film-of-the-book" is a standard phenomenon of the industry. Puig's *Kiss of the Spider Woman* and Thomson's *Suspects* use film to present fiction.

59. I am using Barthes's terms from *S/Z;* see 4-6. The self-consciousness of postmodernist texts, with their attendant invitation to readers to become "producers," makes them distinctively "writerly" texts in this categorisation.

60. I refer to the meanings played upon throughout the text but summarised in the Author to Mensch letter of Part 6, 654: letters as letters of the alphabet, epistles to readers, and the phenomenon of literature.

61. Calvino, *If on a winter's night a traveler,* 200.

62. Patricia Waugh, *Metafiction,* 35.

CHAPTER 4

Strategies of Influence: Intertextual Infiltration in Robert Kroetsch's *What the Crow Said* [1]

GHOSTS OF THE PAST

> I want to avoid both meaning and conclusiveness. And one way to achieve this is to keep *retelling,* keep transforming the story. It is the old trick of Proteus or the trickster figure. [2]

Protean transformations of "the story": although there are many ways of theorising influence, its existence is as inescapable as its diversity is problematic. Whether one conceptualises the press of history, tradition, mythology, story, or the inheritance as a debilitating weight upon present performance, a cause of *anxiety* or of *exhaustion,* or as an inviting playing field whose configurations change remarkably and whose detail compels reformulations, "it" is the provisional and alterable context, ground idea, narrative impulse or construct for the play of meaning. While analyses of texts and the production of meanings may be formal, historical, aesthetic, or philosophical, it is because texts are variously contextual, embedded in the discursive formations of their origins and reception, that they also have cultural and political dimensions involving questions of position, range of reference and focus. Further, since distinctions can be drawn between the contextual fields that a text may be said to signal overtly *in itself* and the contexts that may be constructed in the performance of a reading, the site is always open to changing interpretations. Just as authors shall deliberately or unconsciously invoke predecessors and contexts for reception of their writing, so readers discover meanings

188   *Theories of Play and Postmodern Fiction*

according to the baggage of texts, experience and expectation that constitutes their particular coding. Intertextual possibilities are expansive and it is a commonplace of postmodernist practice (following Barthes, Derrida, Bloom and Kristeva) to acknowledge influence and to perceive the text not as transparent product of an author-creator, its meaning single and clear, but, rather as a "mosaic of quotations,"[3] its capacity for meanings variable and complex. Via pastiche and parody, citation and interaction, ghosts of the past inhabit new texts, re-appearing like old "familiars" to play the devil against the undivided Word and, as Borges suggests in the conceit of "Pierre Menard, Author of the *Quixote*," the "new" text, though verbally identical with the "original," is "almost infinitely richer";[4] alternatively, Cervantes' *Don Quixote* is transformed by three centuries of literary-cultural accretion, displacement, supplementarity, change. The site of meaning is never still.

Within an overview that holds play as endemic to culture, refuses the opposition of play to seriousness, and emphasizes literature as interactive process, a site of complex exchanges, I have argued that Pynchon's *Gravity's Rainbow* is, in its extraordinary range of procedures as well as reference, a definitive example of the decentered text and that Barth's *LETTERS* games not only with letters but also with "the world" as it is represented in language. Each text exemplifies the play that is in language and invites readers to a cooperative examination of the ways of communication and relationships between literature and cultural contexts. Difference is value and the regenerative qualities of these subversive texts displace the past by rereading it as variable constructions of the past.

In this chapter, having addressed already the processes of influence as an area of interest in *Gravity's Rainbow* and *LETTERS,* I wish to take a specific and more confined example of overt intertextual play, the example of Robert Kroetsch's *What the Crow Said* in its appropriation of strategies of Latin American "magical realism" as they are defined in Gabriel García Márquez's *One Hundred Years of Solitude.* Kroetsch acknowledges this influence: "I think that particular text, *One Hundred Years of Solitude,* is what triggered me into *What the Crow Said.* "[5] It is an influence shared by Canadian West Coaster, Jack Hodgins, notably in his novel *The Invention of the World,*[6] and his view of the excitement of literary borrowings and connections supports

Strategies of Influence 189

Kroetsch's initiative and reinforces the theory of intertextual infiltration presented by Barthes and Kristeva:

> That coastline that goes past Vancouver and past my house goes right down past Fuentes' Mexico and Vargas Llosa's Peru and Márquez's Columbia, and I don't want to make too much of it but there is that connection which is as tangible as the CPR lines across Canada, as far as literature is concerned. All literatures are foreign literatures and, as I think I've said somewhere else, you're faced with the choice of being influenced by nothing, and writing in a vacuum, by pretending that the West Coast native culture is your own, or by deciding that all literature in the world is yours equally, and to be touched—if that's what influence means—to be touched by any work that excites you no matter where it comes from. [7]

Although Hodgins comments upon deliberate writerly choices, whereas the theory of intertextuality expressed by Barthes and Kristeva emphasizes the inevitability of influence as residual to the operations of language, his enthusiasm for the possibilities of borrowing sets a very positive basis for action by readers as well as by writers. It is an enthusiasm that Kroetsch shares: "I really take pleasure in that sense of influence. You meet writers who are afraid of being influenced. It should be the opposite: writers should be afraid of *not* being influenced."[8] And, as I interpret the possibilities of this process, there is no necessary contradiction between the ways of influence, in their limited "grounding," and the openness of discontinuities or what Derrida has defined as the Nietzschean affirmation, "the joyous affirmation of the play of the world and of the innocence of becoming, the affirmation of a world of signs without fault, without truth, and without origin which is offered to an active interpretation."[9] Against the constraints of local geography, history, culture and time, although not in ignorance of them, a text's capacity for meanings can be refined and explored, complicated and expanded, against ending. Accepting the play of the supplement, or trace, in language allows the game to happen against nostalgia over lost origins or the impulse towards final meaning—these forms of closure.

Kroetsch has suggested that Canadian writing "takes place between the vastness of (closed) cosmologies and the fragments found in the open field of the archaeological site." In this middle ground where the

190   *Theories of Play and Postmodern Fiction*

writing "comes to a genealogy that refuses origin," there is "the welcome dream of Babel."[10] Applauding openness against both the reductiveness of national stereotyping and perceptions of the literary text as a place of fixed meaning, he repeats a preference evident in his fiction and in his criticism. The place *between* is the place of diversity and difference. With its emphasis upon process and (con)fusion, or the interplay of systems and detail, tradition and innovation, inheritance and experimentation, this "place" in its ambiguity and in the interests of transforming the story simultaneously invites and resists definition. Hence there occurs the double bind that Robert Lecker perceives as the central and enabling characteristic of Kroetsch's writing, the dialectical interplay of varied sets of oppositions which produces ambivalence as "the hallmark of the borderman's art."[11] One important aspect of this multiplicity is the "presence" of other writers in Kroetsch's work, a presence he acknowledges readily—Ovid, Cervantes, Joyce, Faulkner, and above all Conrad[12]—and, indeed, there are recognizable traces of their influence, thematically and strategically, in the novels. Kroetsch's strong interest in displacement, substitution and playful transformation, together with his inclusion of mythological allusions and the crafting of fragments which may contain entire stories, might be traced to Ovid; his interest in oral story-telling and the rural community, and his mixing of myth and history as categories, or his edging of the notionally real into the fantastic, suggest the influence of Faulkner and Hardy; his making incompletion and uncertainty the focus of character, meaning and the presentational process itself—this self-conscious and self-reflexive attention to the telling in recognition of the duplicity of language—are reminders of Conrad's Marlow. Kroetsch's self-reflexive fiction, while replaying variations on Cervantes and Sterne, can also be considered in the company of contemporary metafiction: the works of Nabokov, Borges, Beckett, Barth, Calvino, Pynchon, and so on. Intertextual inscriptions proliferate overtly in the fiction and as variable frames by which readers may participate as co-"authors" of the texts. So the succession of wanderers, Michael Hornyak, Johnnie Backstrom, Hazard Lepage, Jeremy Sadness, William Dawe and Dorf repeat traditional quest motifs only by ironic displacement of them, by acknowledging the classical pattern while simultaneously uninventing it through comic eroticism, tricksterism and parody—or, as Kroetsch has described his play upon this inheritance, by intruding "the shabbiness of Ovid . . . his inconsistencies"[13] into the supposed

Strategies of Influence 191

coherence of story. It is not just that the priapic wanderers are defined in ironic pairings with oppositional characters whose affiliation with centrism, convention and order serves as a control upon their deconstructive energy. The liaisons are complicated, and the binaries challenged, by the parodic representation of the control group too, particularly Demeter Proudfoot, Mark Madham, Anna Dawe and Karen Strike, whose ordering activities as characters are displaced by the concentrations on contingency and discontinuities in the texts that present them. They, and the narratives "they" create as surrogate writers, recorders and mediators of the flawed quest, are as unsettling of the inheritance as the odd "heroes" of their attention.

Ironically misnamed Demeter's pedantic attention to dates, lists, numbers and his card index, as a check on the odyssean wanderer, parodies rather than confirms objectivity and the dream of verisimilitudinous narrative. Become the madman in the bathtub, this biographer's pursuit of "the naked truth" (172) and his faith in mimesis are subverted by a postmodernist epistemology that emphasizes comic absurdity and uncertainty against the constraints of empiricism, causal explanation and linear form. Transferring its ironic play upon the Homeric epic to 1945 and the Great Plains of North America, *The Studhorse Man* thus complicates the reading game not only by dramatising the conflict between opposing systems of perception and value but by presenting this dramatisation in a text more in sympathy with the Lepage motto "NOTHING IN MODERATION" (120) than with Demeter Proudfoot's preference for "an ordered world" (61).[14] Similarly, the formal intricacies of *Gone Indian* favour the wanderer, both character and signifier, by deconstructing the metaphysical implications of orderly chronological narrative. Paradoxically, the possibilities of Jeremy Sadness's flight "west," against cultural accretions and the dead ends of convention, are accentuated by his minder's zeal for codes and explanation—if the research student as surrogate son defies his professorial supervisor and the paternal tradition, it is also the case that the taped reports, in their fragmentariness and spontaneity, resist the mediation of Madham's epistolary frame in his attempt to explain everything. Against the imperatives of beginnings and endings as explanatory conventions, the intersection of different narrative forms asserts the contingencies of process. Against "his" attempts as academic supervisor, Professor Mark Madham is undone, and even converted, by the tricksterism of his text.

192   *Theories of Play and Postmodern Fiction*

In this consideration of intertextual unsettlings, *Badlands* and *Alibi* are of particular interest because of their presentation, against traditional mythological forms and centuries of repetitions, of the female quester. More than mediators of the male adventure story, Anna Dawe and Karen Strike have the role of active agent as storyteller, of maker not muse. So for this "not Penelope," Anna Dawe: "I bought my gin by the case, bought and read my books by the parcel, imagined to myself a past, an ancestor, a legend, a vision, a fate" (3).[15] Bumping into the badlands of William Dawe's expedition, with Indian woman Anna Yellowbird and cases of Gordon's gin aboard the Mercedes-Benz, she is the investigator *and* story-maker, a female insurgent into the Homeric and Conradian journey into the underworld or darkness of time, consciousness and representation. Presenting Anna Dawe's telling as imaginative reconstruction, as story rather than report, *Badlands* questions the idea of "reality" as a given just as it acknowledges by displacement the traditions of quest within which and against which its meanings are extended. *Alibi,* too, plays with the inheritance. Seemingly conventional, a narrative in journal form presented as the tellings of a male narrator, it is, rather, a work of considerable contrivance in which the "male" story is the product of a female editorializer. Just as the idea of a "valid" Dorf journal is subverted by the uncertainty of Karen Strike's part as editor/creator, narrative coherence and conventions of characterization, structure and point of view are unsettled. Typically, Kroetsch's work self-consciously acknowledges and displaces the literary legacy by references that emphasize the interplay as an open process.[16]

The possibilities for pursuit are many, the "mosaic of quotations" extensive and growing. But in *What the Crow Said,* it is the magical realism of Latin-American writing, and of García Márquez's work in particular, that provides the leading reverberations. Reading *What the Crow Said* through the text of *One Hundred Years of Solitude* helps to elucidate Kroetsch's narrative strategies in this ludic and self-reflexive novel, his recreation of a rural Alberta in mythic terms and out of an oral tradition of story-telling.

COLLUSIONS: MACAWS AT THE SNOWLINE

The development of Latin-American fiction since the 1940s,[17] from a largely social-realist tradition of mimetic intention and regional focus,

Strategies of Influence

193

shows signs of extensive literary influence (particularly that of Kafka, Proust, Joyce, and Faulkner together with renewed attention to Cervantes and Rabelais) upon an exotic physical and cultural landscape. In addition to their being influenced by European and American writing, the writers of Latin America find inspiration in new Latin-American writing, in the work of their near contemporaries. [18] So, for example, although Borges's precise asceticism may not be evident in the exuberant writings of Vargas Llosa, Infante, Fuentes, Cortázar, Carpentier, García Márquez, and Puig, his sceptical treatment of knowledge and language as fields for elaborate games is immediately apparent in their work. Like his, though not with the same economy, their writings too acknowledge the artifice and power of language and present reality as a construct with which not only fabulists, but also philosophers, historians, schoolteachers, and politicians play.

Acknowledging the influence of writing upon writing, and the curious relationships between cultures and their expression in literature, what characteristics in Latin-American experience may contribute to *lo real maravilloso?* What produces this literature "more exotic than a collection of macaws"?[19] The explanation offered by Cuban novelist Alejo Carpentier indicates the inseparability of myth and history, and the sense in which "the real" is a product of the processes of its construction:

> The fact is that, in the virginity of its landscape, in its coming together, in its ontology, in the Faustian presence of Indian and Negro, in the sense of revelation arising from its recent discovery, in the fertile mixtures of race which it engendered, [Latin] America is very far from having used up its abundance of mythologies. . . . For what is the story of [Latin] America if not a chronicle of the marvelous in the real?[20]

Carpentier wrote this essay in 1949. The ideas are expanded in a lecture given in the Caracas Athenaeum on May 22, 1975, and translated as "The Baroque and the Marvelous Real." He defines the baroque as a spirit and style appearing in all periods, associating it with expression of the extraordinary and strange, involving mutability, proliferation, excess, variety and crowding. Manifest in painting, architecture, sculpture and literature, it may well, he suggests, invade the very citadel of classicism itself. For Carpentier, magical realism is the Latin

194   *Theories of Play and Postmodern Fiction*

American expression of this baroque spirit, the expression of an inheritance developed from the meeting of Empire and native cultures and developed over centuries with continuing emphasis upon the extraordinary in the local and particular. If this preserves the capacity for wonder and amazement at the world's variety, it does so not naively but with erudition to match the enthusiasm of its expression. Again, in 1975, Carpentier comes back to the particular fascination of the Latin American realities—which is also to say, the particular modes of perception of their creative interpreters:

> We have forged a language appropriate to the expression of our realities, and the events that await us will find that we, the novelists of Latin America, are the witnesses, historians, and interpreters of our great Latin American reality. We have prepared ourselves for this, we have studied our classics, our authors, and our history. In order to express our moment in America, we have sought and found our maturity. We will be the classics of an enormous baroque world that still holds the most extraordinary surprises for us and for the world. (107-8)

Latin America has a most diverse topography with climatic extremes and a varied human calendar, a perplexed history of invasion, revolutions and civil wars, foreign development and exploitation, machismo, passion and the exoticism of carnival to colour its pages.[21] From this abundance, and drawing upon oral traditions of story-telling which intermingle the magic of dreaming with the trivia of daily existence, the writers create their countries of the mind in which boundaries between fact and fantasy become as intangible as the point of origin in Derrida's complication of the genealogy of texts:

> In its syntax and its lexicon, in its spacing, by its punctuation, its lacunae, its margins, the historical appurtenance of a text is never a straight line. It is neither causality by contagion, nor the simple accumulation of layers. Nor even the pure juxtaposition of borrowed pieces. And if a text always gives itself a certain representation of its own roots, those roots live only by that representation by never touching the soil, so to speak. [22]

Strategies of Influence 195

No straight line or simple accumulation of layers, or of borrowings: in its movement from garden state to windstorm, Eden to Apocalypse, *One Hundred Years of Solitude* presents an historical chronicle so mythologized that human history itself may seem to be reincarnated in the gossipy domestic detail of the generations of Buendias in Macondo. Although the text may be read as an imaginative recreation of the history of Colombia, centred upon García Márquez's birthplace, Aracataca, its merging of the "marvellous" and the "real," together with its concentration on magical motifs and patterns, creates a collective mythic consciousness that transcends while not denying specificities of place and time. However much Macondo and its people are inspired by García Márquez's memories of Aracataca, the text invites a reading in terms of other texts, (his)story in terms of other histories/stories, from biblical to textbook history, Ovid to Borges. Ovid, Cervantes, and Rabelais, and, from the twentieth century, particularly Conrad, Woolf, Kafka, Faulkner and Borges: it is not surprising that these are the writers whose influence García Márquez acknowledges,[23] since their concentrations on magical transformation, on uncertainty and its correlatives (possibility and multiplicity), and, above all, on the trickeries of language and story-telling, subvert naturalism to create more fantastic realities. Traces of such explorers of dream and myth and language are evident in his fiction, in the stories as well as the longer works. Because the predecessor texts are themselves intertextual, notions of origin are (as Derrida suggests) complicated and reading is challenging, more a matter of trading cards with the devil than accepting the undivided word of God.

By the circuitous paths of influence, then, the world is brought to Macondo and is represented in Macondo's mythology. Alternatively, Macondo is a metaphor for the world—provided that, in the complicated processes of exchange, allowance is also made for its relevance to Colombian history. Similarly, the elaborate formal conceit by which Melquiades' mysterious parchments become the text we read locates the final Aureliano, their decipherer and reader, as the metatextual equivalent of all readers of *One Hundred Years of Solitude*. Trained on Seneca and Ovid by the wise Catalonian bookstore proprietor and former professor of classical literature, Aureliano discovers that "literature was the best plaything that had ever been invented to make fun of people."[24] Self-reflexive of the linguistic play

196   *Theories of Play and Postmodern Fiction*

of the text, this "discovery" also stands as a cautionary note against narrowly reductive readings.

What, then, are the strategies by which García Márquez's text creates its sense of the fantastic, and to what extent are these replicated in *What the Crow Said?* The following comparative discussion concentrates on narrative strategies in order to look, in turn, at narrative voice and position, perspectives on time, and techniques contributing to the creation of character and community. Of course *What the Crow Said* communicates "up front,"[25] as it were, and in its "own" right; it may be read independently of *One Hundred Years of Solitude* as a "Canadian" text that dabbles with stories told by farm boys and biblical accretions, or the reconstructed suspicions, dreams, events and narratives that constitute local lore. But the connections reemphasize the elements of conceptual play and, since both works are concerned self-reflexively with the nature of meaning, to trace this intertextuality is to focus upon the central epistemological concern.

Attempting to define the fantastic, Todorov suggests that reader uncertainty is its primary condition, that a text must persuade the reader to consider its world of characters as a world of living persons but to hesitate between natural and supernatural explanations of events.[26] Its dissolution of boundaries, between natural and supernatural, real and fantastic, to the extent that the fantastic is presented as real, is the definitive characteristic of *One Hundred Years of Solitude* and the source of its mythology and its wonder. A similar dissolution marks Kroetsch's narrative method in *What the Crow Said.* Each text makes exuberant use of hyperbole, blends dream and waking, suspends the notion of time as linear progression, dissolves the boundary between life and death, and involves the reader in its self-reflexive reminders of text as artifice, explanation as uncertain, and multiple possibilities as the condition of communication in language. Presented by an all-comprehending narrator who is able to interweave past, present, and future, to anticipate events, and to function as imperturbable reporter of the fantastic and the mundane in the same guise of fidelity to fact, each text illuminates "the dance between myth and reality [. . .] the two dancing together,"[27] inviting the reader not to observe and judge, but to join in the dance.

Narrative position, then, providing perspectives on time and character, establishes the main framework not only for writer as artificer, but for reader as participant in a deconstructive-reconstructive

Strategies of Influence

activity, and Kroetsch's comment on this position indicates the appropriateness of *One Hundred Years of Solitude* as reading screen: "When I was writing *What the Crow Said,* beginning *Years later . . .,* suddenly just with that phrase, I had available to me all that people said years later, that whole fabric of gossip and story."[28] The first sentence of *What the Crow Said*—"People, years later, blamed everything on the bees; it was the bees, they said, seducing Vera Lang, that started everything" (7)—evokes the first sentence of *One Hundred Years of Solitude*—"Many years later, as he faced the firing squad, Colonel Aureliano Buendía was to remember that distant afternoon when his father took him to discover ice" (7). The connections are not merely semantic; rather, each sentence introduces the perspective of an omniscient narrator, prepares for free play in the treatment of time (to the point of timelessness), and adds signposts to the narrative that alert reader expectation and promise surprises in presentation. A game is on; the play begins.

Kroetsch's interest in an Albertan oral tradition ("I have to [go] back and rehear Alberta in a quite different way")[29] is a means of taking story back to folklore origins, to that treasure-house of anecdote and exaggeration, either real or imagined, where humour and spontaneity and superstition are less inhibited by scientific rationalization, and where the free flow of dream and imagination may be naturalized as the very condition of waking reality. Because of the withdrawn, omniscient narrator-as-faithful-reporter, the fantastic is not overtly mediated by any sceptical censor, and Kroetsch's interest in origins, new-world naming, and story-telling (this process of relearning Alberta, what we are or might be, via a creative archaeological dig) produces a process that mythologizes, and a narrative that is mythic. His repeated emphasis that this process is an exercise in un-naming, un-creating, and un-inventing, an exercise represented in the self-reflexive and parodic foregrounding of artifice in the novels, is equivalent to the deconstructionists' problematization of notions of origin, truth, and closure.[30] In *One Hundred Years of Solitude,* the similar narrative position also arises from an interest in oral story-telling and alternative, unofficial perspectives on social-political history.[31] It facilitates the text's presentation of wonder together with the ambiguities of nostalgia, its combination of mythological or folk perspectives with a twentieth-century "detachment" that mixes indulgence with criticism, dream with denunciation. García Márquez's attribution of influence to his maternal

198   *Theories of Play and Postmodern Fiction*

grandparents, in particular to his grandmother's story-telling, is well known—"Everything I have written I knew or I had heard before I was eight years old"—and, a willing interviewee, he has supplied prosaic explanations for the origins of such fabulism in the text as acts of levitation, and the sky filling with yellow butterflies.[32] Even so, although interesting and plausible, such explanations remain outside the text, and they do not reduce the magic of its conception and language which are better read, for example, via Ovid, Kafka, or Borges. The surreal is the real when José Arcadio Buendía proclaims ice "the great invention of our time" (22), when Remedios the Beauty appears amidst clouds of yellow butterflies, when a trickle of blood negotiates the labyrinth of streets to convey news of a death, and so on. Dissolving conventional distinctions between time past and future, truth and falsehood, and the fabulous and the real, all reported via an imperturbable narrative voice pedantic in its attention to detail, the text creates its colourful and primitive folk consciousness, wherein experience of ice is indeed a marvel, and the absurd pronouncement, "The earth is round like an orange" (10), signifies madness. It is in the overlap of the real and the surreal, that author and reader collude on the textual play, tacitly acknowledging the intertexts and their simultaneous deconstruction and reconstruction of the text at hand and the realities that this text prefigures.

A central focus in each text, then, the manner in which time is treated in *One Hundred Years of Solitude* is also discoverable in *What the Crow Said.* Set against the chronological progression of six generations of family saga, and the numbered sequence of pages in which that saga is created, is the discovery that Melquiades (gypsy, magus, prophet, muse, persona) has written this family history one hundred years ahead of time. Furthermore, he "had not put events in the order of man's conventional time, but had concentrated a century of daily episodes in such a way that they coexisted in one instant" (382). Granting Melquiades this miraculous foresight is the in-text equivalent of declaring its narrator's omniscience. The omniscient narrator exercises characteristics of Coyote *and* God, with power to compress, make leaps backwards and forwards, predict and summarize in ways that dislocate linear progression and simple perspectives on temporal-spatial relations. The strategy produces complex structures that involve cyclical patterns, the idea of time repeating itself and the pervasive sense of myth. The notion that one hundred years of time can exist in

Strategies of Influence 199

an instant is a sophisticated one, and it becomes a precise metatextual acknowledgement, an indication of the nature of the text itself as "total" source and container of those *cien anos.* Because the pages of the text coexist, they evoke simultaneously family founders José Arcadio Buendía and Ursula Iguaran, the final Aureliano, and all between as textual signifiers awaiting a reader to select their page. Melquiades' foreknowledge is supplemented by the prophetic insight of other characters: their anticipation is based upon sensitivity and memory, although presented as both natural and mystical. So, for example, 145-year-old Pilar Ternera anticipates recurrences in the circling patterns of the Buendía family history:

> There was no mystery in the heart of a Buendía that was impenetrable for her because a century of cards and experience had taught her that the history of the family was a machine with unavoidable repetitions, a turning wheel that would have gone on spinning into eternity were it not for the progressive and irremediable wearing of the axle. (364-65)

Also, Ursula, Earth Mother, witness to her great-grandson José Arcadio Segundo's radicalism, exclaims "Just like Aureliano [her son] . . . It's as if the world were repeating itself" (275). Shaped by recurrences and the crossing of boundaries between reality and fantasy and life and death, the timelessness (the artifice) of *One Hundred Years of Solitude* as fable transcends the minutiae of change in its seasonal, social, political, and historical aspects. That timelessness is most appropriately symbolized in the eternal fragment of Melquiades' room, where it is always March and always Monday, the room in which the parchments (the text) are written *and* deciphered, the hypothetical fixed point where writer and reader collaborate to produce the text. It is pertinent in this representation of the place of creativity as a magical space that it be an intersection of perspectives (by turns seen as supernaturally fresh and dust free, a waste-heap stinking with the smell of rotten memories, the chamber-pot room and a haven) as well as the schoolroom of Aureliano's reading instruction. Metaphor for the scene of writing (and also of reading), it is context dependent *and* transcendent, product *and* source, the product of history and literature and language which it, in turn, reconstructs with ebullient difference.

200 *Theories of Play and Postmodern Fiction*

Mythical Macondo, Colombia; mythical Big Indian, Alberta. As struggling wordsmith and rememberer of the future (because Gutenberg has made all memory of the past irrelevant), Liebhaber is prophet and chronicler of *What the Crow Said,* a comical Melquiades. Here, too, prophecy provides textual signposts, fragmenting simple linear narrative and reinforcing awareness of the text as artifice, and of meaning as a cultural construction. When, remembering the future, Liebhaber remembers the night that Martin Lang will die and, later, the coming of "one godawful nut-buster of a flood" (145), the narrative method, as in *One Hundred Years of Solitude,* subverts (with Todorov's uncertainty about explanation) conventional naturalism to introduce supernaturalism, and to contribute to the text's myth-making. So Liebhaber carries the burden of Martin Lang's frozen corpse and converses with him across the boundary of life and death, just as José Arcadio Buendía converses with regular visitor Prudencio Aguilar, the man he killed in a duel of honour. Liebhaber's projected flood comes to the municipality of Bigknife after a period of searing wind during "The War Against the Sky" and constitutes a variation on the fantastic struggles of humankind against the elements in *One Hundred Years of Solitude.* In each text, the community's struggle for survival against natural forces (their trial) invokes a common archetypal pattern, a mythological subtext that presents the idea of timelessness through its emphasis upon ancient forms and their repeatability and is part of each author's acknowledged desire to return to "origins." That the pattern's meaning and significance depend on echo and allusion, or the intertextual inscriptions which create the archaeological site, also indicates the instability of the sign and the incessant dialectic between particular and general (or other) aspects of textuality. As Derrida suggests, in a characteristic assertion of the unceasing play of intertextuality which simultaneously creates and erodes meaning, "This interweaving, this textile, is the *text* produced only in the transformation of another text. Nothing, neither among the elements nor within the system, is anywhere ever simply present or absent. There are only, everywhere, differences and traces of traces."[33] Foucault is more optimistic than Derrida about pinning down the traces but, either way, the tracking of meanings is a more exciting prospect than the closure of fixed definition, a contract which would limit discourse to the possibilities permitted by that particular definitional framework. Thus, just as *One Hundred Years of Solitude* presents in displaced

Strategies of Influence   201

forms its reading of Colombian social and political history with references to population increases, growth of towns, foreign influence, the impact of technological change, the history of the United Tropical Fruit Company, civil wars and the fortunes of particular political figures, it also invokes larger narrative patterns and symbolic markers (the movement from origin to end, Eden to Apocalypse, and the dialectics of nature and culture, love and death, past and present, desire and loss, memory and forgetting) that create relationships between this story and others, this national story and patterns in world history, or the conceptual and linguistic play between specific history and myth-making. Similarly, with the ambiguous location of its Big Indian community and its attention to ritual and folklore, desire and dreaming, birth, madness, death and story-making, *What the Crow Said* exceeds the restrictions of conventional text-book history for its magical realist plays upon constructions of the past as symbolic remembering.

García Márquez's style of magical realism is also evident in Kroetsch's presentation of characters and event in *What the Crow Said,* and the opening sentence establishes the perspective that this text, as a whole, elaborates: "People, years later, blamed everything on the bees; it was the bees, they said, seducing Vera Lang, that started everything" (7). The fabulous is made real; Vera Lang *is* seduced by the bees; the supernatural event is made the explanation of natural phenomena as myth becomes reality. Vera's mysterious pregnancy and her aloofness from men ("men are a bunch of useless bastards" [14]) are explained in the fabulous erotics of signifiers that recall Zeus's courting of Danäe in the form of a shower of gold: "they knew no man would satisfy her. Not one. No mortal man would satisfy her" (13). When townsfolk link peculiarities in the seasons and unusual events with Vera Lang, who is beautiful and cold, she becomes their scapegoat and the object for repressed male desire. As Liebhaber, spokesman, tries to explain to the crow: "She was pretending not to possess the beautiful but mortal body that had once been naked to the bees. . . . 'The whole country is bitched'" (64). So stories can serve as explanations, and *What the Crow Said,* like *One Hundred Years of Solitude,* is a novel about story-making, about the stories that people create, bullshit and beauty that arise from explorations of self and society; and within the linguistic play which deconstructs fixed definitions, character is as uncertain a concept, a literary construct, as any other. Set amongst traditional images of springtime fertility, and against such recognizable rituals of

202   *Theories of Play and Postmodern Fiction*

farm life as Old Lady Lang's attention in the cellar to sprouting potatoes and Tiddy Lang's work keeping the bull from the cows' paddock, Vera's impregnation by bees celebrates not only passion but also the rhythms of seasonal change and flow, growth and regeneration in ways that paradoxically re-emphasize the familiar by introducing the marvellous, bringing the mythologically-charged golden swarm to "the whole nectar of her world-old virgin body" (12). Obsessed with bees, "arrogantly pregnant" (37), constructing her strange newspaper reports, giving birth, continuing to provoke desire, taking a succession of husbands who die remarkable deaths, afloat in a drifting granary on the flooded river, Vera Lang is a figure of fable, Keats's "belle dame sans merci" in a prairies culture. When this queen bee is united with Marvin Straw the hangman as maddened and desiring lover, high farce contends with figurative resolution in Kroetsch's play upon antitheses.

The fabulism of García Márquez's presentation of the Buendías in *One Hundred Years of Solitude,* and especially Petra Cotes' association with supernatural fertility, is evoked in the pattern of marvellous fecundity produced by Vera's seduction by the bees and emphasized in the procession of remarkable pregnancies at the Lang farm. Desire contends with death, and the resulting fluctuations in each text are attended by Earth Mother figures (Ursula Iguaran and Tiddy Lang). Reading men's fortunes in her roles as mysterious prophet and gossipy folk historian, Old Lady Lang becomes Melquiades metamorphosed. Inspiring male desire, variously associated with death, and combining Eros and Thanatos, Vera Lang symbolizes the eternal struggle between love and death which is also central to the generations of Buendías. In its delineation of these contending forces, Kroetsch's text repeatedly reveals its magical realism in ways that recall the predecessor text. Fabulously pregnant by O'Holleran's absent phallus, Rose, as creator of cemeteries for dead birds and the family crockery, evokes memories of the Buendías' solitude and their "hereditary vice of making something just to unmake it" (352); the repressed sensuality of Amaranta and earth-eating Rebeca is repeated in Kroetsch's portrait of Rita Lang, epistolean, whose erotic letters to imprisoned men (the replies to which all lie unopened and arranged in shoe boxes under her bed) are representative of sensualist and author, desire and dream:

> She imagined them all, her faithful men, ripping open the scented
> envelopes that she so carefully slipped into the mail: Rita, bent at the

Strategies of Influence 203

table, slowly unbuttoning her blouse, furtive and wanton, lifting a nipple to her mouth. The quick flash of her tongue against the rising nipple, the motion of her pen. On and on she wrote, driving her imprisoned lovers to the edge of a terrible dream, a terrible flying. (213)

Pietro Crespi's suicide and Colonel Gerineldo Márquez's lonely solitude, results of Amaranta's masochistic self-denial, become, in *What the Crow Said,* the bizarre obsession of hangman Marvin Straw for Vera Lang and that final terrible flight of prisoner Jerry Lapanne's thirty-ninth escape attempt in his quest for Rita Lang: a flight that ends ludicrously when his flying machine, Liebhaber's boat piloted by Vera's Boy, and the centre piling of the CNR bridge miraculously coincide at the same instant! Again, then, it is not so much the dialectic between love and death itself which connects the texts but, rather, close similarities in the manner in which oppositions are presented, a manner which, in play, naturalizes exaggeration, grotesquerie, and the magical.

García Márquez's aphorisms are a type of language play which, in the manner of their idiosyncratic invention, are a form suited to conveying strange discovery; consequently, in *One Hundred Years of Solitude,* they are credited to his explorers and teachers. Creating wonder, they are also parodic because they mingle time scales, innocence, and sophistication: "Science has eliminated distance" (Melquíades 8); "The earth is round, like an orange" (José Arcadio Buendía 10); "The world must be all fucked up [. . .] when men travel first class and literature goes as freight" (the wise Catalonian 368); "Friends are a bunch of bastards!" (Aureliano 380). That Kroetsch should find this form so useful indicates shared interests and intentions, combining folk humour and invention with a parodic, self-conscious wit: "men are a bunch of useless bastards" (Vera Lang 14); "The sprocket wheel of being is jammed" (Father Basil 52); "Tomorrow will be just as miserable as today" (the crow 82); "Men live, men die. . . . And that is the truth of it" (Father Basil 138). Because he has "delivered a three-hour harangue to a deserted church, having confused Saturday and Sunday" (51), accidentally preached a burial sermon at a wedding, and pronounced as his newest theological discovery the existence of a God, Father Basil as deliverer of aphorisms and sole representative of organized religion is also the figure of its parody. Bizarre aphorisms are the device by which this character is created and,

204 *Theories of Play and Postmodern Fiction*

as in *One Hundred Years of Solitude,* the playful subversion of conventional meaning and wisdom is central not only to representations of character but also to the re-mythologization of a community. In magical realism, frameworks of authority are deconstructed and recreated in new and fabulous configurations.

García Márquez's strategy of presenting very precise but bizarre numbers and meticulous descriptions too extraordinary for rational belief creates magical realism and mythology by parodying social realist attempts at verisimilitude in narrative. If the proliferation of fine detail in a text comes from an author's holding up the mirror to nature, what is the source of a proliferation of fine but *extraordinary* detail? Is this form of playful exaggeration another parody of standard authorities over truth? Defining the fantastic, Todorov emphasizes uncertainty of understanding, hesitation between the uncanny and the marvellous as categories of explanation; Alejo Carpentier says that in *lo real maravilloso americano* the (allegedly) fantastic inheres in natural and human realities. Typically in magical realist texts, the banal is made strange by excessive concentration on fine detail (the stuff of realism) with apparent exaggeration (the hyperbole of magical realism). In this labyrinth of intertextual influence, Macondo's rain, lasting four years and eleven months and two days, and Meme's return from boarding school with four nuns and sixty-eight classmates, necessitating seventy-two extra chamber-pots, may be said to prompt Liebhaber's passing out in the can thirty-two times, the schmier game which lasts exactly 151 days in four different locations, and Jerry Lapanne's eating of 420 pounds of brick and stone over two years in an attempt to escape prison and find Rita Lang. Similarly, there are formal links between the supernatural proliferation of Aureliano Segundo's animals, the cinematic close-up of the slaughter of striking workers, or the eating contest in *One Hundred Years of Solitude,* and Vera Lang's bee swarms, Tiddy Lang's periods of mourning, or the series of battles in "The War Against the Sky" in *What the Crow Said.* The injury list is a fine example of that finnicky excess and parodically self-conscious humour masquerading as the record of empirical observation that typifies the conceptual play:

> Liebhaber looked about him and realized that every male over the age of sixteen in the Municipality of Bigknife had been injured or maimed or had suffered a related illness in The War Against the Sky.

Strategies of Influence 205

> Gunshot wounds had crippled grown men, robbed youths of fingers
> and toes. Exploding shotgun barrels had scarred handsome faces and
> ripped at biceps and elbows. Wise and confident men, driven to drink,
> had missed the curve in the road down into the valley, had sheared off
> powerline poles, had plunged over the banks of coulees, into boulders
> and gullies. One hundred and seventeen people had in six hours
> suffered horsefly bites. Hunters had turned over in boats, had been
> chewed up by the propellors of outboard motors; one group had clung
> all night, in rough water, to a drifting gasoline drum. Trees had fallen
> on the injured who sought shelter in the bush; the endless wind had
> lifted granaries and haystacks before astonished eyes, had grimly
> worn the sanest citizens looney. (178)

A third-person narration but refracted through Liebhaber's viewpoint,
the list is pedantic, as if in the interests of accuracy, and also ridiculous.
While it includes believable prairies accidents, these take on, through
compression and through exaggeration, the deflated mock heroic mode
that links contemporary magical realism with a long history through
Gothic and medieval romance to the supernatural in classical Greek
epic.

Another strategy common to the mythologizing of both Macondo
and Big Indian is the presentation of the remote community as set
against rumours and evidence of a bigger world beyond. That
presentation is largely accomplished by investing mundane things with
wonder. When the gypsies bring ice, telescopes, magnets,
daguerreotypes, and then cinema, phonographs, and the telephone to
Macondo:

> It was as if God had decided to put to the test every capacity for
> surprise and was keeping the inhabitants of Macondo in a permanent
> alternation between excitement and disappointment, doubt and
> revelation, to such an extreme that no one knew for certain where the
> limits of reality lay. (210)

Similarly, there is Isador Heck's return to Big Indian with stories of
other places:

> Heck, when asked about the world beyond the municipality, would
> start to answer then he'd say "It would make a pig laugh," and he'd

206   *Theories of Play and Postmodern Fiction*

> burst into uncontrollable laughter. When finally he got control of his
> laughter, he sometimes told, in the beer parlor, of airplanes that flew
> without propellers, of highways that were made of solid cement but
> soared through the air. Then everyone else in the beer parlor broke
> into uncontrollable laughter. (142)

But Heck, former sceptic, has toured as a man shot from a cannon, and
from this God's-eye view "it struck him clearly, everything existed"
(142). Complicating the processes and authority of meaning, and
substituting possibilities for limitations and wonder for certainty, the
texts emphasize relativism as an implicit philosophical sub-stratum to
the fabulist play of their surfaces. As Derrida says, "There is not a
single signified that escapes, even if recaptured, the play of signifying
references that constitute language. The advent of writing is the advent
of this play."[34] Within the society of the text, the ordinary (by
conventional standards) is made fabulous, just as the fabulous (by
conventional standards) is made ordinary. In magical realism, magical
things (seduction by bees, metamorphosis, speaking with the dead,
fabulous pregnancies) happen.

THE TEMPTATION OF MEANING

The pervasive element of play in *What the Crow Said* is partly
indicated, then, in this reading of intertextuality, in the extent to which
the text incorporates García Márquez's style of magical realism. As a
decidedly self-reflexive and postmodernist work, it proceeds against
ending, as Kroetsch has acknowledged in interview: "I think that novel
is my own personal struggle with the temptation of meaning, and it's
the reader's struggle too. Some readers were so compelled to impose on
it a total explanation instead of allowing the . . . game to happen." And,
he later adds, "We know enough rules to be in the game but we don't
know enough to *really play* the game and that's where we're at."[35]
Endgames are complex, and Kroetsch's comment implies his advocacy
of a type of play which, involving writer, text, and reader, necessarily
involves bringing certain paraphernalia to the game: a (de)construction
kit which would include (though not be exhausted by) *One Hundred
Years of Solitude,* itself an intertextual funhouse, together with an
interest in language, society, history and story-making. In its challenge
by inversion, misrule, and jestful exuberance to official, and necessarily

Strategies of Influence 207

limiting codes, the carnival aspects of this play certainly recall Bakhtin's emphasis on the regenerative power of the carnivalesque. It is a mode of being-in-the-world and of textual construction with which Kroetsch is well acquainted;[36] it is also a reading perspective which *What the Crow Said* invites, and a leading part of its intertextual reach. When Bakhtin defines carnival laughter as universal, mocking and restorative, these terms provide an indication of the serious play of the comic in Kroetsch's work:

> Carnival laughter is the laughter of all the people. Second, it is universal in scope; it is directed at all and everyone, including the carnival's participants. The entire world is seen in its droll aspect, in its gay relativity. Third, this laughter is ambivalent: it is gay, triumphant, and at the same time mocking, deriding. It asserts and denies, buries and revives. (11-12)

Displacing old hierarchies of authority and truth as well as rank, privilege and traditional cultural arrangements, the carnivalesque allows for what is idiosyncratic and different. But Bakhtin emphasizes its affirmative aspect. If in its medieval context, the carnival permitted satirical expression and temporary subversion of regular social roles, arrangements and knowledge constructions, the *carnivalesque* emphasizes the turn, moment or expression of that radical cultural poetics that is simultaneously destructive and reconstructive, transgressive and regenerative. In *What the Crow Said,* Kroetsch's investigation of prairie story-making mixes sceptical laughter and parody with affection, his interrogation of the foolish and ludicrous with a restorative interest in the interplays between frailty and strength, absurdity and insight. In the absence of certainty, without the tight controls of absolute game-rules, texts (and life) proceed and interest lies in the myriad permutations and possibilities of play between beginning and ending.

One may take various approaches to the question of meaning in *What the Crow Said,* none of which can definitively conclude the possibilities for meaning which reside in such diverse concerns of the text as the unending and infinitely variable struggle of love versus death; male-female relationships, together with simple gender stereotyping and its mocking subversion; the archaeological pursuit of a return to origins, to archetypes, or into dreams and the unconscious—

208   *Theories of Play and Postmodern Fiction*

concerns also central to *One Hundred Years of Solitude* as this discussion has implied. Suggesting that *What the Crow Said* is his struggle with the *temptation* of meaning, Kroetsch defines the temptation that preoccupies so many of his male characters: JG is mysteriously silent but able to communicate with the crow, and he attempts to fly above the earth like the crow; Joe Lightning, inspired by the example of JG and of the crow, wants to communicate with an eagle; Isador Heck's cannon flights have given him a bird's-eye view of the earth and a new arrogance about the nature of existence. But this band of male questers, so the pattern of events suggests, are ludicrous overreachers and their quests for knowledge end in farce, with variously ignominious falls to earth. JG, Joe Lightning, Skandl, and Jerry Lapanne, in their varied aspirations to be crow, fly and plummet absurdly: their flights are presented in male metaphors and, consistent with the traditional symbolism, they are away from the female earth of their source, responsibility and inevitable return. In this text, however, the talking crow is taunting, insolent, and vulgar, offering obscenities not answers as a bird linked more with tricksterism than with death or with mysterious knowledge. Magical Melquiades, gypsy prophet, associated with crow because he wears a black hat ("with a brim like the wings of a crow" [322]) and because his powers transgress the boundary between life and death, is domesticated and vulgarized by his deflationary reincarnation as the black crow who mocks questers. Kroetsch's crow is no gifted chronicler of generational history, no clairvoyant, no source of wisdom. Indeed from "Liebhaber, you don't know your ass from your elbow" (64) to "A bunch of raving idiots" (88) it is the voice of amused cynicism and disparagement, one whose contemplation accentuates the comical absurdity of Big Indian society and not answers to its predicaments.

In terms of the temptation of meaning, then, Liebhaber's compromise and Tiddy Lang's solidity are the best temptations that *What the Crow Said* offers. Persistent in his offer of love, struggling to remember the future (and, therefore, not bound by the past), even attempting to fertilize the barren sky that offers no answers by firing off volleys of Vera's bees, Liebhaber, the having lover, is at last granted his return to Tiddy Lang, to the text's Earth Mother: "Tiddy, then, taking every man who had ever loved her" (215). The text's answer is no surprise, though Kroetsch's deployment of conventional gender stereotypes is not as *au fait* with current politics as are the writerly

Strategies of Influence 209

strategies of his narrative. Or is this parodic too? The female earth figure accepts the male voyager in an existential sharing of the sensual moment: Tiddy, "with no imagination at all, dreaming the world" (216), accepts Liebhaber, "happy. He cannot remember anything" (217). Around the two, life continues in its forms of loneliness, sensuality, and hope, providing no guarantee against over-reaching and pain, but offering, in thematic terms, the process of living as a defense against the temptation of meaning, and offering as well the engaging complexities of a text which refutes reductive summaries in its play of possibilities. As the figure associated directly with language, Liebhaber's attempts "to disentangle himself from the tyranny of rote" (69) and his view that Gutenberg "made memory of the past irrelevant" (68) serve to foreground deconstructively the intriguing processes of language as a means of presentation, ordering and communication. It is by merging fact and fiction, by offering creative forays into the past as history that magical realist texts draw attention to matters of perception and communication.

Setting type for an edition of the *Big Indian Signal* while surrounded by floodwaters, Liebhaber refuses to mention the flood; instead, he refers to spring rains and remarks that "boating excursions might become a regular Saturday night event along the banks of the Big-knife" (204). The artifice and power of the printed word, the authority of the writer to prescribe reality, and the consequent reminder that the text's presented versions of reality are fictions are all foregrounded in *What the Crow Said* as they are in *One Hundred Years of Solitude*. In its attention to the gossipy local newspaper and to Liebhaber's struggle with words, as well as in its brand of magical realism generally, *What the Crow Said* invites reader participation in the exploration of meaning by emphasizing the ways in which the text may be deconstructed.[37] One of these is the tracing of influence, the consideration of "traces"[38] in the texts which draw attention to the processes of signification, de-center or de-privilege authority, and complicate the whole question of meaning. The processes of textual interrogation are, as Derrida has persistently argued, theoretically endless, even though as Foucault's work shows, with Derrida's, that aggressive and painstaking investigation of the archive can provide provisional insights into discursive formations and holds upon the play of textuality.

210   *Theories of Play and Postmodern Fiction*

In this discussion of modes of play in *What the Crow Said,* I have concentrated on magical realism and on *One Hundred Years of Solitude* because it is the most important single literary influence upon Kroetsch's text. Although appreciation of the later work does not depend upon knowledge of this "source," it is extended by it. One of the challenges, and joys, of being a reader lies in making connections, some of which may be figured self-consciously in the play of the text:

> I'm not inventing the novel so much as writing in a tradition, though I choose to misquote in order to write my novel. I am taking material from the readers. They have that material with them, so I'm taking it and offering it back—and one of the models I hear operating is the notion of gift. I see the relationship between reader and writer as a gift exchange. And it's not a one way thing. In a sense, readers have to give me this material which, in true gift fashion, demands its return. I have to give back those stories and I expect a kind of responsibility on the part of the author and the reader, and the kind of joy and pleasure that should go with gift giving. [39]

As Kroetsch suggests, readers indeed carry about a wealth of narrative material—products of folk stories, mythology, anecdote, literature and life experience—and in the mazy processes of its recyclings with variation, story-making offers the enchantment of the familiar as strange or, alternatively, flashes of recognition within the apparently different. Textuality is inevitably hybrid. Reading *What the Crow Said* as not only a self-conscious exploration of Canadian place and story-telling, but as a magical realist text that signals *One Hundred Years of Solitude* as a particular literary antecedent refreshes both in the two-way charge of intertextual exchange. In each text, the processes of deconstructing and un-naming question received meanings by their reconstruction of alternative narratives; and, as the processes demonstrate, meanings are mobile, not fixed. There is considerable play in the possibilities, and some writers (and many readers) "will most mornings, choose to be Coyote." [40]

NOTES

1. An earlier version of this chapter was published under the title of "Novelist as Trickster: The Magical Presence of Gabriel García Márquez in

Strategies of Influence

211

Robert Kroetsch's *What the Crow Said,"* *Essays on Canadian Writing,* No.34, Spring 1987, 92-110.

2. Robert Kroetsch in Shirley Newman and Robert Wilson, *Labyrinths of Voice: Conversations with Robert Kroetsch,* 130-1. In the now-considerable range of critical attention to Kroetsch's work, this study remains an invaluable point of reference.

3. The phrase is Julia Kristeva's; see her *Desire in Language: A Semiotic Approach to Literature and Art,* 66. There are obvious links with Barthes's statement: "The text is a tissue of quotations drawn from the innumerable centres of culture" ("The Death of the Author," in *Image, Music, Text,* 146). Such perceptions of textuality are underwritten, of course, by poststructuralist linguistics and, in particular, by Derrida et al.

4. Jorge Luis Borges, *Labyrinths,* 69. Despite different emphases in discussions of magical realism, many of which focus on exuberance and excess rather than erudite invention, Borges remains inspirational, more than a point of occasional citation. For one reading of Borges' influence upon directions in magical realism during the late 1930s and the 1940s, see Angel Flores, "Magical Realism in Spanish America," in Zamora and Faris, *Magical Realism: Theory, History, Community.*

5. Brian Edwards, "Narrative as Gift Exchange: Talking with Robert Kroetsch," 76. In addition, see Kroetsch's *The Crow Journals,* 18-19 and 29. In the *Journals,* Kroetsch notes: "Márquez has cracked the problem of how to tell a story in third person again. Voice: a calm distancing that enables him to forget the conventions of realism" (29).

6. Hodgins' *The Invention of the World* is an obvious example of magical realist writing in which fabulism contends with banality and the specifics are also (as the title suggests) emblematic.

7. Peter O'Brien, ed., *So To Speak: Interviews with Contemporary Canadian Writers,* 212-3. It is not just the citational detail of this comment that is important but the perception that all literatures are "foreign literatures," a perception that does not neglect the local but which, rather, allows other shaping forces, connections and influences their value in our appreciation of that local both as "local" and as "other." It is a perception, and an enthusiasm, that distinguishes Latin American magical realism.

8. Kroetsch in *Labyrinths of Voice,* p.24. While conceding the inevitability of influence, since it is part of the very fabric of language and literature, I share Kroetsch's enthusiasm for self-conscious analysis and articulation of the resources. Formalized and debated as "tradition," the divided senses of connection may be theorised and traced so differently, as feminist and

212 *Theories of Play and Postmodern Fiction*

postcolonialist discussions have shown. But however the connections are made, perceived, extolled or deplored, the vacuum is no site for literary activity.

9. Jacques Derrida, "Structure, Sign and Play," in *Writing and Difference*, 292. I come back frequently to Derrida's early statement. It is energizing. Nevertheless, it is a decided misinterpretation, in the negative sense, to perceive his work as unconcerned with "fault," "truth" and "origin," as concerned only with some sort of unrestricted "freeplay of signifiers." As I have already suggested, we do not escape these concepts but, as Derrida demonstrates, we can continue to question their authority and efficacy.

10. Robert Kroetsch, "Beyond Nationalism: A Prologue," *Mosaic* 14.2, 1981, xi. Reprinted in *Robert Kroetsch: Essays, Open Letter*, 83-9. Kroetsch's critical writings have been disseminated variously—see *The Lovely Treachery of Words*.

11. Robert Lecker, *Robert Kroetsch*, 20. Lecker's study of Kroetsch's work is well worth consideration. An updated bibliography of Kroetsch criticism has been produced by Dennis Cooley, University of Manitoba. For a variety of recent essays, see *Open Letter*, Ninth Series, Nos. 5-6, Spring-Summer 1996, *Kroetsch at Niederbronn*.

12. As one would expect, the list is elastic. Discussing the question of influence, Kroetsch has referred as well to García Márquez. See *Labyrinths of Voice*, especially 6-16, and Geoff Hancock, "An Interview with Robert Kroetsch." In the Hancock interview, Kroetsch emphasizes his interest in "foregrounding the language" thereby to invite the reader into the process of creating fiction: "I'm interested in sharing with the reader the fact that I'm making a fiction" (42).

13. Kroetsch, in *Labyrinths of Voice*, 184. The formulation is interesting. The classical writer, his fragmentary texts, is introduced as influence and as authority or marker into the divided procedures of postmodernist fiction. Under whatever label they've been categorized, writers of fiction have an impressive history of allusion and replay, of allowing the past (in its language and literature) into the pages of contemporary production. Since Aeschylus supped at the Homeric feast, the procedure has remained more-or-less inescapable.

14. Readers of *The Studhorse Man* have also noted Kroetsch's demythologising of the West and the Western. Certainly Hazard Lepage may be read as anti-hero, as a parody of the traditional western traveller—his heroic wound is a buckshot charge in the arse and his hazardous exploits end when he is killed by his own horse. See Dick Harrison, ed., *Crossing Frontiers: Papers in American and Canadian Western Literature*, Ch.VII.

Strategies of Influence 213

15. References are to the New Press edition (Toronto: General Publishing Co., 1982). Of all Kroetsch's fiction, *Badlands* has perhaps attracted most attention. Apart from the interest of the writer taking a flatboat trip down the Red Deer River in southern Alberta, revisiting some of those sites of palaeontological discovery that have made the area so famous, excavating some of that bonebeds history, *Badlands* is a fascinating example of intertextual cross-cutting. For a very precise and very well-informed analysis of influence in this novel, see Simone Vauthier's "*Badlands:* Where Are the Voices Coming From?"

16. Discussions with Kroetsch of the question of "influence" and its places in his fiction may be seen in *Labyrinths of Voice,* particularly the first part of this four-part study, and in "Narrative as Gift Exchange." In the latter, in answer to the question "to what extent does reading of the text depend upon knowledge of the prior text?," Kroetsch indicates, as one would expect, an attitude to intertextual play that invites readers to make connections while not insisting on the necessity to do so:

"I would certainly try to write a text so that a reader could read it without recognising the parallel. I want a text to live primarily up front in its own terms and, as I said, as a game and with a play of its own. The discovery or recognition of these other parallels is amplification, it's not basic to it." ("Narrative as Gift Exchange," 80.)

The issue must remain open. While it is possible to read Joyce's *Ulysses* and White's *The Aunt's Story,* for example, without prior knowledge of *The Odyssey,* the reading experience (and the texts' capacity for meanings) is enriched considerably by awareness of the associations.

17. There are many useful studies of this development: see D.P. Gallagher, *Modern Latin American Literature;* Regina Janes, *Gabriel García Márquez: Revolutions in Wonderland,* especially chapter 1; Alastair Reid, "Basilisks' Eggs"; Gordon Brotherston, *The Emergence of the Latin American Novel;* Gerald Martin, *Journeys Through the Labyrinth;* Philip Swanson ed., *Landmarks in Modern Latin American Fiction.*

18. *One Hundred Years of Solitude,* for example, includes names of characters from novels written by Cortázar, Carpentier and Fuentes. For details of these and discussions of their effects, see Gallagher, 144-63 and Clive Griffin, "The Humour of *One Hundred Years of Solitude*" in *Gabriel García Márquez: New Readings* edited by Bernard McGuirk and Richard Cardwell. Greg Price's interviews in *Latin America: The Writer's Journey* with leading Latin American writers (though not including García Márquez) shows very clearly not only their erudition and their appreciation of world literature in

214 *Theories of Play and Postmodern Fiction*

general but also, and in particular, their attention to "local" Latin American literary production. This influence appears frequently in references, allusions and language play in the fiction of Vargas Llosa, Carpentier, Cortázar, Fuentes, García Márquez and Puig.

19. The phrase is Robert Wilson's and I wish to pay tribute to the essay from which it comes, "On The Boundary of The Magic and the Real: Notes on Inter-American Fiction." In this essay, he provides a fine introduction to *What the Crow Said* within the context of some of the main characteristics of magical realism. Grateful for his comments on the relationships, I am attempting in this chapter to take particular note of literary strategies, aspects of play and implications for reading.

20. As cited by Reid, "Basilisks' Eggs," 180, 183. Carpentier's essay is available in another translation in Zamora and Faris, *Magical Realism: Theory, History, Community.*

21. This sense of exotic abundance is encapsulated in García Márquez's references to "the Caribbean":

"The Caribbean taught me to look at reality in a different way, to accept the supernatural as part of our everyday life. The Caribbean is a distinctive world whose first work of magical literature was *The Diary of Christopher Columbus,* a book which tells of fabulous plants and mythological societies. The history of the Caribbean is full of magic—a magic brought by black slaves from Africa but also by Swedish, Dutch and English pirates who thought nothing of setting up an Opera House in New Orleans or filling women's teeth with diamonds."

The comment is included within a discussion of readings and influences in Plinio Apuleyo Mendoza and Gabriel García Márquez, *The Fragrance of Guava,* 52.

22. Derrida, *Of Grammatology,* 101. In addition, for further examples of Derrida's deconstructive analyses of the operations of language, see *Writing and Difference* and *Positions.*

23. See Reid, "Basilisks' Eggs"; Mendoza and García Márquez, *The Fragrance of Guava,* 46-52; William Kennedy, "García at Noon and Beyond," 69-71.

24. All page references are to Gregory Rabassa's translation of *Cien Anos de Soledad.* It is significant that this statement should come at page 357, late confirmation of what characterizes this text from the start—and one may well suspect that the indefatigable reader, hunting assiduously for connections and for meanings, is included amongst those people.

25. See note 16.

Strategies of Influence

26. Tzvetan Todorov, *The Fantastic: A Structural Approach to a Literary Genre,* 24-40. Considered as a literary genre, fantasy covers a wide range of forms. Rather than situate magical realism as a sub-genre of fantasy, I prefer to view it as a mode of presentation that uses some of the techniques traditionally associated with fantasy but which is recognizable by virtue of a number of strategies peculiar to it. Those strategies are evident in *One Hundred Years of Solitude,* which has come to be regarded as the definitive example, and it is one of the tasks of this intertextual study to analyse them.

27. Kroetsch, in *Labyrinths of Voice,* 122. As legions of commentators demonstrate, these terms are provocative and their significations always yet to be agreed. But there is sound heuristic value in seeing them as interrelated, one the flip side of the other in a two-way process of conceptual influence. If *myth* signifies the larger view, an accretion of perspectives and narratives gathered over time and informing particular *reality,* as it has itself been informed by various realities, the interaction serves to remind us about ways of seeing. As Barthes suggests (in *Mythologies),* myth may be seen as a mode of language use.

28. *Labyrinths of Voice,* 169.

29. *Labyrinths of Voice,* 39. This subject recurs in Kroetsch's reflections upon life and literature. In particular, see "On Being an Albertan Writer" in *Robert Kroetsch: Essays* and *The Lovely Treachery of Words.*

30. See Geoff Hancock, "An Interview with Robert Kroetsch" and Kroetsch's "Unhiding the Hidden: Recent Canadian Fiction." The essay is reprinted in *Robert Kroetsch: Essays, Open Letter,* spring 1983, Fifth Series, No. 4—a special issue of *Open Letter* that brings together a variety of Kroetsch's critical essays.

31. This is a recurrent emphasis in García Márquez's comments about the work. See, for example, Reid's "Basilisk's Eggs," and Mendoza and García Márquez, *The Fragrance of Guava,* chapter 8.

32. See Reid, "Basilisk's Eggs,"186 and 191. Such explanations focus not so much on acts of perception as on modes of narration. Attention to oral traditions and to folklore commonly emphasize the local as variously fanciful and colorful. There is a strong attraction in the gossipy and partial methods of storytelling associated with local communities and oral traditions (and grandparents).

33. Jacques Derrida, *Positions,* 26. As I have emphasized, it is important to note that Derrida's deconstruction of the metaphysics of presence does not substitute mere absence. Rather, dismantling the truth claims associated with the prioritising of speech and presence (over writing and absence), he turns

216 *Theories of Play and Postmodern Fiction*

attention back to interactive complications and, therefore, to positionality and the play of language.

34. Derrida, *Of Grammatology,* 7. Associating this "play" overtly with movement, Derrida's work allows it immeasurable seriousness as the inescapable mode of operations in language.

35. *Labyrinths of Voice,* 15 and 163.

36. In their exuberance, and particularly because of the inversions they practice upon traditional social arrangements and literary constructions of them, Kroetsch's novels invite consideration in terms of the carnivalesque. Kroetsch discusses the carnivalesque himself in "Carnival and Violence: A Meditation," in *Robert Kroetsch: Essays,* 111-22.

37. "I'm interested in sharing with the reader the fact that I'm making a fiction. One of the assumptions of old style realism is that the novel isn't fiction," Kroetsch in "An Interview with Robert Kroetsch," with Geoff Hancock, 42.

38. Consider Derrida's viewing the text as "henceforth no longer a finished corpus of writing, some content enclosed in a book or its margins, but a differential network, a fabric of traces referring endlessly to something other than itself, to other differential traces"—"Living On: Border Lines," *Deconstruction and Criticism.* Ed. Harold Bloom et al., 84.

39. "Narrative as Gift Exchange," 84. Contemporary theorising emphasizes in various ways the fluidity of exchanges against older "top/down" models of communication. The whole rhetoric of reception theory, for example, decapitalizes the author to draw attention to interactive processes of exchange. If it is overtly democratic and egalitarian, in its rhetoric, there is yet no question that ideology and authority remain in the processes, albeit in different ways.

40. "The artist him/her self in the long run, given the choice of being God or Coyote will, most mornings, choose to be Coyote."

From Robert Kroetsch and Diane Bessai, "Death Is a Happy Ending: A Dialogue in Thirteen Parts," in *Figures in a Ground: Canadian Essays on Modern Literature Collected in Honor of Sheila Watson.* Ed. Diane Bessai and David Jackel, 206-15.

CHAPTER 5

Revisioning the Carnivalesque: The Cultural Combinations of Angela Carter's *Nights at the Circus*

THE INTERVIEW AS INTRODUCTION

> For me the main thing in a narrative is not the explanation of an extraordinary event, but the *order of things* that this extraordinary event produces in itself and around it; the pattern, the symmetry, the network of images deposited around it, as in the formation of a crystal.
>
> Italo Calvino[1]

> "Think of him as the amanuensis of all those whose tales we've yet to tell him, the histories of those women who would otherwise go down nameless and forgotten, erased from history as if they had never been, so that he too, will put his poor shoulder to the wheel and help to give the world a little turn into the new era that begins tomorrow."
>
> Angela Carter[2]

Although only three characters are presented in the opening scene of *Nights at the Circus,* many more participate in the references that offer this dressing room interview as an elaborately allusive beginning. The "bricolage" creates its own deconstruction of the idea of single origin and Fevvers (christened Sophie), winged aerealiste and interviewee, is the music hall freak as a spiralling collection of stories; "Cockney Venus," "Helen of the High Wire," *L'Ange Anglaise* and "the Angel of Death"; she is the mysteriously abandoned orphan become famous for flying, particularly for the lazy sensuality of her slow-motion triple

218 *Theories of Play and Postmodern Fiction*

somersault, a performance (like the writer's) that is controlled and exuberant, defies gravity, shows off her parts and invites suspension of disbelief. Combining biblical and classical reference with the interventions of later folk culture, the fantasies of supernatural origin and the power of flight, Fevvers is the winged creature in tawdry detail, the dream (and Freud's interpretation of it) vulgarised as music hall entertainment. Lizzie, her London-born Italian companion, is the ex-whore as minder, the Marxist-feminist maternal substitute with the air of a "terrier bitch" and the pecuniary instincts of an accountant. In some of her parts a challenge to motherhood's association with conservative morality and protection, she nevertheless presents, in the dream of a "happy ending," the ideology of traditional romance in shabby attire. Jack Walser, itinerant journalist as bemused interviewer, the male presence in this extraordinary meeting, is "Ishmael with an expense account," the writer as note-taker/maker, a reference combining the picaro's passion for change with not only Ishmael's notable ambivalence towards the object of fascination but also the play between empiricism and imagination that marks the postmodernist turn in Melville's big book. As the scene proceeds in Fevvers' dressing room, this "mistresspiece of exquisitely feminine squalor" marked by its soiled underwear, marine aroma and signs of excessive celebration, the grand gestures of her guffawing, farting, gluttony, belching and bawdy story-telling would situate the young reporter as nervous male visitor. But Walser is a travelling "man of action," an *American;* given neither to introspection nor judgement but generous to the lie and experienced in enchantments and illusions, a connoisseur of tall tales (Fevvers *is* six feet two in her stockings), he is well credentialled to trade quips. "Is she fact or is she fiction?" He has come armed with writerly scepticism — this interview is one for a series entitled *provisionally* "Great Humbugs of the World" and, having watched her in performance, he even muses upon the possibility of the fabulous bird-woman being a genuine miracle while pretending to be a hoax to gain credit in a secular world.

This auspicious opening sets a style of literary largesse. In the self-conscious exuberance of its detail and the discursive play with which character and concepts are introduced, Carter's late Victorian setting is a product of Austen, Dickens and Rabelais. Witty, exotic and vulgar, expansive and parodic, the text presents the interview as a performance, Fevvers' performance for Walser and the text's for the reader as a double act in disarming duplicity. If the references to Colette and to

Revisioning the Carnivalesque

Alfred Jarry introduce, respectively, literary associations with worldly sexuality and scatological performance, those to the myth of Leda and the Swan and Helen of Troy are of much greater significance. Introducing the idea of extraordinary origins and elevated status, they invoke the whole world of the Homeric epics and their classical offspring. Against that Helen, this one "launched a thousand quips, mostly on the lewd side" (8) and against the status and solemnity of Western Literature's classical "origins" and patriarchal tradition, Carter launches this comic feminist revision set, significantly, in 1899, in the apocalyptic moment at "the fag-end, the smouldering cigar-butt, of a nineteenth century" (11) and focused upon a strange female figure with "all the éclat of a new era about to take off" (11). The dressing-room interview encompasses all of Part One, London, offering Fevvers' history as she presents it to Walser, this Ishmael of American journalism on assignment back across "the herring pond," revisiting an updated European Gothic and scribbling all the while in his note book. The digressive mode with its abundance of stories within stories, their vernacular variety and such a range of literary-cultural reference foreground this story-making as a highly self-conscious encounter with divided European traditions. The wholly female world of Ma Nelson's brothel, "we were all suffragists in that house" (38), rewrites sexual exploitation with an edge of solidarity, independence and comedy as if to offer "new" space for female power against "old" histories of male control. Situated against the brothel's litany of light-hearted revels, and with its cellar darkness, woman monsters, peculiar gentlemen clientele and the proprietress as the very figure of the lugubrious and macabre, Madame Schreck's museum is a symbol of degenerate Victoriana, a parodic replay of arch Gothic excess. While Toussaint plays appropriately ghastly organ crescendoes for fascinated clients, it is in Fevvers' descriptions of Madame Schreck that Carter pulls out the stops, summoning no less than Lady Macbeth, Virgil and Dante to the spectacle of this weird mistress of a dark place of fascination and duplicity. Her exaggerated and self-parodic rhetoric reaches its ludicrous climax in the voice of Mr Rosencreutz, the Schreck Museum customer who is especially fixed on Fevvers:

> "Queen of ambiguities, goddess of in-between states, being on the borderline of species, manifestation of Arioriph, Venus, Achamatoth, Sophia [. . . .] Lady of the hub of the celestial wheel, creature half of

220   *Theories of Play and Postmodern Fiction*

> earth and half of air, virgin and whore, reconciler of fundament and
> firmament, reconciler of opposing states through the mediation of
> your ambivalent body, reconciler of the grand opposites of death and
> life . . ." (81).

Mocked by Fevvers in the story that frames this speech as her
recollection, the Rosencreutzian exaggerations, albeit as excess, turn us
back to the winged woman as a freak of nature, mythological symbol
and challenge not only to categories and ideologies of normality but
also to the oppositional strategies that accompany difference.

In the following discussion, I wish to emphasise the
interrelationship between playfulness and seriousness in Angela
Carter's feminist/deconstructive play upon forms and concepts by
looking at strategies of combination in *Nights at the Circus*. In
interview, she has pointed to this combinatory process as a form of self-
conscious *bricolage:*

> Writing is for me a process, a long work-in-progress; much of my
> writing has been in exploration of narrative genres in search of a form
> which would be viable as a vehicle of ideas. Emphasizing artificiality,
> choosing forms which explicitly assume it, which are indeed based on
> the foregrounding of their artificiality, has seemed to me a possible
> solution. Besides, I have an academic training as a medievalist, and
> the allegorical form of narration came to me so to say naturally, it
> was familiar [. . .] I have also indulged in a sort of intellectual
> bricolage—great fun; revisiting and reutilizing our cultural heritage,
> as though it were a big junk shop, a gigantic scrapyard. (Bono 43)

Demonstrating that there need be no division between entertainment
and cultural commentary, and enacting its postmodernist levelling of
distinctions between high and popular culture, the text is a leading
example of contemporary carnivalesque. Bahktin's theory and
criticism, in particular his discussions of dialogism and the
carnivalesque, help to define the place and modes of play in Carter's
work. They are multifarious. Her writing resists labels. Not fantasy
though it uses the fantastic, and not social realism, although attentive to
important cultural issues, *Nights at the Circus* offers a linguistic
equivalent to circus variety in performance.

Revisioning the Carnivalesque *221*

FEMINIST DECONSTRUCTIONS: ENTERTAINMENT AND CULTURAL CRITICISM

Offering an arch branch of entertainment together with social criticism, Carter's fiction, from the "adult fairy tales" of *The Bloody Chamber* collection to the black humorist and feminist deconstruction of gender in *The Passion of New Eve,* confuses generic categories. Together with the exotic fabulation, stylistic flourishes and delight in the play of rhetoric that seem most overtly to characterise her work as "fantasy," there are always indicators of insistent cultural analysis. In her role of writer as entertainer, she is simultaneously the writer as literary and social critic; there is no contradiction between:

> I don't mind being called a spell-binder. Telling stories is a perfectly honourable thing to do. One is in the entertainment business. . . . [3]

and

> This investigation of the social fictions that regulate our lives—what Blake called the "mind-forg'd manacles"—is what I've concerned myself with consciously since that time [the 1960s]. (I realise, now, I must always have sensed that something was badly wrong with the versions of reality I was offered that took certain aspects of my being *as* a woman for granted. . . .) [4]

In this respect, in the self-conscious turn against literary categories, in the transgression of brand-names, in the mixing of "mimesis" and "fantasy" or the "real" and the "surreal" in ways that question the usefulness of the distinctions themselves, Carter's work is decidedly postmodernist. Since poststructuralist theory and critical practice have challenged the mimetic contract traditionally held to define the texts of classic realism [5], the distinction between mimesis and fantasy is itself, as a consequence, negotiable. If what is usually held to be "real and normal" is uncertain, and even moreso its representation in writing, so too are decisions about fantasy as that which departs from "consensus reality," [6] or for which explanation is radically problematic. [7] The issues are important, and for two reasons. First, their consideration focuses attention not just upon aesthetic theory but upon writing strategies and processes of communication. Second, by challenging conservative

222   *Theories of Play and Postmodern Fiction*

measures of social realism, seriousness and relevance, they make it difficult to dismiss as escapist or peripheral that which is labelled "fantasy," "surreal," "Gothic" or *mere* entertainment.

In its concentration upon the unconscious and the psychic life of the individual, psychoanalysis has recovered dreams, imagination and fantasy as subjects for serious analysis. Introducing the notion of "psychical reality," Freud attempts not so much to deconstruct the opposition between subjective phenomena and material or external reality as to accord the subjective the importance commonly attached to that "objective" reality:

> Whether we are to attribute *reality* to unconscious wishes, I cannot say. It must be denied, of course, to any transitional or intermediate thoughts. If we look at unconscious wishes reduced to their most fundamental and truest shape, we shall have to conclude, no doubt, that *psychical* reality is a particular form of existence which is not to be confused with *material* reality. [8]

So fantasies (as dreams and day dreams) are texts to be deciphered and the distinction between *manifest* and *latent* content invites attention to the play of differences, the work of interpretation and the nature of meaning and significance. Although it is not my intention to concentrate upon psychoanalytic theory and practice in this analysis of modes of play in Carter's text, it is the case that Freud's work upon fantasy not only accords it central importance in individual and social practice, regenerating it as a subject for study, but that it also offers interpretative strategies that continue to influence our perceptions of language and meaning. Even so, and as Derrida points out in "Freud and the Scene of Writing,"[9] psychoanalysis is a rhetoric and, as with philosophy and literature, its rhetorical modes can be considered against its (mis)use as an explanatory system and with a hold on solutions. Lacan's equation of "condensation" and "displacement" with metaphor and metonymy emphasizes the rhetorical status of Freud's concepts, but there remains the problem of weighing apparent primary function against secondary elaboration or the tendency in psychoanalysis to search the origin, another function of desire and power that would seek to close the discourse. Intersections that focus upon discourse in its openness and complexity are certainly possible between a psychoanalytic literary criticism that is textual and rhetorical

Revisioning the Carnivalesque

and poststructuralist refusals to concede final answers. Paradoxically, in its formalism the collusion may offer opportunities "beyond formalism" for analysis of the play between language and cultural reference.[10]

When invitations to play are presented against the threat of death as literal or symbolic sub-text, an edge of seriousness sharpens the offer, adding urgency to the promise of exuberance. In deferral of *that* conclusion, against the fear of oblivion (or subjection) represented in silence, blank and closure, diversions crowd the text. So, for example, Marvell's "Now let us sport us while we may" and Pynchon's "Now everybody—," invitations offered against the immanence of "grave" and "rocket," define not only the interrelationship of play and seriousness in those texts but also the salutary force of scepticism. Acknowledgement of the endgame, though not necessarily as a preparation for it, focuses attention upon the process which shall be its displacement and deferral so that, although old gravity may not be overcome, "yet we will make him run."

Angela Carter's fictions present such a variety of comic-erotic displacements of death. Acknowledging Stoker, Shelley, Poe and Hoffmann amongst its literary ancestors, her work does so via Carroll, Dinesen and García Márquez,[11] for hers is a gamesome and self-reflexive intervention upon this inheritance, a postmodern Gothic in which fantasy is not so much domesticated as used with arch self-consciousness. Against vicarious experience of terror in face of the unknown, the supernatural or threats of suffering and death, her readers are offered self-conscious plays upon these subjects as they may be turned to entertainment and cultural commentary including, always, the leading matters of sexuality, gender, identity and the operations of power. In the extravagance of its detail, "The Bloody Chamber," Carter's "Bluebeard" reconsidered, plays out the old story of sexuality, temptation, betrayal and punishment as an ambiguous "adult tale." This *rite de passage* may be terrible with fascination but not all travellers suffer exotic deaths. In this revision, the causeway linking castle and mainland, the dangerous world of the Marquis and the protective familiarity of mother's apartment, carries not only the young bride to her meeting with sexual experience, temptation and threat of death but also hard-riding mother, the female figure as saviour. And, in the new dispensation, the red mark of "shame" signifies refusal of the prohibition.[12] Against the long narrative of patriarchal repression and female guilt, revisionist Eves, or Eve reinterpreted, would be foolish

224   *Theories of Play and Postmodern Fiction*

not to transgress. There is a similar conceptual play in "Black Venus," in Carter's presentation of the relationship between Baudelaire and Jeanne Duval, white poet and black muse, with references to the Fall: "every child, who, offered the choice between virtue and knowledge, will always choose knowledge, always the hard way."[13] Against the corruptions of this relationship which is presented as a meeting between European decadence and native innocence, in which the black goddess is by turns romanticised and abused, there is an ambiguous erotics of transgression. Its conclusion maintains that ambiguity with the image of Jeanne Duval, returned to Martinique after Baudelaire's early death, dispensing, until her own death, "to the most privileged of the colonial administration, at a not excessive price, the veritable, the authentic, the true Baudelairean syphilis" (23). The female triumph may be hollow but not the measured language of its expression. In *The Passion of New Eve*,[14] these ironies multiply in Carter's dismantling of the cultural construction of gender as young Englishman Evelyn is transformed into Eve, and Hollywood beauty and dream creation Tristessa de St. Ange is revealed to be a male transvestite, the figure of a male fantasy of desire and feminity. Here, death is nothing less than the apocalyptic destruction of western patriarchal civilization attended by a many-breasted and gross fertility goddess: "'Woman has been the antithesis in the dialectic of creation quite long enough . . . I'm about to make a start on the feminisation of Father Time'" (67). The emasculation is a beginning, with reconstructed Eve having experienced rape by Zero, "the great Platonic hermaphrodite" (148), together with Tristessa in the desert, and Mother's evacuation of the role of great female principle and matriarchal goddess, this sequence of "experiences" that confuse gender categories and challenge essentialist notions of the self. Thus, as Ricarda Schmidt points out, Eve's cave journey "does not only serve the deconstruction of both patriarchal and matriarchal symbols of woman, it is also a visionary journey" (65). Anti-evolutionary, a journey back in time that incorporates the vision of the legendary bird the archaeopteryx as a symbolic wholeness combining contraries, it leads into her looking to the place of birth, via water: "We start from our conclusions. I arrived on that continent by air and I left it by water; earth and fire I leave behind me" (191). The writing is provocatively affirmative and self parodic, a gaudy demythologising in which Carter reworks old images in an excess of vulgarity and black comedy. In each of these texts, her feminist deconstructions resituate the narrative

Revisioning the Carnivalesque 225

inheritance while demonstrating, in the process, possibilities for self-delight and for instruction in the darkest of places. Nevertheless, against this reading, doubts remain. Carter criticism has become very concerned about perceived ambiguities in her position(s) and production and it is easy to see why this should occur given the different political profiles and preferences of her readers and her own shifty predilections in the works of fiction.[15] Does she reject or refurbish sado-masochism, soft pornography and inherent "male" systems of desire and authority? Does the feminist come up short in her revisionist attention to the literary-cultural-political inheritance? As Derrida's work reminds us, there is no escaping (in acts of deconstruction, demythologizing, or revisionist politics of whatever type) not only the earlier referential links, paradigms, constructions and language against which the new work situates itself but also, ironically, possible collusion with it. And as Elaine Jordan suggests, "Angela Carter is a writer of contradictions" (123), one whose ironic yoking together of heterogeneous categories and effects invites our creative misreading of the interplays. Even so, working within and against the inheritance of folk, Gothic and Romance traditions, patriarchal authority and the pornographic, she presents difference and re-making (particularly in terms of gender, identity, self-definition and cultural authority) in ways that emphasize these as issues that must remain contentious in society and in literature. There is no utopian idealism in her work.

There are many instances in Carter's fiction, then, where play sports with death in feminist revisions of received cultural structures and practices, and as the preparation and process of other beginnings. Exhibiting an imagination that is wild *and* disciplined, concentrating upon heterogeneity and difference, she offers not so much a new discourse as examples of familiar concepts and forms used against themselves. These acts of appropriation and displacement accord with Julia Kristeva's view that "A feminist practice can only be [. . .] at odds with what already exists so that we may say 'that's not it' and 'that's still not it'"[16] Because they simultaneously acknowledge and interrogate the inheritance, reworkings with difference keep open the opportunities for continuing dialogue. In "The Bloody Chamber," the fairy tale is reconceived as arch feminist Gothic, "Black Venus" remakes the biographical sketch as a comic-erotic integration of fact

226   *Theories of Play and Postmodern Fiction*

and fancy, and *The Passion of New Eve* presents a picaresque deconstruction of Western mythology on the subject of sexual identity.

Many of these things come together and, to be consistent with the rhetoric and the politics, fall apart in *Nights at the Circus*. Its apocalyptic moment is emphasized in the first chapter:

> For we are at the fag-end, the smouldering cigar-butt of a nineteenth century which is just about to be ground out in the ashtray of history. It is the final, waning season of the year of Our Lord, eighteen hundred and ninety nine. And Fevvers has all the *éclat* of a new era about to take off. (11)

Its main figure is Fevvers the remarkable aerealiste, the woman with wings who carries upon her feathered shoulders such a weight of literary-mythological reference. Its notional location shifts from London to Petersburg to Siberia in an unfinished picaresque movement that projects the Land of the Rising Sun, the democratic heartland of North America. . . . Its cultural frame is a makeshift construction of freak show, brothel, music hall and circus, places of entertainment that specialize in artifice, dissimulation and role-play. Its mode is carnivalesque. Whereas Alice finds her play-world down the rabbit hole and through the looking glass, Fevvers is deposited/hatched in a basket on the steps of a London brothel. Carroll offers play as a reproach to earnestness and pomposity in the "adult" world of work, maintaining a separation that is challenged by Carter's texts. Her "Victorian" novel rereads the world in terms of the play of its constructs, unpicking the preposterous "real" in surreal and parodic elaborations of its status, exemplifying Huizinga's attribution of significance:

> The play concept as such is of a higher order than seriousness. For seriousness seeks to exclude play, whereas play can very well include seriousness.[17]

Presenting the spirit of carnival together with so many of its articulations, *Nights at the Circus* offers the complexities, and play, of the dialogical in this overt form of a combinatory carnivalesque. Conceived dialogically, with an emphasis upon interactive operations or the play of differences within language and between language and social practice, "carnival" is, as Bakhtin has argued, a special form of

Revisioning the Carnivalesque

borderline activity, "life itself, but shaped according to a certain pattern of play."[18] His work provides a pertinent theoretical framework for analysis of Carter's writing in general, with its characteristic interplay of rhetorical exuberance and social criticism, but for *Nights in the Circus* in particular.

In this chapter, I have suggested that the boundaries between "mimesis" and "fantasy" are always negotiable, that the supposedly fantastic invades the supposedly real, and that there are many examples in Carter's fiction of the fantastic, in play, used against the repressive, in death. The following consideration of *Nights at the Circus* concentrates upon strategies of play in terms of Bakhtin's theory of the dialogical and the carnivalesque.[19] Incorporating the fantastic within the ambivalence of its social commentary, this text is not only an example of contemporary carnivalesque, a work in which the regenerative power of laughter does not allow seriousness to atrophy, but a feminist revision of its open-ended possibilities.

JUGGLING WITH LANGUAGE: THE CIRCUS AND THE CARNIVALESQUE

"Chief, let me invite you to spend a few nights at the circus!"

Emphasizing the magic of spectacle, the circus is a place of diversion. Its acts are presented large in a space made special by the illusion— enhanced by the familiar circus trappings of sawdust and glitter, wires, lights, music and the smell of excrement. Associating performance with the grand gestures of elaborate role-playing and trickery, it offers a place apart where skill and danger consort with deception and the confidence game is an essential element in the contract. Gathered in darkness about the ring, the audience participates in a carnival atmosphere that is significantly different from the exchange situation of film, dramatic performance, concerts or opera. The Big Top is a site of folk culture, a formal legacy of carnival pageants and market-place performance which, like them, is organized around laughter. *Writing* about the circus, Carter works variations upon an old entertainment tradition and Walser's invitation, "Chief, let me invite you to spend a few nights at the circus!" is a metatextual form of her text's embrace of its readers—in hope of thrills, wonder and games against the imperatives of workaday social organization. Like Borges's "labyrinth"

228   *Theories of Play and Postmodern Fiction*

and Barth's "funhouse," Carter's "circus" is a scene for distraction, a place of play but one in which there are opportunities for instruction as well as amusement and entertainment.

When Bakhtin defines folk carnival humour of the Middle Ages and Renaissance in three forms, ritual spectacles, comic verbal compositions and varieties of billingsgate, he emphasizes the comic aspect as that which distinguishes the carnivalesque by marking not only its separation from life in its sober aspect but also its special energy: "carnival is the people's second life, organized on the basis of laughter. It is a festive life."[20] But if carnival spectacles, and manifestations of them in literature and in oral culture, "offered a completely different, nonofficial, extraecclesiastical and extrapolitical aspect of the world, of man, and of human relationships [. . .] a second world and a second life outside officialdom," (6) it is also the case that the forms are defined in dialectical interplay with "officialdom." In Bakhtin's analysis, the "comic" and "serious" aspects of medieval life are interactive; the relationship is dialogical. This doubleness informs *Nights at the Circus* where the carnivalesque is not only instrumental but turned to social issues.

Offered at the end of Part One, Walser's "Chief, let me invite you to spend a few nights at the circus!" concludes the London dressing room scene. Although it introduces "circus," literally, and the picaresque structure of Parts Two and Three, the invitation embraces retrospectively and metaphorically the detail of Part One, the collection of stories in which Fevvers is displayed and note-taking Walser, attendant at the shrine, is sufficiently intrigued as to want to run away with the circus. As the "normal" participant-observer through whose reactions the extraordinary is accentuated, this "Ishmael" is plunged into carnivalesque excesses from the start. The interview is presented as a comic-erotic performance in which language of the marketplace combined with easy literary erudition is the staple of both Fevvers' and Lizzie's storytelling, "two Scheherezades, both intent on impacting a thousand stories into the single night" (40) and the in-text audience of one, Walser, is extended by co-option of readers to the spectacle. Filling in Fevvers' story from hatching to wing sprout, first flight and life amongst London whores, the tellings mix billingsgate with artful allusions that accentuate the duplicities of narration and compel readers into the game by complicating the narrative mixture; along with the bizarre details of brothel activities, "In a brothel bred, sir, and proud of

Revisioning the Carnivalesque 229

it" (22), such items as Fevvers' particular fascination with a picture of Leda and the Swan, reference to the fate of Icarus, Prospero's wand, the influence of Baudelaire, "funeral baked meat," Virgil in Hell, this rag-and-bone shop of the heart and "summer is icumen today" add the grab-bag of a lit. student's borrowings to sophisticate the linguistic play. In this text, "the morn in russet mantle clad/Walks o'er the dew of yon high eastward hill" can become "the Fructifying disc is just now nudging his way up the backside of yonder hillock!" (82) The greasepaint prose is spread as thick as Fevvers' layers, and the "exquisite" squalor of the dressing room is matched by the first-person narratives that create Ma Nelson's brothel and Madame Schreck's establishment as a collection of the stories of their inmates. Carnivalesque vulgarity, this discourse of unrestraint against conservative social customs, is represented as a source of energy and regeneration. Low brothel adventure is displaced by laughter and, in the parody of their tellings, the stories of Ma Nelson, Fanny Four-Eyes, Sleeping Beauty, the Wiltshire Wonder and Albert/Albertine offer an "otherworld" and ambiguous perspective on serious matters of social relationships and practice. So Ma Nelson, brothel-keeper, is also a feminist:

> "Oh, my little one, I think you must be the pure child of the century that just now is waiting in the wings, the New Age in which no women will be bound down to the ground." And then she wept. (25)

Deposited "hatched" on the brothel steps, thereby symbolically escaping the Law of the Father, a miraculous combination, Fevvers' role changes from Cupid, "the gilded *sign* of love" (23), to the Winged Victory. Affirming Fevvers' statement "we were all suffragists in that house; oh, Nelson was a one for 'Votes for Women'" (38), this confirmation creates an image of strident female nature as the basis for renewal and political action:

> "Does that seem strange to you? That the caged bird should want to see the end of cages, sir?" queried Lizzie, with an edge of steel in her voice."Let me tell you that it was a wholly female world within Ma Nelson's door. Even the dog who guarded it was a bitch and all the cats were females, one or the other of 'em always in kitten, or newly given birth, so that a sub-text of fertility underwrote the glittering

230   *Theories of Play and Postmodern Fiction*

> sterility of the pleasure of the flesh available in the academy. Life
> within those walls was governed by a sweet and loving reason. I
> never saw a single blow exchanged between any of the sisterhood
> who reared me, nor heard a cross word or a voice raised in anger."
> (39)

The story-tellers offer solidarity and economic necessity as their
justification; but sexual commerce and female deprivation are also
presented in the intermingling of clichés and their parody that ridicules
"male" peculiarities and celebrates female knowledge. Mr.
Rosencreutz's weird genital obsession is made absurd by Fevvers'
narration: "'H'm. This is some kind of heretical possibly Manichean
version of neo-Platonic Rosicrucianism, thinks I to myself; tread
carefully, girlie! I exhort myself'" (77); Madame Schreck's "museum"
is an establishment that specialises in artifice, a place of play designed
to cater to the appetites of its disparaged male clientele; and Fevvers'
amusement at her patrons' stupidity is sustained by the promise of cash
returns. The flamboyant detail of Part One presents brothel culture as a
source of feminist messages as well as comedy.

The dressing room setting and Walser's location as listener/note-
taker create the context of exchange. Presenting this male as a well-
credentialled listener by virtue of his wandering, inquisitiveness and
talent with words, and concentrating on his point of view in the third-
person narration, Carter accentuates the processes of story-telling by
the tactic of interruption. Asking questions, offering occasional
observations, trying to piece the parts together, sceptical and amazed,
Walser scribbles on. Submitted to heavy aromas and sexual bantering,
to Fevvers' gargantuan farting, yawning and belching, he is the willing
victim of an excess of grotesque bodily realism transformed by comic-
erotic fascination and the pressure of uncertainty. In the interests of
observation and explanation, he will join the circus and become, in the
picaresque development of Parts Two and Three, less a register of
amazement than another contributor to the heteroglossic performance.[21]

A structure composed of tensions, since its emphasis upon the
varieties of on-the-road movement must contend with social-cultural
constructions as sites of meaning, the picaresque deals typically with
constraint as well as freedom. Against the apparent confinement of
identities fixed in relationships and place, journeying is an overt form
of the mobility of concepts and signifiers. Although it is situated amidst

Revisioning the Carnivalesque 231

the Siberian wanderings of Part Three, Fevvers' observation may be applied to the operations of all parts of the mobile text: "'Young as I am, it's been a picaresque life; will there be no end to it? Is my fate to be a female Quixote, with Liz my Sancho Panza?'" (245). As the brothel is a site of interplay, of dialogism at "work," so too are the Imperial Circus and the interrupted Grand Tour in the rhetorical exuberance and discontinuous narratives that simultaneously present and deconstruct structures for the representation of meaning.

How could this text resist the image of circus as microcosm:

> What a cheap, convenient, expressionist device, this sawdust ring, this little O! Round like an eye, with a still vortex in the centre; but give it a little rub as if it were Aladdin's wishing lamp and, instantly, the circus ring turns into that durably metaphoric, uroboric snake with its tail in its mouth, wheel that turns full circle, the wheel whose end is its beginning, the wheel of fortune, the potter's wheel on which our clay is formed, the wheel of life on which we are all broken. O! of wonder; O! of grief. Walser thrilled, as always, to the shop-soiled yet polyvalent romance of the image. (107)

Typically, Carter replays the cliché self-consciously, allowing it a continuing place in the construction of meanings while emphasizing its ambiguous properties. The magic circle that intermingles French perfume with the "aroma of horse dung and lion piss" (105) and offers activity as entertainment, presents the play element in heightened form. Participating in the "Ludic Game," Walser's feelings of writerly liberation in his role as clown reflect the licence taken by the text in general: "Walser's very self, as he had known it, departed from him, he experienced the freedom that lies behind the mask, within dissimulation, the freedom to juggle with being, and, indeed, with the language which is vital to our being, that lies at the heart of the burlesque" (103). Again, in a structural replay of Part One, the central figure is the focus of a range of stories crossed by the continuing double interest of love story and sexual politics, the romance tradition and its feminist revision. And in the burlesque mode, comic invention mixes readily with parody. As Linda Hutcheon suggests in her references to *Nights at the Circus* in *A Poetics of Postmodernism,* this border-crossing is provocative both as image and extrapolation: "The multi-ringed circus becomes the pluralized and paradoxical metaphor

232   *Theories of Play and Postmodern Fiction*

for a decentered world where there is only ex-centricity. Angela Carter's *Nights at the Circus* combines this freak-circus framework with contestings of narrative centering: it straddles the border between the imaginary/fantastic (with her winged woman protagonist) and the realistic/historical, between a unified biographically structured plot and a decentered narration, with its wandering point of view and extensive digressions" (61). As I have suggested with reference to transgression, the carnivalesque, deconstruction, and the critical edges of postmodernist aesthetics and practice, the place of play, critique, and idiosyncratic invention is the place between—a location that acknowledges centers (history, tradition, reality, truth) even as it interrogates their claims to authority. Creative intervention, new forms, revised cultural arrangements and the politics of play can not occur in a vacuum. To be meaningfully off-center, to seek new modes of play, involves an initial acknowledgement of those old rules of the game.

Presenting in Colonel Kearney a comically exaggerated portrait of the American entrepreneur as carnival shyster, Carter establishes an extravagant framework for the circus troupe. This emblematic Uncle Sam of stars and stripes dress, dollar bill belt buckle, and grand plans for travel and the Ludic Game, has the energetic vulgarity of a side-show spruiker. With Sybil the fantastic pig as his partner, such mottos as "a fool and his money is soon parted!" (101), "the bigger the humbug, the better the public likes it" (147) and "Bamboozlem" (147), and with a vision of his "free Amurrican circus" (103) circumnavigating the globe, Kearney is a parody of New World commercialism as confidence game. A similarly exaggerated play with old forms marks the troupe as the recognisable figures of circus tradition, the animal trainers, strongman, trapeze artists and clowns, are particularised in the short narratives of their discontents. The "Princess of Abyssinia" is distinguished by her scarred body and silence; classical pianist as tamer of tigers, small, dark and formidable, she consorts with danger: "their heavy heads between their paws among the bloody bones, a beautiful still-life or *nature morte* of orange tawny shapes composed around the Princess's open Bechstein grand; they drowsed like unawakened desire, like unlit fire" (154). The Strong Man's absurdity is emphasized in the farcical scene of his introduction, fucking the Ape-Man's woman as a background copulatory chorus to Walser's communication with the preternaturally-knowing apes. High-

Revisioning the Carnivalesque

wire family, the Charivaris, fulfil the trapeze artist tradition of arrogance and jealousy in their failed attempt to scuttle Fevvers:

> The historic tribe, who rope-danced before Nero, Charlemagne, the Borgias, Napoleon . . . the Charivaris will now enter a long slow eclipse. Finally, forced to emigrate, two millennia of circus art will peter out in a pizza concession on Mott Street. (161)

Above all, the clowns, traditional exemplars of the carnivalesque, are an ambiguous symbol of merriment, these quintessential figures for play interrelated with work, comedy with seriousness, laughter with despair:

> "We are the whores of mirth, for, like a whore, we know what we are; we know we are mere hirelings hard at work and yet those who hire us see us as beings perpetually at play." (119)

Priapic and anal, the Rabelaisian excesses of the clowns' dance and of Buffo the Great as a drunken Lord of Misrule, embody carnival parody. Transforming grotesquerie and fear of death through the regenerative power of laughter, they offer ambiguous possibilities of renewal; in the emblematic figure of Buffo as the ambiguous scapegoat for human repressions, merriment is subverted by madness.

The combination of play with seriousness characteristic of Carter's work in general is demonstrated in the inversions. Writing "against the grain," in resistance to the pattern of male overlord/female victim and with a parodic zeal that allows sympathy a place with her virtuoso delight in language, she offers messages in sequences that challenge male first-ness. Mignon's history is a waif's sad progress. From the orphanage to her roles impersonating the dead for Herr M. and as the Ape-Man's woman, she is the female victim of varieties of male exploitation, "the broken blossom of the present tense" (140). But brought to the Princess so that she might sing to the tigers, she is rescued from subservience through her singing and the sisterhood:

> "The cruel sex threw her away like a soiled glove," said Fevvers. "— but us girls 'ave gone and sent her to the cleaner's!" Lizzie concluded triumphantly. (155)

234   *Theories of Play and Postmodern Fiction*

Making music with the Princess, even in the remote "Conservatoire of Transbaikalia," charming not only tigers but also a newly contrite Samson, Mignon's Orphic powers are a glorification of female regeneration: "Under that unseasonable sun, or under the influence of the voice and the piano, all the wilderness was stirring as if with new life" (250). Similarly, when the "army of lovers" (217) break out of Countess P's bizarre House of Correction they represent the power of female love against repression. Each found guilty of killing a husband, theirs is an assertion against male cultural forms, their liberation symbolised in the destruction of time and in the white Siberian landscape they enter.

But lest the "message" appear too reductive, what turns are made in the main text of Fevvers' winged progress? Presented in Part One as a parody of the romance heroine, a Mae West [22] with wings to whom "the music of the spheres was the jingling of cash registers" (12), Fevvers' remarkable stature is matched by her vulgarity, boldness and eroticism. As the female hero, an artist of the high trapeze, she travels and she escapes all male attempts to pinion her. Fussed about by Lizzie, but confident of her strength, she is the independent female figure as star attraction, her singularity as a literary character the product of an exuberant rhetoric. In narrative moves that sustain the elements of Gothic romance and vaudevillean exaggeration, Fevvers escapes the mad scientist figures, Rosencreutz and the Grand Duke, and then the Russian outlaws who see in her a bizarre promise of relief—"nobility of spirit hand in hand with absence of analysis, that's what always buggered up the working class" (232) and not only Fevvers, but Lizzie too, becomes an existential sceptic in the text's liberating mixture of perspectives and styles:

> "Here we are," opined Liz, "lodged up the arsehole of the universe with a bunch of scabby bandits so sunk in false consciousness they thought the Queen of England would shed a tear for them if only she knew their misery . . ." (234).

Moved audaciously from one scrape to another, her narrative progress held together by the threads of circus performance and the accretion of stories, Fevvers may seem to be the exemplary figurehead of a "New Age" of female independence (25), as Lizzie's hope fulfilled, though only under her watchful guidance. For Lizzie is the text's leading

Revisioning the Carnivalesque

235

feminist, the Sancho Panza who must be vigilant lest her astounding charge fall victim to sentimentality, nostalgia or the romance convention of a "happy ending." What can the writer do with Walser and the romance? Will the custom applying to the Prince who rescues the Princess from the dragon's lair apply as well to the trapeze artist who rescues the clown? The penultimate chapter reunites the leads in this discontinuous "love story," but Lizzie's complication of the context underlines the tension upon which the extravagance of *Nights at the Circus* turns:

> "Those of us who learned the lessons of experience have ended their journeys already. Some who'll never learn are tumbling back to civilisation as fast as they can as blissfully unenlightened as they ever were. But, as for you, Sophie, you seem to have adopted the motto: to travel hopefully is better than to arrive."
>
> "How?" asked Fevvers carefully, "have you reached this conclusion?"
>
> "It's a fool's errand, Sophie. From that fleeting glimpse we caught of your fancy boy mounted on a reindeer and wearing a frock, it would seem he is not the man he was. Nothing left, Sophia! Nothing there. . . . But it's me who is the bigger fool than you, because at least you're going off after him of your own free will while I tag along behind you through the middle of nowhere only because of the bonds of old affection."
>
> "I am," she added sourly, "the slave of your freedom." (279)

The "lessons of experience" are interpreted differently, of course, and just as "confinement" and "freedom" are unstable concepts, "free will" is an old cliché that invites the work of ideological deconstruction. It is by virtue of its self-consciousness about ideology and choice that the text maintains its open-endedness. Fevvers may provide another cliché, "'I'll *sit* on him, I'll hatch him out, I'll make a new man of him'" (281) but it contends with "'Think of him as the amanuensis of all those whose tales we've yet to tell him, the histories of those women who would otherwise go down nameless and forgotten, erased from history as if they had never been . . .'" (285). Bolstered figuratively by the New Year's Eve setting, the possibility of fresh starts, rather than conclusions, is supported by the tornado of Fevvers' laughter "across the entire globe, as if a spontaneous response to the giant comedy that

236 *Theories of Play and Postmodern Fiction*

endlessly unfolded beneath it" (295). Fevvers laughs in recollection that she had fooled Walser on the subject of her "virginity," having him believe she was the "only fully-feathered intacta in the history of the world." Better, it is implied, acknowledgement of the varieties of experience than the idea of unscribbled innocence; better this revelation, and equal treatment between the sexes, than repressive male fantasies of idealized womanhood. It is not just that comic exuberance is the text's answer to atrophy but that self-conscious and self-reflexive play, supported by a picaresque structure that displaces arrival (and endings) by travel (and processes), are the means by which Carter presents social-political questions as a continuing interaction of perspectives with both comic and serious aspects. Fantastic figure, emblematic, assertive, Fevvers symbolizes, against reductive role-play, femininity and freedom or "the freedom which lies behind the mask, within dissimulation, the freedom to juggle with being, and indeed, with the language which is vital to our being, that lies at the heart of the burlesque" (103).

THE HYBRID TEXT: A REVISED SCHEDULE

Nights at the Circus is a text in which the dominant mode of play is combination. Against the privileging of any particular generic form or discourse, its interassociation of literary high culture and folk humour, carnivalesque diversion and sexual/cultural politics, romance conventions and their parody, is a form of combination that preserves the heterogeneity of elements against the pressures of appropriation and homogenisation. Resisting categorical definition and emphasizing process, it retains a rebellious edge. The text is hybrid, an example of Bakhtin's sense of the dialogical in a carnivalesque mixture of entertainment and message:

> Languages of heteroglossia, like mirrors that face each other, each reflecting in its own way a piece, a tiny corner of the world, force us to guess at and grasp for a world behind their mutually reflecting aspects that is broader, more multi-levelled, containing more and varied horizons than would be available to a single language or a single mirror. [23]

Revisioning the Carnivalesque

As Bakhtin observes, the author of a text is the one who employs "the languages of heteroglossia" but, just as this intersection resists simple object analysis and all claims of definitive truth, it prevents construction of the author as a unified concept with authority over meaning. The double-voicedness by which one senses the difference between narrator and author is multiplied in the range of speech and reference associated with characters. Always, the play of language exceeds its users. As entertainer and social commentator, Angela Carter offers in *Nights at the Circus* the *jouissance* of language play with ambiguous cultural criticism

Part of the conceptual framework that Bakhtin defines in the concepts of dialogism, polyphony and heteroglossia, "carnival" involves the interactive double play of parody or travesty; subversive of the serious world of "official" regulations and practices, its mocking provides for the possibility of change; the "old" and ideas of the "new" coexist in a state of shifty tension. In this discussion, I have argued that Carter's *Nights at the Circus* is carnivalesque in mode and concerned with carnival subjects.

But what contribution can this exercise in criticism make to theories of play? As Robert Wilson points out, the carnivalesque may be distinguished, for the purposes of understanding its characteristics and for its application in textual analysis, by comparison with Derridean freeplay. In this view "purposefulness: the presence or absence of an intention"[24] differentiates the two. Situated within the Schillerian tradition of purposeful play, carnival implies particular choice and shaping of action (by carnival participants) whereas Derrida emphasizes freeplay in language as an inevitable condition of its operations. While any text may be considered in terms of Derrida's perceptions of the complex and theoretically endless "freeplay" of signifiers not all texts are carnivalesque in the Bakhtinian sense with its emphasis upon the double plays of comic exaggeration and invention. Although Derridean deconstruction is in its first moves linguistic and even formalist, in its concentration upon *différance,* trace, supplement, graft and the erosion of truth claims, the processes may be turned to specific cultural contexts and political interests as Derrida demonstrates so clearly. On the other hand, because carnival is more immediately concerned with overt cultural operations in its various plays upon hierarchies, ritual and the workings of power in discourse and culture, it engages the social. It is a point of conjecture whether it is revolutionary

238 *Theories of Play and Postmodern Fiction*

or conservative in its effects, a means of unsettling the status quo or a form of licensed revel that is always contained by the larger social calendar that continues beyond it.[25] Carnival laughter may indeed signify ridicule or affirmation, by turns seeming to promote discontinuity and change and the celebration of old patterns. But there are distinctions to be made between folk carnival as a social practice, the source of Bakhtin's theory in particular carnival events, and carnival and carnivalesque as items of interest and practice in literary texts. It is the image of spontaneous and exuberant carnival laughter as a *shared* ritual that Bakhtin affirms so nostalgically:

> Carnival does not know footlights, in the sense that it does not acknowledge any distinction between actors and spectators. Footlights would destroy a carnival, as the absence of footlights would destroy a theatrical performance. Carnival is not a spectacle seen by the people; they live in it, and everyone participates because its very idea embraces all the people. While carnival lasts, there is no other life outside it [. . .] It has a universal spirit; it is a special condition of the entire world, of the world's revival and renewal, in which all take part. (7)

Swept up in the atmosphere, the participant's individuality is lost to the spirit of communal festivity. But the question of representation, whether in Rabelais, Cervantes, Sterne or Carter, necessarily introduces the "footlights" and carnivalesque texts separate actor-characters from spectator-readers. Despite Bakhtin's emphasis upon identification of carnival participants with the action, the sense of difference which would distinguish at least a self-conscious carnivalist is accentuated unavoidably in literary manifestations. Whether the text is perceived as relatively close to the context of its carnivalesque subject, as in Rabelais, or as a more belated (re)construction, as in Carter, attention is drawn to language, to its ambiguities vis-a-vis subject matter and to the processes of reception. Although Walser's role as interviewer in Part One of *Nights at the Circus* formalizes the question of spectator position, it is the play of rhetoric that most signals difference, displacing the social real for the heteroglossia of language.

Resisting monologism by emphasizing the polyphonic intersection of languages in discourse, attending to ideology and affirming the regenerative power of laughter, Bakhtin's work provides not only a

Revisioning the Carnivalesque 239

rhetoric of play but also processes for textual criticism. While agreeing with Robert Wilson that carnival is "both a distinctive and a powerful idea"[26] in the family of play concepts, I am more optimistic than he is about its usefulness for analysis of particular texts. But if analysis is to attend to the carnivalesque in its dividedness and to ambivalence at the heart of carnival laughter, that is, to the particularities of performance and context, it is necessary to recall Bakhtin's repeated emphases upon the complexities of language operations:

> —at any given moment of its historical existence, language is heteroglot from top to bottom: it represents the co-existence of socio-ideological contradictions between the present and the past, between differing epochs of the past, between different socio-ideological groups in the present, between tendencies, schools, circles and so forth, all given a bodily form. These "languages" of heteroglossia intersect each other in a variety of ways, forming new socially typifying "languages." [27]

Seeing Rabelais's work as an expression of folk humour and wisdom that is heterogeneous in its language mixture, Bakhtin's emphasis upon the struggle between "lower" cultural forms and "higher" official practices simultaneously acknowledges and complicates distinctions of social class by defining the official and the carnival as "Two aspects of the world, the serious and the laughing aspect, [which] coexisted in their consciousness."[28] If laughter opposes dogmatism, fanaticism, pedantry and the like, it does so by restoring the ambivalence of dialogical interplay rather than by replacing one form of single meaning or position with another. Decisions about the nature of laughter, its subjects, directions and effects, involve critical judgements that take account of contexts of expression and reception. So, for example, Bakhtin explains Rabelais's inclusion of bawdy jokes at the expense of woman as not only a feature of the popular comic aspect of the Gallic tradition but also as a characteristic marked by ambivalence, as much concerned with regeneration as degradation: "We must note that the image of the woman in the 'Gallic tradition,' like other images in this tradition, is given on the level of ambivalent laughter, at once mocking, destructive and joyfully reasserting. Can it be said that this tradition offers a negative, hostile attitude toward woman? Obviously not. The image is ambivalent."[29] Taking this historical perspective, and

240   *Theories of Play and Postmodern Fiction*

considering the attribution of bawdy jokes to characters in the works, Bakhtin exonerates Rabelais; but, as Wayne Booth points out, "this exoneration of carnival laughter is conducted by and for men"[30] and the general manner of address in *Gargantua and Pantagruel* is to an exclusively male audience. Further, to cite tradition as the grounds of exoneration emphasizes the place for feminist interventions upon that male hegemony.

In what ways may Angela Carter be said to have feminised the carnivalesque? Rabelais and Bakhtin omit the female voice. It is not that woman is excluded from Rabelais' writing, but that she is the subject of a range of references and propositions rather than their author. As Booth notes, "An easy and useless case for the charge of sexism could be made—and indeed it has often been made—simply by listing the immense number of moments in which women are degraded, mocked, humiliated, or explicitly pronounced as inferior to men" (57); but, as he also points out, in weighing the charge one should consider who utters such propositions and in what tone and circumstances, as well as alternative and more favorable images of woman such as those associated with the Abbey of Thélème at the end of *Gargantua,* and the preponderance of satirical attacks on males. Even so, this simplified balance sheet mode of criticism is unfair to the works' ironies and to the test of ideological positions; when Bakhtin emphasizes the positive aspects of "grotesque realism" and the therapeutic power of laughter, "we" may choose to include men and women as beneficiaries of the healing process. It remains the case, nevertheless, that because the female point of view in its own right is excluded, such largesse does not refute patriarchal authority so much as bear the stamp of its imprimatur, and the carnivalesque presented in the writings of Rabelais and theorised by Bakhtin is a male discourse. Carter's intervention varies this discourse. Inscribing female points of view, she extends the opportunities and modes of play by presenting traditional carnival subjects from other angles. The moves are complementary. Woman becomes bawdy story-teller and social critic, not just in the person of the author but in the range of female characters whose voices add different versions of grotesque realism to the carnival collection. In their variations upon popular comic tradition and romance conventions, Fevvers' farting, belching and sexual banter, and the stories of brothel culture and circus performance offer a female revision of the carnivalesque in which woman is no longer the butt but the instigator of

Revisioning the Carnivalesque 241

laughter. She has at her disposal not only the ambiguous legacy of a split tradition that has represented woman as whore and madonna, object of sin and salvation, but opportunities for "feminist" parody and play that use the energies of the carnivalesque for a revised performance schedule.

In *Beyond Good and Evil,* Nietzsche claims the moment for:

> a carnival in the grand style, for the laughter and high spirits of the most spiritual revelry, for the transcendental heights of the highest nonsense and the Aristophanean derision of the world. Perhaps this is where we shall discover the realm of our *invention,* that realm in which we, too, can still be original, say, as parodists of world history and God's buffoons—perhaps, even if nothing else today has any future, our *laughter* may yet have a future.[31]

Combining acknowledgement with scepticism in the ambiguous double-plays of its referencing, parody's inventions are made upon the cultural inheritance. One may attempt to laugh God or the Devil out of sorts but not out of court; whatever exhilaration that laughter provides, it is edged with the other, with the practices and texts of its provocation. So in *Nights at the Circus* laughter is enriched by the literary-cultural frameworks that Carter incorporates or which the text invites to the discourse. A leading example of contemporary carnivalesque, it affirms the value of laughter for serious purposes.

NOTES

1. Italo Calvino, "Definition of Territories: Fantasy" in *The Uses of Literature,* 73. In The *Castle of Crossed Destinies* where the travellers use tarot cards to construct their narratives, Calvino provides an apt demonstration piece.

2. Angela Carter, *Nights at the Circus,* 285. This quotation emphasizes not only the feminist revisionism so central to this text, but also the *fin de siècle* setting with its sense of a new beginning.

3. John Haffenden, *Novelists in Interview,* 82. The comment is in reply to Haffenden's suggestion that Carter's use of folklore might give some readers impressions of "dream-realities, or perhaps escapist fantasies or just spell-binding excursions," as if these are unrelated to "the real" of life in society.

4. Angela Carter, "Notes from the Front Line," in M. Wandor ed., *On Gender and Writing,* 70. This essay presents a strong sense of Carter's

242   *Theories of Play and Postmodern Fiction*

commitment to an open-ended feminism, to the need for continuing interrogation of constructions of gender and representations of female identity, history and cultural positions.

5. For particular examples of critical readings, see Barthes's *S/Z,* Jonathan Culler's *Flaubert: The Uses of Uncertainty* and Barbara Johnson's *The Critical Difference: Essays in the Contemporary Rhetoric of Reading.*

6. Kathryn Hume, *Fantasy and Mimesis: Responses to Reality in Western Literature,* 21. In her survey of definitions of fantasy (see Chapter 1), Hume favours those that are "inclusive" rather than "exclusive," those definitions that are broadest and, therefore, include the widest range of texts. Her own proposition is that literature is the product of two impulses, *mimesis* (the desire to imitate social realities) and *fantasy* (the desire to change those "realities"), and that most literature includes elements of both. To the extent that it challenges the sweep of exclusive definitions (and their appropriation of texts), the view of fantasy as an element rather than a definitive category opens taxonomy and practice.

7. Todorov's definition of the fantastic emphasizes uncertainty or hesitation in explanation. See Tzvetan Todorov, *The Fantastic: A Structural Approach to a Literary Genre.* The quotation from Calvino, used as an epigraph to this chapter, comes from his short response to Todorov's study.

8. Sigmund Freud, *The Interpretation of Dreams* in *The Standard Edition of the Complete Psychological Works of Sigmund Freud,* ed. J. Strachey, IV-V, 620.

9. In Derrida's *Writing and Difference,* 196-231. Considering the long history of the problematic relationship between psychoanalysis, see Lionel Trilling's *Freud and Literature* (1940) and Harold Bloom's "Freud and the Sublime: A Catastrophe Theory of Creativity" in *Agon: Towards a Theory of Revisionism* (1982).

10. In "The Idea of a Psychoanalytic Literary Criticism," Peter Brooks explores the possibilities for its application to literary criticism of refusing psychoanalysis a position of privilege as an explanatory procedure. He considers the concept of transference for what it may offer to understanding of the reading process: "The text conceived as transference should allow us to illuminate and work through that which is at issue in the situation of the speaker, or the story of the narrator—that is what must be rethought, reordered, interpreted from his discourse. Transference and interpretation are in fact interdependent and we cannot assign priority to one over the other"—*Discourse in Psychoanalysis and Literature,* ed. Shlomith Rimmon-Kenan, 13. See also

Revisioning the Carnivalesque   243

Cynthia Chase's "'Transference' as trope and persuasion" in the same collection, 211-32.

11. In interview, Carter mentions a variety of literary influences, many of which readers might perceive in her texts themselves. Dinesen, and others, have helped shape the fairy tale revisions of *The Bloody Chamber,* for example, and the influence of Latin American magical realism is a factor in *Nights at the Circus.* See Haffenden, *Novelists in Interview,* 80-5. Although tracing the paths of influence involves more or less informed guess-work, Carter's texts often advertise at least part of their range in direct references and allusions. As I indicate in this chapter, the range in *Nights at the Circus* is extensive.

12. It is a long history, of course. Revisionist interpretation champions Eve as the necessary transgressor of patriarchal law, as the rebellious figure who acts in the spirit of daring and imagination, in quest of knowledge, against constraints of the God-authored system.

13. Angela Carter, *Black Venus,* 9. For an effective reading of this story, one that situates it with respect to Baudelaire's biography, colonialism, marketing of the Venus image and idea, and Carter's "postcolonial" revision, see Jill Matus, "Blonde, Black and Hottentot Venus: Context and Critique in Angela Carter's 'Black Venus'." For a most fascinating overview of nineteenth-century (and early twentieth-century) interests in and constructions of black bodies, see Robyn Gardner's "Different Bodies."

14. For a comparative reading of *The Passion of New Eve* and Carter's earlier novel *The Infernal Desire Machines of Doctor Hoffman* (1972) that examines closely Carter's "charting of the unconscious processes of Western society," see David Punter's "Angela Carter: Supersessions of the Masculine." Unpicking Carter's attention to sexuality and gender, Punter points out that her focus on the struggle between Eros and Thanatos shifts from specific histories in the earlier work to the social processes of gender construction in the second. It is the case that against the desire for climax, ending and dissolution of self-differentiation, Carter's work, in its ironies, offers increasing self-consciousness and provisionality or continuation of the search for identity and meaning under the sign (in *The Passion of the New Eve)* of the broken phallus. There are no guaranteed happy endings or, as Punter suggests in a later piece, "There is no future tense in Carter's novels: beyond the present, all we can fairly and fearfully suspect is recurrence, the turning of a wheel on which that which began separate will remain separate" (1991 145). Even so, there is extraordinary diversion along the way. On this matter of keeping on, see also Elaine Jordan, "The Dangers of Angela Carter" and Ricarda Schmidt, "The Journey of the Subject in Angela Carter's Fiction." In "The Body of the City:

244   *Theories of Play and Postmodern Fiction*

Angela Carter's *The Passion of New Eve"* Nicoletta Vallorani provides an astute concentration on spatial concepts, moving from the carnivalization of Eve/lyn's body through the constructions of New York, Beulah and Zero's Town to emphasize gendered associations between urban space and bodies.

15. See, for example, Patricia Duncker, "Re-imagining the Fairy Tale: Angela Carter's Bloody Chambers," Susanne Kappeller, *The Pornography of Representation* 133-37, Robert Clark, "Angela Carter's Desire Machine" and Elaine Jordan's response to these studies, "The Dangers of Angela Carter."

16. Elaine Marks and Isabelle de Courtivron, eds., *New French Feminisms: An Anthology.* Xavière Gauthier's interview with Kristeva "Oscillation du 'pouvoir' au 'refus'," originally published in *Tel Quel,* is translated and included in the Marks and Courtivron anthology, 166-67.

17. Huizinga, *Homo Ludens,* 45. I have commented on the importance, and the resistances, of Huizinga's study. It is certainly necessary to move beyond simple play-seriousness oppositions to begin to theorize not only the cultural value of play, but also the necessarily changing ways in which seriousness will be articulated and understood.

18. Bakhtin, *Rabelais and His World,* 7.

19. For his own work on dialogism, see M.M. Bakhtin *The Dialogic Imagination,* especially "Discourse in the Novel"; and the theory of the carnivalesque, which may be seen as an example of dialogical interaction, is presented in *Rabelais and His World.*

20. Bakhtin, *Rabelais and His World,* 8. The extent to which this "second" life shapes and invades the first, so that they are not so much distinctly separated as variously interrelated, remains a matter of debate.

21. Bakhtin uses "heteroglossia" in his essay "Discourse in the Novel," in *The Dialogic Imagination.* Opposing the idea of unity in origins or performance and the principle of homogenisation with respect to discourse, it suggests the heterogeneity of language styles and their cultural commerce that he sees operating in the novel in particular. It has become popular in conceptualising the varieties of language performance in postmodernist fictions.

22. "I'm a great admirer of Mae West. The way Mae West controls the audience-response towards herself in her movies is quite extraordinary. Fevvers is supposed to have something of Mae West's baboon or gunslinger's walk . . ."—Angela Carter in Haffenden, *Novelists in Interview,* 88.

23. Bakhtin, "Discourse in the Novel," in *The Dialogic Imagination,* 414-5.

24. Robert R. Wilson, "Play, Transgression and Carnival: Bakhtin and Derrida on *Scriptor Ludens,*" 84. In this typically careful consideration of play

Revisioning the Carnivalesque 245

concepts, Robert Wilson argues that the carnivalesque is interactive rather than transgressive in the manner of Derridean freeplay. Seeing it in terms of cultural action and reaction, he emphasizes the tension between oppositions as a state of play that is "free, voluntary and creative" (86) rather than transgressive, and he is sceptical of its value for textual analysis.

25. This point is also raised by Michael Bernstein with respect to one dominant form of carnivalesque literature, the Saturnalian dialogue: "What is striking in the literary tradition of the Saturnalian dialogue, from its classical origins until long after the Renaissance, is how rarely the laughter ('festive', 'universal', and 'ambivalent' in Bakhtin's triad [p.11]) actually challenges the audience's own sense of judgment and values. In part, no doubt, this is due to the formally authorized nature of the festival suggesting, in fact, that the ruling conventions permit themselves to be mocked, due to a full confidence in their power to emerge still more firmly entrenched the following morning." — Michael André Bernstein, "When the Carnival Turns Bitter: Preliminary Reflections upon the Abject Hero," 290. Concentrating on Diderot's *Le Neveu de Rameau*, Bernstein reviews the carnivalesque in terms of the "abject hero" with the result that darker aspects of the typology of laughter are emphasized against the regenerative.

26. Wilson, "Play, Transgression and Carnival," 87. Cf. Wilson's later formulation in *In Palamedes' Shadow: Explorations in Play, Game, & Narrative Theory,* chapter 2.

27. Bakhtin, "Discourse in the Novel," 291.

28. Bakhtin, *Rabelais and His World,* 96. Regarding the "carnival" and the "official" as two interrelated *aspects* of social condition, rather than as fixed indicators of class, Bakhtin creates this more flexible, and complex, perspective upon play. Comic and serious, it supports change and ambivalence against monologic definitions.

29. Ibid., 241.

30. Wayne C. Booth, "Freedom of Interpretation: Bakhtin and the Challenge of Feminist Criticism," 63. One of the most interesting aspects of Booth's paper, is the repudiation of freedom from ideological taint together with his emphasis upon subjective critical judgment. In this light, the "answer" to the dilemma of understanding Rabelais's text lies neither in the appeal to single historical placement nor in its avoidance, but in allowing the many voices to be heard.

31. Friedrich Nietzsche, *Beyond Good and Evil,* sec. 233, 150. I am grateful to Michael Bernstein, "When the Carnival Turns Bitter," 284, for this reference.

CHAPTER 6

Deceptive Constructions:
The Art of Building in
Peter Carey's *Illywhacker*

THE ENGINEER AND THE BRICOLEUR

He built like a jazz musician. He restated and reworked the melody of
the old emporium. The creaking galleries were gone now, but you
saw them still, in your imagination. He built like a liar, like a
spider—steel ladders and walkways, catwalks, cages in mid-air, in
racks on walls, tumbling like waterfalls, in a gallery spanning empty
spaces like a stainless Bridge of Sighs.[1]

Educated by Herbert Badgery in the "trickery and deception" (547) of a
city, Hissao the builder adds dissimulation and parody to his
inheritance of the "Australian" skill in improvisation. When
Illywhacker ends with the reconstruction in Sydney, "city of illusions,"
of The Best Pet Shop in the World, financed by Japanese money,
designed by Hissao, and exhibiting its Australians (shearers, lifesavers,
inventors, manufacturers, bushmen, aboriginals, artists, and writers) in
cages, it re-focuses a leading metaphor in Carey's text. Combining the
idea of Australians on display with the idea of building, and text, as
products of "bricolage," this novel pet-shop (and the novel as pet-shop)
presents the double play of parody together with its postmodernist
pastiche upon early twentieth-century Australian history. As hindsight
with difference, it is an exercise in refiguring tradition, with inventive
duplicity. If Badgery's improvisatory prowess signifies the national
skill in making do with materials at hand, *Illywhacker* is a literary
equivalent: writing as the canny embezzlement of other writing or the

248 *Theories of Play and Postmodern Fiction*

text as a tissue of messed-about quotations.[2] It renovates history by opening constructions of the past to new building regulations more in line with Barth's funhouse and the Bonaventure Hotel than with the dun-coloured offspring of traditional realism.

Hissao's innovatory practice, building "like a liar, like a spider," appeals to the imagination. It recalls Barthes' definition of the pleasure of the text as a composition in the making:

> "Text" means "Tissue"; but whereas hitherto we have always taken this tissue as product, a ready-made veil, behind which lies, more or less hidden, meaning (truth), we are now emphasizing, in the tissue, the generative idea that the text is made, is worked out in a perpetual interweaving; lost in this tissue—this texture—the subject unmakes himself, like a spider dissolving in the constructive secretions of its web.[3]

Barthes' emphasis upon construction as a process of making and unmaking, or displacement and difference, coincides with Derrida's description of decentering—"We will therefore not return to dissemination as if it were the centre of the web"[4]—and Carey's big book makes play with the traditional "Australian" inheritance offering a decentered structure that favours ingenuity in building detail. Herbert Badgery's preoccupation with building houses is analogous to building the historical text and old preoccupations with constructing a national consciousness. Each is tacked together, a construction composed of bits and pieces, borrowings, multi-cultural detritus—an exercise in bricolage. In postmodernist terms, the postcolonial imperative must recognize difference and, addressing the historical "subject," Carey and Bail, in Australia, find opportunity to acknowledge and displace the processes of national caricature.[5]

Murray Bail's forays into great Australian traditions help to particularise the modes of play in Carey's renovations and, as introduction, I will refer briefly to Bail's "The Drover's Wife," *Homesickness* and *Holden's Performance.*[6] Paying court to Lawson's icon of the bush tradition, and to Drysdale's painting, "The Drover's Wife" is a proliferation of texts which, taken together, question the currency not of Lawson's story nor of Drysdale's painting but of constructions of representativeness made upon them. In its artifice, in replacing the omniscient narrator with "Gordon," Adelaide dentist, who

Deceptive Constructions 249

has lost "Hazel" to a drover, it draws attention to cultural semiotics and reading frames in a spirit of playful dissimulation. It is a form of play whose critical effect depends upon the reader's appreciation of Lawson's text and its revered place in Australian literature and in constructions of the bush tradition. This deconstructive unsettling of national markers continues in *Homesickness,* and most notably in the absurdist heterogeneity of its band of thirteen tourists abroad. Differentiated by name, status, speech, and sexual preference, they are "multicultural," heterosexual and homosexual, hedonistic and ascetic, brash and introverted, humourless and comic, but "Australian." Self-consciously ridiculous their museum-hopping international grand tour may be, in its bizarre emphasis upon "Australian" graffiti, artefacts, and values as measures of nostalgia and of worth, but there is the disturbing implication that, amidst the fun, the parody strikes a mark. The check-list satire is polished as well as inventive, and, as Don Anderson suggests, *Homesickness* "delights in its own ludic potentialities."[7] Its profusion of naming becomes, paradoxically, an exercise in unnaming, and, against homogeneity, the text presents a persuasive case for difference. As the tourists are moved from Africa to England, South America, the United States and Russia, it is increasingly apparent that *they* are the exhibit, a travelling exhibition, and that not only national identity but character itself is held to be a provisional construction, a product of choices from a mobile range of possibilities. It is not so much a case of reality resisting attempts to represent it in language as that the "real" is that which we construct and apprehend in language. In tourism, Bail emphasizes the passing parade and the question of perspective:

> The tourist keeps going, one leg after the other, or stands waiting, queued. You embody the Human Condition. Stop. Keep going. Searching. For what? It is always a grand sight. (177)

So, as Barthes suggests, "lost in this tissue—this texture—the subject unmakes himself"[8] and "the text passes: it is a nomination in the course of becoming, a tireless approximation."[9] Along the way, in *Homesickness,* the proliferation of slogans, quips and allusions denotes opportunities for play with language and culture against the gravity of identity and ending. And, because the figures constitute so varied a raid on images from Australian popular culture, they provide not simply a

250   Theories of Play and Postmodern Fiction

comic iconography but also a critique of ideological processes. The "innocent" third-person narrative simultaneously invites and targets readers—welcomed to the display of tourists on parade, alerted to the mobility of signifiers and to their mismatches with whole truth, we may recognize our complicity in the construction and transmission of emblems. What sharper suggestion of the mobility and reach of signs, their insufficiency and their tenacity, than this exchange as the travellers are about to leave a remote African village:

> Mrs Cathcart bent down before getting in.
> "And what's this little tacker's name?"
> The boy pointed to himself:
> "Oxford University Press."
> "She means your name," Doug put in, encouraging.
> The boy nodded.
> "Oxford University Press."
> "That's nice. Doug, give him a coin. What would
> you like to be, dear, when you grow up?"
> The boy looked up at Mrs Cathcart. The driver
> began revving the four-cylinder engine.
> "A tourist." (52)

When the travels end, with the tourists gathered in a completely bare museum, lit by harsh white light, Bail underscores the text's elaborations on centrism and decentering, cultural formations and discontinuity, movement and return: "Gradually, standing quietly, they began to see themselves. Possibilities included the past and the near future . . ." (317). In its ludic attention to cultural markers and to matters of connection and transformation, *Homesickness* offers a view of culture and identity as networks of discursive formations, as shifting and shifty constructions that invite intervention.

Holden's Performance maintains this parodic exploration of cultural markers while narrowing the geographical range. Reliable enough, mechanical, home-grown and dull, a figure of the car whose name he bears, Holden Shadbolt is an Australia's Own Product whose travels are confined to Adelaide, Sydney and Canberra, where human conduct is influenced by the city grid and Bail's artful lessons in geometry sacrifice the intricacies of mathematics to the invective of cultural commentary. From the straight lines of Adelaide's "puritanical

Deceptive Constructions 251

streets" and the "logic of *plain thinking*" (2), Holden's moves to Sydney's irregularities, and to Canberra, where national power is "reinforced by a psycho-geometric townplan of lawned circles and spokes, parliaments and palaces at the end of perfectly straight vistas" (215), are somnambulistic changes in direction. They prescribe this automaton's progress as a comic exercise in cultural analysis. Adelaide-trained on a high-fibre diet of ground galley proofs of the *Advertiser,* Holden's photographic memory and unblinking reliability suit not only the black and white world of Manly's Epic Theatre but, in turn, his position as watchful chauffeur to the Minister for the Interior and his selection for Colonel Light's training squad of unobtrusive bodyguards to the Prime Minister. Flat by comparison with Uncle Vern, Frank McBee, Alex Screech and Sid Hoadley, and emblem of the great Australian blankness in his inarticulate and uncritical passage, Holden is a negative figure, one part of a national caricature presented against the absurdist cartography of Bail's city scapes and three decades or so of very reduced cultural history. This Australia is a place of distances, sprawl, and odd collisions, in which human conduct is a product of geomorphic detail and the operations of chance:

> This problem of emptiness in vast space . . . it allowed, extremes of simplicities and acts of God. Dry old continent, flat as a board. With few obstacles to slow down and give texture to a thought, to deeds and to speech itself, angles of chance could intersect with little interruption, without explanation; a paradise for the gambler and fatalist.
>
> The straight lines had been introduced to superimpose some sort of order; an illusion of order. (350)

Whereas the gambler dices with chance, and the fatalist has *considered* possibilities against predetermination, Holden's performance is an unreflexive procession, the mechanical ideal of a reliable engine:

> *Ability to idle all day. Slight overheating.*
> *Stand for hours in the sun. No complaints.*
> *Can go all day on a meat pie.* (353)

But Bail's text, in its reflexiveness, subverts the dominant conceit, displacing *by placing* the totalising figure of the engineering marvel. It

252   *Theories of Play and Postmodern Fiction*

uses the metaphor of the engineer to unpick it, and the processes recall Derrida's deconstruction of Lévi-Strauss's oppositional figures:

> If one calls *bricolage* the necessity of borrowing one's concepts from the text of a heritage which is more or less coherent or ruined, it must be said that every discourse is *bricoleur*. The engineer, whom Lévi-Strauss opposes to the *bricoleur,* should be the one to construct the totality of his language, syntax, and lexicon. In this sense the engineer is a myth. A subject who supposedly would be the absolute origin of his own discourse and supposedly would construct it "out of nothing," "out of whole cloth," would be the creator of the verb, the verb itself. The notion of the engineer who supposedly breaks with all forms of *bricolage* is therefore a theological idea; and since Lévi-Strauss tells us elsewhere that *bricolage* is mythopoetic, the odds are that the engineer is a myth produced by the *bricoleur.*[10]

Dismantling notions of origin and priority, and decentering authority by emphasizing limitation, difference and interplay, Derrida's argument obliterates neither "engineer" nor "bricoleur" but, rather, practices claiming privilege in unity. Constructed from a heritage "which is more or less coherent or ruined," Bail's mechanistic model is the engineering product of a bricoleur's discourse. As the figures of engineer and bricoleur are interdependent, each a supplement that complicates the other, so too in Bail's play with Holden as a marker within cultural traditions more interesting in their heterogeneity than for figures that reduce the critical difference.

In these texts, Bail offers postmodernist visitations upon cultural history, constructions that acknowledge "Australia" in its dividedness by putting the signs on display as signs. There is slippage within operations of the sign, a language game, which, displayed, draws attention to naming more as a play of differences than a matching of equivalences. In "The Drover's Wife," *Homesickness* and *Holden's Performance,* it is the self-consciousness of Bail's presentation of the markers, and the rituals, that invites readers to consider not only their pertinence within Australian cultural traditions but also their attraction as items of play. I read this as self-consciousness based not upon identity and independence but, rather, upon incertitude and the positive recognition of provisionality. In such a construction, as Derrida argues often, meaning involves play: "play *includes* the work of meaning or

Deceptive Constructions

the meaning of work, and includes them not in terms of *knowledge*, but in terms of *inscription:* meaning is a *function* of play, is inscribed in a certain place in the configuration of a meaningless play."[11]

THE ARCHITECT OF ILLUSION

In *Illywhacker,* the figure of building foregrounds explicitly the idea of construction as bricolage. I have suggested that this emphasis on process, and, therefore, on the product in its plurality and dividedness, indicates the play in postmodernism.[12] By displaying scaffolding, or layers, or cultural accretions, in the metonymic slide between building and text, it opens the building/text to inspections mindful of artifice and ontological concerns. The invitations alert readers to the challenges of reading against completion, to reading as a game in which the rules can shift, styles of play are important, and all results are provisional— which is not to deny the operations of power in the discourse. Discussing "the social construction of (un)reality," in his study of postmodernist fiction, Brian McHale uses the building metaphor as a definitional figure: "It is precisely by foregrounding the skeleton of layers [. . .] that postmodernist fiction achieves its aesthetic effects and sustains interest, in the process modeling the complex ontological landscape of our experience."[13] Acknowledging cultural markers in ways that also interrogate their reliability as measures of identity, Bail's texts are examples of urbanely self-conscious postmodernist writing. They deconstruct the identikit. Sharing this interest in the Australian heritage and the ways of cultural definition, Peter Carey provides in *Illywhacker* the special duplicity (and challenge) of a narrator whose particular talent is lying. Speiler, con-man, bullshit-artist, Herbert Badgery is a figure of the writer as trickster; his story is an artful version of twentieth-century Australian history—past-ness refigured according to new building specifications or cultural cartography of a postmodernist turn. In the following discussion, I will argue that Carey's representation, in Badgery, of the author as bricoleur exemplifies the play in postmodernist construction by featuring the positive possibilities in collusion against totalties.

"Call me Ishmael" is the invitation to a journey composed not just of passing strange adventure but of considerable craft in the switching rhetoric of its telling. It is not just that Melville's narrator is given to disappearances and returns, but that the grand project is tricked out (re-

254   *Theories of Play and Postmodern Fiction*

presented) in such a parade of styles that linguistic play subverts simple identity and the critical difference is brought forward in this presentation of "speech" as writing. It is immediately apparent that "My name is Herbert Badgery" (11) is closer to Melville's model than to the "David Copperfield kind of crap" from which Salinger's Holden Caulfield attempts to distinguish his introduction, and difference.[14] When *Illywhacker* begins by declaring itself the work of a con-man who adds that he is 139 years old, growing tits, addicted to lying and relieved to have found an outlet (this novel) for his special talent, the reader is bludgeoned about the artifice of narration and instructed to enjoy the performance: "my advice is to not waste your time with your red pen, to try to pull apart the strands of lies and truth, but to relax and enjoy the show" (11). Characteristic of postmodernist textuality, this dissembling about "truth" or, rather, its rejection as the ideal of a God-authored system, opens the way to multifarious and self-conscious story-making. Against THE WORD, words are unleashed, liars are licensed, History receives a deconstructive shot and the past can be fashioned not just as a source book for narrative but as the product itself of narrative constructions. Carey's narrator is street-smart, a wandering part-time car salesman and survivor educated in the school of hard knocks, whose book learning post-dates experiences as aviator, salesman, builder and theatrical performer, whose gaol term allows time for a B.A. by correspondence, and whose lover tells him, in a reaffirmation of the duplicity of character and text: "You have invented yourself, Mr Badgery, and that is why I like you. You are what they call a confidence man. You can be anything you want" (91). In further signals of this text's redeployment with difference of received narratives of Australian culture, the cast is an assembly of yarn-spinners, aspiring poets, epistoleans and novelists. Collectively, they advertise the telling, providing evidence of the irresistible attractions of lying. Having before him such examples of the poet as his wife Phoebe, history mistress Annette Davidson and Horace Dunlop the Rawleigh's man, this trio of odd interlacings, the "King of Liars" concludes that poets "sit like spiders in the centre of their pretty webs" (204). Had Carey's Badgery read Barthes's reference to the subject unmaking himself in writing "like a spider dissolving in the constructive secretions of its web"?

But it is via "poem" as an instructive figure, and the metonymic play between writing and building, that *Illywhacker* foregrounds its

Deceptive Constructions 255

deceptive constructions. "But now I know," says the lying narrator as he constructs a cage for the king parrot, "a poem can take any form, can be a sleight of hand, a magician's trick, be built from string and paper, fish or animals, bricks and wire" (201) and "Phoebe's great poem was not built from words but from corrugated iron and chicken wire. She did not even build it herself but had me, her labourer, saw and hammer and make it for her. She had me rhyme a cage with a room, a bird with a person, feathers with skin, my home with a gaol . . ." (205). It is a small shift to prose and to the involvement of three generations of Badgerys in their changing construction of the Best Pet Shop in the World with its caged Australiana on display, sustained at first by American dollars and finally by its new owners, the Mitsubishi Company. In this liars' tradition, builders are inventive:

> Spawned by lies, suckled on dreams, infested with dragons, my children could never have been normal, only extraordinary. Had they enjoyed the benefits of books and distinguished visitors they might have grown as famous as they deserved. . . . But as it was they had no books, no brainy visitors. They made their futures in the same way that people fossicking in a tip must build a life, from the materials that come to hand. They made their philosophies from fencing wire and grew eccentrically . . . (359).

The images recall Vance Joy, Harry's absent father, inspiration and muse, from Carey's earlier novel *Bliss*. It is in tip-fossicking Vance that Harry finds his pattern and the Joys their bohemian notoriety, their difference: "Seen fossicking at the tip they were granted the right to eccentricity normally given only to aristocrats . . ." (17). Suckled on stories, Harry Joy much prefers his father's to those he heard in church "about Heaven and Hell and the tortures of Jesus" (15). In particular, Vance tells about New York, "most beautiful and terrible city on earth," which after the next flood will provide its secular lesson, "a bible of buildings, a much better bible, a holy place which only the very learned will know how to read" (18). So there is a talent required not only of builders, working "from the materials that come to hand" but also of interpreters. And in their repetitions of the figure, the texts provide playful readers' guides, cryptic invitations to tip-fossicking that simultaneously hold the connection between building houses, texts and

256 *Theories of Play and Postmodern Fiction*

identity while affirming tricks, illusion, conceits and discontinuities as measures of the art.

But with such emphasis upon the liar's art and the artifice of buildings, what connections are there between Carey's text, which begins so ostentatiously with the lie, and popular versions of Australian cultural history? Calvino's Marco Polo builds fantastic constructions in words, and they exist not in stone and timber but as invisible cities of the imagination, confined to language and to new reading configurations: "Only in Marco Polo's accounts was Kublai Khan able to discern, through the walls and towers destined to crumble, the tracery of a pattern so subtle it could escape the termites' gnawing."[15] In *The Castle of Crossed Destinies,* the stories his travellers build from tarot symbols may touch upon familiars from world literature, but this pictorial mode of narrative construction also displaces all cultural grounds. There is a significant difference between Calvino's art of building, in these collections, and Pynchon's "zone" in *Gravity's Rainbow,* which Brian McHale holds as "paradigmatic for the heterotopian space of postmodernist writing":

> As the novel unfolds, our world and the "other world" mingle with increasing intimacy, hallucinations and fantasies become real, metaphors become literal, the fictional worlds of the mass media— the movies, comic-books—thrust themselves into the midst of historical reality. The zone, in short, becomes plural:
> Isn't this an "interface" here? a meeting surface for two worlds . . . sure, but *which two?* (45)

Although one may quibble with McHale's "real," it is the case that in Pynchon's zone the collection of cultural paraphernalia—place names, events, film, song, books, people—colludes with the fictitious in subversion of its own reliability not as historical reference but as sign of the actual. In chapter two, I have argued that Pynchon's text effectively disassembles History. Carey's building strategies in *Illywhacker* fall between Calvino's world-conjuring and Pynchon's deployment of the "real" as fantastic. Exploiting the licence for dissimulation created by Badgery as ebullient and unreliable narrator, the text deals in trickery; but, on the other hand, its style of geographic and cultural reference situates events within a colourful version of early twentieth-century culture, a traveller's progress in which the

Deceptive Constructions 257

cartography mixes text-book exactitude with an illywhacker's flair for invention. From details of Geelong, Colac, Ballarat, Bacchus Marsh, and Melbourne, to the Mallee and to Sydney, and with reference to early aviation, conscription, religious issues, the T-model Ford, travelling theatricals, the 1930s depression, political movements and changes in national commercial relationships, Carey offers the surprise of the known defamiliarised by particularity and story. The results fulfil an epigraph's promise, the quotation from Twain:

> Australian history . . . . does not read like history, but like the most beautiful lies; and all of a fresh new sort, no mouldy old stale ones. It is full of surprises and adventures, the incongruities, and contradictions, and incredibilities; but they are all true, they all happened. (7)

The interplay of "lies" and "truth" presents not only a demonstration of the con-man's art, evidence of the instabilities of rhetoric and skills of persuasion. Allowing for recognitions, for "truths," by situating the narrative in Australian history, it invites reconsiderations of that inheritance by emphasizing opportunities for interpretation. Whether the building materials consist of the mud and wire netting, wooden crates, and galvanized iron of Herbert Badgery's obsession with houses, or the words of his story-telling, the emphasis on "architecture" dismantles the product. Claiming the privileged narrative space and freedom of the "liar's art" (11), "enthusiasm" as his great talent in life (158) and his "salesman's sense of history" (343), narrator Badgery's rush of story telling embodies Carey's deconstructive plays with local history. In Book 1, for example, names of cities, towns, streets, buildings and institutions proliferate like old familiars, with such cultural markers as Victoria's Western District squattocracy, Geelong's private schools and the city's class consciousness, the *Geelong Advertiser,* the Shearers' Strike, debates on the rabbit issue, Ford motor cars, the mountains of north-east Victoria (Timbertop country), Ballarat's hotels, and Melbourne's street grid and its cultural spaces lacing the invented with interpolations of *the real.* This is the author Carey, who lived in Bacchus Marsh, was a border at Geelong Grammar School and a frequent enough visitor to Ballarat and to Melbourne, revisiting with parodic invention the ambiguous attractions of those familiar sites displaced in time together with some of the narratives of

258   *Theories of Play and Postmodern Fiction*

their (de)construction. History mistress Annette Davidson and Phoebe McGrath, student, are located at the Hermitage Church of England Girls' Grammar School, sister institution to Geelong Grammar School during Carey's student days and, like the boys' school, associated with Western District squatters, wealth, privilege and Englishness. Hardly representing old landed wealth as the daughter of a former bullocky and an ex-barmaid, Phoebe's emergence as a beauty gives an edge to her transgressions:

> The boys from College and Grammar not only seemed to overcome their distaste for her vulgar background, but gave her presents of school scarves. And when the anxiously awaited invitations to the prestigious end-of-year dances began, at last, to arrive, slipped into the green-felt letter rack, to be collected and displayed like trophies on study walls, the little "horror" had more than her share. But by then Annette (cautious, careful Annette) had taken the house in Villamente Street, West Geelong, and Phoebe gave not a fig for the Manisides or Chirnfolds or the Osters or any of the other social luminaries of the Western District. She attended no dances and created a perfect scandal by tearing up an invitation to the Geelong Grammar School dance, before witnesses. She might as well have spat in the altar wine. (15)

There is a Villamante Street in West Geelong; Manifold, Chirnside and Austin are amongst those names from the Western District; Hermitage girls attended Geelong College and Geelong Grammar dances; the parody reinvents a history. Similarly, Herbert Badgery's perambulations and flights are set upon a landscape of specific cultural signs—Melbourne Road, Ryrie Street, Malop Street, Kardinia Park, Belmont Common, Barwon Heads and Colac. As "ground" for the narrative's focus on business schemes, work, relationships, attitudes, dreams and dissatisfactions, they emphasize the self-conscious history-making of this 1919-23 "love story" (12). It is appropriate that the solidity of Melbourne's cityscape is contrasted with the Maribyrnong River valley, the city centre's street names, rectangular grid and particular buildings with west suburban mudflats as the site for Badgery's bower-bird construction of a family love-nest composed from a church hall stolen from Brighton Methodists, spare wing sections from the Morris Farman aeroplane, carpet foraged from Port

Deceptive Constructions

259

Melbourne tip, and a water tank "borrowed" from an Essendon building site. Typically, in its inventiveness, the eccentric/ex-centric draws attention not just to its antithesis in the idea of the historically verifiable "real" but also to mediations of that real wrought by memory, selection, perspective and language.

The text even includes its "education of an architect," in Herbert Badgery's instruction of Hissao, the one whose name evokes all snakes and dragon influences in its peculiar reptilian collection and, as well, prefigures the Japanese connection in this generation's entrepreneurial activity:

> An architect must have the ability to convince people that his schemes are worth it. The better he is the more he needs charm, enthusiasm, variable walks, accents, all the salesman's tools of trade.
>
> I showed him, most important of all, the sort of city it was—full of trickery and deception. If you push against it too hard you will find yourself leaning against empty air [. . .] and I had him do drawings, of buildings that lied about their height, their age, and most particularly their location. There was not one that did not pretend itself huddled in some European capital with weak sun in summer and ice in winter. (546-7)

So the supreme architect of illusion, instructed in Sydney as the city of illusions—this hybrid of European borrowings—fulfils three generations of Badgery promise in "opening out the pet shop, living out the destiny I had mapped for him when I took him to the South Pylon of the Bridge [. . .] he was building a masterpiece" (597). Its display in cages of lifesavers, inventors, manufacturers, bushmen, aboriginals, artists and writers as the genuine Australiana repositions the text's long journey through markers of Australian culture. Questioning ideas of the typical, like Bail's redeployment of the images, its play with caricature satirizes identikit national formations to encourage attention to particularity and difference. When Carey returns to a Sydney context in *The Tax Inspector,* with its concentration on the bizarre Catchprice family of the western suburbs, the microcosmic family presents a much darker vision of the city. Amidst the talk of deals, debts, dirty money and public corruption, and linked emblematically with them, are the secrets of incest within the family, Benny Catchprice's sexual fantasies and the Gothic cellar beneath Catchprice Motors. Here in this

260   *Theories of Play and Postmodern Fiction*

threatening underworld of the city and the damaged psyche, Maria
Takis, the tax inspector, faces her obsessive young captor: "It was like a
subway tunnel in here. She could smell her own death in the stink of
the water. Even while she had fought to stop his grandmother being
committed, all this—the innards of Catchprice Motors—had been here,
underneath her feet" (259). This lower bodily view of the city is a much
darker carnivalesque than the ebullient parody in *Illywhacker* but, like
the earlier work, it questions comfortable assertions of reality.

The work of fiction reminds us that the actual world is more
inconclusive, more open to refigurings, discoveries and new
combinations than it is sometimes held to be. Complex and
heterogeneous, it invites and resists attempts at settlement. As Doreen
Maitre suggests in *Literature and Possible Worlds,* "By the
presentation of worlds which in some ways invite us to take them for
the actual world, the novel makes us aware of both the continuities and
the discontinuities between the actual and the possible" (117). I have
argued that Carey's emphasis upon building acknowledges this play
between continuities and discontinuities. The play elements are in the
text and in the culture that it both addresses and re-dresses. To extend
this argument, I wish to turn attention to the other side of the figure of
building as bricolage to examine, more specifically, the text's focus on
language and writing.

THE THEFT OF HISTORY

Late in *Illywhacker,* and after she has read his notebooks (now that he
has taught himself to be an author as "the only scheme available"),
Leah Goldstein complains that Herbert Badgery treats history badly:

> A hundred things come to me, things that amused me at the time,
> touched me—and now I see they were only excuses to thieve things
> from me. And even then you have not done me the honour of thieving
> things whole but have taken a bit here, a bit there, snipped, altered,
> and so on. You have stolen like a barbarian, slashing a bunch of
> grapes from the middle of a canvas. (549)

He has, she alleges, not only misappropriated her ideas but so
misrepresented the truth that events and people, the detail and the tone,
are gross distortions of actuality. Badgery is the liar, discovering in

Deceptive Constructions 261

writing the ideal outlet for his talent. She is the one with the liar's lump, "the callus where her HB pencil fitted against her finger" (552). In this altercation between "writers," Carey stages a battle that the text has enjoined from the start, its postmodernist polemic against naive constructions of truth-telling.

In Part One, and with respect to the writings of Derrida and Foucault in particular, I have suggested that the variable concept of "play" is important in contemporary historiography. In consideration of the problematics of position and selection, together with the slippages in language itself, history is seen as an always divided construct and not a seamless record of the actual. If we can agree with Rodolphe Gasché that there is no need for post-structuralism to rediscover history "because history was never lost,"[16] it is necessary, nevertheless, to address the relationships between history, culture, and writing. As the debates demonstrate, these issues are not solved in any simple sense; rather, there are persuasions, variations, provisional agreements, and degrees of consensus, and the discourse outruns answers, as it should. Although Leah Goldstein may seem to present merely a common, and simple, complaint about selection and perspective, in alleging that Badgery's theft transgresses her text, the Chinese box structure situates *her* letter of complaint within *his* illywhacker performance. Her charges are reminders of the text and textual processes: "And why have you been so unfair to us, to yourself most of all? [. . . .] Why do you pose as the great criminal, the cynic? [. . . .] You have left out everything worth loving about the emporium. You left out the pianola. And when you leave out the pianola you leave out the very possibility of joy, and suddenly there is a dreadful place, gloomy, oppressive, without music [. . . .] You have treated us all badly, as if we were your creatures" (549-50). The exchange demonstrates again the artifice of the real and the unavoidable infidelity of words to history and to culture if they are perceived as givens rather than as constructs. Similarly, the "social realist" style that Graeme Turner sees in the first part of *Illywhacker,*[17] the style that traditionally privileges history, is not only preceded and framed by Herbert Badgery's opening declaration of his addiction to lying but is variously qualified, as it proceeds, by the excesses of a storyteller whose reliability everywhere contends with his enthusiasm for exaggeration. In *Illywhacker* the fantastic does not gradually replace a social realist mode; it is introduced from the start.

262   *Theories of Play and Postmodern Fiction*

For the purposes of this context, Frank Lentricchia's discussion of Derrida's work creates a useful perspective for the analysis of writing's relationship with "history" in Carey's novel. While regarding Derrida's deconstructive work as thoroughly formalist, Lentricchia emphasizes as well his historical consciousness. He allows (at least) two different emphases in interpretation of this work, that which encourages "the pleasure-oriented formalism of the Yale critics" (the common Marxist formulation of Anglo-American deconstruction), and his view that Derrida initiates a new historical project, one that Lentricchia finds already underway in Foucault's writing.[18] He does not, therefore, condemn Derridean deconstruction to any ahistorical, apolitical, acultural wasteland of self-delighting freeplay; rather, emphasizing Derrida's interrogation of the play of signification from within writing, and on temporal and cultural "grounds," he acknowledges his attention to authorities and to contexts, and quotes, approvingly:

> I didn't say there was no center, that we could get along without the center. I believe that the center is a function, not a being—a reality, but a function. And this function is absolutely indispensable. The subject is absolutely indispensable. I don't destroy the subject; I situate it.[19]

Derrida's work does not deny "authorities" or "centers"—rather, he characteristically refuses their power to specify the limits of meaning. This is not, then, a denial of history but a reminder that it involves heterogeneity, fragmentation, and difference, and that constructions or readings of history must take account of its *writing*. In Lentricchia's words, "Put as boldly as possible, Derrida's point is that once we have turned away from various ontological centerings of writing, we do not turn to free-play in the blue, as the Yale formalists have done. Rather, it would appear that our historical labours have just begun" (175). To labour with the play of difference is to attend to circumstance, context, ideology and rhetoric, and in awareness of the seriousness of play in language and of choices in its use.

In *Illywhacker*, then, the theft of history is that act of appropriation which uses the past selectively, in play, to construct new configurations that are always already "old" as part of a discourse that precedes *and* succeeds them. Herbert Badgery's alleged appropriations of Leah Goldstein's alleged history resemble Carey's raids upon an Australian

Deceptive Constructions 263

cultural inheritance, which is itself a very divided narrative. In either instance, there are points of contact and difference; that which is ordered in its representation of history can be shown to be only seeming whole and unified, an exercise in writerly bricolage that by bearing/baring the stamp of its rhetoricity invites not demolition but more thinking/writing.

The text's address to writing, its self-referencing, provides notice of language as a medium for duplicity. And, as Helen Daniel observes, the formal arrangements draw attention sharply to the text's constructed-ness and artifice:

> With his "salesman's sense of history," Herbert's telling of it is in the true illywhacker style, playing on all its high points, teasing out its tangles where major strands knot together, interrupting the narrative to go back to some earlier episode or run ahead to anticipate some later development, telling yarns within yarns, running off at tangents and detours when they promise richer tales . . . (177).

With its repetitive emphasis upon "lying," *Illywhacker* suits Daniel's template in *Liars: Australian New Novelists*. Badgery's opening declaration presents Epimenides' paradox, "All Cretans are liars," and the text appears to offer "splendid new fictions at every turn, lies which are beautiful and noble, some subsistence lies, some mean and ignoble, snivelling things, noisome, some simply bullshit" (168). But the terminology deals unavoidably with "truth" and, with that measure as the provenance of lies, there is always the challenge of attending sufficiently closely to the duplicity of language as it complicates the simple opposition of "truth" and "lie." As some commentators have argued, notwithstanding the importance of Daniel's study, there is a totalising rhetoric at work within her discoveries of the liars' arts:

> Daniel's fallacious assumption of a correspondence between nature (its conceptual paradigm) and fiction runs throughout *Liars*. Peter Carey is said to display, in all his stories, a "translucency, through which we glimpse the infinite onion of the universe, with all its layers of reality" (159). What the reader discovers, it should be answered, is more fiction: complex, multilayered, playful fiction. [20]

264   *Theories of Play and Postmodern Fiction*

In its self-conscious attention to language and to acts of writing, this "playful fiction" represents the 'historical novel' in its dividedness, and with recognition of the reader's complicity in the art of building new constructions, in language, upon the uncertain foundations of a cultural inheritance.

This recognition is everywhere apparent in *Illywhacker*. It is not just signalled in the overt "Dear Reader" gestures that present this text's revisions of the ancient and playful "contract," revisions that also deconstruct any sense of homogeneity in reception by their emphasis upon dissembling:

> But for the rest of it, you may as well know, lying is my main subject, my specialty, my skill. (11)

> In a moment I must tell you how, competing with my son for the affection of a woman, I misused the valuable art I had learned from Goon. Tse Ying . . . (209)

> —no use at all in you skipping pages, racing ahead, hoping for a bit of hanky-panky. (227)

> My greatest wish is to show you my brave and optimistic boy struggling against the handicap of his conception and upbringing towards success. (436)

> Lucky man, you say, to be so old and frail and yet, at the same time, to inspire such devotion. Bullshit, professor. (490)

> You, my dear sticky-beak, already know the conditions of life on the fourth gallery, but for me it was a revelation. (521)

And so on. As is usually the case, such "direct" addresses paradoxically deconstruct unities, of "reader" and of narrator, by using the conventions of decorum in communication to displace, as pretence, the "contract" of communication. They do not advertise reliability and truth; rather, the guise of confessional intimacy displays its artifice and invites readers to the novel exchange as a process of decidedly playful collusion. They are an obvious narrative strategy and, like structural arrangements that disrupt simple linear construction and its

Deceptive Constructions

associations, they question not so much the idea as the grounds of representation. But, beyond this, they also point to the more fundamental recognition that the play against closure is in the language.

In the fissures of words, in the inexactitude of matches and in the conjurings, there are opportunities for continuing play. Those approximations of reference that allow Herbert Badgery's flighty self-constructions hold for the simultaneous demolition and renovation of language: "There is nothing like a bit of opening out to get people to declare their position. You'll find that this does not happen until the bricks are actually falling . . ." (532). And with ontological confinements suspended, the opportunities for play are considerable: "There is no God. There is only me, Herbert Badgery, enthroned high above Pitt Street while angels or parrots trill attendance" (572). Writing displaces speech as the illywhacker becomes novelist and, in the pastiche of "Australian" markers, culture is refigured as a linguistic construction. "Badgery's" spiel draws attention not to Carey but to language. It dismisses neither history nor culture; rather, the "voice" emphasizes the (dis)continuous work of shaping forces and the desirability of open-endedness in addresses that bring the "past" forward to the present. There is an exuberance in language in Carey's inventive play with ideas and in the range of allusions to twentieth-century Australian culture. The stories about Melbourne and the Victoria Market, selling cannons and T-model Fords, snakes and dragons, Molly Rourke and the electric invigorator, the Kaletskys in Sydney, travels across Victoria, Charles's trade in animals and birds, and the peculiar history of the Pet Shop, create a vivid impression of the mobile text in its sweep of cultural reference. And the mobility is reflexive: "town to town, dancing, writing letters. I cannot stay still anywhere. It is not a country where you can rest. It is a black man's country: sharp stones, rocks, sticks, bull ants, flies. We can only move around it like tourists" (323). In their movements "abroad," Bail's tourists gather bizarre markers of "Australia" in parody of national identity. In Carey's use of the figure, the mobility again resists the idea of unity. As his characters criss-cross the cultural landscape of three generations of selective Australian history, the mobility of the signifiers emphasizes difference. *Illywhacker* is the work of one who has learned that "a poem can take any form, can be a sleight of hand, a magician's trick, be built from string and paper, fish or animals, bricks and wire" (201).

266 *Theories of Play and Postmodern Fiction*

The Depression years of the 1930s evoke in Australian cultural remembrance immediate images of poverty, unemployment, population movement and profound uncertainty. Focusing on the Badgerys' wandering, Carey's attention to the 1930s intermixes familiar symbolic markers and his illywhacker's localism:

> I would rather fill my history with great men and women, philosophers, scientists, intellectuals, artists, but I confess myself incapable of so vast a lie. I am stuck with Badgery & Goldstein (Theatricals) wandering through the 1930s like flies on the face of a great painting, travelling up and down the curlicues of frame, complaining that our legs are like lead and the glare from all that gilt is wearying our eyes, arguing about the nature of life and our place in the world while—I now know—Niels Bohr was postulating the presence of the neutrino, while matter itself was being proved insubstantial, while Hitler—that black spider—was weaving his unholy lies. (326)

The emphasis upon perspectives, the local and the international as well as shifts in time and their effects upon understanding, are important. Just as history may be arranged in terms of large themes, movements, periods, developments and famous events and figures, it is also composed of any number of local inflections. If small detail writes back against grand narratives in cultural appreciation, it is also the case that selection, ordering and communication vary from public consensus to the variable idiosyncracies of individual particularity. Presenting Leah Goldstein travelling the Victorian countryside with Herbert Badgery, emphasizing precisely this shifting play of perspectives, Carey underscores the central emphasis in *Illywhacker* upon the inevitability of the liar's art and story-making in constructions of cultural history:

> But she saw the landscape with Herbert's eyes. It was his, not hers. She could feel nothing for the place, and only sense the things he had told her: how he had flown there, crash-landed here, sold a car to a spud cockie there, at Bungaree. Even Ballarat had been like that. She had seen it as one might see a triple-exposed photograph: streets in which Grigson drove, Mrs Ester strode and through which the horse dragged Molly's mother's coffin. All of this she saw, but it was nothing to do with her. (351)

Deceptive Constructions 267

Landscape and experience are so multiply inscribed, so variously coded, that attributions of meaning and value are, beyond individual choosing, matters for continuing negotiation. Carey's 1930s context is an amalgam, a travelling show, put together with respect to his leading characters' acts of getting by in tough times, making do (in signal Badgery fashion) with what comes to hand, with the Snake Act in pubs, part-time work with the Nathan Schick Show in Ballarat, Charles's skill with birds and animals, tip-fossicking desperation and illywhacker cunning. There are clear links between this self-conscious revisionism, with its play between nostalgia and satire, and Hissao's reconstruction of the Best Pet Shop in the World. Building like a jazz musician, a liar, a spider, he fulfils the illywhacker's ideal of creative improvisation, deception and salesmanship in the absurdist image of caged Australians on display as a live exhibition for paying customers. A reflection on the text's play with history and recalling Bail's parody of national stereotypes in *Homesickness* and *Holden's Performance,* it refigures the spatial and conceptual metaphors of labyrinth (Pynchon), funhouse (Barth) and circus (Carter) to offer all of the ambiguities of the "pet shop": "And you can say it is simply hate that has made Hissao put so many of his fellow countrymen and women on display. Yet he has not only fed them and paid them well, he has chosen them, the types, with great affection. There is a spirit in this place. It is this that excites the visitors" (599). But, the text invites, who's to trust an illywhacker?

One of the most remarkable images in Carey's *Oscar and Lucinda* is the figure of Lucinda prowling the 'tween decks of *Leviathan* looking for a game. Presenting the young heiress as a compulsive gambler, and the Rev Oscar Hopkins as an obsessive, Carey concentrates again on ideas of play, chance and gamesome opportunity—the gambler's addiction—in rewriting "Australian" historical fiction. Having taken to cards "like a duck to water" (166), gambled with the odds in England, and driven to desperation on the home passage by a freak of the *Leviathan*'s ventilation system, Lucinda is the female hero with a double passion. Associated with the gambling streak, she knows the contradictory fascination of glass:

> she did not have to be told, on the day she saw the works at Darling Harbour, that glass is a thing in disguise, an actor, is not solid at all, but a liquid, that an old sheet of glass will not only take on a royal

268   *Theories of Play and Postmodern Fiction*

and purplish tinge but will reveal its true liquid nature by having grown fatter at the bottom and thinner at the top, and that even while it is as frail as the ice on a Parramatta puddle, it is stronger under compression than Sydney sandstone, that it is invisible, solid, in short, a joyous and paradoxical thing, as good a material as any to build a life from. (135)

It is, in other words, another work of fiction. Double-dealing, duplicitous, a thing of fascinating appearances whose reality is both illusory *and* tenacious, it is variously interpretable—another "mould of fashion, glass of form." Orchestrating his gamblers' educations, Oscar's in England and Lucinda's in Australia, towards the climactic mid-ocean meeting of their double confession, and the eventual imago of the glass church, Carey juggles with large narrative interpretations of European, and Christian, experience of the Southern Continent. Granting Oscar a gambler's perception of meaning, "'Our whole faith is a wager, Miss Leplastrier [. . .] we bet that there is a God. We bet our life on it. We calculate the odds, the return . . .'" (261), opens again the closed text of History. Like Herbert Badgery's lies, it refigures the cultural inheritance as the multi-faceted construction of networks of narrative, the "product" as a field of play. In *The Unusual Life of Tristan Smith* Carey's concerns with particularities of Australian history are subsumed in a phantasmagoria of the world history of imperialism and empire presented symbolically in the relationship between colonial Efica and colonising Voorstand and with attention to questions of power, influence, ideas about history, individual displacement and negotiations of meaning, significance and identity. Introducing quest themes, Tristan Smith/Bruder Mouse as grotesquely misshapen hero, political intrigue, Sirkus performance, riddles, deception and the solace of love, the picaresque narrative is Tristan's story. Surreal in its excesses, exploring contemporary postcolonial concerns in the displaced forms of its mix of fable, symbol, myth and satire, this fiction shows Carey tempering history with bizarre imaginings. Addressing the national and international, historical and visionary, this fiction, like *Illywhacker,* also focuses upon the instabilities, uncertainties, needs and small triumphs of individuals. Despite the elaborate frameworking and theatricality, its play with concepts and with language, it comes back to the intimacies of those *petit récits* that, in Lyotard's definition of the

Deceptive Constructions 269

postmodern, replace the grand narratives of human knowledge and progress.

From the early short fiction to *The Unusual Life of Tristan Smith,* Carey's work, his inventive bricolage, refigures *the* Australian experience as an open site for further constructions. Whereas in Bail's texts, it is polished cartoonist exaggerations that question the stereotypes of a "national" culture, Carey's displacements are the results of careful detail turned, finally, to extremities. Presented with a self-conscious edge of exaggeration, as entertainment and as commentary, his cultural landscapes are remarkable for their coupling of difference and familiarity, and, in Herbert Badgery's building and lying, as in Oscar's and Lucinda's gambling and Tristan Smith's role as Bruder Mouse, he creates figures that are emblematic as well as particular. In the processes of their artful play with "national" constructions, his texts disassemble the past as a reliable concept; they offer the attractions of new building permits unconstrained by regulations that limit the play of signification to measuring a construction's strength according to the quality of its truth-claim.

NOTES

1. Peter Carey, *Illywhacker,* 597. The image is self-reflexive of the text's artifice, its negotiations between the empirical and the imaginary.

2. This is a borrowing of Roland Barthes's definition of texts as the products of "bricolage." See *S/Z,* 4-14.

3. Roland Barthes, *The Pleasure of the Text,* 64. The image has many connections—with Derrida's attention to language and writing, Iser's notion of textual meaning as a cooperative product involving the reader, and such famous literary emphases upon weaving/making as *The Odyssey* and *Moby-Dick.*

4. Jacques Derrida, *Dissemination,* 269.

5. The debate and the constructions are international, of course, and I have discussed Canadian examples, in particular, in addition to the Australian context. See "Alberta and the Bush: The Deconstruction of National Identity in Postmodernist Canadian and Australian Fiction" which concentrates on the fiction of Robert Kroetsch and Murray Bail, "Prospero's Art: Zest and Instruction in Recent Canadian and Australian Fiction," and "Deconstructing 'Canadian Literature': Essays in Theory and Criticism."

6. "The Drover's Wife" is included in Bail's short fiction collection *Contemporary Portraits.*

270   *Theories of Play and Postmodern Fiction*

7. Don Anderson, review of *Homesickness,* in *Westerly.*

8. Barthes, *The Pleasure of the Text,* 64

9. Barthes, *S/Z,* 11.

10. Derrida, "Structure, Sign and Play in the Discourse of the Human Sciences," in *Writing and Difference,* 285.

11. Derrida, "From Restricted to General Economy: A Hegelianism without Reserve," in *Writing and Difference,* 260.

12. While acknowledging Linda Hutcheon's emphasis upon a "mimesis of process" in metafiction (or narcissistic narrative), it is also necessary to attend to the "product"—though in its instability as "process," this exchange model of textual negotiation. See Linda Hutcheon, *Narcissistic Narrative: The Metafictional Paradox,* 5.

13. Brian McHale, *Postmodernist Fiction,* 39.

14. J.D. Salinger, *The Catcher in the Rye,* 5.

15. Italo Calvino, *Invisible Cities,* 10

16. Rodolphe Gasché, "Of Aesthetics and Historical Determination," in *Post-Structuralism and the Question of History,* ed. Derek Attridge et al., 159.

17. See Graeme Turner "American Dreaming: The Fiction of Peter Carey," 434. Turner's case for placing Carey's fiction in an American context on the basis of stylistics is supported not only by reference to the American metafictionists, but also by Carey's own references to American culture and influence. Central in "American Dreams," *Bliss* and *Illywhacker,* it receives a vigorous postcolonial emphasis in the displaced terms of *The Unusual Life of Tristan Smith.*

18. This analysis draws upon Lentricchia's discussions in *After the New Criticism,* of 1980. Similar concerns about cultural context inform his later study *Criticism and Social Change* in which he prefers Kenneth Burke's emphasis upon the operations of power in discourse, and his platform for social change, to the political conservatism he reads in de Man's work:

"Deconstruction is conservatism by default—in Paul de Man it teaches the many ways to say that there is nothing to be done. The mood is all from early T.S. Eliot. We are Prufrocks all, all hollow men, who inhabit the wasteland that we know now is the humanities way of the modern university:

'Paralyzed force, gesture without motion'" (p.51).

Derridean deconstruction is excluded.

19. *After the New Criticism,* 174. A popular comment for those wishing to answer the charge of unlicensed freeplay in Derrida's work, it is a response he made following presentation of the epochal paper "Structure, Sign and Play in the Discourse of the Human Sciences." See *The Structuralist Controversy,* 271.

Deceptive Constructions   *271*

20. Robert R. Wilson "Theory as Template: The New Australian Novel," a review of *Liars,* 169. See also Greg Manning, "A Litany of Lies: A Look at Australia's New Fiction," 5-6.

Interlude

This, therefore, will not have been an answer.[1] As I have attempted to argue in this study, play is antithetical to rest. Associated with movement rather than conclusion, involving the action of enquiry and process while resisting resolution, its definitions are, by definition, provisional. To hold that play is endemic to culture is to emphasize change, interrogation, difference and heterogeneity. To analyse the places of play in literature involves not just attention to shifting relationships in the creation and reception of texts but acknowledgement of the play *in* language and opportunities for play *with* language.

After Genesis, "Babel" is usually associated with the confusion of tongues,[2] with the differences *between* languages that result from their dispersal. But there is a more subtle and pervasive sense of difference *within,* and it relates not just to incompletion (of the tower) but to the instability of components:

> The "tower of Babel" does not merely figure the irreducible multiplicity of tongues; it exhibits an incompletion, the impossibility of finishing, of totalizing, of saturating, of completing something on the order of edification, architectural construction, system and architectonics.[3]

Derrida's is an important contribution to theories of play. Recognition of the constructed-ness of cultural forms, including language as the building material of meanings, directs attention to the operations of difference and opportunities for intervention. It encourages continuing productivity, mindful that each achievement is incomplete, and that it, in turn, invites disassembly and reconstitution.

274   *Theories of Play and Postmodern Fiction*

Although play may be exuberant, it is only a much reduced notion that defines it against seriousness and, in consequence, regards it as peripheral to such *important* cultural matters as privilege and deprivation, material production and distribution, operations of power and the constitution of knowledge. When it is located within the processes of discourse, as the factor that deprivileges all forms of essentialism, encourages enquiry, and promotes difference, its political-historical-cultural relevance may be recognized. Play has no provenance apart from its manifestations in cultural processes; the study of play is the study of cultural forms and activities in their dividedness.

In this concentration on particular examples of postmodernist fiction, I have attempted to situate the texts as cultural artefacts while noting those characteristics that resist simple geographical/historical location. Strategies of combination, decentering and cultural revisionism acknowledge *and* displace the markers of identification. Incorporating reference and offering connections, the texts also transform those borrowings so that the notion of origin as explanation gives way to questions of transaction and negotiation in the pursuit of meanings and, if one wishes, the attribution of significance. What the texts have in common, their postmodernist badge, are their varying degrees of overt self-consciousness about language as not just the divided host of meanings but as an instrument of revision, entertainment, and play. In their networks of connection, *Gravity's Rainbow, LETTERS, What the Crow Said, Nights at the Circus,* and *Illywhacker* summon cultural reference in ways that dispossess it of any final claims on truth by emphasizing the shifty grounds of rhetoric, intricacies of context, and the duplicities of communication. As Pynchon's story suggests, "I love you" is not the guarantee but the temptation of meaning and, as an exchange between lovers or between texts and readers, it prefigures much by masking plenty. The lovers' discourse is fraught with play and that is its enchantment. Regardless of their intention, texts beckon and dissemble; to think otherwise is to be a dupe of the "game," a poor player whose strutting and fretting may be caused by too ready an acceptance of the role of narratee, implied reader, intended reader, superreader, or some other such refinement of *position.* Possibilities for exchange exceed the apparent narrative construction; beyond up-front conceptions of narrator, focaliser, or point of view, any ghostly identikit of the author in the wings has still

Interlude 275

to contend with the divided operations of reference. There's the rub, and, in play, the opportunities for engagement never end. Revelation is a beginning. There is no postlude.

NOTES

1. A variation upon the quotation from Derrida's *Dissemination* used as an epigraph to Part I, Chapter 1.

2. See "Genesis," Chapter 11.

3. Derrida, "Des Tours de Babel," in *Difference in Translation*, 165.

Bibliography

Abrams, M.H. "The Deconstructive Angel." *Critical Inquiry* 3.3 (1977): 425-38.

Aeschylus. *The Oresteia.* Ed. Robert Fagles. Harmondsworth: Penguin, 1979.

Alter, Robert. "The New American Novel." *Commentary* 60 (1975): 44-51.

Alter, Robert. *Partial Magic: The Novel as a Self-Conscious Genre.* Berkeley: U of California P, 1975.

Ames, Christopher. "Power and the Obscene Word: Discourses of Extremity in Thomas Pynchon's *Gravity's Rainbow.*" *Contemporary Literature* 31.2 (1990): 191-207.

Anderson, Don. Review of *Homesickness. Westerly* 4 (1980): 94-6.

Arac, Jonathan, Wlad Godzich, and Wallace Martin, eds. *The Yale Critics: Deconstruction in America.* Theory and History of Literature 6. Minneapolis: U of Minnesota P, 1983.

Arac, Jonathan, ed. *Postmodernism and Politics.* Manchester: Manchester UP, 1986.

Aristophanes. *The Frogs.* Trans. David Barrett. Harmondsworth: Penguin, 1967.

Attridge, Derek, et al. *Post-Structuralism and the Question of History.* Cambridge: Cambridge UP, 1987.

Auerbach, Erich. *Mimesis: The Representation of Reality in Western Literature.* Trans. Willard R. Trask. Princeton: Princeton UP, 1968.

Avedon, Elliott M., and Brian Sutton-Smith. *The Study of Games.* New York: John Wiley & Sons, 1971.

Axelos, Kostas. "Planetary Interlude." *Yale French Studies* 41 (1968): 6-18.

Axelos, Kostas. "The Set's Game-Play of Sets." *Yale French Studies* 58 (1979): 95-101.

Bail, Murray. *Contemporary Portraits.* St. Lucia: U of Queensland P,1975.

Bail, Murray. *Homesickness.* Ringwood: Penguin, 1980.

278 *Bibliography*

Bail, Murray. *Holden's Performance.* Ringwood: Viking/Penguin, 1987.

Bakhtin, Mikhail. "The Role of Games in Rabelais." Trans. Hélène Iswolsky. *Yale French Studies,* 41 (1968): 124-32.

Bakhtin, Mikhail. *Rabelais and His World.* Trans. Hélène Iswolsky. Cambridge, Mass.: M.I.T. P, 1968.

Bakhtin, Mikhail. *The Dialogic Imagination.* Trans. Caryl Emerson and Michael Holquist. Austin: U of Texas P, 1981.

Barth, John. "The Literature of Exhaustion." *The Atlantic* 220.2 (August 1967): 29-34.

Barth, John. *The Floating Opera.* 1956; New York: Doubleday, 1967.

Barth, John. *The End of the Road.* 1958; Harmondsworth: Penguin, 1967.

Barth, John. *The Sot-Weed Factor.* 1960; New York: Grosset & Dunlap, 1970.

Barth, John. "Muse, Spare Me." *Book Week* 26 September (1965): 28-9.

Barth, John. *Giles Goat-Boy.* 1966; Harmondsworth: Penguin, 1967.

Barth, John. *Lost in the Funhouse.* 1968; New York: Bantam Books, 1969.

Barth, John. *Chimera.* 1972; London: Quartet Books, 1977.

Barth, John. *LETTERS.* 1979; London: Secker & Warburg, 1980.

Barth, John. "The Literature of Replenishment." *Atlantic* (January 1980): 65-71.

Barth, John. *Sabbatical: A Romance.* New York: Putnam, 1982.

Barth, John. *The Friday Book: Essays and Other Nonfiction.* New York: Putnam, 1984.

Barth, John. *The Tidewater Tales.* 1988; New York: Ballantine Books, 1988.

Barth, John. *The Last Voyage of Somebody the Sailor.* Boston: Little, Brown, 1991.

Barth, John. *Once upon a Time: A Floating Opera.* London: Hodder & Stoughton, 1994.

Barth, John. *Further Fridays: Essays, Lectures, and Other Nonfiction 1984-94.* Boston: Little, Brown & Co., 1995.

Barth, John. *On with the Story.* Boston: Little, Brown & Co., 1996.

Barthes, Roland. *S/Z.* 1970. Trans. Richard Miller. New York: Hill and Wang, 1975.

Barthes, Roland.*The Pleasure of the Text.* 1973. Trans. Richard Miller. New York: Hill and Wang, 1975.

Barthes, Roland. *Roland Barthes by Roland Barthes.* 1975. Trans. Richard Howard. New York: Hill and Wang, 1977.

Barthes, Roland. *Image, Music, Text.* Trans. Stephen Heath. New York: Hill and Wang, 1977.

Bibliography 279

Barthes, Roland. *A Lover's Discourse: Fragments.* 1977. Trans. Richard Howard. New York: Hill and Wang, 1978.

Baudrillard, Jean. *Simulations.* New York: Semiotext(e), 1983a.

Baudrillard, Jean. "The Ecstasy of Communication." *The Anti-Aesthetic: Essays in Postmodern Culture.* Ed. Hal Foster, 126-33.

Baudrillard, Jean. *Cool Memories.* London: Verso, 1990.

Beaujour, Michael. "The Game of Poetics." *Game, Play, Literature.* Ed. Jacques Ehrmann. Boston: Beacon P, 1971, 58-67.

Bellamy, Joe David. "Having It Both Ways: A Conversation between John Barth and Joe David Bellamy." *New American Review* 15 (1972): 134-50.

Belsey, Catherine. *Critical Practice.* London: Methuen, 1980.

Bell, Michael. "Narration as Action: Goethe's 'Bekenntnisse einer Schonen Seele' and Angela Carter's *Nights at the Circus.*" *German Life and Letters.* 45.1 (1992): 16-32.

Bennett, David. "Wrapping Up Postmodernism: The Subject of Consumption Versus the Subject of Cognition." *Postmodern Conditions.* Ed. Andrew Milner et al. Clayton, Victoria: Monash U, 1988, 15-36.

Berman, Neil David. *Playful Fictions and Fictional Players: Games, Sport and Survival in Contemporary American Fiction.* Port Washington, New York: Kennikat P, 1981.

Berne, Eric. *Games People Play.* New York: Grove P, 1964.

Bernstein, Michael André. "When the Carnival Turns Bitter: Preliminary Reflections upon the Abject Hero." *Critical Inquiry* 10.2 (1983): 283-305.

Berressem, Hanjo. *Pynchon's Poetics: Interfacing Theory and Text.* Urbana: U of Illinois P, 1993.

Bertens, Hans. *The Idea of the Postmodern.* London: Routledge, 1995.

Bessai, Diane, and David Jackel. *Figures in a Ground: Canadian Essays on Modern Literature Collected in Honor of Sheila Watson.* Saskatoon: Western Producer Prairie, 1978.

Blake, Kathleen. *Play, Games and Sport: The Literary Works of Lewis Carroll.* Ithaca: Cornell UP, 1974.

Bleich, David. *Subjective Criticism.* Baltimore: Johns Hopkins UP, 1978.

Bloom, Harold. *The Anxiety of Influence: A Theory of Poetry.* New York: Oxford UP, 1973.

Bloom, Harold, et al. *Deconstruction and Criticism.* New York: Seabury P, 1979.

Bloom, Harold. *Agon: Towards a Theory of Revisionism.* New York: Oxford UP, 1982.

280   *Bibliography*

Bono, Paola. "The Passion for Sexual Difference: On (Re)Reading Angela Carter's *The Passion of New Eve.*" *Tessera* 11, Winter (1991): 31-46.

Booth, Wayne. "Preserving the Exemplar." *Critical Inquiry* 3.3 (1977): 407-23.

Booth, Wayne. "Freedom of Interpretation: Bakhtin and the Challenge of Feminist Criticism." *Critical Inquiry* 9.1 (1982): 45-76.

Borges, Jorge Luis. *Labyrinths.* Ed. Donald A. Yates and James E. Irby. Harmondsworth: Penguin, 1970.

Bowen, Zack. *A Reader's Guide to John Barth.* Westport, Conn. & London: Greenwood P, 1994.

Bowering, George. *Burning Water.* Toronto: General Publishing, 1980.

Bowering, George. *Caprice.* Markham, Ontario: Penguin/Viking, 1987.

Brooks, Peter. "The Idea of Psychoanalytic Literary Criticism."*Discourse in Psychoanalysis and Literature.* Ed. Shlomith Rimmon-Kenan. London: Methuen, 1987, 1-18.

Brotherston, G. *The Emergence of the Latin American Novel.* Cambridge: Cambridge UP, 1977.

Brown, Norman O. *Life Against Death: The Psychoanalytic Meaning of History.* Middletown, Conn.: Wesleyan UP, 1959.

Bruss, Elizabeth. "The Game of Literature and Some Literary Games." *New Literary History* 9 (1977):153-72.

Burke, Ruth E. *The Game of Poetics: Ludic Criticism and Postmodern Fiction.* NewYork:Peter Lang,1994.

Caillois, Roger. *Man, Play and Games.* Trans. Meyer Barash. London: Thames & Hudson, 1962.

Caillois, Roger. "Riddles and Images." *Game, Play, Literature.* Ed. Jacques Ehrmann. Boston: Beacon P, 1971, 148-58.

Calinescu, Roger. *Rereading.* New Haven: Yale UP, 1993.

Calvino, Italo. *The Castle of Crossed Destinies.* 1969. Trans. William Weaver. London: Picador, 1978.

Calvino, Italo. *Invisible Cities.* 1972. Trans. William Weaver. London: Picador, 1979.

Calvino, Italo. *If on a winter's night a traveler.* 1979. Trans. William Weaver. London: Picador, 1982.

Calvino, Italo. *The Uses of Literature.* 1982. Trans. Patrick Creagh. Orlando: Harcourt Brace Jovanovich, 1986.

Carey, Peter. *War Crimes.* St Lucia: U of Queensland P, 1979.

Carey, Peter. *Bliss.* London: Picador, 1981.

Carey, Peter. *Illywhacker.* St Lucia: U of Queensland P, 1985.

Carey, Peter. *Oscar and Lucinda.* St Lucia: U of Queensland P, 1988.

Bibliography 281

Carey, Peter. *The Tax Inspector.* St Lucia: U of Queensland P, 1991.

Carey, Peter. *The Unusual Life of Tristan Smith.* New York: Random House, 1995.

Carpentier, Alejo. "On the Marvelous Real in America." Zamora and Faris, eds., *Magical Realism: Theory, History, Community,* 75-88.

Carpentier, Alejo. "The Baroque and the Marvelous Real." Zamora and Faris ed., *Magical Realism: Theory, History, Community,* 89-108.

Carroll, David, ed. *The States of "Theory": History, Art and Critical Discourse.* New York: Columbia UP, 1990.

Carter, Angela. *The Infernal Desire Machines of Doctor Hoffman.* 1972. Harmondsworth: Penguin, 1982.

Carter, Angela. *The Passion of New Eve.* 1977. London: Virago, 1982.

Carter, Angela. *The Sadeian Woman: An Exercise in Cultural History.* London: Virago, 1979.

Carter, Angela. *The Bloody Chamber And Other Adult Tales.* 1979. New York: Harper Colophon, 1981.

Carter, Angela. "Notes from the Front Line." M. Wandor, ed., *On Gender and Writing.* London: Pandora Press, 1983.

Carter, Angela. *Nights at the Circus.* 1984. London: Picador, 1985.

Carter, Angela. *Black Venus.* 1985. London: Picador, 1986.

Carter, Angela. *Wise Children.* London: Chatto and Windus, 1991.

Cervantes Saavedra, Miguel de. *Don Quixote.* 1604/14. Trans. Samuel Putnam. New York: Viking Press, 1949.

Chambers, Ross. "Rules and Moves." *Canadian Review of Comparative Literature.* 19.1-2 (March/June 1992): 95-100.

Chase, Cynthia. "'Transference' as trope and persuasion." *Discourse in Psychoanalysis and Literature.* Ed. Shlomith Rimmon-Kenan. London: Methuen, 1987, 211-32.

Clark, Robert. "Angela Carter's Desire Machine." *Women's Studies* 14 (1987): 147-61.

Clerc, Charles, ed. *Approaches to Gravity's Rainbow.* Columbus: Ohio State UP, 1983.

Cohen, Ralph. "Do Postmodern Genres Exist?" *Genre* XX 3-4 (1987): 241-57.

Cooper, Peter L. *Signs and Symptoms: Thomas Pynchon and the Contemporary World.* Berkeley: U of California P, 1983.

Coover, Robert. *The Universal Baseball Association.* New York: Random House, 1968.

Coover, Robert. *Pricksongs and Descants.* 1969. London: Picador, 1973.

Coover, Robert. *The Public Burning.* 1977. Harmondsworth: Penguin, 1978.

282   *Bibliography*

Cosenza, Joseph A. "Reader-Baiting in *Gravity's Rainbow." Massachusetts Studies in English* 9.1 (1984): 44-53.

Cowart, David. "'Sacrificial Ape': King Kong and his antitypes in *Gravity's Rainbow." Literature and Psychology* 28 (1978): 112-8.

Cowart, David. *Thomas Pynchon: The Art of Allusion.* Carbondale: Southern Illinois UP, 1980.

Crosman, Robert. "Do Readers Make Meaning?" *The Reader in The Text: Essays on Audience and Interpretation.* Eds. Susan R. Suleiman and Inge Crosman. Princeton: Princeton UP, 1980, 149-64.

Culler, Jonathan. *Flaubert: The Uses of Uncertainty.* Ithaca: Cornell UP, 1974.

Culler, Jonathan. *Structuralist Poetics.* London: Routledge and Kegan Paul, 1975.

Culler, Jonathan. "Prolegomena to a Theory of Reading." *The Reader in the Text: Essays on Audience and Interpretation.* Eds. Susan R. Suleiman and Inge Crosman. Princeton: Princeton UP, 1980, 46-66.

Culler, Jonathan. *The Pursuit of Signs: Semiotics, Literature, Deconstruction.* London: Routledge & Kegan Paul, 1981.

Culler, Jonathan. *On Deconstruction: Theory and Criticism After Structuralism.* Ithaca: Cornell UP, 1982.

Culler, Jonathan. *Barthes.* London: Fontana, 1983.

Daniel, Helen. *Liars: Australian New Novelists.* Ringwood: Penguin, 1988.

de Man, Paul. *Blindness and Insight: Essays in the Rhetoric of Contemporary Criticism.* London: Methuen, 1983.

de Saussure, Ferdinand. *Course in General Linguistics.* Trans. W. Baskin. London: Fontana/Collins, 1974.

Deleuze, Gilles. *Nietzsche and Philosophy.* Trans. Hugh Tomlinson. London: Athlone P, 1983.

Derrida, Jacques. *Speech and Phenomena, and Other Essays on Husserl's Theory of Signs.* 1967; Trans. David B. Allison. Evanston, Ill.: Northwestern UP, 1973.

Derrida, Jacques. *Of Grammatology.* 1967; Trans. Gayatri Chakravorty Spivak. Baltimore: Johns Hopkins UP, 1976.

Derrida, Jacques.*Writing and Difference.* 1967; Trans. Alan Bass. London: Routledge and Kegan Paul, 1978.

Derrida, Jacques. *Dissemination.* 1972; Trans. Barbara Johnson. Chicago: U of Chicago P, 1981.

Derrida, Jacques. *Positions.* 1972; Trans. Alan Bass. Chicago: U of Chicago P, 1981.

Bibliography

Derrida, Jacques. "The White Mythology: Metaphor in the Text of Philosophy." *New Literary History* V1.1 (1974): 7-74.

Derrida, Jacques. "Living On: Border Lines." *Deconstruction and Criticism.* Ed. Harold Bloom et al. New York: Seabury Press, 1974.

Derrida, Jacques. "The Supplement of Copula: Philosophy *before* Linguistics." *Textual Strategies: Perspectives in Post-Structuralist Criticism.* Ed. Josué V. Harari. Ithaca: Cornell UP, 1979, 82-121.

Derrida, Jacques. "Des Tours de Babel." *Difference in Translation.* Ed. Joseph F. Graham. Ithaca: Cornell UP, 1985, 165-207.

Derrida, Jacques. *The Ear of the Other: Texts, and Discussions.* Trans. and ed. Christie V. McDonald, Claude Lévesque and Peggy Kamuf. New York: Schocken Books, 1985.

Derrida, Jacques. *The Post Card: From Socrates to Freud and Beyond.* Trans. Alan Bass. Chicago: U of Chicago P, 1987.

Derrida, Jacques. *Limited Inc.* Trans. Samuel Weber. Evanston, Ill.: Northwestern UP, 1988.

Derrida, Jacques. "Some Statements and Truisms about Neologisms, Newisms, Postisms, Parasitisms, and other Small Seismisms." *The States of "Theory."* Ed. David Carroll, 63-94.

Detweiler, Robert. "Games and Play in Modern American Fiction." *Contemporary Literature* 17.1 (1976): 44-62.

Dilthey, Wilhelm. *W. Dilthey: Selected Writings.* Ed. H.P. Rickman. London: Cambridge University Press, 1976.

Docherty, Thomas, ed. *Postmodernism: A Reader.* Hemel Hempstead: Harvester Wheatsheaf, 1993.

Douglas, Alfred. *The Tarot.* Harmondsworth: Penguin, 1973.

Dreyfus, Hubert L., and Paul Rabinow, eds. *Michel Foucault: Beyond Structuralism and Hermeneutics.* Chicago: U of Chicago P, 1982.

Duncker, Patricia. "Re-imagining the Fairy Tales: Angela Carter's Bloody Chambers." *Literature and History: A Journal for the Humanities* 10.1 (1984): 3-14.

Eagleton, Terry. *Criticism and Ideology.* 1976; London: Verso, 1978.

Eagleton, Terry. "Marxism and Deconstruction." *Contemporary Literature* 22 (1981): 477-88.

Eagleton, Terry. "The Revolt of the Reader." *New Literary History* XIII (1982): 449-52.

Eagleton, Terry. *Literary Theory: An Introduction.* Oxford: Blackwell, 1983.

Eagleton, Terry. *Against the Grain: Essays 1975-1985.* London: Verso, 1986.

Edwards, Brian. "Mixing Media: Film as Metaphor in Pynchon's *Gravity's Rainbow.*" *Australasian Journal of American Studies* 1.3 (1982): 1-15.

Edwards, Brian. Review of *The Play of the World. Canadian Review of Comparative Literature* XII.2 (1985): 361-4.

Edwards, Brian. "Alberta and the Bush: The Deconstruction of National Identity in Postmodernist Canadian and Australian Fiction." *Line* 6 (1985): 72-82.

Edwards, Brian. "Deconstructing the Artist and the Art: Barth and Calvino at Play in the Funhouse of Language." *Canadian Review of Comparative Literature* XII.2 (1985): 264-86.

Edwards, Brian. "Novelist as Trickster: The Magical Presence of Gabriel García Márquez in Robert Kroetsch's *What the Crow Said.*" *Essays on Canadian Writing* 34 (1987): 92-110.

Edwards, Brian. "Narrative as Gift Exchange: Talking with Robert Kroetsch." *Mattoid* 28 (1987) 75-89.

Edwards, Brian. "Tradition and Duplicity: George Bowering's *Caprice* and Peter Carey's *Illywhacker.*" Presentation to Association for Canadian Studies in Australia and New Zealand Conference, Australian National University, July 1988.

Edwards, Brian. "Deconstructing 'Canadian Literature': Essays in Theory and Criticism." *West Coast Line* 3 (1990): 150-58.

Edwards, Brian. "Prospero's Art: Zest and Instruction in Recent Canadian and Australian Fiction." *Australian-Canadian Studies* 9.1/2 (1990): 79-90.

Edwards, Brian. "Deceptive Constructions: The Art of Building in Peter Carey's *Illywhacker.*" *Australian and New Zealand Studies in Canada* 4 (1990): 39-56.

Edwards, Brian. "Playing with Theory" (Review of R. Rawdon Wilson, *In Palamedes' Shadow: Explorations in Play, Game, & Narrative Theory*) *Mattoid* 39 (1991): 127-34.

Edwards, Brian. "Figures of Difference: History, Historicism and Critical Practice." *Canadian Review of Comparative Literature* XIX.1/2 (1992): 155-68.

Edwards, Brian. "Artifice and Desire: Narrative Striptease in *The Puppeteer.*" *Open Letter* Ninth Series 5-6 (1996): 219-28.

Edwards, Brian. "Rigged Play: Pynchon's *Gravity's Rainbow* as Decentered Text." *Canadian Review of Comparative Literature* XXIII. 2 (1996): 277-305.

Ehrmann, Jacques, ed. *Game, Play, Literature.* Boston: Beacon P, 1968.

Bibliography 285

Eliade, Mircea. *Cosmos and History: The Myth of the Eternal Return.* Trans. Willard R. Trask. New York: Harper & Row, 1959.

Eliade, Mircea. *Myths, Dreams and Mysteries.* Trans. Philip Mairet. London: Collins, 1968.

Eliot, T.S. "Tradition and the Individual Talent." *Selected Prose of T.S. Eliot.* Ed. Frank Kermode. London: Faber, 1975.

Eliot, T.S. "The Metaphysical Poets." *Selected Prose of T.S. Eliot.* Ed. Frank Kermode. London: Faber, 1975.

Ellis, M.J. *Why People Play.* New Jersey: Prentice-Hall, 1973.

Empson, William. *Seven Types of Ambiguity.* Harmondsworth: Penguin, 1961.

Enck, John. "John Barth. An Interview." *Contemporary Literature* 6 (1965): 3-14.

Euripides. *The Bacchae.* Trans. G.S. Kirk. Englewood Cliffs, N.J.: Prentice-Hall, 1970.

Farina, Richard. *Been Down So Long It Looks Like Up To Me.* New York: Random House, 1966.

Faris, Wendy B. "Scheherazade's Children: Magical Realism and Postmodernist Fiction." *Magical Realism: Theory, History, Community.* Eds. Lois Parkinson Zamora and Wendy B. Faris. 163-90.

Farwell, Harold. "John Barth's Tenuous Affirmation: 'The Absurd Unending Possibility of Love'." *The Georgia Review* XXVIII (1974): 290-306.

Felperin, Howard. *Beyond Deconstruction: The Uses and Abuses of Literary Theory.* Oxford: Clarendon P, 1985.

Fetterly, Judith. *The Resisting Reader: A Feminist Approach to American Fiction.* Bloomington: Indiana UP, 1978.

Feyerabend, Paul. *Against Method.* London: New Left Books, 1975.

Fielding, Henry. *Tom Jones.* 1749; New York: Random House, 1950.

Fink, Eugen. *Das Spiel als Weltsymbol.* Stuttgart: B. Umbreit, 1960.

Fink, Eugen. "The Oasis of Happiness: Toward an Ontology of Play." *Games, Play and Literature.* Ed. Jacques Ehrmann. Boston: Beacon P, 1968, 19-30.

Fish, Stanley. "Literature in the Reader: Affective Stylistics." *New Literary History* 2.1 (1970): 123-62.

Fish, Stanley. "Interpreting the Variorum." *Critical Inquiry* 2 (1976): 465-85.

Fish, Stanley. *Is There a Text in This Class?* Cambridge, Mass.: Harvard UP, 1980.

Fish, Stanley. "Why No One's Afraid of Wolfgang Iser." *Diacritics* (1981): 2-13.

286   *Bibliography*

Fogel, Stan, & Gordon Slethaug. *Understanding John Barth.* Columbia: U of
    South Carolina P, 1990.
Foster, Hal, ed. *The Anti-Aesthetic: Essays on Postmodern Culture.* Port
    Townsend, Wash.: Bay P, 1983.
Foucault, Michel. *Madness and Civilization: A History of Insanity in the Age of
    Reason.* Trans. R. Howard. New York: Vintage/Random House, 1973.
Foucault, Michel. *The Birth of the Clinic: An Archaeology of Medical
    Perception.* Trans. A.M. Sheridan-Smith. New York: Vintage/Random
    House, 1975.
Foucault, Michel. *The Archaeology of Knowledge.* Trans. A.M. Sheridan-
    Smith. New York: Harper & Row, 1976.
Foucault, Michel. *Language, Counter-Memory, Practice.* Ed. Donald F.
    Bouchard, and trans. Bouchard and Sherry Simon. Ithaca: Cornell UP,
    1977.
Foucault, Michel. *Discipline and Punish: The Birth of the Prison.* Trans. Alan
    Sheridan. New York: Vintage/Random House, 1979.
Foucault, Michel. *The History of Sexuality.* Trans. Robert Hurley. New York:
    Vintage/Random House, 1980.
Fowles, John. *The Magus.* 1966; London: Pan Books, 1968.
Fowles, John. *The French Lieutenant's Woman.* 1969; London: Panther Books,
    1971.
Fowles, John. *The Ebony Tower.* 1974; London: Panther Books, 1975.
Fowles, John. *Daniel Martin.* 1977; London: Triad/Panther, 1978.
Fowles, John. *Mantissa.* 1982; London: Triad/Panther, 1984.
Freud, Sigmund. *Jokes and Their Relation to the Unconscious.* Trans. James
    Strachey. New York: Norton, 1960.
Freud, Sigmund. *The Interpretation of Dreams.* Trans. J. Strachey, *The
    Standard Edition of the Complete Psychological Works of Sigmund Freud*
    London: Hogarth P, 1953-74, vol. IV-V.
Freud, Sigmund. *Civilisation and Its Discontents.* Trans. J. Rivière. London:
    Hogarth P, 1975.
Freund, Elizabeth. *The Return of the Reader.* London: Methuen, 1987.
Frye, Northrop. *Anatomy of Criticism.* Princeton: Princeton UP, 1957.
Frye, Northrop. *Fables of Identity: Studies in Poetic Mythology.* New York:
    Harcourt & Brace, 1963.
Gadamer, Hans-Georg. *Truth and Method.* Trans. Garrett Barden and John
    Cumming. New York: Seabury P, 1975.
Gadamer, Hans-Georg. *Dialogue and Dialectic.* Trans. P. Christopher Smith.
    New Haven: Yale UP, 1980.

Bibliography 287

Gallagher, D.P. *Modern Latin American Literature.* London: Oxford UP, 1973.

García Márquez, Gabriel. *Leaf Storm and Other Stories.* Trans. Gregory Rabassa. New York: Avon, 1973.

García Márquez, Gabriel. *No One Writes to the Colonel.* 1961; Trans. J.S. Bernstein. London: Jonathan Cape, 1971.

García Márquez, Gabriel. *One Hundred Years of Solitude.* 1967; Trans. Gregory Rabassa. Harmondsworth: Penguin, 1972.

García Márquez, Gabriel. *The Autumn of the Patriarch.* 1975; Trans. Gregory Rabassa. London: Jonathan Cape, 1977.

García Márquez, Gabriel. *Chronicle of a Death Foretold.* Trans. Gregory Rabassa. London: Picador, 1983.

Gardner, Robyn. "Saying the Subject (or Slaying the Subject) of Postmodernism." Unpublished paper presented to Honours Seminar, "Cultural Theory/Cultural Practice," Deakin University, 1988.

Gardner, Robyn. "Different Bodies." *Mattoid* 50, The Body Issue (1996):6-32.

Gasché, Rodolphe. "Deconstruction as Criticism." *Glyph* 6 (1979): 177-216.

Gasché, Rodolphe.*The Tain of the Mirror: Derrida and the Philosophy of Reason.* Cambridge, Mass.: Harvard UP, 1986.

Gasché, Rodolphe. "Of Aesthetics and Historical Determination." *Post-Structuralism and the Question of History.* Ed. Derek Attridge et al. Cambridge: Cambridge UP, 1987, 139-61.

Gasset, Ortega y. *The Dehumanisation of Art and Other Essays on Art, Culture and Literature.* Princeton: Princeton UP, 1968.

Gauthier, Xavière. "Oscillation du 'pouvoir' au 'refus'." *New French Feminisms: an Anthology.* Eds. Elaine Marks and Isabelle de Courtivron. New York: Hill & Wang, 1978, 166-7.

Gezari, Janet K. "Roman et problème chez Nabokov." *Poetique* 17 (1974)

Graff, Gerald. "The Myth of the Postmodernist Breakthrough." *Triquarterly* 33 (1973): 383-417.

Graff, Gerald. "Fear and Trembling at Yale." *The American Scholar* Autumn (1977): 467-78.

Graff, Gerald. "Under Our Belt and off Our Back: Barth's *LETTERS* and Postmodern Fiction." *Triquarterly* 52 (1981): 150-64.

Graham, Joseph F. *Difference in Translation.* Ithaca: Cornell UP, 1985.

Green, Geoffrey, Donald J. Greiner & Larry McCaffery, eds. *The Vineland Papers.* Normal, Ill.: Dalkey Archive P, 1994.

Greene, Gayle and Coppelia Kahn eds. *Making a Difference: Feminist Literary Criticism.* London: Methuen, 1985.

288 *Bibliography*

Griffin, Clive. "The Humour of *One Hundred Years of Solitude.*" *Gabriel García Márquez: New Readings.* Eds. Bernard McGuirk and Richard Cardwell. Cambridge: Cambridge UP, 1987, 81-94.

Gross, Beverley. "The Anti-Novels of John Barth." *Chicago Review* XX (1968): 95-109.

Guinness, G., and A. Hurley eds. *Auctor Ludens: Essays on Play in Literature.* Philadelphia: John Benjamins, 1986.

Habermas, Jurgen. *Knowledge and Human Interests.* London: Heinemann, 1972.

Habermas, Jurgen. "Modernity Versus Postmodernity." *New German Critique* 22 (1981): 3-14.

Habermas, Jurgen. "Modernity—An Incomplete Project." *The Anti-Aesthetic: Essays on Postmodern Culture.* Ed. Hal Foster. Port Townsend, Wash.: Bay P, 1983, 3-15.

Haffenden, John. *Novelists in Interview.* London: Methuen, 1985.

Hancock, Geoff. "An Interview with Robert Kroetsch." *Canadian Fiction Magazine* 24-5 (1977): 33-52.

Hans, James S. *The Play of the World.* Amherst: U of Massachusetts P, 1981.

Harari, Josué V. *Textual Strategies: Perspectives in Post-Structuralist Criticism.* Ithaca: Cornell UP, 1979.

Harris, Charles B. *Passionate Virtuosity: The Fiction of John Barth.* Urbana and Chicago: U of Illinois P, 1983.

Harrison, Dick, ed. *Crossing Frontiers: Papers in American and Canadian Western Literature.* Edmonton: U of Alberta P, 1979.

Hartman, Geoffrey. "Literary Criticism and Its Discontents." *Critical Inquiry* 3 (1976): 203-20.

Hartman, Geoffrey. *Criticism in the Wilderness.* New Haven: Yale UP, 1980.

Hartman, Geoffrey. *Saving the Text: Literature, Derrida, Philosophy.* Baltimore: Johns Hopkins UP, 1981.

Hassan, Ihab. *The Dismemberment of Orpheus.* Madison, Wisconsin: U of Wisconsin P, 1982.

Hassan, Ihab. *The Postmodern Turn: Essays in Postmodern Theory and Culture.* Cleveland: Ohio State UP, 1987.

Heidegger, Martin. *Der Satz vom Grund.* Pfullingen: Verlag Günther Neske, 1957.

Hendin, Josephine. *Vulnerable People: A View of American Fiction Since 1945.* New York: Oxford UP, 1978.

Hirsch, E.D. *Validity in Interpretation.* New Haven: Yale UP, 1967.

Hirsch, E.D. *The Philosophy of Composition.* Chicago: U of Chicago P, 1977.

Bibliography   *289*

Hite, Molly. *Ideas of Order in the Novels of Thomas Pynchon.* Columbus: Ohio State UP, 1983.

Hodgins, Jack. *The Invention of the World.* New York: Harcourt Brace Jovanovitch, 1978.

Holland, Norman. *5 Readers Reading.* New Haven: Yale UP, 1975.

Holland, Norman. "Unity Identity Text Self." *PMLA* 90 (1975): 813-22.

Holquist, Michael. "The Carnival of Discourse: Baxtin and Simultaneity." *Canadian Review of Comparative Literature* XII.2 (1985): 220-34.

Holub, Robert. *Reception Theory: A Critical Introduction.* London: Methuen, 1984.

Horvath, Brooke. "Linguistic Distancing in *Gravity's Rainbow.*" *Pynchon Notes* 8 (1982): 5-22.

Huizinga, Johan. *Homo Ludens. A Study of the Play Element in Culture.* Trans. R.F.C. Hull. London: Paladin, 1970.

Hume, Kathryn. *Fantasy and Mimesis: Responses to Reality in Western Literature.* London: Methuen, 1984.

Hutcheon, Linda. "The Carnivalesque and Contemporary Narrative: Popular Culture and the 'Erotic'." *University of Ottawa Review* 53.1 (1983): 83-94.

Hutcheon, Linda. *Narcissistic Narrative: The Metafictional Paradox.* London: Methuen, 1984.

Hutcheon, Linda. "The Pastime of Past Time: Fiction, History, Historiographic Metafiction." *Genre,* XX, no.3-4 (1987): 285-305.

Hutcheon, Linda. *A Poetics of Postmodernism: History, Theory, Fiction.* New York & London: Routledge, 1988.

Hutcheon, Linda. *The Politics of Postmodernism.* New York & London, Routledge, 1989.

Hutchinson, Peter. *Games Authors Play.* London: Methuen, 1983.

Ingarden, Roman. *The Cognition of the Literary Work.* 1937; Trans. Ruth Ann Crowly and Kenneth R. Olsen. Evanston, Ill.: Northwestern UP, 1973.

Iser, Wolfgang. *The Implied Reader: Patterns in Prose Fiction.* Baltimore: Johns Hopkins UP, 1974.

Iser, Wolfgang. *The Act of Reading: A Theory of Aesthetic Response.* Baltimore: Johns Hopkins UP, 1978.

Jameson, Fredric. "Postmodernism, or the Cultural Logic of Late Capitalism." *New Left Review* 146 (1984): 53-93.

Jameson, Fredric. "Postmodernism and Consumer Society." *Postmodernism and Its Discontents.* Ed. E. Ann Kaplan. London: Verso, 1988, 13-29.

Jameson, Fredric. "Marxism and Postmodernism." *New Left Review* 176 (1989): 31-45.

290 *Bibliography*

Jameson, Fredric. *Postmodernism, or, the Cultural Logic of Late Capitalism.* Durham, NC: Duke UP, 1991.

Janes, Regina. *Gabriel García Márquez: Revolutions in Wonderland.* Columbia: U of Missouri P, 1981.

Jauss, Hans Robert. *Toward An Aesthetic of Reception.* Trans. Timothy Bahti. Minneapolis: U of Minnesota P, 1982.

Johnson, Barbara. *The Critical Difference. Essays in the Contemporary Rhetoric of Reading.* Baltimore: Johns Hopkins UP, 1980.

Johnson, Barbara. "Translator's Introduction," to Jacques Derrida, *Dissemination.* Chicago: U of Chicago P, 1981.

Jordan, Elaine. "The Dangers of Angela Carter." *New Feminist Discourses.* Ed. Isobel Armstrong. 1992. 119-33.

Jordan, Elaine. "Down the Road, or History Rehearsed." *Postmodernism and the Re-Reading of Modernity.* Eds. Francis Barker et al. Manchester: Manchester UP, 1992. 159-79.

Kaplan, E. Ann, ed. *Postmodernism and Its Discontents.* London: Verso, 1988.

Kappeler, Susanne. *The Pornography of Representation.* London: Polity P, 1986.

Kaufmann, Walter, ed. *The Portable Nietzsche.* Harmondsworth: Penguin/ Viking, 1976.

Kearney, R., ed. *Dialogues with Contemporary Continental Thinkers.* Manchester: Manchester UP, 1984.

Kellner, Douglas. *Postmodernism/Jameson/Critique.* Washington, D.C.: Maisonneuve P, 1989.

Kendrick, Walter. "The Real Magic of Angela Carter." *Contemporary British Women Writers: Narrative Strategies.* Ed. Robert Hosmer. New York: 1993. 66-84.

Kennedy, William. "García at Noon and Beyond." *The Observer* 10 Dec. (1972): 69-71.

Kermode, Frank, ed. *Selected Prose of T.S. Eliot.* London: Faber, 1975.

Kermode, Frank. *The Sense of an Ending.* New York: Oxford UP, 1967.

Kern, Edith. *The Absolute Comic.* New York: Columbia UP, 1980.

Kierkegaard, Soren. *Concluding Unscientific Postscript.* Trans. D.F. Swenson and W. Lowrie. Princeton: Princeton UP, 1968.

Kolodny, Annette. "Dancing Through the Minefield: Some Observations On the Theory, Practice and Politics of a Feminist Literary Criticism." *Feminist Studies* 6.1 (1980); reprinted in Showalter, ed. *The New Feminist Criticism.* London: Virago, 1986, 144-67.

Bibliography 291

Kracauer, Siegfried. *From Caligari to Hitler: A Psychological Study of the German Film.* Princeton: Princeton UP, 1974.

Krafft, John M. *Historical Imagination in the Novels of Thomas Pynchon.* Dissertation, State University of New York at Buffalo, 1978.

Kristeva, Julia. *Desire in Language: A Semiotic Approach to Literature and Art.* Ed. Leon S. Roudiez; trans. Thomas Gora, Alice Jardine, and Leon Roudiez. New York: Columbia UP, 1980.

Kroetsch, Robert. *But We Are Exiles.* 1965; Toronto: Macmillan, 1977.

Kroetsch, Robert. *The Words of My Roaring.* London: Macmillan, 1966.

Kroetsch, Robert. *The Studhorse Man.* 1970; Markham: Paperjacks, 1977.

Kroetsch, Robert. *The Crow Journals.* Edmonton: NeWest P, 1980.

Kroetsch, Robert. *Badlands.* 1975. Toronto: General Publishing, 1982.

Kroetsch, Robert. *What the Crow Said.* Don Mills, Ontario: General Publishing, 1978.

Kroetsch, Robert. *Alibi.* 1983. Toronto: General Publishing, 1984.

Kroetsch, Robert. *Robert Kroetsch: Essays. Open Letter* Spring (1983).

Kroetsch, Robert. *Completed Field Notes: The Long Poems of Robert Kroetsch.* Toronto: McClelland & Stewart, 1989.

Kroetsch, Robert. *The Lovely Treachery of Words.* Toronto: Oxford UP, 1989.

Kroetsch, Robert. *The Puppeteer.* Toronto: Random House, 1992.

Kroetsch, Robert. *A Likely Story: The Writing Life.* Red Deer: Red Deer College P, 1995.

Kuhn, Thomas. *The Structure of Scientific Revolutions.* Chicago: U of Chicago P, 1962.

Lavenda, Robert H. "From Festival of Progress to Masque of Degradation: Carnival in Caracas as a Changing Metaphor for Social Reality." *Play and Culture.* Ed. Helen B. Schwartzman. West Point, N.Y.: Leisure Press, 1980, 19-28.

Le Clair, Thomas. "John Barth's *The Floating Opera:* Death and the Craft of Fiction." *University of Texas Studies in Language and Literature* 14 (1973): 711-30.

Lecker, Robert. *Robert Kroetsch.* Boston: Twayne Publishers, 1986.

Leitch, Vincent. *Deconstructive Criticism.* London: Hutchinson, 1983.

Lentricchia, Frank. *After the New Criticism.* Chicago: U of Chicago P, 1980.

Lentricchia, Frank. *Criticism and Social Change.* Chicago: U of Chicago P, 1983.

Leverenz, David. "On Trying to Read *Gravity's Rainbow.*" *Mindful Pleasures: Essays on Thomas Pynchon.* Eds. George Levine and David Leverenz. Boston: Little, Brown, 1976, 229-49.

292 *Bibliography*

Levine, George, and David Leverenz eds. *Mindful Pleasures: Essays on Thomas Pynchon.* Boston: Little, Brown, 1976.

Levine, George. "V-2." *Pynchon: A Collection of Critical Essays.* Ed. Edward Mendelson. Englewood Cliffs, N.J.: Prentice-Hall, 1978, 178-90.

Lippman, Bertram. "The Reader of Movies: Thomas Pynchon's *Gravity's Rainbow." University of Denver Quarterly* 12.1 (1977): 1-46.

Lord, George de Forest. *Heroic Mockery: Variations on Epic Themes from Homer to Joyce.* Newark: U of Delaware P, 1977.

Lyotard, Jean-François. *The Postmodern Condition: A Report on Knowledge.* Trans. Geoff Bennington and Brian Massumi. Minneapolis: U of Minnesota P, 1984.

Lyotard, Jean-François and Jean-Loup Thébaud. *Just Gaming.* Trans. Wlad Godzich. Manchester: Manchester UP, 1985.

Lyotard, Jean-François. "Complexity and the Sublime." *Postmodernism:ICA Documents 5.* Ed. Lisa Appignanesi, 10-12.

McGuirk, Bernard and Richard Cardwell, eds. *Gabriel García Márquez: New Readings.* Cambridge: Cambridge UP, 1987.

McHale, Brian. *Postmodernist Fiction.* London: Methuen, 1987.

McHale, Brian. *Constructing Postmodernism.* London: Routledge, 1992.

McKenzie, James. "Pole-Vaulting in Top Hats: a Public Conversation with John Barth, William Gass, and Ishmael Reed." *Modern Fiction Studies* 22.2 (1976): 131-51.

Macherey, Pierre. *A Theory of Literary Production.* Trans. Geoffrey Wall. London: Routledge & Kegan Paul, 1978.

Macksey, Richard and Eugenio Donato, eds. *The Structuralist Controversy: The Languages of Criticism and the Sciences of Man.* Baltimore: Johns Hopkins UP, 1970.

Maitre, Doreen. *Literature and Possible Worlds.* London: Pembridge Press/Middlesex Polytechnic Press, 1983.

Manning, Greg. "A Litany of Lies: A Look at Australia's New Fiction."*The Age Monthly Review* 8:3 (1988): 5-6.

Marks, Elaine and Isabelle de Courtivron, eds. *New French Feminisms: An Anthology.* New York: Hill & Wang, 1978.

Marino, James A.G. "An Annotated Bibliography of Play and Literature." *Canadian Review of Comparative Literature* XII.2 (1985): 306-53.

Martin, Gerald. *Journeys Through the Labyrinth.* London: Verso, 1989.

Matus, Jill. "Blonde, Black and Hottentot Venus: Context and Critique in Angela Carter's 'Black Venus'." *Studies in Short Fiction* 28.4 (1991): 467-76.

Bibliography 293

Melville, Herman. *Moby-Dick.* 1851; New York: Norton, 1967.

Mendelson, Edward. "Gravity's Encyclopedia." *Mindful Pleasures: Essays on Thomas Pynchon.* Ed. George Levine and David Leverenz. Boston: Little, Brown, 1976, 161-95.

Mendelson, Edward, ed. *Pynchon: A Collection of Critical Essays.* Englewood Cliffs, N.J.: Prentice-Hall, 1978.

Mendoza, Plinio Apuleyo and Gabriel García Márquez. *The Fragrance of Guava.* Trans. Ann Wright. London: Verso, 1983.

Michaels, Walter Benn. "The Interpreter's Self: Pierce on the Cartesian Subject." *Georgia Review* XXXI.2 (1977): 383-402.

Millar, S. *The Psychology of Play.* Baltimore: Penguin, 1968.

Miller, J. Hillis. "Stevens Rock and Criticism as Cure, II." *Georgia Review* 30 (1976): 330-48.

Miller, J. Hillis. "Ariadne's Thread: Repetition and the Narrative Line." *Critical Inquiry* 3 (1976): 57-78.

Miller, J. Hillis. "The Critic as Host." *Critical Inquiry* 3 (1977): 439-47.

Milner, Andrew et al., eds. *Postmodern Conditions.* Clayton, Victoria: Monash University, 1988.

Moi, Toril. *Sexual/Textual Politics: Feminist Literary Theory.* London: Methuen, 1985.

Morrell, David. *John Barth: An Introduction.* University Park: Pennsylvania State UP, 1976.

Morris, Meaghan. *The Pirate's Fiancée: Feminism, Reading,Postmodernism.* London: Verso, 1988.

Morrisette, Bruce. *The Novels of Robbe-Grillet.* Ithaca: Cornell UP, 1971.

Morisette, Bruce. "Games and Game Structures in Robbe-Grillet." *Game, Play, Literature.* Ed. Jacques Ehrmann. Boston: Beacon P, 1971, 159-67.

Motte, Warren. *The Poetics of Experiment: A Study of the Work of Georges Perec.* Lexington, Ky.: French Forum Monographs, 1984.

Motte, Warren, trans. and ed. *Oulipo: A Primer of Potential Literature.* Lincoln: U of Nebraska P, 1986.

Motte, Warren. *Playtexts: Ludics in Contemporary Literature.* Lincoln: U of Nebraska P, 1995.

Neuman, Shirley and Robert Wilson. *Labyrinths of Voice: Conversations with Robert Kroetsch.* Edmonton: Ne West P, 1982.

Neumann, Erich. *The Great Mother: An Analysis of the Archetype.* Trans. Ralph Manheim, Princeton: Princeton UP, 1972.

Neumann, John V. and Oskar Morgenstern. *Theory of Games and Economic Behaviour.* Princeton: Princeton UP, 1944.

294 *Bibliography*

Nietzsche, Fredric. *Philosophy in the Tragic Age of the Greeks.* Trans. Marianne Cowan. Washington, D.C.: Regnery Gateway, 1962.

Nietzsche, Friedrich. *Beyond Good and Evil.* Trans. Walter Kaufmann. New York: Random House, 1966.

Nietzsche, Friedrich. *The Will to Power.* Trans. Walter Kaufmann. New York: Random House, 1968.

Nietzsche, Friedrich. *The Portable Nietzsche.* Ed. Walter Kaufmann. Harmondsworth: Viking/Penguin, 1976.

Noland, Richard W. "John Barth and the Novel of Comic Nihilism." *Wisconsin Studies in Contemporary Literature* 7 (1966): 239-57.

Norris, Christopher. *Deconstruction: Theory and Practice.* London: Methuen, 1982.

Norris, Christopher. "Deconstruction Against Itself: Derrida and Nietzsche." *Diacritics* Winter (1986): 61-9.

Norris, Christopher. *Derrida.* London: Fontana, 1987.

Norris, Christopher. *What's Wrong with Postmodernism?: Critical Theory and the Ends of Philosophy.* London & New York: Harvester Wheatsheaf, 1990.

O'Brien, Peter, ed. *So To Speak: Interviews with Contemporary Canadian Writers.* Montreal: Vehicule P, 1987.

Ozier, Lance W. "Antipointsman/Antimexico: Some Mathematical Imagery in *Gravity's Rainbow.*" *Critique* 16.2 (1974): 73-90.

Ozier, Lance W. "The Calculus of Transformation: More Mathematical Imagery in *Gravity's Rainbow.*" *Twentieth Century Literature* 21.2 (1975): 193-210.

Pearce, Richard, ed. *Critical Essays on Thomas Pynchon.* Boston: G.K. Hall & Co., 1981.

Pease, Donald. "J. Hillis Miller: The Other Victorian at Yale." *The Yale Critics.* Eds. Jonathan Arac et al. Minneapolis: U of Minnesota P, 1983, 69-74.

Plato. *The Republic.* Trans. Benjamin Jowett. New York: Random House, 1937.

Poirier, Richard. "Rocket Power." *Saturday Review of the Arts* 3 March 1973, 59-64.

Poirier, Richard. "The Importance of Thomas Pynchon." *Twentieth Century Literature* 21.2 (1975): 151-62.

Popper, Karl. *The Logic of Scientific Discovery.* London: Hutchinson, 1959.

Popper, Karl. *Objective Knowledge.* Oxford: Oxford UP, 1972.

Pratt, Mary Louise. "Interpretive Strategies/Strategic Interpretations: On Anglo-American Reader-Response Criticism." *Postmodernism and Politics.* Ed. Jonathan Arac. Manchester: Manchester UP, 1986, 26-54.

Bibliography

Price, Greg. *Latin America: The Writer's Journey.* London: Hamish Hamilton, 1990.

Prince, Alan. "An Interview with John Barth." *Prism* Spring (1968): 42-62.

Puig, Manuel. *Kiss of the Spider Woman.* 1976; Trans. Thomas Colchie. London: Arena, 1984.

Punter, David. "Angela Carter: Supersessions of the Masculine." *Critique: Studies in Modern Fiction* 25.4 (1984): 209-22.

Punter, David. "Essential Imaginings: the Novels of Angela Carter and Russell Hoban." *The British and Irish Novel Since 1960.* Ed. James Acheson. New York: St. Martins P, 1991. 142-58.

Pynchon, Thomas. "The Small Rain." *Cornell Writer* 6.2 (1959): 14-32.

Pynchon, Thomas. "Mortality and Mercy in Vienna." *Epoch* 9 (1959):195-213.

Pynchon, Thomas. "Entropy." *Kenyon Review* 22 (1960): 277-92.

Pynchon, Thomas. "Low-lands." *New World Writing* 16 (1960): 85-108.

Pynchon, Thomas. "Under the Rose." *Noble Savage* 3 (1961): 223-51.

Pynchon, Thomas. *V.* 1963; London: Picador, 1975.

Pynchon, Thomas. "A Journey into the Mind of Watts." *New York Times Magazine,* 12 June (1966): 34-5, 78, 80-2, 84.

Pynchon, Thomas. *The Crying of Lot 49.* 1966; Harmondsworth: Penguin, 1974.

Pynchon, Thomas. "The Shrink Flips." *Cavalier* 16 (1966): 32-3, 88-92.

Pynchon, Thomas. *Gravity's Rainbow.* 1973; London: Picador, 1975.

Pynchon, Thomas. *Slow Learner.* London: Picador, 1985.

Pynchon, Thomas. *Vineland.* Boston: Little, Brown, 1990.

Radar, Edmond. "A Genealogy. Play, Folklore and Art." *Diogenes* 103 (1978): 78-99.

Rapoport, Anatol. *Fights, Games and Debates.* Ann Arbor: U of Michigan P, 1960.

Rapoport, Anatol. *Two-Person Game Theory.* Ann Arbor: U of Michigan P, 1966.

Rapoport, Anatol, ed. *Game Theory as a Theory of Conflict Resolution.* Dordrecht: D. Reidel Publishing Co., 1974.

Ray, William. *Literary Meaning: From Phenomenology to Deconstruction.* Oxford: Blackwell, 1984.

Readings, Bill. *Introducing Lyotard: Art and Politics.* London: Routledge, 1991.

Reid, Alastair. "Basilisks' Eggs." *New Yorker* 8 Nov. (1976): 175-208.

Reilly, Charlie. "An Interview with John Barth." *Contemporary Literature* 22.1 (1981): 5-8.

296 *Bibliography*

Retallack, Joan."Post-Scriptum-High-Modern." *Genre* XX.3-4 (1987): 483-512.

Richardson, Samuel. *Pamela, or Virtue Rewarded.* 1740; London: Dent, 1914.

Rimmon-Kenan, Shlomith. *Discourse in Psychoanalysis and Literature.* London: Methuen, 1987.

Roberts, John M. et al. "Games in Culture." *American Anthropologist* 61 (1959): 597-605.

Ruthven, Kenneth K. *Myth.* London: Methuen, 1976.

Ryan, Michael. *Marxism and Deconstruction.* Baltimore: Johns Hopkins UP, 1982.

Said, Edward. "The Problem of Textuality: Two Exemplary Positions." *Critical Inquiry* 4.4 (1978): 673-714.

Said, Edward. *The World, the Text, and the Critic.* Cambridge, Mass.: Harvard UP, 1983.

Said, Edward. *Culture and Imperialism.* London: Chatto & Windus, 1993.

Salinger, J.D. *The Catcher in the Rye.* Harmondsworth: Penguin, 1958.

Sanders, Scott. "Pynchon's Paranoid History." *Twentieth Century Literature* 21.2 (1975): 177-92.

Saussure, Ferdinand de. *Course in General Linguistics.* London: Peter Owen, 1960.

Schaub, Thomas. *Pynchon: The Voice of Ambiguity.* Chicago: U of Illinois P, 1981.

Schiller, Friedrich. *On the Aesthetic Education of Man.* Ed. and trans. Elizabeth M. Wilkinson and L.A. Willoughby. Oxford: Oxford UP, 1967.

Schmidt, Ricarda. "The Journey of the Subject in Angela Carter's Fiction." *Textual Practice* 3.1 (1989): 56-75.

Scholes, Robert. *The Fabulators.* New York: Oxford UP, 1976.

Scholes, Robert. *Fabulation and Metafiction.* Chicago: U of Illinois P, 1979.

Schulz, Max F. "Barth, *Letters,* and the Great Tradition." *Genre* 14.1 (1981): 95-115.

Schwartzman, Helen B., ed. *Play and Culture.* West Point, N.Y.: Leisure Press, 1980.

Sharratt, Bernard. *Reading Relations: Structures of Literary Production.* Brighton: Harvester P, 1982.

Showalter, Elaine, ed. *The New Feminist Criticism.* London: Virago, 1986.

Siegel, Carol. "Postmodern Women Novelists Review Victorian Male Masochism." *Genders* 11 (1991): 1-16.

Siegel, Mark. *Pynchon: Creative Paranoia in Gravity's Rainbow.* Port Washington, N.Y.: Kennikat P, 1978.

Bibliography 297

Simmon, Scott. "Beyond the Theatre of War: *Gravity's Rainbow* as Film." *Literature/Film Quarterly* 6.4 (1978): 347-63.

Slade, Joseph. *Thomas Pynchon.* New York: Warner Paperback Library, 1974.

Slade, Joseph. "Escaping Rationalization: Options for the Self in *Gravity's Rainbow.*" *Critique* 18.3 (1977): 27-38.

Smith, Joseph H. and William Kerrigan. *Taking Chances: Derrida, Psychoanalysis and Literature.* Baltimore: Johns Hopkins UP, 1984.

Smith, Mack. "The Paracinematic Reality of *Gravity's Rainbow.*" *Pynchon Notes* 9 (1982): 17-37.

Smith, Marcus and Khachig Tololyan. "The New Jeremiah: *Gravity's Rainbow.*" *Critical Essays on Thomas Pynchon.* Ed. Richard Pearce. Boston: G.K. Hall & Co., 1981, 169-86.

Smith, Thomas S. "Performing in the Zone: The Presentation of Historical Crisis in *Gravity's Rainbow.*" *Clio* 12.3 (1983): 245-60.

Spanos, William V., Paul A. Bové and Daniel O'Hara, eds. *The Question of Textuality: Strategies of Reading in Contemporary American Criticism.* Bloomington: Indiana UP, 1982.

Spariosu, Mihai. *Literature, Mimesis and Play: Essays in Literary Theory.* Tübingen: Gunter Narr Verlag, 1982.

Spariosu, Mihai. *Dionysus Reborn: Play and the Aesthetic Dimension in Modern Philosophical and Scientific Discourse.* Ithaca: Cornell UP, 1989.

Spariosu, Mihai. *God of Many Names: Play, Poetry and Power in Hellenic Thought from Homer to Aristotle.* Durham: Duke UP, 1991.

Spivak, Gayatri Chakravorty. *In Other Words. Essays in Cultural Politics.* London: Methuen, 1987.

Stark, John. *The Literature of Exhaustion: Borges, Nabokov and Barth.* Durham: Duke UP, 1974.

Stark, John. *Pynchon's Fictions: Thomas Pynchon and the Literature of Information.* Athens, Ohio: Ohio UP, 1980.

Steele, Peter. *Jonathan Swift: Preacher and Jester.* Oxford: Clarendon P, 1978.

Steele, Peter. "Scriptor Ludens: The Notion and Some Instances." *Canadian Review of Comparative Literature* XII.2 (1985): 235-63.

Steiner, George. Introduction to Huizinga's *Homo Ludens. A Study of the Play Element in Civilization.* London: Paladin, 1970.

Sterne, Laurence. *The Life and Opinions of Tristram Shandy, Gentleman.* 1759-67; London: Macdonald, 1949.

Storey, Robert F. *Pierrot: A Critical History of the Mask.* Princeton: Princeton UP, 1978.

298   *Bibliography*

Stove, David. *Popper and After: Four Modern Irrationalists.* Oxford: Pergamon Press, 1982.

Suleiman, Susan R. and Inge Crosman, eds. *The Reader in the Text: Essays on Audience and Interpretation.* Princeton: Princeton UP, 1980.

Suits, Bernard. *The Grasshopper: Games, Life and Utopia.* Toronto: U of Toronto P, 1978.

Suits, Bernard. "The Detective Story: A Case Study of Games in Literature." *Canadian Review of Comparative Literature* XII.2 (1985): 200-19.

Sutcliffe, Denham. "Worth a Guilty Conscience." *Kenyon Review* 23.1 (1961): 181-4.

Swanson, Philip, ed. *Landmarks in Modern Latin American Fiction.* London: Routledge, 1990.

Tanner, Tony. *Thomas Pynchon.* London: Methuen, 1982.

Tatham, Campbell. "John Barth and the Aesthetics of Artifice." *Contemporary Literature* 12 (1971): 60-73.

Taylor, Mark C. *Deconstruction in Context: Literature and Philosophy.* Chicago: U of Chicago P, 1986.

Tharpe, Jac. *John Barth: The Comic Sublimity of Paradox.* Carbondale: Southern Illinois UP, 1974.

Thiher, Allen. *Words in Reflection. Modern Language Theory and Postmodern Fiction.* Chicago: U of Chicago P, 1984.

Thomson, David. *Suspects.* 1985; London: Picador, 1986.

Todorov, Tzvetan. *The Fantastic: A Structural Approach to a Literary Genre.* 1970; Trans. Richard Howard. Ithaca: Cornell UP, 1975.

Todorov, Tzvetan. "On Literary Genesis." *Yale French Studies* 58 (1979): 213-35.

Tompkins, Jane P., ed. *Reader-Response Criticism: From Formalism to Post-Structuralism.* Baltimore: Johns Hopkins UP, 1980.

Turner, Rory. "Subjects and Symbols: Transformations of Identity in *Nights at the Circus.*" *Folklore Forum* 20.1/2 (1987): 39-60.

Vallorani, Nicoletta. "The Body of the City: Angela Carter's *The Passion of New Eve.*" *Science Fiction Studies.* 21.3 (1994): 365-79.

Vauthier, Simone. "*Badlands:* Where Are the Voices Coming From?" *Open Letter* Ninth Series 5-6 (1996): 159-75.

Vitanza, Victor J. "The Novelist as Topologist: John Barth's *Lost in the Funhouse.*" *Texas Studies in Language and Literature* XIX.1 (1977): 83-97.

Waldmeir, Joseph J., ed. *Critical Essays on John Barth.* Boston: G.K. Hall & Co., 1980.

Bibliography 299

Walkiewicz, E. P. *John Barth.* Boston: G. K. Hall & Co, 1986.

Walton, Kendall L. *Mimesis as Make-Believe: On the Foundations of the Representational Arts.* Cambridge, Mass.: Harvard UP, 1990.

Wandor, M. ed. *On Gender and Writing.* London: Pandora Press, 1983.

Waugh, Patricia. *Metafiction: The Theory and Practice of Self-Conscious Fiction.* London: Methuen, 1984.

Weisenburger, Steven. "The End of History? Thomas Pynchon and the Uses of the Past." *Critical Essays on Thomas Pynchon.* Ed. Richard Pearce. Boston: G.K. Hall & Co., 1981, 140-56.

Westervelt, Linda A. "A Place Dependent on Ourselves: The Reader as System-Builder in *Gravity's Rainbow.*" *Texas Studies in Literature and Language* 22.1 (1980): 69-90.

Weixlmann, Joe and Sher Weixlmann, "Barth and Barthelme Recycle the Perseus Myth: A Study in Literary Ecology." *Modern Fiction Studies* 25.2 (1979): 191-207.

White, Hayden. *Metahistory: The Historical Imagination in Nineteenth-Century Europe.* Baltimore: Johns Hopkins UP, 1973.

White, Hayden. *Tropics of Discourse: Essays in Cultural Criticism.* Baltimore: Johns Hopkins UP, 1978.

Wilson, Robert Rawdon. "Spooking Oedipa: On Godgames." *Canadian Review of Comparative Literature* 4.2 (1977): 186-204.

Wilson, Robert Rawdon. "On the Boundary of the Magic and the Real: Notes on Inter-American Fiction." *The Compass* 6 (1979) 37-53.

Wilson, Robert Rawdon. "Three Prolusions: Towards a Game Model in Literary Theory." *Canadian Review of Comparative Literature* 8.1 (1981): 79-92.

Wilson, Robert Rawdon. "Godgames and Labyrinths: The Logic of Entrapment." *Mosaic* XV.4 (1982): 1-22.

Wilson, Robert Rawdon. "In Palamedes' Shadow: Game and Play Concepts Today." *Canadian Review of Comparative Literature* XII.2 (1985): 177-99.

Wilson, Robert Rawdon. "Play, Transgression and Carnival: Bakhtin and Derrida on 'Scriptor Ludens'." *Mosaic* XIX.1 (1986): 73-89.

Wilson, Robert Rawdon. "Theory as Template: The New Australian Novel." *Mattoid* 33 (1989): 159-75.

Wilson, Robert Rawdon. "SLIP PAGE: Angela Carter, in/out/in the Postmodern Nexus." *Ariel: A Review of International English Literature.* 20.4 (1989): 96-114.

Wilson, Robert Rawdon. *In Palamedes' Shadow: Explorations in Play, Game, & Narrative Theory.* Boston: Northeastern UP, 1990.

Wimsatt, W.K. "Belinda Ludens: Strife and Play in 'The Rape of the Lock'." *New Literary History* 4 (1973): 357-74.

Winnicott, D. W. *Playing and Reality.* New York: Basic Books, 1971.

Wittgenstein, Ludwig. *Philosophical Investigations.* Trans. G.E.M. Anscombe. Oxford: Blackwell, 1968.

Zamora, Lois Parkinson & Wendy B. Faris., eds. *Magical Realism: Theory, History, Community.* Durham & London: Duke UP, 1995.

Ziegler, Heide. *John Barth.* London: Methuen, 1987.

Index

Abrams, M.H. 8n8, 42, 60–1
The Act of Reading 41
After the New Criticism 41
Alibi 191
allusion xv, 4, 5, 67, 98, 100, 122,
    158, 176
Anderson, Don 249
The Anti-Aesthetic 87n2
The Anxiety of Influence 8n12, 178n2,
    187
Arac, Jonathan 52n15, 73n18
archaeological 65–6, 102–3, 121, 197,
    207
The Archaeology of Knowledge
    52n18, 66
Aristophanes 18
Aristotle xvi, 17
Auctor Ludens 32n10
Austen, Jane 24, 218
author
    authorial intention 4
    as bricoleur 253
    death of 67, 132
    identity 165–7
Avedon, E.M. 32n6
Axelos, Kostas 13, 21, 32n8

The Bacchae 18

Badlands 192, 213n15
Bail, Murray xvi, 248–53, 259, 265,
    267
Bakhtin, Mikhail 26–9, 33n17, 36n41,
    112–3, 207, 220, 226–7, 228–
    41
Barth, John 141–85, 187, 188, 190,
    267
    and exhaustion 5, 15, 92, 119,
    137n47, 141–2
    and replenishment 8n12, 83, 142,
    145, 153, 160, 174–8
Barthes, Roland xvi, 4, 23, 35n34/35,
    42, 43, 50n4, 66–8, 83, 115,
    127, 132, 134n16, 157, 165,
    185n59, 188, 189, 211n3,
    215n27, 242n5, 248, 254
Bataille, Georges 56
Baudrillard, Jean 4, 11, 81, 88n5
Beaujour, Michel 30n1
Beckett, Samuel 190
*Been Down So Long It Looks Like Up
    To Me* 138n57
Bennett, David 86
Berman, Neil David 33n17
Berne, Eric 13
Bernstein, Michael 245n25
Berressem, Hanjo 123

302   *Index*

Beyond Deconstruction 73n20
Beyond Good and Evil 241
binarism xii, 21, 82, 92, 95, 97–100,
    104, 118, 122, 133n9, 145,
    177, 190, 191, 219–20, 221,
    239
Black Venus 224, 225
Blake, Kathleen 33n17
Blanchot, Maurice 56
Bleich, David 51n6
Bliss 255
The Bloody Chamber 221, 225
Bloom, Harold 8n5, 8n12, 178n2, 188,
    242n9
Booth, Wayne 8n8, 42, 61, 240
Borges, Jorge Luis 15, 44, 119,
    137n47, 141, 177, 179n2, 188,
    190, 193, 195, 198, 227
Bowen, Zack 181n9
Bowering, George 178
Bradbury, Malcolm 185n53,
bricolage xvi, 23, 46, 217, 220, 247–8,
    252, 253, 269
Brooks, Peter 242n10
Brotherston, Gordon 213n17
Bruss, Elizabeth 15
Burke, Ruth 31n2
Burning Water 178

Caillois, Roger xiii, 13, 20–1, 27,
    35n28
Calinescu, Matei 50n4
Calvino, Italo 15, 17, 39–40, 48–9,
    177, 190, 217, 256
Carey, Peter xvi, 247–71
carnivalesque 27–9, 102, 112–3, 207,
    216n36, 220, 226, 227–36,
    237–41, 260
Carpentier, Alejo 193–4, 204, 213n18

Carroll, David 75n31
Carroll, Lewis 17, 223, 226
Carter, Angela xvi, 217–45, 267
The Castle of Crossed Destinies 17,
    256
Cervantes, Miguel de 5, 188, 190,
    193, 194, 238
character 99–101, 148–67, 162–4,
    182n21, 201, 254
Chase, Cynthia 243n10
chess 107–8
Chimera 142, 159, 160, 178
circus xvi, 227–8, 231–4, 267
Civilization and Its Discontents 117
Cixous, Hélène 65
Clark, Robert 244n15
Clerc, Charles 123, 127
closure xiv, 58, 69, 92, 94
comic 98, 112, 171, 190, 204, 207,
    208, 218–20, 223, 228, 237,
    239, 250, 251
Conrad, Joseph 190, 192, 195
context 4, 5, 11, 29–30, 39, 57, 69, 99
Cooley, Dennis 212n11
Cooper, Peter L. 132n2
Coover, Robert 15, 17, 178
Cortázar, Julio 17, 193, 213n18
Cosenza, Joseph A. 139n64
Course in General Linguistics 35n33
Cowart, David 123, 134n19, 138n54
The Critical Difference 69
Crosman, Robert 40
The Crying of Lot 49 43, 91, 100, 113,
    115
Culler, Jonathan 40, 45–6, 51n6, 68–
    9, 70, 167, 242n5

Daniel, Helen 263
Das Spiel als Weltsymbol 34n23

Index

decentering xiii, 61, 62, 64, 93–4, 95, 125, 248, 250, 252, 262
deconstruction xi, xiii, 6, 24, 26, 47–8, 55–75, 92, 94, 100, 105, 143, 146, 157, 197, 206, 217, 224, 249, 253, 257–8
   and feminism 64–5
   and genealogy 66
   and history 167–72
   and literary criticism 56, 68–70
   and marxism 62–4
   as reading practice 56–8, 63
   and textuality 57
Deconstruction in Context 56
de Man, Paul 8n5
The Death of the Novel 180n5
The Defense 13, 17
Deleuze, Gilles 34n19
Derrida, Jacques xiii, xvi, 3, 4, 6, 17, 19, 23, 24, 26, 29, 33n19, 35n35, 36n40, 42, 56, 70, 83, 85, 94, 95, 115, 116, 151, 188, 189, 194, 195, 200, 206, 209, 215n33, 216n38, 222, 225, 237, 242n9, 248, 252, 261, 262, 273
   on writing and play 57–62, 69–70
Dialogue and Dialectic 34n20
dialogism 27, 220, 226–7, 231, 237, 239
Dickens, Charles 218
différance 57–8, 95, 100
difference 30, 56, 57, 62–3, 79, 81, 82, 83, 86, 94, 99, 116, 188, 199, 200, 220, 222, 225, 238, 248, 249, 252, 254, 259, 265, 273
Dilthey, Wilhelm 135n23
Dionysus Reborn 31n2

displacement 6, 86, 93–4, 97, 99, 101–2, 123
Dissemination 3, 34n20, 57, 248, 273n1
diversity xiv, 93
   and inclusiveness 102–3, 106
Don Quixote 5, 15, 44, 188
dreamwork 103, 110, 194, 195, 197, 202–3, 207, 218, 222, 241n3
Duncker, Patricia 244n15
duplicity xiv, 58

Eagleton, Terry 62
Edwards, Brian 34n25, 211n5
Ehrmann, Jacques xiii, 11, 19–21, 22, 30, 34n23, 106, 108
Eliade, Mircea 135n30, 169
Eliot, T.S. 5, 35n35, 67, 148
Ellis, M.J. 21, 35n30/31
Empson, William 45
Enck, John 180n7
The End of the Road 143, 151–3, 159, 163
"Entropy" 3, 44, 115
epistolary 144–5, 147, 191
epistoleans 147–67, 254
Euripides 18
exchange xi, xvii, 3, 11, 14, 80, 82, 210

Fabulation and Metafiction 134n19
Famous Last Words 178
fantasy 194–6, 204, 220–3, 227, 242n6, 256, 261
Farina, Richard 138n57
Faulkner, William 190, 193, 195
Felperin, Howard 73n20
feminism 219, 223–8, 240, 241n4
   and deconstruction 64

304 Index

Fetterly, Judith 64
Feyerabend, Paul 32n13
Fielding, Henry 23, 143, 166
film 123–7
Findley, Timothy 178
Fink, Eugen 30n1, 34n23
Fish, Stanley 41–5, 52n13, 53n20
5 Readers Reading 51n6
Flaubert, Gustave 24
The Floating Opera 143, 148–51, 163, 173
Flores, Angel 211n4
Fogel, Stan 181n9
Foster, Hal 87n2
Foucault, Michel 44, 62, 65–6, 83, 102–3, 115, 200, 209, 261, 262
Fowles, John 33n15, 171, 184n53
freeplay 21, 42, 95, 237, 262
Freud, Sigmund 26, 116, 117, 222, 242n8
Freund, Elizabeth 50n4, 52n15
The Frogs 18
Frye, Northrop 5, 35n35, 67
Fuentes, Carlos 193, 213n18
funhouse xv, 142, 145, 165, 167, 228, 248, 267

Gadamer, Hans-Georg 19, 33n19, 35n27, 135n23
Gallagher, D.P. 213n17
game 12–17
    and carnival 27–8
    classification 12–3
    game theory 13–5
    godgame 33n15, 93, 137n47
    in *Gravity's Rainbow* 107–12
    of history 169
    language games 24–6

literary games 15–6
    as metaphor 14–5
    novel as game 147
    and play 16
    of reading 15, 191, 253
Game, Play, Literature 30n1
Games Authors Play 16, 33n18
Games People Play 13
García Márquez, Gabriel 188, 193–210, 223
Gardner, Robyn 80, 243n13
Gasché, Rodolphe 56, 261
Gauthier, Xavière 244n16
genealogical 66, 92, 103, 190
Gerst, Angela 183n38
Gezari, Janet K. 33n17
Giles Goat-Boy 142, 156–9, 168
Glas 4, 58
God of Many Names 31n2
Gone Indian 191
Graff, Gerald 37n47
The Grasshopper: Games, Life and Utopia 11, 31n4
Gravity's Rainbow xiv–xv, 82, 91–139, 178, 188, 256
Greene, Gayle 74n22
Griffin, Clive 213n18
Gross, Beverley 180n9
Guinness, G. 33n17

Habermas, Jurgen 80, 135n23
Haffenden, John 241n3, 243n11, 244n22
Hancock, Geoff 212n12, 215n30
Hans, James xiii, 19, 21
Hardy, Thomas 190
Harris, Charles B. 159, 179n2, 182n21, 185n57
Harrison, Dick 212n14

Index

Hartman, Geoffrey 4, 35n35, 47, 51n7, 58, 60
Hassan, Ihab xiv, 83–6
Hesiod 11, 17
heterogeneity 22, 63, 79, 82, 83, 106
Hirsch, E.D. 72n16
history 44, 94, 101–6, 115–6, 145, 155, 167, 193–4, 251, 253, 254, 256, 257–9, 260–9
Hite, Molly 134n18
Hodgins, Jack 188–9
Hoffmann, E.T.A. 223
Holden's Performance 248, 250–3, 267
Holland, Norman 51n6, 53n24
Holquist, Michael 37n46
Holub, Robert 50n4
Homer 11, 17, 18, 192, 219
Homesickness 248–50, 267
Homo Ludens 19
Hopscotch 17
Horvath, Brooke 114
Huizinga, Johan xiii, 19–20, 27, 34n27, 226
Hume, Katherine 242n6
Husserl, Edmund 56
Hutcheon, Linda 181n15, 185n56, 231–2, 270n12
Hutchinson, Peter 16, 33n18
hybridity xvi, 162, 210, 236–41
identity 4, 56, 155, 249

If on a winter's night a traveler 39–40, 48–9, 177–8
The Iliad 11, 13, 18
Illywhacker xvi, 253–69
The Implied Reader 43
In Palamedes' Shadow 22, 31n2
inclusiveness 100

incompletion 25, 120, 190, 253
indeterminacy xiv, 26, 57, 69, 84
The Infernal Desire Machine of Doctor Hoffman 243n14
influence xiii, 98, 187–90, 197–8, 213n16
Ingarden, Roman 49n3
intertextuality xv, 29–30, 58, 67, 100, 148, 153, 163, 173, 188–210, 218–9
The Invention of the World 188
Irigaray, Luce 65
Iser, Wolfgang 41–5

Jameson, Fredric 81–3, 86, 167
Janes, Regina 213n17
Jauss, Hans Robert 45
Jencks, Charles 83
jeu libre 12, 133n11
Johnson, Barbara 37n50, 69, 132n8, 242n5
Jordan, Elaine 225, 243n14, 244n15
jouissance 68, 80, 83, 86, 237
Joyce, James xv, 190, 193

Kafka, Franz 193, 195, 198
Kaplan, E. Ann 88n4
Kappeller, Susanne 244n15
Kellner, Douglas 88n4
Kennedy, William 214n23
Kierkegaard, Soren 56
Kolodny, Annette 65, 73n21
Kracauer, Siegfried 139n63
Krafft, John M. 102
Kristeva, Julia 27, 36n42, 65, 188, 189, 225
Kroetsch, Robert 187–216
Kuhn, Thomas 32n13

306   *Index*

labyrinth 93, 118–9, 121, 204, 227, 267
Labyrinths of Voice 187, 211n8, 212n12, 212n13
Lacan, Jacques 26, 222
language 24–5, 29, 113–32, 146, 190, 193, 238–40, 263–5
The Last Voyage of Somebody the Sailor 146, 148, 159, 162
laughter 27–9, 112–3, 207, 227–30, 238–41
Lavenda, Robert 28, 36n43
The Laws 18
Lawson, Henry 248–9
Lecker, Robert 190
LeClair, Thomas 180n9
Leitch, Vincent 56
Lentricchia, Frank 41, 61, 262
letters 144–7, 165
LETTERS xv, 47, 141–85, 188
Leverenz, David 132n2
Lévi-Strauss, Claude 252
Levine, George 139n63
Limited Inc 61–2, 74n31
Lippman, Bertram 139n63
Literature and Possible Worlds 260
Lost in the Funhouse 141, 142, 159–62, 163, 164, 171
'Low-lands' 96
Lyotard, Jean-François xiv, 79–81, 83, 101–2, 268

Macherey, Pierre 73n18
magical realism 188–210
The Magus 33n15, 188n53
Maitre, Doreen 260
Mantissa 171–2
Marino, A.G. 33n17
Marks, Elaine 244n16

Martin, Gerald 213n17
Marvell, Andrew 223
Marx, Karl 150, 157, 169
Matus, Jill 243n13
McHale, Brian 253, 256
McKenzie, James 180n7
Melville, Herman 117–8, 119–20, 253–4
Mendelson, Edward 133n14, 134n19, 138n55
Mendoza, Plinio A. 214n20, 214n23
metafiction 96, 106, 145, 157, 167–74, 181n15
metahistory 65, 103, 167–74
Metahistory 52n19
Middlemarch 43
Millar, S. 35n32
Miller, J. Hillis 8n9, 67
Milner, Andrew 89n10
mimesis 92, 94, 181n15, 172, 191, 221, 227
misreading 61, 225
Moby-Dick 117–8, 253–4
Moi, Toril 73n22
Morisette, Bruce 30n1, 33n17
Morrell, David 181n9
Motte, Warren 19, 31n2, 33n17, 34n26
Mulligan Stew 178
myth 160, 190, 193–6, 200, 215n27, 219

Nabokov, Vladimir 13, 15, 17, 137n47, 190
narcissistic narrative 145, 270
narrative
    artifice 143–4
    connections 150, 210
    and history 103

Index

patterns 150, 151, 154–6
recycling 142, 159
self-consciousness 178
narrator 127–30, 147–67, 192, 196–7, 198–9, 205, 237, 253, 254–7
Neuman, Shirley 211n2
New Criticism 70
The New Feminist Criticism 73n21
Nietzsche, Friedrich xiii, 19, 24, 33n19, 34n20, 56, 65, 71n4, 71n13, 115, 241
Nietzsche and Philosophy 34n19
Nights at the Circus xvi, 217–45
Noland, Richard W. 180n9
Norris, Christopher 73n19, 75n32

O'Brien, Peter 211n7
The Odyssey xv, 13, 18
Of Grammatology 7n3, 57, 214n22, 216n34
On the Aesthetic Education of Man 31n3
On Deconstruction 46
Once Upon a Time: A Floating Opera 148, 150, 159, 162
One Hundred Years of Solitude xv, 188, 192–210
The Oresteia 18
Oscar and Lucinda 267–8
Oulipo 15, 33n17
Ovid 190, 194, 198

Pale Fire 178
paranoia 98, 101, 106, 110
parody 14, 27, 80, 97, 116, 126, 155–6, 157, 175, 190–1, 197, 203, 209, 219–20, 230, 236–7, 247, 249, 250, 258, 260, 265

The Passion of New Eve 221, 224, 226, 243n14
pastiche 83, 247
Philosophical Investigations 24, 35n38
Philosophy in the Tragic Age of the Greeks 33n19
picaresque 230–1, 236
Plato xiii, xvi, 17–9
play
   as *agon* 18
   and art 22–3
   and the carnivalesque 26–9, 112–3, 207
   and combination 236, 260
   and culture 19–21, 29
   as defence 107
   of differences 23, 62–3, 99, 199–200, 222, 238, 248–9, 265
   and game 11–12, 106–13
   with history xv, 86, 101–5, 115–6, 155–6, 169–72, 195, 257–9, 260–9
   as interplay xi–xii, 18, 79, 192, 252
   of language xiii, 17, 24–5, 101, 104, 114–30, 155, 203, 206, 209, 263
   as *paidia* 18
   and psychoanalytic theory 26
   and reading 17, 24, 152, 264–5
   and resistance 95, 122, 145
   and seriousness xiii, 19, 93, 119, 174, 207, 220, 223, 226, 233, 262, 274
   of signification xiii, 4, 57
   as subversion 113, 122, 204
   and transgression 82
   as verbal contest 19

308   *Index*

of the world 17, 21
The Play of the World 21
*Playtexts: Ludics in Contemporary
   Literature* 34n26
The Pleasure of the Text 66, 68
Poe, Edgar A. 223
Poirier, Richard 137n50
Popper, Karl 32n13
The Post Card 58–60
postcolonialism xi, 212n8, 248, 268
The Postmodern Condition 87n1
postmodernism xiv, 12, 79–89, 123,
   232, 253
Postmodernism and Its Discontents
   88n4
Postmodernism/Jameson/Critique
   88n4
Postmodernist Fiction 253, 256
poststructuralism xi, 55, 84, 120, 223
Pratt, Mary Louise 43
Price, Greg 213n18
Prince, Alan 180n7
process xii, 67, 99, 175, 190, 210,
   253, 261, 273
Proust, Marcel 193
Puig, Manuel 127, 176, 193, 214n18
Punter, David 243n14
Pynchon, Thomas xiv–xv, 4, 15, 43,
   82, 91–139, 188, 190, 223,
   256, 267
Pynchon: The Voice of Ambiguity
   132n2

quest 99–100

Rabelais, François 27, 193, 194, 218,
   238, 239
Rabelais and His World 36n41
Radar, Edmond 22

Rapoport, Anatol 32n14
Ray, William 51n6
The Reader in the Text 40
reader response 6, 39–53
Reader Response Criticism 40
reading xiii, 5–6, 119, 130–2, 152,
   174, 195–6, 209, 210, 228,
   250, 255–6, 264
   as game 253
   character as reader 162–4
   erotics 68
   instruction 166
   and play 24
   as process 66–7
   as rereading 176–8
   and voyeurism 147
realism/reality 142–3, 192, 193–4,
   197–8. 204, 209, 221, 249,
   256, 259, 260, 261
reason 79, 80, 110
Reception Theory 50n4
Reid, Alastair 213n17, 214n20,
   215n31, 215n32
Reilly, Charles 180n5, 182n21
replay 146, 150, 151, 163
The Republic 18
Rereading 50n4, 188
The Return of the Reader 50n4
Richardson, Samuel 147, 148, 166
Rimmon-Kenan, Shlomith 242n10
rocket 99, 103–4, 115, 120
role-play 112, 127, 171, 226, 236
Rorty, Richard 87n2
The Rustle of Language 50n4
Ryan, Michael 63

Sabbatical: A Romance 146, 148, 150,
   159, 162, 174
Said, Edward 65, 167

Index

309

Salinger, J.D. 254
Sartre, Jean-Paul 56
Saussure, Ferdinand de 23, 35n33, 56, 58
Schaub, Thomas 120, 123, 128, 131, 133n2, 133n14, 135n30, 138n54
Schiller, Friedrich 11, 13, 31n3, 237
Schmidt, Ricarda 224, 243n14
Scholes, Robert 134n19
Schwartzman, Helen B. 36n43
Searle, John 61
self-consciousness xi, 5, 86, 252, 253, 254, 258, 267, 269, 274
Sexual/Textual Politics 73n22
Shelley, Mary 223
Showalter, Elaine 73n21
Siegel, Mark 132n4, 132n6
Signs and Symptoms 132n2
Simmon, Scott 138n55
Slade, Joseph 133n14
Smith, Mack 138n54
Smith, Marcus 134n19
Smith, Thomas 105
Smollett, Tobias 143, 166
Sophocles 18
Sorrentino, Gilbert 127
The Sot-Weed Factor 92, 142, 154–6, 163, 173
Spariosu, Mihai xiii, 11, 17–20, 31n2
Speech and Phenomena 71n11/12
spieltrieb 11
Spivak, Gayatri C. 64
Stark, John D. 139n63, 189n9
Steiner, George 16, 19
Stendhal 24
Sterne, Laurence 39, 47, 143, 148, 166, 190, 238
Stoker, Bram 223

Stove, David 32n13
The Studhorse Man 191
Suits, Bernard xiii, 11, 16, 17, 21, 31n4, 32n6
Sukenik, Ron 180n5
Suleiman, Susan 40
supplement 29, 57, 67, 69, 95, 120
Sutcliffe, Denham 183n30
Swanson, Philip 213n17
S/Z 4, 43, 50n4, 53n21, 66–8, 134n16, 242n5, 248

The Tain of the Mirror 56
Tanner, Tony 137n50, 139n71
Tatham, Campbell 179n2
The Tax Inspector 259–60
Taylor, Mark 56
textuality 3, 21, 39, 57, 200, 209–10
Tharpe, Jac 180n9
Thiher, Allen 25, 35n33, 36n39
Thomas Pynchon: The Art of Allusion 134n19
Thomson, David 127, 176
The Thousand and One Nights 55
Through the Looking Glass 17
The Tidewater Tales 146, 148, 150, 159, 162, 174
time 103, 126, 196–9, 266
Todorov, Tzvetan 200, 204, 242n7
Tololyan, Khachig 134n19
Tom Jones 15, 46–7
Tompkins, Jane 40
Tractus Logico-Philosophicus 24
tricksterism 187, 190–1, 208, 253–4, 257
Trilling, Lionel 242n9
Tristram Shandy 15, 39
Tropics of Discourse 52n19
Truth and Method 33n19

Turner, Graeme 261
Twain, Mark 257

Ulysses xv, 43, 213n16
uncertainty 56, 82, 91–2, 96, 115, 120, 175, 190, 191, 195, 196, 201, 204, 207, 230, 252, 264
The Universal Baseball Association 17
The Unusual Life of Tristan Smith 268

V 91, 96, 113, 115
Validity in Interpretation 72n16
Vallorani, Nicoletta 244n14
Vargas Llosa, Mario 193, 214n18
Vauthier, Simone 213n15
Vineland 113

Walton, Kendall 50n4
Waugh, Patricia 178
Weisenburger, Steven 104, 134n19

Weixlmann, Joe 181n19
What the Crow Said xv, 187–216
White, Hayden 44, 65, 103, 168
White, Patrick 213n16
Why People Play 21
Wilson, Robert R. xiii, 13–4, 16, 22, 28, 30n2, 31n4, 32n11, 33n15, 36n45, 37n46, 136n39, 137n47, 211n2, 214n19, 237, 239, 263
Wimsatt, W.K. 33n17
Wittgenstein, Ludwig xiii, 16, 24–6, 35n38, 56
Wittig, Monique 65
Woolf, Virginia 195
writing 3, 57, 69, 254, 261–5
Writing and Difference 17, 33n19, 57, 70, 71n8/9, 94, 95, 214n22, 252–3

The Yale Critics 73n18